3 0012 00147849 3

On the Verge of Want

A unique insight into living conditions along Ireland's Western seaboard in the late 19th century

On the Verge of Want

A unique insight into living conditions along Ireland's Western seaboard in the late 19th century

Compiled and Edited by
James Morrissey

Crannóg Books

First published in 2001 by
Crannóg Books, 28 Foxrock Avenue, Dublin 18, Ireland.
E-mail address: crannogbooks@eircom.net

Library of Congress Cataloging-in-Publication Data is available for this book

A CIP catalogue record for this book is available from the British Library

ISBN 0 9512826 3 8

Book Design and Cover by Paul McElheron & Associates, Dublin
Editorial and indexing by Carole C. Devaney, Dublin
Printed in Ireland by Colour Books, Dublin

CONTENTS

INTRODUCTION

The Congested Districts Board was established by the Land Act of 1891 to provide assistance to 'congested districts' – areas regarded as exceptionally poor and undeveloped – along the west coast of Ireland.

The Board was set up following a visit in 1890 to the West of Ireland by Arthur Balfour, Chief Secretary for Ireland. The plight of the people he saw and met left Balfour in no doubt that assistance was needed.

Following his visit, Balfour said: 'The general impression left upon the casual traveller is that you are dealing with a population not congested in the sense of being crowded, but congested by not being able to draw from their holdings a safe and sufficient livelihood for themselves and their children, whose condition trembles constantly on the verge of want, and when the potato crop fails, goes over that margin and becomes one of extreme and even dangerous destitution.'

The first Annual Report of the Congested Districts Board, published in December 1892, outlined the conditions that prevailed among inhabitants of congested districts. Almost all inhabitants possessed small plots of land from which they made a meagre living. Secondary sources of income included sea-fishing, sale of seaweed, wage-earning in England, Scotland and elsewhere, weaving, knitting, sewing, sale of turf and illicit whiskey, and donations from relatives in America. As the Report states:

> 'Residents along the seashore have many advantages arising from fishing, gathering seaweed for kelp and manure, and from cheap carriage by sea for flour, meal and other commodities; but, on the other hand, peat for fuel has often to be brought a great distance by those living on the seashore, and rough grazing for cattle and sheep is frequently not available there. People dwelling inland either depend almost altogether on their farms, or else they regularly migrate for some months of the year in search of employment in England and Scotland, or even America in rare instances. In some inland mountain glens where the inhabitants have very small patches of land tilled in primitive and unskilled methods, where their cattle and sheep have deteriorated in breeding and diminished in numbers, where little effort is made by the men to earn money through migratory labour or otherwise – in such mountain glens are to be found those people who endure the most comfortless and cheerless lives of all the inhabitants of congested districts in Ireland. In a "good year" they are little more than free from the dread of hunger, while a complete or partial failure of their crop involves as a consequence proportionately greater or less suffering from insufficient food.'

The Annual Report provides figures of estimated receipts and expenditure of typical families living in different congested districts. For example, a family in 'comparatively good circumstances', deriving receipts from both agriculture and fishing, would have an annual income totalling £48 3*s.* 4*d.*, made up of:

	£	*s.*	*d.*
Sale of oats	4	10	0
Sale of potatoes	6	13	4
Sale of 2 two year old cattle	12	0	0
Sale of 3 pigs	4	10	0
Sale of 1 foal	5	0	0
Sale of eggs	7	10	0
Sale of butter	1	0	0
Sale of 10 lambs	4	0	0
Sale of fish	3	0	0

The expenditure for this family would be £37 2*s.* 0*d.*, with clothes, groceries, rent and tobacco among the main items. Home produce consumed by the family was valued at £10.

But a family in 'very poor circumstances' would be forced to survive on an income of £9 16*s.* 0*d.*, while their expenditure would be £10 19*s.* 0*d.* Home produce consumed by such a family was valued at between £12 and £17.

The Annual Report goes on the explain that:

> 'Even in the most prosperous of the congested districts, the standard of living is low, the diet being altogether vegetable, with the exception of salt fish at times, which is used more as a relish than as an article of food.
>
> 'The houses, furniture and bedding are too often unhealthy, mean and comfortless, and the week-day clothing is frequently ragged and scanty. With the exception of shop-keepers, very many families are on the same low level with regard to resources, but some families are so utterly unfortunate as to have either no able-bodied men among them or else too few to provide for their wants.
>
> 'The farms, or rather holdings, are small in extent, and from 2 to 4 statute acres are planted with potatoes and oats. The rents for these plots vary from a few shillings to £6 a year . . . The methods of cultivation are usually primitive and bad, there being no rotation of crops, drainage is insufficient, there is an inadequate supply of suitable manure, and the weeding of crops is neglected. The breeds of livestock are worn out and of little value, and the kinds of poultry are capable of much improvement.'

The Report declares that suggestions and projects for areas 'may be wise and good but nothing can come of them except failure, unless perserverance in hearty work is shown by people who rarely had an adequate motive for steady hard work'.

But the level of income at the disposal of the Board was at a rate of only a few shillings per year for each family and the Board pronounced: 'Prosperity is not to be conferred through money payments by the Board: it must be earned by the people themselves, for the Board's funds are only sufficient to provide instruction and opportunities for those who are willing to struggle hard to improve their condition.'

A congested district was defined as one where more than 20 per cent of the population of a county live in Electoral Divisions of which the total ratable value, when divided by the number of people living there, resulted in a sum of less than £1 10*s.* for each individual. Counties along the western seaboard fell into the category of 'congested districts'.

The following is a list of Congested Districts Counties from the Board's first Annual Report of 1892. The number of congested districts was increased in subsequent years.

Co.	**No. of Cong. Distr.**	**Area in Statute Acres**	**Pop. in 1891**	**Poor Law Valuation per head of Pop.**		
				£	*s.*	*d.*
Donegal	19¼	824,132	110,220		18	0
Leitrim	4½	174.004	35,250	1	6	8
Sligo	2⅓	148,099	32,565	1	5	5
Roscommon	5⅓	104,862	26,185	1	2	9
Mayo	18⅝	893,480	143,201		18	3
Galway	14¼	564,958	75,248		17	10
Kerry	13	661,042	86,981	1	1	7
Cork	6	237,992	39,866	1	3	7

In my home town of Kiltimagh, Co. Mayo, there were frequent references to the Congested Districts Board, decades after it ceased to function.

Fr. Denis O'Hara was parish priest of this Co. Mayo town between 1888 and 1923. He was appointed a member of the Congested Districts Board in 1893. To this day, the legacy of Fr. Denis is remembered in Kiltimagh and his enormous economic, social and spiritual contribution. In his book, *History of The Congested Districts Board* (1925), the first Secretary of the Board, W. L. Micks, wrote: 'I have accompanied Fr. Denis through the numbers of clustered hovels in which people lived on their rundale holdings [farms comprised of numerous isolated plots] before the Board's real land work began; and afterwards I have seen the comfortable detached houses and improved compact holdings.'

The story is told of how Fr. Denis set out for Monaghan town in the 1890s to ask the St. Louis nuns to establish a convent in Kiltimagh. When his initial request was rejected, Fr. Denis boldly declared that he was not leaving until the nuns conceded. He waited and they conceded.

He was an inveterate letter-writer, constantly appealing for assistance on behalf of his parishoners. On one occasion, he wrote to *The Freeman* newspaper, highlighting the appalling mistreatment of tenants by a local landlord:

> 'John McEllin was fined five shillings because there was a dog path through the hedge of his own land . . . John Gormally had to work eight days for nothing because he did not go to work the day he was sent for . . . Pat Ruane had a half acre in his own land turned to potatoes. The master did not think he should sow potatoes there and commanded him to leave down the sods again with his hands, and with his hands the poor man turned every sod . . . Pat McHugh was fined for venturing to ask how much he would be paid for the days worked for him [the landlord] . . . Pat Duddy had to pay £5 to be allowed sleep in his father's house because he gave up a holding of land which he could not hold on account of the high rent.'

In his book, Micks wrote that the approach of Fr. Denis was gentle, persuasive, practical and sensible. His personal income 'went back wisely to the people for their improvement' and Micks concluded 'there never was, in my judgement, a more kindly unselfish generous man'.

Before the Congested Districts Board provided any form of assistance, Balfour recommended to his Board colleagues that a survey of the congested districts be conducted.

The first Annual Report of the Congested Districts Board records in 1892:

> 'After much consideration it was decided that a careful survey of the condition of the various localities should be undertaken by Members and Inspectors of the Board. A list of districts, or natural areas, was drawn up, and with respect to each district it was determined that "a minute examination into the existing condition of the inhabitants should be undertaken, by which their means of livelihood, the quality of the soil, the amount of land (if any) now available for extension of holdings, the fishing accommodation in existence, the possibility of increasing it, the number of migratory labourers, the character and extent of local industries, and other relevant particulars should be carefully recorded". Numerous other distinctions between one district and another were also mentioned, but the above enumeration of matters for inquiry will suffice to explain the object in view.'

The task of compiling a list of natural geographic divisions, together with the various headings for gathering information for the survey (later to be known as base line reports), was given to W. L. Micks. A total of 84 divisions were identified and a team of inspectors was appointed solely for compiling the reports. Micks wrote letters of appointment to each inspector and stated 'it is right to mention that they [the Board] will regard all your reports and observations as confidential'.

When I first read these reports some years ago, I immediately felt that they provided a wonderful 'mirror' of life in the West of Ireland from just over a century ago. Thus, a selection of the base line reports are printed here in full, faithfully retaining the format and words of the original documents. Only obvious spelling mistakes and minor inconsistencies have been corrected. All other documents are treated similarly, so that the reader can fully savour these historical treasures. A number of photographs of the period have also been included in the reports to illustrate contemporary scenes and living conditions.

James Morrissey

ACKNOWLEDGEMENTS

In a letter dated 15 January 1927, W. L. Micks, first Secretary of the Congested Districts Board and author of *History of the Congested Districts Board*, wrote: 'I wish to present to the Library of Trinity College Dublin a bound folio volume of 84 printed reports made to the Congested Districts Board between the years 1892 and 1898 by highly qualified and specially selected Inspectors on the condition at that time of the congested districts and the inhabitants.'

He concluded by stating that 'these reports are a most valuable and authentic source of information to historians and social inquirers in the future'. Trinity College has been home to these reports ever since.

Some years ago, I accessed these reports and immediately realised that they provided a unique insight into life in the West of Ireland and along our west coast generally. A selection of the reports form the basis of this book.

Without the foresight of W. L. Micks and the safe-keeping of the material by Trinity College Dublin, this book could not have been undertaken.

The author is grateful to the Board of Trinity College Dublin for permission to reproduce selected reports; to David Micks, grandson of W. L. Micks for his co-operation; to the Royal Irish Academy, the Royal Dublin Society, the National Library in Dublin and the Ulster Museum for valuable additional material.

Thanks also to Ronan Menton for inputting the text and to Colour Books for printing *On the Verge of Want.*

The skilled editorial and indexing services provided by Carole Devaney and the design excellence of Paul McElheron were delivered with professionalism and genuine interest.

Finally, to Heather and my family – thank you.

J. M.

MEMBERS OF THE CONGESTED DISTRICTS BOARD FOR IRELAND

William L. Micks

First Secretary of the Congested Districts Board, established in 1891, Micks was appointed an honorary member of the Board in 1909 and a 'permanent' (paid) member in 1910. He remained with the Board up to the date of its dissolution in 1923 and recorded its work in his book *History of The Congested Districts Board*, published in 1925.

Sir Henry Doran

An agriculturalist and engineer, Doran worked as an inspector with the Congested Districts Board before becoming Chief Land Inspector. He was appointed a permanent member of the Board in 1910 and remained in that position until its dissolution in 1923.

The Rev. Fr. Denis O'Hara

Parish priest of Kiltimagh, Co. Mayo, Fr. Denis was a member of the Congested Districts Board from 1893 to 1922. He promoted the Parish Committee Scheme for improving houses and helped transform Kiltimagh into 'a brisk busy well-ordered little country town', according to W. L. Micks.

F. G. Townsend Gahan

Townsend Gahan was a civil engineer and one of the first to be appointed to the outdoor staff of the Congested Districts Board. He worked in Donegal and Mayo. Later appointed a senior inspector, he remained with the Board until 1923.

Arthur Balfour

As Chief Secretary for Ireland, Balfour visited the West in 1890 to see at first hand the plight of the people. According to W. L. Micks, Balfour 'has the credit of being the first British Minister who acknowledged in a practical way that the universal poverty of the West of Ireland was a disgrace to the British government'.

Francis S. Sheridan

A barrister, Sheridan was employed by the Board from its foundation in 1891 to its dissolution in 1923. He was appointed Assistant Secretary in 1910 and subsequently Secretary in 1921.

MAP OF IRELAND, SHOWING THE DISTRICTS SCHEDULED AS CONGESTED

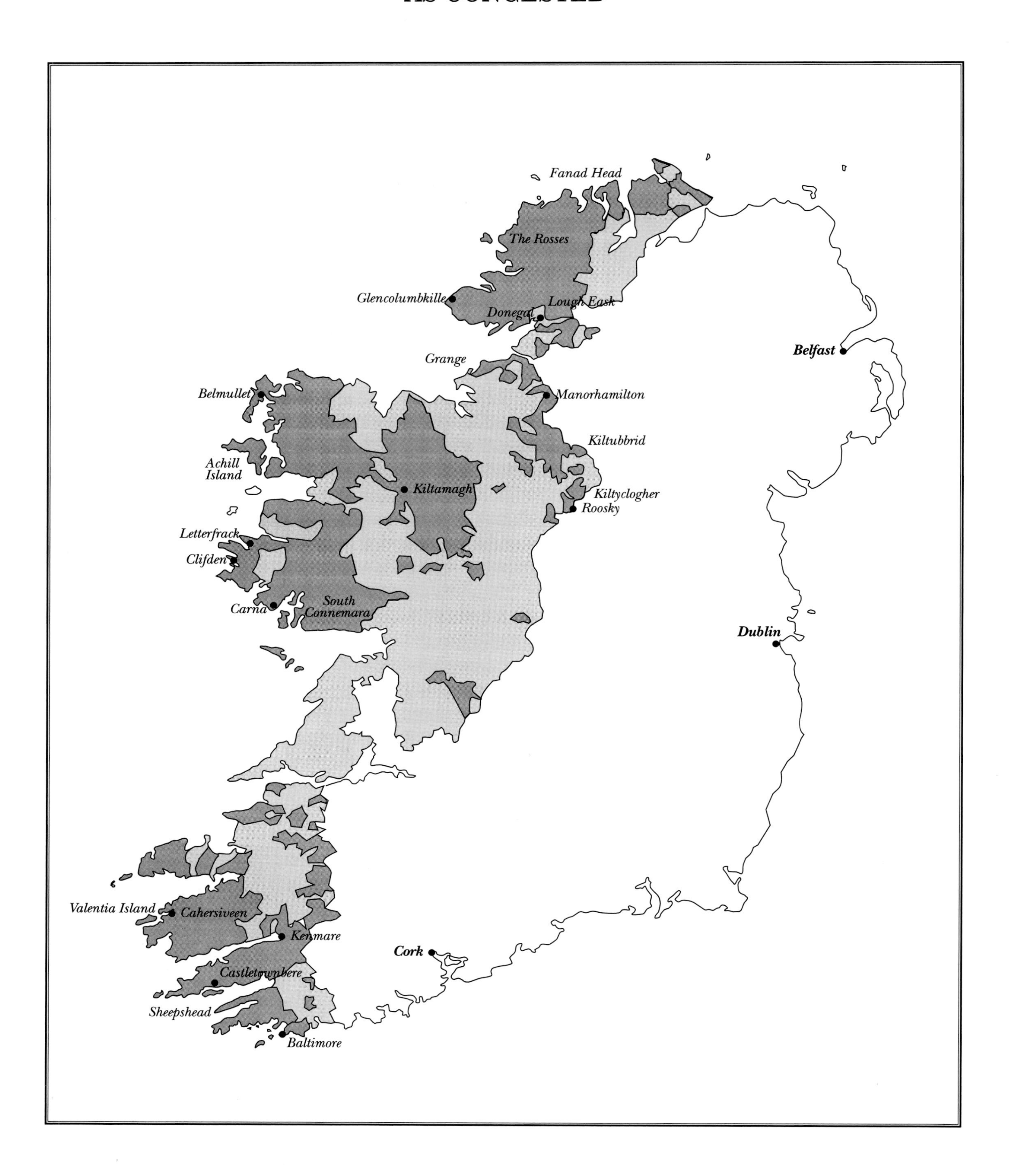

Districts scheduled under 1891 Act

Districts scheduled under 1909 Act

THE "CONGESTED DISTRICTS" AND THE WORK OF THE CONGESTED DISTRICTS BOARD

BY

FRANCIS S. SHERIDAN, *Barrister-at-Law,*
Chief Clerk to the Congested Districts Board.

[FEBRUARY 1915]

When allusion is made to the "congested districts" of Ireland, people who do not know the districts are likely to ask "what is meant by the congested districts?" For it is not at all a title that is self-explanatory (being rather a misnomer), and it is consequently essential that the position should be made clear from the first so that the circumstances of the districts may be understood as far as it is possible to understand the condition of a locality without careful study on the spot.

The term "congested districts" was not applied because the land is thickly populated and overcrowded. On the contrary the density of the population is very low, being only 89 persons per square mile as compared with 134 for all Ireland. The districts were first called "congested" by those mistaken philanthropists who recommended emigration of the inhabitants instead of development of local resources and possibilities. The name has since stuck to the districts. One ought simply to think of the congested districts as being exceptionally poor and undeveloped. The technical and legal definition will be alluded to later on.

§ I. THE ORIGIN OF THE CONGESTED DISTRICTS.

It is impossible to give a faithful description without going a little into history. Certain essential facts as they exist need to be traced to their source in order that a just estimate be formed of the reason why the people of the congested districts are so poor, and also why progress cannot be rapid owing to defective education and to a consequent want of initiative. In considering the ameliorative work of the Congested Districts Board, particularly in relation to the purchase and resale of land, it must be remembered that the Board is not dealing merely with the natural circumstances of a backward people in an out-of-the-way part of Ireland, but rather with unnatural conditions created many generations ago and allowed to continue until our own time without any remedial efforts.

The accompanying map of Ireland* will illustrate the portion of the country committed to the charge of the Congested Districts Board, and subsequent statistics will show the relative position of the congested districts to the rest of Ireland.

During the period from Philip and Mary to Cromwell – particularly in the time of the last-mentioned – re-arrangements of the confiscated lands of Ireland were made to reward the adventurers in the various campaigns against the Irish, and clearances of the "fat lands" were carried out to make way for the "planters" to whom grants of these desirable lands were given – the "innocent" Irish ploughmen and labourers being permitted to remain in the neighbouring "lean lands" to till for the newly endowed proprietors.

Under the Settlement Act of Cromwell's Parliament in September 1653, the owners of selected lands and their retainees in Ulster, Leinster, and Munster who had not maintained a "constant good affection" to the Parliament were ordered under penalty of death to leave their homes before the 1st. May, 1654, with their families, cattle and belongings, and to proceed to occupy lands of little or no value to be allocated to them across the Shannon in Connacht, where they had to wait and "negotiate" for new lands. These proscribed Catholic people included the best blood of the country – Irish nobility and gentry and also the descendants of the old English – Norman settlers who had stood by the King in his war with the Parliament.

To ensure that the migrated persons would not disturb the new occupiers in possession of their old estates, a belt of country four miles wide (afterwards reduced to one mile and known as the "mile line") was drawn right around

* The accompanying map of Ireland referred to here in Sheridan's Report, showing the Districts scheduled as Congested, is reproduced on page xii of this book.

Connacht including the sea-shore, and the lands in the belt were given only to Cromwellians who could be relied upon, like herds, to keep the migrants within the boundary. Thus the new inhabitants of Connacht and the few old ones who had survived the previous war were cooped within the confines of the Western Province and could not get out by land or sea, for they were forbidden to leave it. Subject to certain modifications as to succession during the operation of the succeeding Penal Laws, which need not be gone into here, the land in Connacht had by order of the Government to be divided at death equally between all the sons of the new settlers there. As the years rolled on, therefore, the tendency was to make all the inhabitants (landlords and tenants alike) poorer by continual sub-division, and as there were no industries or emigration – agriculture being virtually the only occupation – the position of the tillers of the soil as well as the owners became gradually weakened.

Somewhat similar stories might be told of the clearances in Ulster and Munster in the reigns of James I and Elizabeth and the driving West of the Irish people to make way for the Government nominees to whom the confiscated lands were assigned, and in this way was laid the foundation of the congested districts as we now know them. In a word, therefore, the problem set to the Congested Districts Board may be said to lie in undoing the evolutionary results of the work of Elizabeth, James I, and Cromwell. But no Government at the present time could propose to exercise the same summary powers that Cromwell possessed, and thus make as rapid progress in their operations as he did in his time. Moreover he dealt with proprietors of lands who took their families and retainers with them *en bloc* whereas the Board are dealing with landlords and tenants individually – having consequently to face a much more difficult and detailed task – and do it in a complicated legal way.

After the Cromwellian "settlement", things were undecided for a time, for the migrants to Connacht naturally hoped, on the restoration of Charles II to get back to their old estates. But the "planters" were influential in England, whereas the dispossessed Irish were not, and on the whole the recent grantees were confirmed in their lands purely as a matter of expediency. In a couple of generations the new Connacht families had become rooted in the soil, and although an attempt was made to do justice to them in the reign of James II, it fell through on his abdication.

As time went on a cleavage developed between the landlords and their tenants in Connacht, which was accentuated through the operation of the Penal Laws. The Government facilitated the landlords in affording special and stringent legislation for the recovery of whatever rents were demanded, and the tenants in the West became impoverished upon their infertile lands through increase of population and continual sub-division. The tenants suffered hardships from landlords and their agents who by demanding increases of rent killed any motive for effecting improvements in farms. In the time of the Georges it became usual for landlords to live away from their estates and this tendency was accentuated by the Act of Union. The estates were left to be managed by agents who were obliged by their employers to make rents rise with their increased expenditure away from home.

The increase in the population of Connacht after the Williamite wars at the end of the 17th. century (by which time the cordon round Connacht had become somewhat relaxed) was, however, slightly retarded by the smuggled emigration of young men to fill the gaps in the Irish Brigade serving on the Continent. After this was disbanded at the close of the French Revolution and prior to the advent of steamships and railways there was no thinning of the ever-increasing population (except by famine, disease, and the Government penal transportation) and thus the poor Connacht peasantry increased and multiplied beyond the capacity of the land to support them in any degree of comfort. Still they struggled on as long as they could make ends meet, for farming was remunerative in the early years of the 19th. century owing to the demand and high prices for Irish food-stuffs during the Napoleonic wars. But afterwards the people of the West were barely able to exist, the potato being their staple food. The population of Ireland increased from just over four millions in 1792 to about 8½ millions during the ensuing half-century, and naturally the West with its "long weak families" suffered the strain most.

Various partial famines recurred, culminating in the Great Famine of 1845-8 when the potato failed. The population of the country was reduced and the West was left broken and helpless. Wholesale emigration was then resorted to by the Government and by philanthropists to relieve hunger and suffering. The adult strong departed leaving the very old and very young peasants to continue the struggle, most of the young remaining only until those who had emigrated were able to send home the passage money to help them in turn to seek a better livelihood across the seas than they could get at home. Rents increased while prices for corn and cattle dropped below the standard of the previous war-time. The absolutely destitute were compelled to enter the workhouses erected under the Poor Law System introduced into the country a short time before (1838) and thus were the congested districts brought into the condition in which they were found by Mr. Arthur Balfour when in 1890 he as Chief Secretary for Ireland visited the West to see for himself how matters stood, and to investigate on the spot the causes of the Land War which had been raging for several years.

Up to 1869 other causes besides poverty contributed to the discontent of the people. Tithes or tithe rent charges had to be paid for the upkeep of the Established Church, in which the vast majority of the people did not worship, and relief was only obtained by the Church Disestablishment Act of 1869. From that on, however, the main cause of trouble was in the inability of the land-holders to pay their rents, and wholesale evictions followed. But a whole country cannot be evicted, and the Government faced the problem by the establishment of the Land Commission in 1881 to fix "fair rents," to compel landlords to cease from making arbitrary increase in rents and to restrict the power of landlords to evict (I).

Owing to legal difficulties in carrying out the spirit of the "fair rent" idea in the Land Laws, several amending Acts were passed, but it was soon apparent that these Land Laws were at best only palliative, and that the land of Ireland – and particularly the West of Ireland – under modern conditions of life was unable to support both landlords and tenants: one class had to go. The Government therefore decided in 1885 as a matter of policy to adopt a larger scheme of Land Purchase – a system which had been already adopted in a small way under the Acts of 1869, 1870, and 1881.

It is not germane to this necessarily short paper regarding the congested districts to examine very closely the several Land Purchase Acts (II) and the various financial and other schemes involved in the work of carrying out the bloodless revolution of transferring the land of Ireland from the *dual* ownership of landlord and tenant to the *single* ownership of tenant-purchaser, but it may be mentioned that the Act of 1885, associated with the name of a distinguished Irishman, the late Lord Ashbourne, was financed in cash, while the Acts of 1891 and 1896 were financed in land stock. The Act of 1903 was again a cash transaction, while the Act of 1909 was mainly a reversion to payments in stock. There is no doubt that *cash* is the most satisfactory method of procedure if practicable, but the difficulty was and is to raise it in such amounts and at such short notice as the purchase scheme of Ireland demands. Hence the Government have had to resort to stock finance with its disadvantages. It may here be stated that in the whole scheme of land purchase, Ireland has only the use of the credit of the United Kingdom of Great Britain and Ireland, for every shilling advanced under the scheme is to be repaid with interest by the purchasing tenants. And so far the British Exchequer has lost nothing in bad debts, while it is an interesting fact that in the congested districts – the poorest section of Ireland – there have not been any losses by failure to meet the Land Commission annuities.

§ 2. THE ESTABLISHMENT OF THE CONGESTED DISTRICTS BOARD.

When Mr. Balfour had completed his tour of the West and noted the condition of the people, he had in mind the districts that needed the special help it was proposed to give in order to lift them out of the slough of misery to which they had been condemned by the force of circumstances over which they had little or no control. In describing his experiences in a speech at Liverpool on the 19th. November, 1890, Mr. Balfour said: "The general impression left upon a casual traveller is that you are dealing with a population not congested in the sense of being crowded, but congested by not being able to draw from their holdings a safe and sufficient livelihood for themselves and their children, whose condition trembles constantly on the verge of want, and when the potato crop fails, goes over that margin and becomes one of extreme and even dangerous destitution."

These were the people and the districts he wished the Government to help, feeling that in the light of history they had an equitable claim to special consideration by Great Britain, but the difficulty was to segregate the districts without arbitrarily selecting them. After considering several plans he decided upon the ratio of population to valuation as the test of congestion to be adopted, and accordingly in the Land Act of 1891 establishing the Congested Districts Board, it is defined that: "Where at the commencement of this Act more than twenty per cent of the population of a County, or in the case of the County Cork of either Riding thereof, live in Electoral Divisions of which the total ratable value, when divided by the number of the population, gives a sum of less than one pound ten shillings for each individual, those Divisions . . . shall form a separate County (in this Act referred to as a Congested Districts County)."

This definition brought in areas sparsely populated as well as congested ones with dense population, but the test failed to include several suitable areas for treatment.

Thus were established the congested districts as scheduled in 1891. The annual income placed at the disposal of the Board at first was £41,250, being interest at 2¾ per cent. on £1,500,000 of the Church Surplus Fund consequent on the Disestablishment of the Irish Church. It may be noted that this Endowment was made from a purely Irish Fund. In addition about £6,000 a year was provided from Parliamentary funds for the Administrative Staff. The administration of two small Loan Funds was also handed over to the Board – the Irish Reproductive Loan Fund, and the Sea and Coast Fishery Fund, amounting to about £66,000 and £18,000 respectively in cash, securities, and outstanding loans.

In the early years the Board's operations were regarded as being only experimental, for if the efforts failed in their objects the income was considered enough to risk, whereas if Parliament approved of what was done, more funds would be forthcoming. As it turned out, the Board's utility was very generally admitted and accordingly a new grant of £25,000

(I) See the article on "The Fair Rent Provisions of the Irish Land Acts," by A.P. Magill, in the *Bulletin of Economic and Social Intelligence* of January 1914.

(II) For articles relating to these Acts see the *Bulletin of Economic and Social Intelligence* of January 1912 and June 1913.

(gross) a year was made by Parliament in 1899 but on conditions that reduced it to about £15,000 (nett). A further increase of £20,000 per annum was made under the Purchase Act of 1903 out of the Ireland Development Grant; and as a result of the finding of the Dudley Royal Commission of 1906 the Board was reconstructed and made a corporate body in 1909 and the income was increased to £250,000 a year less £19,000 a year paid to the Department of Agriculture, as will be explained later on.

The Board now consists of 14 members, of whom three are *ex-officio* – the Chief Secretary, the Under Secretary, and the Vice President of the Department of Agriculture and Technical Instruction. Nine are nominated and honorary members, and the remaining two are permanent members in receipt of a salary in respect of the duties discharged by them under the Congested Districts Acts. Under the Act of 1909 the extent of the area of the congested districts has been greatly increased over that scheduled by the Act of 1891, as shown on the map. The following Table gives some of the comparative conditions of the original scheduled area, of the recently added portions, and of the remainder of Ireland:

TABLE I. – *Area and Population of the Congested Districts.*

	Original Congested Districts (1891)	Congested Districts added in 1909 (including Towns)	Total Congested Districts in 1911	Rest of Ireland (including Cities and Towns)	Approximate ratio between present Congested Districts and rest of Ireland
Area (in acres)	3,608,569	4,053,910	7,662,479	13,192,243	1 to 2
Population in 1911	466,372	594,486	1,060,858	3,329,361	1 to 3
Ratable Valuation 1911	£591,168	£1,787,242	£2,378,410	£13,235,603	1 to 6

It will be noticed that the Act of 1909 more than doubled the original area and population of the congested districts and that the present area is more than one-third of Ireland while the population is about one-fourth. The ratable valuation is, however, only about one-sixth of all Ireland, thus indicating the relative poverty of the Board's districts. They are also mainly rural, the population of the towns only amounting to 85,391 out of the 1,060,858. There are only three towns in the congested districts with a population over 10,000, namely: Galway, 13,255; Sligo 11,163; and Tralee 10,300. This shows the absence of industries other than agriculture and fishing. At present the Board's resources are mainly devoted to operations under the land purchase and resale enactments.

Before dealing in detail with the efforts of the Board in reviving rural activities, it should be stated that the first step taken by the Board in 1892 was to institute a comprehensive survey of the economic condition of the scheduled districts – to form a base line from which progress could afterwards be measured, as well as to indicate the course of action which might be best suited for the different circumstances of the various districts, for the special characteristics of the localities have to be borne in mind in framing schemes of improvement. For example, the development of fisheries was obviously the work to be undertaken in one district, the improvement of agriculture in another, while in a third the undertaking of engineering works was necessary for opening up a backward locality and the assisting of steamer services was found to supply a necessary link in the chain of connection between isolated places and ports of distribution.

In starting operation the Board adopted the principle of "helping the people to help themselves." No mere charity or eleemosynary aid was given, and the establishment of "relief works" to alleviate temporary or exceptional distress, though frequently urged, was always refused. It was fully realised that such temporising expedients were only demoralising in their effect, and they formed no part of the programme of re-generation adopted by the Board. No project that was not considered likely to be reproductive directly or indirectly was supported. The Board's efforts were to raise the mode of life from the submerged condition to which it had been reduced to that of a virile, progressive, self-supporting and self-respecting community.

The duties undertaken by the Board were divided mainly into sections appertaining to the purchase and resale of land; agriculture; fisheries; industries; works and miscellaneous undertakings. These again had to be subdivided as the exigencies of circumstances demanded, and taking the main divisions seriatim the following summary of the work accomplished will indicate the Board's objects and procedure.

EDITOR'S NOTE: The final part of Sheridan's Report, with a concluding summary of the Board's operations, may be found on pages 229-38 of this book.

CONGESTED DISTRICTS BOARD FOR IRELAND

COUNTY OF DONEGAL – UNION OF MILFORD

REPORT OF MR. GAHAN, *Inspector*

DISTRICT

OF

FANAD

STATISTICAL TABLE

ELECTORAL DIVISION.	Area in Statute Acres.	Poor Law Valuation.	Number of Ratings at and under £10 and above £4 Valuation.	Number of Ratings at and under £4 Valuation.	Population in 1891.	Number of Families in 1891.	Number of Families on Holdings exceeding £2 and under £4 Valuation.	Number of Families on Holdings at and under £2 Valuation.	Number of Families in very poor circumstances.	Number of Families which have no Cattle.
		£								*
Carrowkeel,	6,920	1,537	69	59	1,064	181	37	22	6	7
Fanad North,	7,763	1,146	73	187	1,757	296	126	61	7	7
Fanad West,	5,818	1,199	95	134	1,408	256	64	70	11	12
Greenfort,	3,727	1,033	60	59	796	145	28	31	8	4
Killygarvan,	3,089	486	53	48	488	97	37	11	10	3
Knockalla,	4,328	925	79	95	1,005	195	71	24	7	6
TOTALS,	31,645	£6,326	429	582	6,518	1,170	363	219	49	39

* Several of these are Cotters. Nearly every man who has land has cattle; some few have "grazers," and some few cattle "on milk."

(1.) Whether inland or maritime.

This district, owing to its peculiar physical formation, has a very extended coast-line, if by "coast-line" shore touched by salt water is meant. The Electoral Divisions of Fanad North and Fanad West are almost insular – the neck of land connecting Fanad West to the mainland being a little under a mile broad. The district is bounded on the north-east for a distance of fifteen miles by Lough Swilly. From Fanad lighthouse to Ballyhoorisky the extreme north-west of the district is nine miles, washed by the Atlantic. From Rinmore Point to Kindrum, along the shore of Mulroy Bay, is twenty miles, and from Keadew Bridge to Kerryheel is four miles, or a total coast-line of forty-eight statute miles.

(2.) Average quantity of land cultivated on holdings at and under £4 valuation, under (*a*) oats, (*b*) potatoes, (*c*) meadow, (*d*) green crops.

On holdings of, say £3 10*s*. valuation, about six acres would be cultivated, consisting of four acres of oats, one and a half acres potatoes, and half an acre turnips.

On holdings at £2 valuation and under, three acres oats, and one or one and a half acres potatoes, and no turnips, would be cultivated. The amount of meadow land is so small that it need not be considered, not one man in twenty has any meadow. The beasts get straw in the winter instead of hay. Straw, rising sometimes to 3*s*. 6*d*. and 4*s*. a cwt. Cabbages are grown by most farmers, sometimes in a separate plot, sometimes with potatoes. Very few grow mangle-wurzel, and very few flax. This latter as a crop is dying out.

(3.) Extent of mountain or moor grazing, and rights possessed by tenants, whether in common or otherwise.

The extent of mountain or moor grazing may be stated to be as follows:–

Electoral Division.	Extent of Mountain and Moor Grazing.	Remarks.
	Acres.	
Carrowkeel, . . .	4,200	Divided, sheep common.
Fanad North, . . .	4,500	Divided. Lord Leitrim has large fenced area of mountain this year, let to tenants. About 1,000 acres sheep common.
Fanad West, . . .	2,500	Divided generally.
Greenfort, . . .	1,700	Divided. Sheep on mountain common.
Knockalla, . . .	2,300	Common generally.
Killygarvan, . . .	1,500	Divided and Common.
Total, . . .	16,700	

(4.) Extent and description of land, if any, which could be profitably reclaimed and added to existing adjoining holdings.

There is not much land in this district which would be suitable for reclamation, though generally in the mountainous portions there are lands attached to holdings which if properly reclaimed might be profitably cultivated. This applies more especially to Carrowkeel, Knockalla, and the upland portions of Killygarvan Electoral Divisions. In Fanad, North and West, the population is more crowded, and all the available land is cultivated, some being obliged to rent patches from larger farmers further inland, to set their potatoes in. Nearly every farm in the district might be better drained, though on account of the sandy nature of the soil, drainage is not so deficient in this district as in many others.

(5.) Particulars as to any suitable land in district which could be obtained, and to which families could be migrated with a reasonable prospect of success.

There is, so far as I could ascertain, no suitable land for a migration scheme in the district.

(6.) Method of cultivation, manures, rotation of crops, etc., etc.

In this district farm cultivation is much more advanced than in the districts of Teelin, Glencolumbkille, and Glenties.

Potatoes are almost invariably cultivated in drills. The quantity of corn grown greatly exceeds that of potatoes. Turnips are always found on the larger holdings and often on the smaller ones. Flax is grown by a few, but not to the same extent as in former years. Mangle-wurzel is grown by the larger farmers. A species of vetch is also grown by a few. Cabbages are cultivated by most, sometimes in "gardens" near the house, sometimes in fields by themselves, and sometimes with potatoes. Along the sea-coast barley is generally sown with oats, as the people say they get a better crop by so doing, such a crop goes by the local term of "Pracas."

The land is prepared for potatoes in the beginning of April. Any people who have early potatoes set them about the 8th. From the 8th till the 15th corn is generally sown, and after the corn, or about the 20th of April, the later potatoes are set. If it is a wet spring they may be later still. The corn land of last year is the potato land of this year, and *vice versa*. In the poorer portions of the district, where they cannot afford to manure their extra corn land, a second corn crop is taken off without any manure. Those who can afford it buy special manures, of which there is a large quantity sold in the district – about 200 or 300 tons. The quantity of turnips grown hardly constitutes a rotation, but this year's turnip land will next year be corn, and following year potatoes. Corn is grown in large quantities, as it is the chief food for cattle, there being, as I have already stated, almost no meadow land in the district. The grain goes to feed the horses, cattle, and fowl sometimes. The straw is given to horses and cattle, and, along with cabbage and potatoes, forms their winter fodder. Farm-yard manure is used generally through the district. Seaweed is a little used in one or two places, but not generally. They think it induces the rot in the potatoes. Lime is not much used:– 1st, because it is scarce; and 2nd, because there is such a great scarcity of turf to burn it with. It is found in the townland of Springfield in Greenfort Electoral Division, and in Carngarrow in Knockalla Electoral Division. If kilns could be established and lime burnt for the people in different localities it would be of immense benefit, as it is very useful for the corn crop as a manure. The lime might be sold to the people at a moderate price.

(7.) General information with regard to stock, and suggestions as to improvement of breeds – (*a*) cattle, (*b*) sheep, (*c*) horses and donkeys, (*d*) pigs, (*e*) poultry, etc., etc.

The stock of the district is, as a rule, poor.

Cattle.– The cattle belong to the old Irish breed, and are of a small, low type, being impoverished by repeated in-breeding. The price runs from £2 to £3 10*s*. at present. The bulls are very small, ill-looking animals; their descendants could not possibly have any good points about them. It is worthy of remark that at Milford fair in July, some heifers from local cows, crossed with Polled Angus bulls, fetched £5 10*s*., while larger local cattle were only going for £3 and £3 10*s*. The Board have one Shorthorn bull in the district at Ballyhernan, Kildrum, Fanad West, which the people seem to appreciate. Some think the Galloway would be more suited to the district than the Polled Angus. The cattle are no better housed in this district than in others. The byres are dirty, badly constructed, and draughty. The cattle are generally kept in all night, summer and winter, for the sake of the manure. Owing to the absence of hay in the district, the cattle are often badly fed in the winter when the straw fails.

Sheep.– These are of the white-faced Irish breed, small and poor generally. In some one or two cases on better farms I saw some good Border Leicesters. The wool on these sheep is finer than on the Scotch sheep, but Scotch sheep seem to me to be more suitable to the district. However, opinion seems to be divided in the matter. It is suggested:–

I. Introduce some Border Leicester rams along the coast-line, locating them, on the same principle as the bulls, with respectable farmers.

II. Into the mountainous portions of the district introduce a number of Scotch rams, and if possible some ewes letting the former run with the sheep, and selling the latter.

Horses.– There are a large number of horses in the district, many of them large coarse animals, but not at all suitable for the farmers who own them. I believe Lord Leitrim has a Clydesdale stallion at Mulroy; but it is not a breed at all suitable for the peasantry, even when crossed with their small mares. A stallion, Hackney or Suffolk Punch, located at Rosnakill (a central point, but not a "Congested" Electoral Division) would be of immense service to the people.

Lord Leitrim has an Arab stallion, but it is considered rather too small.

Donkeys.– There are more in this district than in the western districts, and they are not despised here as they are there. I would suggest the introduction of stallions of good quality.

Pigs.– There are a good many pigs in the district, most farmers keeping two, and the better off ones three or four.

The breed might be improved by crossing with three-quarter bred Yorkshires.

The number of pigs in this district as in others depends on the spring prices and the potato crop.

Poultry.– The poultry are of the usual local breed but are good layers. Indeed the Fanad poultry are generally considered to lay larger eggs than others, this is only hearsay, as any eggs I saw seemed to me to be of the usual small size; they, however, get very nearly Derry prices for their eggs, the present price being 8½*d*., while in Carrick and Glencolumbkille at present they are 5½*d*. and 6*d*. per dozen. An improvement in the breed might be tried, Minorcas and Plymouth Rocks ought to do well in the locality.

Poultry are fed on Indian meal and potatoes, getting very little grain, and herein lies the principal fault of the country farmers. The birds lay wonderfully well – considering everything. I fancy that the fact of their always having the house to lay in, with the warmth of the fire in the room, may have something to say to this.

There are a number of geese reared in the district, and an improvement in these would be much appreciated. Very few turkeys are reared in the district.

The stock of the district is, as a rule, poor. Below I give general statistics as to number of cattle, sheep, &c.:–

Electoral Division.	Poultry					Cattle	Sheep	Pigs	Horses	Asses
	Hens	Ducks	Geese	Turkeys	Total					
Carrowkeel,	2,430	900	960	100	4,390	1,086	905	250	100	60
Fanad North,	3,330	1,350	1,400	50	6,130	1,480	600	300	60	85
Fanad West,	2,960	1,200	700	100	4,960	1,536	1,586	350	150	70
Greenfort,	2,175	870	650	100	3,795	1,160	725	290	100	30
Killygarvan,	1,164	388	250	25	1,827	485	388	90	50	15
Knockalla,	2,240	780	500	50	3,570	975	1,950	150	100	40
Totals,	14,299	5,488	4,460	425	24,672	6,722	6,154	1,430	560	300

The great majority of the horses have carts.
The donkeys generally have creels but some have carts.
The totals of geese and pigs is the *summer* total. Pigs are bought from May till August, and sold from October to February.

(8.) Markets and fairs for cattle and produce of district; also statement as to where the people obtain food and other supplies, and the prevailing custom with regard to the disposal of butter, eggs, and poultry; to what extent are they sold in the first instance to local shopkeepers and dealers, and, generally speaking, how old are the eggs when sold to the first buyer, and about how old when they reach their ultimate destination in Great Britain.

The principal markets are Rathmullan, Ramelton (not actually in the district), and Kerrykeel. There is also a market in Milford. The principal fairs are Ramelton, Milford, Kerrykeel, and Tamney, of these Kerrykeel is the only fair actually in the district.

In Fanad West some supplies are obtained from Tamney, such as meal, flour, &c. These are generally carted up from Milford where they come by steamer. In Fanad North most of the meal, flour, &c. is obtained at Portsalon, where it sometimes comes direct from Derry and sometimes from Milford.

Carrowkeel Electoral Division is generally supplied from Kerrykeel and Portsalon. Greenfort Electoral Division is supplied from Portsalon and Tamney; Knockalla Electoral Division from Rathmullan generally, and Killygarvan Electoral Division from Rathmullan and Kerrykeel. Tea, tobacco, snuff, and sugar and all other small groceries, as salt, soap, &c., are obtained at small local shops.

Eggs are always sold to the local shop-keepers, or if near a village or town they are sold there. The price for eggs in this district is much higher than in the western districts, it being almost up to Derry market prices.

Butter is sometimes made in butts of 75 lbs. to 100 lbs., and sometimes sold in portions of 1 lb. and 2 lbs. to the dealer as it is made. He then puts it all into a butt when he has 100 lbs. gathered, and sends it away. This plan of mixing the butter is very bad, and it is principally owing to this that butter has that seamy appearance when cut transversely. Eightpence and ninepence is about the average price for butter.

A fair number of poultry are exported from Portsalon and Milford, those from Portsalon going direct to Londonderry and on to Liverpool or elsewhere. The prices given are various, ranging from 4*d.* to 1*s.*, each.

The eggs (except when near a village) are invariably sold to local dealers. Their age depends very much on the person to whom they are sold; but generally speaking, the eggs from this district get to the market earlier than those from the more western districts. A steamer runs from Portsalon to Fahan twice weekly. If a man has been gathering eggs for a week he sends them away by her and they get to Derry the same day. Suppose the egg was kept, before being sold to the dealer, for one week; that would make the egg a fortnight old before it got to Derry, and generally speaking, that may be looked upon as being the average extreme age of an egg before reaching Derry. If the eggs are sold to itinerant vendors, these often keep the eggs over on chance of a rise in price, and then it is impossible to say what the age of the egg would be. The eggs are generally sent forward from Londonderry to Glasgow, and to Liverpool and elsewhere in England. I should think the average extreme age would be three weeks for the English market, and the average mean age about a fortnight.

(9.) Rail, steamer, sailing boat, road, postal and telegraph facilities.

The nearest railway station by land is Letterkenny and the nearest by water Fahan – distant thirty-three and eighteen, and fifteen and five miles from the extreme points of the district, respectively. Both the railways are narrow gauge.

The steamer service has already been referred to in a general report on the district.

Coal is brought in by sailing vessels to Milford or Portsalon. Meal and flour are also occasionally brought by them. In the course of years the importation of coal into the district must be a very important item.

The road facilities of the district are not good. Except in one or two instances the roads are hilly and bad. In some cases the hills are so steep as utterly to preclude any idea of taking a load either up or down them – hills with a gradient of one in five being quite common. In Fanad proper the roads are rough and badly kept, apparently no one looks after them at all.

Some of the hills in the Electoral Division of Killygarvan and Knockalla could be easily avoided. At present some of the farmers in Killygarvan have to cart their turf nine miles to their houses, although the distance from the bog is only about four miles. The County is, at present, in arrears with the County Cess, and will not attempt any improvement or alteration of roads; indeed, even with everything paid up, I am afraid "the County" will do very little towards the improvement of the roads of the district.

A road around the base of the Knockalla Mountains, from the County road at the Battery, to the County road in Greenfort Electoral Division (a distance of two and a half miles), thus making a low-level connection between Fanad proper, Rathmullan, and the district, would be a very useful and desirable public work. At present, in winter, owing to the high level of the Glenalla road (500 to 600 feet above sea-level), communication between Fanad and the outer world is almost cut off. The road I have mentioned would also lessen the distance into Fanad proper by some three or four miles. This is, of course, a work which the Grand Jury ought to undertake, as it would benefit such a wide area; but at present, as I have mentioned, the Donegal Grand Jury are much hampered by the very large arrears in County Cess, and are not likely to undertake, at present, public works of any sort.

The postal facilities are very fair. Everywhere, through the district, you can receive and answer a letter on the same day.

There is a telegraph office at Rathmullan and one at Kerrykeel. The latter is the only one in the district. If the wire were extended from Kerrykeel to Tamney and Portsalon, or the telephone from Knockalla Battery carried on to Portsalon, around the mountain, it would be a benefit to the Fanad district. From Knockalla Battery to Portsalon is about four miles. From Kerrykeel to Tamney is four miles, and four more on to Portsalon.

(10.) Employment for labourers in the district, whether temporary or constant, and rate of wage.

There is very little employment for labourers in the district itself. The larger farmers generally have a boy or girl, or both, from the district; but there are not many of these. The rate of wage runs from £5 to £8 the half-year for boys and men, ploughing and mowing for the latter sum, and £2 to £5 for girls, according to their capabilities. There is no constant employment for labourers in the district.

(11.) Migratory labour, average earnings per head, and where earned.

Most of the young men of the district go to Scotland and England for the harvest, and those who do not go there generally hire themselves out in the district known as "the Lagan," between Letterkenny and Derry. Many of the girls hire themselves out to this district also. Some girls, who were able to make 8*s.* a week on shirt sewing, giving it up and going to hire in preference to the sewing work. The rate of wages to labourers in England and Scotland varies from 15*s.* to 25*s.* a week with their keep, any who can do so going back to the same place year after year. The Irishmen are fine workers when away from home, and generally manage to bring home from £7 to £8 at the end of harvest, say November. They also send home money from time to time as they are able. The only drawback to their system of yearly migration is that the morals of those who go over generally descend in the scale. This, I believe, is especially remarkable with young fellows who have remained over two or three seasons. A natural result of this system of migration is that the women at home have to do a large amount of the home harvesting – hay-making, potato digging, etc.

In the Lagan district, boys and girls are hired for the half-year at prices from £5 to £9 for boys and men, and £2 to £6 for girls, all with keep included. The men on the higher wage have to plough, mow, and reap.

The principal "Rabbles" or hiring fairs of the district are Milford on the 23rd of May and 23rd of November, and Letterkenny on the 12th of May and 12th of November respectively. Those farmers who want farm help drive in to these fairs and there engage a boy or girl for the half year. Often the same boy goes to the same farmer year after year. It was at one time the custom for those who were going to hire themselves to have a bunch of straw tied on their caps. Then this fell into disuse, and one straw tied round the hat or held in the mouth or hand was the sign. This custom is, I believe, still in force in some localities.

(12.) Weaving, spinning, knitting, and sewing, whether used locally or sold, and where.

There is a good deal of spinning in the district, and also a good deal of weaving, but mostly for home use; some few make up small webs to sell in Milford fair, but not to any extent. There is a dealer in Milford (Mr. F. Stewart) who gives out wool to the women, who spin it and return it to him spun. He then gives the spun wool to the weavers who make it into flannel, twenty-nine inches wide, at from 2*d.* to 4*d.* a yard. There are about twelve or fourteen weavers in the district, but only a few of these do any work for the fair, the great majority of the flannel made being for home-wear, blankets, etc. There is very little knitting in the district, only the home hosiery. The women's Sunday stockings are generally bought.

The shirt-sewing industry is beginning to develop itself. Messrs. MacIntyre and Hogg have established a centre at Kerrykeel, for which some twenty girls sew. There is also another about to be established in the neighbourhood of Portsalon by the same firm. Messrs. MacIntyre and Hogg first give their girls instructions at their place in Kerrykeel. When a girl is sufficiently skilful with the machine she is given – or rather lent – one at her own house.

A good girl can do five dozen shirts in a week, provided she has a sister or sisters to do the buttonholes and finishings. The pay is – for ordinary shirts, 2*s.* 1*d.* per dozen; for shirts with double plated seam at arms, 2*s.* 3*d.* per dozen; and for those with a diamond piece inserted at the cuffs for buttoning with button and button-hole, 2*s.* 5*d.* per dozen. A girl can, on an average, do four dozen weekly. In the Kerrykeel branch there are twenty-six girls altogether, and the weekly out-put is about 100 dozen. If the shirts are soiled the workers are fined. They are sent off from Milford by the *Melmore* once a week to Derry. So long as a girl has a machine she is responsible for it, and if anything happens to it she will not be given another. If they stop working, the machine must be returned at once. There are at present two machines in the factory returned by girls who preferred going out to hire to continuing the machine work.

(13.) Kelp-burning, and sale of seaweed.

The kelp-burning is a very considerable industry along the coast between Fanad Point and Ballyhoorisky, and is a great source of income to the people. Indeed without it, it is difficult to see how they could exist. There are certain storms at different periods of the year which are looked upon as the time of the kelp seaweed harvest, and the saving and "winning" or drying of the seaweed is of as much importance to the kelp-burners as the saving of his hay is to the farmer. If it is a wet Spring and they cannot get the seaweed dried, the kelp harvest is a failure. As this industry is extensive some account of it may not be out of place. After one of the storms referred to above, every man, woman, and child in the place is in the water saving the weed; any who have carts back them into the water and any who have no carts must creel it up on donkeys, or on their own backs to the grass or sand above high water mark.

It will then be evident that the man who has most help when the kelp harvest is on, has the best chance of making money on it. The kelp-weed gathering goes on for two or three days, and then the various heaps are spread out to dry. Here another difficulty often arises owing to want of space for drying the weed and it is often a source of loss to the kelp-burner. When the weed is dried a rude kiln is constructed of earth and stones, and lit with turf. The weed is then placed on it, and renewed from time to time as that beneath melts away. Some burners run the kelp into rectangular moulds, others just leave it in the rough. When the seaweed is all burnt the kelp is stacked in some convenient place until the dealer comes round, when it is weighed and paid for – the present rate being £4 a ton. On an average, one man can make from 2½ to 4 tons of kelp in the year, some make up to five and six tons where there is a large family all able to work. Kelp is a substance about as heavy as coal or heavier. It is of a dark granular substance easily scored with a knife. The people adulterate it a good deal with sand, at one time it was a common custom to fill the heart of the lump with stones or to put stones through it. This, however, is now done away with, but the sand adulteration is still carried on to a considerable extent. The portion of the weed most fancied for kelp is the long fibrous stalk of the seaweed, but the long flat band seaweed is used also as there is not enough of the former to supply the demand.

Passing from the kelp-makers to the buyers, I would wish to make a few remarks. There is in the kelp trade a curious "ring." Some two or three firms have the monopoly of the trade, and have the Irish coast portioned out – one firm never poaching (as it were) on the others' preserves. By this means the price of kelp has been kept at an abnormally low figure for many years past. A local industry was started at Ramelton some ten or fifteen years ago, and Iodine began to be manufactured. This caused a local rise in the price of kelp, and these firms came in and gave the manager of the business an annuity of £300 a year on condition that the work was discontinued, which it was, and the buildings are now going to ruin. There is at present a rise in the price of kelp, and not for many years have the prices been what they are at present. Still the price is not up to its fair market value which I believe is £7 or £8 a ton. I hear that another reason for the price of kelp keeping so low is the importance of Iodine, manufactured from the refuse of the Nitrate Works in America.

The sale of seaweed is very small indeed. All the kelp-burners get it free and not many use it for manure. Although I have stated that there are two periods of the year when the kelp-weed is obtained, there are some who gather and burn kelp most of the year round. The people along the shore are very strict as to their rights to the seaweed, and a stranger coming to take seaweed from a kelp-burning district would be forcibly made to desist from gathering it.

(14.) Sale of turf, nature and extent of bogs.

The sale of turf is at present prohibited in the district.

The extent of bog is very small – so small indeed that it has become necessary to consider what fuel the people are to have when, in the course of the next few years, the turf gives out altogether. In Fanad North, many farmers are *actually cutting up their grazing land and burning the sods.* In Fanad West they are nearly as badly off, and some in that portion of the Electoral Division known as "Between the Waters" boat their turf a distance of three or four miles, having previously carted it from the bog to the shore, a distance of four miles. At present there are along the shores of Milford Haven, near Cranford, many stacks of turf waiting to be boated over. In Greenfort Electoral Division they are not quite so badly off for turf, but some have to draw it five or six miles from the Knockalla mountains. The principal bog of the district lies in Creeve townland (Knockalla Electoral Division), and in Meentagh townland (Carrowkeel Electoral Division). In these localities all the people of the country around cut their turf. In Creeve bog from 200 to 300 families cart turf away. Those living at the lower side of Killygarvan, above Rathmullan, have to cart round their turf through Rathmullan, as the hills are too steep to take a load over. A peculiarity of the turf-sods of this district, is the great length they are cut, many being two feet and two feet six inches long, when dry. The turf in Creeve and Carrowkeel bogs is of a fair quality as a rule, though some of it is light. There is some turf in Killygarvan Electoral Division, in the quarter of Oughterlin.

(15.) Lobster fishing, number of men and boats employed.

There is very little lobster fishing done in the district, and no boats are exclusively employed at it. About seven or eight boats fish lobsters from time to time. From Lehardan and Fanad and Ballyhoorisky, statistics as to number of fish caught in the district will be found with the general fishing statistics. The lobsters are not of any great size and are sent off by steamer to Liverpool or Glasgow.

(16.) Sea fishing. Facilities for sale of fish, and number of boats and men solely employed in fishing.

Although the coast-line is so extended, this is not a great fishing district, and very few families are solely employed in fishing. Along the coast between Ballyhoorisky and Fanad Point, there are five families solely engaged in fishing, and between Fanad Point and New Bridge there are no families solely engaged in fishing. The boats belonging to these men are as a rule solely for fishing, but sometimes they are used as "wrack" or seaweed boats. The facilities for sale of fish are fair. If there is a big take on, the "hucksters" come with their carts to the shore, but if not, the fish is boated to Buncrana or Rathmullan.

On the coast, between Fanad and Ballyhoorisky, many curraghs are used.

(17.) Number of boats and men employed in carrying turf or seaweed or in fishing. Classification of boats.

There are twenty-eight second class boats and fifteen third class boats in the district registered as fishing boats. Along the coast between Fanad and Ballyhoorisky the third class boats rate as curraghs. The second class boats here rate as third class in Teelin district. Each curragh has a crew of two men, and the other boats four or sometimes five, so that 103 men are engaged in fishing from time to time. These registered boats are also employed in carrying seaweed and turf at different periods of the year. Some of them fish when there are great numbers of fish being taken, others from time to time. Judging by the number of fish caught (of which the particulars are as follows) the fishing of the district does not seem to be very good:–

Lobsters. – 1891-92, 230 dozen.

Cod, Ling. – Cannot obtain accurate return, but they are not taken in any large quantity. They sell at 1*s.* each.

Glasson. – No return of glasson – only used at home.

Haddock. – Taken in fairly large quantities.

Whiting. – Not so numerous as haddock.

Mackerel. – Sometimes taken, but not largely.

Soles. – 1892, 1,716 lbs., £17.

Fluke or Plaice. – 1892, 180 cwt.; value, £85 6*s.* 9*d.* (approximately).

Turbot. – 1892, 238 lbs.; average price, 1*s.*

Herrings. – 1892, 1,450; value, £5 16*s.*

In addition to the above-mentioned forty-three registered boats there are in Fanad West many unregistered boats (about twenty-five or thirty), merely used for turf or seaweed – principally the former. The men cart the turf to the shore at Cranford, and thence boat it across to that portion of Fanad West known as "Between the Waters."

(18.) Fish; whether consumed at home or sold.

Cod and ling when caught are generally sold, either at Rathmullan or Buncrana. Glasson are often salted and eaten at home. Haddock are sometimes eaten fresh, and sometimes sold. The same applies to whiting. Herring are always sold. If there is a take of herrings on, the itinerant vendors come with their carts to the shore, and buy the fish from the boats.

(19.) Extent of fish-curing.

There is no fish-curing carried on in the district.

(20.) Piers and Harbours, existing and suggested, and how far those existing are adapted to wants of district.

There is a pier at Portsalon, in Greenfort Electoral Division, which is the only pier in the district. This pier was constructed some years ago by the Board of Works, and is supposed to be a continuation of the old pier. The present structure is of concrete, and the seaward half of it is at an angle of about 130 degrees with the landward portion. The old pier was left standing and when a sea is running the wall of the old pier causes a nasty back-wash, and must act as a silter. At present the length from the old pier to the angle of the new pier is 130 feet, and from the angle to the end, seventy feet. Any vessels coming to the pier lie at the end as the water is very shoal along the upper portion, owing to the back-wash from the old pier, and also because of this back-wash in a heavy sea, there is a chance of the vessels sustaining damage. As the end portion of the pier is only seventy feet long, none but very small vessels can lie at it. Any vessel of more than sixty feet over all has her stern exposed to the action of the waves round the pier head. At dead low-water springs there is not more than four feet or four feet six inches depth of water off the pier head. The bottom is sandy with clay under the sand. A pretty heavy sea runs here, sometimes with a northerly or north-westerly gale.

In consequence of the foregoing reasons it is extremely difficult to get a vessel to discharge at the quay, and Lord Leitrim's steamer, the *Melmore*, is unable to call at it. Portsalon is, even at present, an important centre for the Fanad District, as when the turf dies out, coal will have to be imported into the district. Besides there is at present a good trade in potatoes, corn, etc., from the district, and an import trade in meal, flour, bran, artificial manures, sugar, etc. If the pier could be lengthened, and all these come by sea, it would be of immense benefit to the community at large. The pier might be lengthened by means of a timber staging, or carrying on the present concrete structure for say another hundred feet. The former would be the cheaper method, but in a sea it would not afford any protection to boats lying behind it.

The *Teredo* is found at Fahan, but from what I could find out it has not appeared at Portsalon. The *Limnoria* has not, to local knowledge, appeared. If these two insects were absent, the life of a greenheart staging would be considerable, as it has stood intact for 19 years in water, and shown no signs of decay. On the other hand, if the *limnoria terebrans*, or the *teredo navalis* appeared, the timber is generally affected inside four years. I estimate that £1,500 ought to put up the timber extension, and about £3,600 the continuation of the present structure in concrete for 100 lineal feet.

A boat-slip is suggested at Fanad Point, beside the lighthouse, but I do not think the project feasible on account of the depth of the water and the amount of blasting which would have to be undertaken for so small a work. There are only some two or three boats altogether at the place.

A boat-slip is suggested at Lahardan, just at the mearing between Killygarvan and Knockalla Electoral Divisions. There are some 12 or 13 boats here, and a slip would be most useful and easily constructed.

A boat-slip is suggested in proximity to Knockalla Battery, but if one were constructed at Lahardan, the Knockalla boats could land their fish there.

(21.) Extent of salmon and freshwater fisheries. Number of men earning their livelihood therefrom.

There are no licensed salmon boats in the district, and no men exclusively gain a livelihood from salmon-fishing.

(22.) Banks and Loan Funds.

There are Banks in Ramelton and Letterkenny, and a monthly branch at Milford. There is no Bank in the district.

There are no Loan Funds in the district.

(23.) Mineral and other resources.

The mineral resources of the district are almost nil. Bog-ore is found in small quantities near Portsalon, but not enough to pay for transport. Limestone is found in Knockalla and Greenfort Electoral Divisions. There is a good deal of kelp burned; probably between 300 and 400 tons leave the district yearly.

(24.) Relative prevalence of cash or credit dealings, length of credit, interest charged, extent of barter, etc., etc.

Food stuffs, as meal, bran, flour, etc., are generally obtained on credit, but tea, tobacco, sugar, snuff, etc., are nearly always paid for as they are bought. The man who does not pay for his bag of meal when he gets it, generally pays by instalments, according as he obtains the money.

The length of credit is for some twelve months, for others six, and for some, perhaps, only a few weeks. It very much depends on the dealer's knowledge of his customer's circumstances. Sometimes if a man was in debt and unable to pay in a year, say, if the dealer sees any chance of his paying in another six months, he lets him run on, but will charge him a correspondingly large interest for the time. The extent of credit varies also with the dealer's knowledge of his customer's circumstances – for some it might run to £15 and £20, and for others only to £4 or £5. The extent of credit is not at present what it used to be, owing to the very low price of cattle and sheep. The interest charged varies with the locality in which the people reside; if they live near the dealer, it will not be so much, if far away it will be more. If a man deals constantly at the same place, he, perhaps, would be charged nothing at all, but I do not think that is very often the case. Generally speaking, 1*s.* per bag of meal, say 13*s.* for six months, or 2*s.* per annum for 13*s.*, or about 15.4 per cent.

There is no barter strictly speaking in the district, *i.e.*, exchange of goods without regard to monetary basis, but all through this district, as through others, eggs are changed for tea, sugar, snuff, &c. Butter likewise and sometimes a load of turf will be exchanged, but this is not supposed to be sold.

The nearest approach to actual barter is when a farmer sends up a cow "on milk" to some mountain farmer who grazes and looks after the cow. In this case the milk is bartered for the grass, being a convenience on both sides, and not having any monetary basis for the transaction.

(25.) Estimated *cash* receipts and expenditure of a family in ordinary circumstances.

The *cash* receipts and expenditure of a family in ordinary circumstances may be estimated as follows:–

Receipts	£	s.	d.	Expenditure	£	s.	d.
Sale of 110 doz. hen eggs at 7*d.*,	3	4	2	Rent, . .	2	10	0
„ 20 doz. duck eggs at 7*d.*, .	0	11	8	County Cess, 7*s.* 1*d.*, and Dog Licence, 2*s.* 6*d.*	0	9	7
„ 6 geese at 2*s.*, . .	0	12	0	7 bags meal at 12*s.* 6*d.* .	4	7	6
„ 15 chickens at 6*d.*, .	0	7	6	12 bags flour at 12*s.* 6*d.* .	7	10	0
„ 100 lbs. butter at 8*d.* .	3	6	8	Bran, . .	1	10	0
„ 2 cows, . .	6	0	0	Patent manure, . .	1	0	0
„ 2 pigs, . .	7	10	0	Turnip seed, . .	0	2	0
„ 3 sheep and lambs, .	2	10	0	1 cow, . .	2	0	0
„ 60 stone potatoes at 3*d.*, .	0	15	0	2 "suckers" (pigs), . .	1	15	0
Two "harvestings", . .	16	0	0	2 sheep, . .	1	0	0
Sale of wool or yarn,. .	0	15	0	Tea, 39 lbs at 2*s.* 4*d.*,. .	4	11	0
	£41	12	0	156 lbs, sugar at 2½*d.*, .	1	12	6
				Parafin oil, 5*s.*, candles. 5*s.*, .	0	10	0
				Salt, 7*s.* 6*d.*, soap, 5*s.*, etc, 10*s.*,	1	2	6
If along the shore – kelp, .	15	0	0	Tobacco, . .	2	12	0
Sale of fish, . .	5	0	0	Intoxicating drink and "treats",	2	0	0
In above case there will probably be only one "harvesting," or perhaps none at all.				Passage to and from England and expenses there deducted from total wage leaving £16 as above.			
Those along the coast would not sell butter. Only 1 cow and 1 pig, no potatoes and no chickens.				Clothes for men, . .	2	10	0
				„ women, . .	2	0	0
				Boots, . .	1	10	0
				Church dues, . .	1	0	0
Cash receipts maritime townlands,	£38	7	10		£41	12	1

(26.) Estimated value of home-grown food consumed, and period during which it lasts.

The potatoes of the district generally last till the end of April. They would last longer but for the fact that many sell the Champions in winter as they begin to get bad when kept very long. Say a man uses 12 stone weekly with his family for 32 weeks, at 3*d.* a stone, and gives his stock 7 stone per week for 20 weeks, or altogether 524 stone at 3*d.* = £6 11*s.*

Then, if he has a ton of oats, he gets half a ton of meal from it at 12*s.* = £6. The majority of the people grow turnips, say 2 roods, producing 8 tons to the acre or 4 tons to half an acre at 8*d.* per cwt. = £2 13*s.* 4*d.*

There is no hay in the district, but straw takes its place, every man having about 4 tons of straw valued at 1*s.* 6*d.* a cwt. = £6.

Each man has up to 15 tons of manure, at 2*s.* 6*d.* a ton = £1 17*s.* 6*d.*

Milk or buttermilk generally is consumed at the rate of two quarts daily at 1*d.*, or allowing for the winter, when there is very little, say 1*s.* weekly, or £2 12*s.* per annum.

Eggs to 3*s.* worth, and butter about 2 lbs. weekly all the year round at 6*d.* = £2 12*s.*

Fowl killed on holidays, &c. = 10*s.*

Cabbage, say 1,000 head at ½*d.* per head = £2 1*s.* 8*d* – showing a total for home-grown food consumed of £31 0*s.* 6*d.* This does not include firing.

(27.) Dietary of people, number of meals daily, and kinds of food throughout the year.

The dietary of the people of this district is very similar to that of other neighbouring districts – potatoes during the winter forming their chief article of diet, and meal when the potatoes are finished. One difference is noticed, that is, that many have a bit of bacon with their dinners, and more oaten-meal stirabout is taken here than in the western districts. There is also more oat-bread made. One reason for this may be the yearly migration to Scotland; another is the much larger quantity of corn grown.

There are three regular meals, and for some, regularly and others irregularly, a fourth meal partaken of between dinner and supper.

Breakfast. – Consists of oaten bread, or flour bread, and tea. If there is a great plenty of potatoes, potatoes are taken as well. Generally before the tea and bread each member of the family has a large bowl of stirabout and buttermilk.

Dinner. – Consists of potatoes, and milk if it is to spare, and a bit of bacon. If it is near the sea, perhaps a bit of dried fish. Tea is taken shortly after. When the potatoes are finished, oaten or more generally Indian meal porridge takes their place.

Extra Meal. – At five o'clock, in the spring and harvest, a fourth meal is taken, consisting of oaten or flour bread and tea.

Supper. – Is taken before going to bed and consists sometimes of potatoes left over from dinner, sometimes of stirabout.

The quantity of tea taken cannot but be injurious to the people, and one may often see children of five and six years of age drinking tea strong enough for any adult. A good deal of salt is taken with the food, and the bread is buttered when the latter is to spare, but generally in the winter months it has to be taken dry.

(28.) Clothing, whether home-made or bought, etc., etc.

The clothing is, as a rule, bought; the shirts, drawers, vests, and petticoats, are generally home-spun. Stockings and socks are generally home-made, but the younger women very often have shop stockings. Many of the men have strong Scotch trousers, some wear corduroys. The Sunday clothes are almost always bought, being obtained either ready-made from the "clothes men" at fairs, or being made by tailor from bought stuff. Three shillings and three and sixpence a yard is the general price given for the stuff; some send their wool away to factories and get cloth back at so much per yard – less the price of the wool, which is generally 6*d.* a pound. The check and fancy shirts worn by the men on Sundays and holidays are always bought. The Sunday dresses of all the younger women are bought at 2*s.* or 2*s.* 6*d.* a yard being given by some, and 1*s.* to 2*s.* by others, according to their means. Three and sixpence is generally paid to the dressmaker, and 3*s.* for trimmings, so that a girl's dress complete comes to about £1 5*s.* or £1 10*s.* This frock will last a year, but they generally have two – one for summer and one for winter, each of which will, with care, last two seasons. Their hats cost about 5*s.* or 7*s.* 6*d.* Men's boots 9*s.*, and women's 5*s.* Some years ago Fanad was celebrated for its shoemakers, but there are very few now owing to the introduction of the cheap boots, as the people think they can get more wear from two pairs of shop boots than from one pair of home-made boots.

Boots are always worn by the men, but not often by the women – a pair of boots will generally last a woman three years.

(29.) Dwellings: kind of houses, home-life and customs, etc., etc.

There is one point that seems to strike one with regard to the houses – that is, the poverty and dirt of many of them in comparison with the large area of cultivated land surrounding them. To look at the land generally one is inclined to say that, comparatively speaking, these men are fairly well off, but again to look at the houses one feels inclined to say they are very poor. The fact of the great portion of the male population being away for a large portion of the year may have something to say to this.

Another noticeable feature is the way in which the houses are grouped in villages – not scattered as in other districts. In this district there are over twenty such little hamlets, as for example Ballyhoorisky thirty-five houses, Glinsk eighteen houses, Leat Beg fifteen houses, Tamney ten houses, Doagh Beg thirty houses. Ballynalost, Ballynabrocky, Arryheernabin, Magheradrumman, all of which have from ten to twenty cottages in the group. These are all in Fanad North and Fanad West. There are several other similar groups in Killygarvan, Carrowkeel, and Knockalla Electoral Divisions.

The houses are, as I have stated, generally poor and not kept clean; they have almost always two rooms, and sometimes a loft. The interior is similar to those in the north-west of the County, in Teelin and Glencolumbkille districts. The bedding is as a rule very bad indeed – that in the room in which the women sleep is better than the other. Irish is spoken by all; but in Killygarvan, Knockalla, Carrowkeel, and Greenfort Electoral Divisions, English is spoken as freely as Irish. In Fanad, North and West, Irish is almost exclusively spoken, but I did not meet any who were unable to speak English.

The home life is very simple. They rise in summer at about seven or later (they are very late risers in Fanad, and one will hardly see smoke at any season of the year before 7 o'clock). The cows are milked and let out and the byres cleaned. Then breakfast. After breakfast work in the fields or digging turf, as the case may be – the women generally working along with the men. Dinner between one and two o'clock, working then till seven o'clock when, in summer, the cows are taken in and milked. The majority of the people keep in their cows all the year round at night for the sake of the manure. After milking, doing up the cows, and cleaning out the byre, they have their supper, and soon after, in the summer, go to bed. As many of the men go away to Scotland, a great deal of the summer work falls on the women who dig the potatoes and reap the corn.

On an average two are hired from every house, either two boys to Scotland or a boy to Scotland and a girl to "the Lagan," and it must also be remembered that in addition to what the boy brings back from Scotland the household expenses have been so much less while he was away. So that if he only brings home say £5, yet during the sixteen weeks he has been away he has saved his family at least 2*s.* 6*d.* weekly.

The effect of the harvest migration I have referred to elsewhere. A good number from this district emigrate to Boston, whereas in other districts New York and Philadelphia have been the favourite centres.

(30.) Character of the people for industry, etc., etc.

The inhabitants of this district are as a rule industrious. They work hard during the earlier part of the year to get their crop in before the time for the English and Scotch work – which begins about May. During the time those harvesting are away, those remaining at home have very little to do till the harvest comes round. The men cut the turf, such as it is, and get it down to the houses, and the potatoes are moulded. If it is a maritime district, kelp is burned during the summer months. The women of this district, unlike those of Glenties, Teelin, and Glencolumbkille districts, have no occupation during the winter months, the knitting of the district being only for home use and the spinning and flannel-making being also local.

The shirt-sewing business is now beginning to make a little way, but Messrs. MacIntyre and Hogg have not got work enough to keep the girls going, even at the low price they give for the work.

(31.) Whether any organized effort has been made to develop the resources or improve the condition of the people. If so, by what means.

There has been up to the present no organized effort made to develop the resources or improve the condition of the people in this district.

(32.) Suggestions as to any possible method for improving the condition of the people in future.

Suggestions as to improvement in stock have been already made in paragraph (7.) of this report, and as to roads and telegraphs in paragraph (9.). This I consider very important for the district.

In the near future the fuel supply will give out and what the people are to do then is a matter for grave consideration. At present, as I have already stated, they are paring sods off the hillsides and grazing fields and stacking them for turf. This is a most deplorable state of affairs, and demands immediate attention. The local landlords will not interfere; first, because they say the people would not mind them, and secondly, because they say that it is a terrible hardship for the poor to have to be without fire, especially in the winter time, which is quite true, and so the work of destruction to the grazing goes on. As far as I can see the only way to stop it is by the importation of fuel, either turf or coal, and selling it at a price within reach of the people. Coal at 13*s.* a ton would be cheaper than turf at 1*s.* 6*d.* a cart. Up to the present the people have had the fuel for nothing, but now those in Fanad at all events must face the fact that they must pay for it. Lord Leitrim sells coal at 12*s.* 6*d.* per ton.

A suggestion as to improvement and lengthening of Portsalon pier has been made in paragraph (20.). A number of fishermen from along the coast fish down by Portsalon and stop there during the night. These men have nowhere to shelter themselves but lie behind boats or walls or wherever they can get shelter. If a shed shelter could be erected in proximity to the pier it would be a great benefit to them.

The issue of pamphlets dealing with various subjects such as Poultry; Dairying; Cattle breeding, and live stock in general; Farm Culture – the best methods of saving manure, &c., would be very advantageous – the pamphlets being a collection of terse, pithy sentences pointing out what to do and what not to do. They would, I think, do a great deal of good. This district owing mainly to the Scotch earnings, and also to the better market prices for produce, is not so poor as the western districts of Glencolumbkille and Teelin.

F. G. TOWNSEND GAHAN,
Inspector.

18th August, 1892.

To

The Congested Districts Board for Ireland.

Ferry crossing at Mulroy Bay, photographed by Robert Welch in July 1894.

CONGESTED DISTRICTS BOARD FOR IRELAND

COUNTY OF DONEGAL – UNION OF GLENTIES

REPORT OF MR. GAHAN, *Inspector*

DISTRICT

OF

GLENCOLUMBKILLE

STATISTICAL TABLE

ELECTORAL DIVISION.	Area in Statute Acres.	Poor Law Valuation.	Number of Ratings at and under £10 and above £4 Valuation.	Number of Ratings at and under £4 Valuation.	Population in 1891.	Number of Families in 1891.	Number of Families on Holdings exceeding £2 and under £4 Valuation.	Number of Families on Holdings at and under £2 Valuation.	Number of Families in very poor circumstances.	Number of Families which have no Cattle.
	A.	£								
Glencolumbkille (part of.)	1,608	82	5	20	147	27	7	13	6	2
Glengesh (part of.)	6,306	342	11	118	666	132	54	64	44	4
Inishkeel,	11,049	246	14	76	514	91	36	40	36	6
Kilgoly,	13,062	619	28	206	1,211	244	72	134	69	30
Malinbeg (part of.)	4,993	352	33	74	587	113	19	55	33	16
TOTALS,	37,018	1,641	91	494	3,125	607	188	306	188	58

(1.) Whether inland or maritime.

This district is adjoining the sea, but the coast is so rugged and precipitous (there being no available harbour in a heavy sea), that the people lead a pastoral and agricultural life.

(2.) Average quantity of land cultivated on holdings at and under £4 valuation, under (*a*) oats, (*b*) potatoes, (*c*) meadow, (*d*) green crops.

In rough ground or rocky hillsides, the proportion of meadow land to tillage is about 2 to 1.

In cases where the holdings are on "bottom land," the proportion is about equal, but these cases are not many. If the land on the holding is fair quality, and well-cultivated, potatoes and corn will cover equal areas; if a rough and poorly-cultivated mountain holding, potatoes will cover three times the area under oats.

In these cases the oats are kept for next year's seeding, and whatever is over, sold or given to stock; the straw is used for thatch or for fodder. When potatoes and corn are equal on the holding, the corn is ground to make oatmeal; the miller being paid by getting one-thirtieth plus one stone, and 1*s.* for drying.

Green crops are not grown at all, as the people cannot fence off their land to prevent them being eaten by sheep. Indeed, the whole question of fencing is one deserving grave consideration, as it is difficult to see how any great progress can be made in agricultural development in the present state of the country, where sheep run in common through all the holdings.

(3.) Extent of mountain or moor grazing, and rights possessed by tenants, whether in common or otherwise.

The tenants have *in common* all the grazing rights over the mountains, about 30,689 statute acres.

Each tenant is supposed to have only a certain proportion of sheep to his "cow's grass," but this rule is not strictly adhered to. The "cow's grass" is a variable quantity ranging from ten acres to one acre according to the quality of the land.

(4.) Extent and description of land, if any, which could be profitably reclaimed and added to existing adjoining holdings.

In the townland of Malinmore on the south side of the village, there is about 200 acres of land which might be reclaimed. It is very exposed, and at present the people cut their turf there. If a "shelter belt" could be got to grow across it to protect it from the sea winds, it might be cultivated profitably.

In the townlands of Glebe, Garveross, Beefan, and Ballard, there is a tract of about eighty acres, at present covered by high spring tides, quite uncultivated. By shutting out the tide which flows in through an opening between rocks about sixty feet wide, and putting on a tidal sluice, the place might be drained, and I think profitably.

In the townland of Meenadreen there is a tract of about fifty acres of good bog-land which might be reclaimed.

In the townland of Laghil there are about eighty acres of bog which might be reclaimed; the elevation above sea-level of both last-mentioned townlands is between 400 and 500 feet.

In the townland of Stranagartan there is land which might be reclaimed: there are four holdings in the townland *very poor.*

In the townland of Meenasillagh there is land which might be reclaimed, about 300 feet above sea-level.

In the townlands of Leamagowra, Stravally, Meenacurrin, Lagunna, Maghera, Owenteskiny, Largybrack, and Lergynasearhagh, and Meenaboll (Glengesh Electoral Division), are bog-lands which might be reclaimed. There is lime in Lougheraherk about three miles off, also in Meentashesk and Lerginacarha close by in small quantities, but with better methods of getting it the stone might be quarried in larger quantities. The eight first-named townlands are all adjoining in the Electoral Division of Inishkeel, and are from 200 to 300 feet above sea-level.

(5.) Particulars as to any suitable land in district which could be obtained, and to which families could be migrated with a reasonable prospect of success.

In the townland of Malinmore (Malinbeg Electoral Division), about 500 feet above sea-level, there is a tract, on the banks and to the southward of Lough Aufa, of about 300 statute acres, which is at present in Mr. Musgrave's hands. It belonged originally to the Malinmore grazing which he bought out a good many years ago at 30*s.* the "cow's grass," a cow's grass in this case being about 6 acres.

This land is at present unfenced, and faces towards the north and north-west, it has everywhere a good slope, but is quite undrained: it is all bog land. I have not thought it expedient to consult with Mr. Musgrave on the matter, so cannot say if he would consent to let the Board have it for their purpose.

In the townland of Croaghacullion, there is a tract of bog land bordering on Lough Lougheraherk sloping towards the west about 400 feet above sea-level: the area of the tract is about seventy acres.

In the townlands of Bangort and Meenasillagh (Kilgoly Electoral Division), there is a tract of bog land 300 acres in extent. Its height above sea-level varies from 300 feet at the head of the valley to 100 feet at the lower end. A portion of this land was once cultivated, but the tenant had to give it up as he had no capital to carry on the necessary reclamation. The land slopes to the south-west and has two streams flowing through it. Lime is to be obtained about a mile distant in Lougheraherk, and there is a plentiful supply of seaweed at Port, only about a mile from the centre of the lands referred to and adjoining their southern extremity. A portion of the land is, I understand, in the landlord's (Mr. McGlade's) hands.

In the townlands of Owenteskiny, Lergynasearhagh, and Largybrack (Iniskeel Electoral Division), there are large tracts of bog land adjoining the Glen and Glengesh rivers which I think might be profitably reclaimed. The land faces to the southward, and there is everywhere a good fall for drainage.

No price so far as I can find out has been yet put on the bog lands except that given by

Mr. Musgrave before referred to, nor did I think it advisable to ask any questions about probable price from the people lest they should come to set a fictitious and absurd value on their bog land (as in the case of the Glenties Railway) which they would undoubtedly do, if they thought there was any likelihood of its being purchased. For interest in farms enormous prices are paid; as much as £150 being paid for a farm, rental only £3 10*s*.; £80, £90, and £100 being frequently paid for farms with a rental not exceeding £2.

(6.) Method of cultivation, manures, rotation of crops, etc., etc.

The general course of cultivation is as follows:–

Seed time is generally from the 1st to the 25th of April. Harvest from September to October. In the end of March, or beginning of April, the land is dug over (there are no ploughs in the district). On the better class farms the last year's corn land is lined into ridges, and the ridges of the potato land dug down, leaving, however, every alternate hollow, to mark the spaces between the corn beds and to act as surface drains. On the smaller farms, the amount under corn being only a fraction of that under potatoes, the same land, year after year, has to yield an impoverished crop to the poor cultivator.

The better class farmers, about the first week in April, plant their potato-seed, three or four to the width of the ridge (about 2 feet 9 inches), and after leaving them awhile "kibbed" in, manure (byre or seaweed) is spread evenly over them, and they are covered with a thin layer of earth; when the tops begin to show some inches above the earth, they are moulded, or earthed up, till the tops are almost covered, and then left till time for digging, no weeding or any other care being given. The corn is scattered broadcast, and harrowed in with a rake or bush. The method of corn culture is the same with all farmers.

The poorer classes vary the process above-mentioned for potatoes as follows:– They have not enough manure to cover the seed-bed, and accordingly only each seed is covered, a handful of manure being pressed down on it. For poor lands they persist in planting four seeds to the width of the ridge, as they imagine they get a better crop out of the land with thicker planting, thus wasting their seed and further impoverishing their land. The manure used is farm-yard manure, and seaweed when they can get it.

There is a great deal of very good lime in the district, suitable for agricultural purposes, and which should be much more largely used than it is. Unfortunately, at present, in most cases the means of access to the quarries are very bad, and also the method of quarrying and burning the lime are crude. If something could be done in the way of establishing kilns near the quarry, and selling it at a low rate, or else quarry the stone for the people, and let them take it away, and burn it for themselves, giving at the same time, means of ingress and egress, it would be a great boon to many, who, at present, never lime their land, simply because they cannot get the limestone without a great deal of trouble, and, to them, expense.

There is lime in the townlands of Altclogh, Kilgoly, Kinnakellew, Lougheraherk, Straboy, Kiltyfanned, Meenacorha, and Meentashesk.

The only rotation is potatoes to oats. In very many cases there is no rotation, but year after year potatoes are taken out of the same land, thus the land becomes completely pauperized of the potato-producing elements, the farm-yard manure laid on year after year only in a small measure restoring them to the land.

When a piece of land is yielding the farmers a bad crop, they generally leave it for two or three years under grass, and break up a new piece. There are no turnips, or cabbages, or mangel wurzel grown, comparatively speaking.

A few farmers plant some cabbage plants, more in those townlands in Glengesh division than in the other townlands.

(7.) General information with regard to stock, and suggestions as to improvement of breeds – (*a*) cattle, (*b*) sheep, (*c*) horses and donkeys, (*d*) pigs, (*e*) poultry, etc., etc.

With regard to the stock of this district:–

Cattle.– These are small and poor, they belong principally to the old Irish breed, very much impoverished by repeated inbreeding. The suggestions made to me have been:–

Try to introduce Kerries, they are hardy and good milkers, and lack of milk is a great want in the country.

Cross Kerries with existing breed, as it is probably that pure Kerries might not thrive in this climate.

Improve the housing and feeding of the cattle; try to introduce some winter green crop. Their food through the winter is wretched, and their housing cold and dirty.

Sheep.– The breed of sheep is very poor and weak from repeated inbreeding; it is difficult to say what particular breed they belong to, but in most cases they have something of the Scotch blackfaced breed. Suggestions:–

Improve with good well-bred Scotch rams, breeding from the best of the indigenous breed.

Improve their food through the winter.

In order to have any success with sheep-breeding, the old rams must be done away with, and in order to do this some drastic measure will have to be adopted. A breed of small white-faced sheep from Connaught was introduced at one time, and throve well.

Pigs.– These are generally large and coarse – $2^1/_2$ cwt. being the fattening weight sought after. They are bought in March and sold in October. I would suggest the improvement of the breed.

Poultry.– It is a good district for poultry, and the breed, though small, thrive wonderfully and lay a great number of eggs considering their treatment. They are fed about nine or ten o'clock in the morning, and once after that, scraps being thrown to them from time to time during the day by some people.

The eggs are very small, ranging from fourpence to sixpence a dozen on an average.

I do not know if larger and better breeds would thrive, they might be tried experimentally in one or two places; but the local breed might be improved as layers, and in size, by careful and judicious management.

Ducks are not largely kept, those that are belong to the small common breed, and lay for about two months in the year.

Geese might be more largely introduced than they are at present. A good number of families keep a pair through the winter, and sell the young birds hatched in the spring to the " gooseman" when he comes round; about 25 score were sold from the district in 1891.

Horses. – The number of horses are very few (being only seventy in number) and are of a very poor class; they are badly fed, badly housed, and often badly treated. They are out in nearly all seasons and are subject to all changes of weather. They average about thirteen hands, and that is about the average height of the entrance into the sheds they are kept in.

Donkeys.– The number of donkeys in the district is wonderfully small, as will be seen from the statistics given below. There is no reason why this hardy and useful little animal should not be introduced and thrive as it does in Mayo, Leitrim, and Roscommon. If some good strong jackasses and a larger number of she-asses were introduced, they would form the nucleus for stocking the district.

Statistics of stock in the district:–

ELECTORAL DIVISION.	POULTRY				Horses	Cattle	Sheep	Asses	Pigs
	Hens	Ducks	Geese	Total					
Glencolumbkille (part of),	326	102	50	478	4	120	520	0	30
Glengesh (part of),	1,333	588	60	1,981	11	435	2,055	3	150
Inishkeel,	1,079	409	60	1,548	21	395	1,710	5	50
Kilgoly,	2,537	548	50	3,135	15	684	2,635	14	250
Malinbeg (part of),	1,236	283	150	1,669	19	344	1,500	4	200
TOTALS,	6,511	1,930	*370	8,811	†70	1,978	8,420	‡26	*680

* The totals of Geese and Pigs vary with the season; the above may be taken as the summer average.

† Of these 25 have no carts.

‡ Of these 21 have no carts.

(8.) Markets and fairs for cattle and produce of district; also statement as to where the people obtain food and other supplies, and the prevailing custom with regard to the disposal of butter, eggs, and poultry;

Kilcar, Ardara, and Carrick are the fairs in the district for the disposal of cattle, sheep, and pigs, also for eggs, butter, &c.; Ardara for tweed, flannels, and homespun; and Carrick, Kilcar, and Ardara for embroidery and knitting – what there is of it.

The supplies of meal, flour, &c., are procured through local dealers, who, in turn, get to what extent are they sold in the first instance to local shopkeepers and dealers, and, generally speaking, how old are the eggs when sold to the first buyer, and about how old when they reach their ultimate destination in Great Britain.

it by sea from Sligo. Thus, meal at 13*s.* a bag in Carrick rises to 14*s.* 6*d.* and 15*s.* in the mountains, owing to additional carriage.

Tea and sugar are obtained from local shops in barter for eggs, and butter (when they have any), and sometimes corn. They get 6*d.* a dozen for their eggs if they deal with the shop in tea, tobacco, &c.; if not, only 5*d.* This is in order to make them buy tea at 3*s.* a pound, and sugar at 3*d.* per pound. Oatmeal is very little used except by those who have corn of their own to grind. Owing to the want of horses or asses they have to carry the meal on their backs to their houses, oftentimes several miles distant.

Eggs are, so to speak, the principal ready money of the district; they are bartered for tea, sugar, tobacco, snuff, and in some cases, flour. If a woman is poor and has no credit, she often goes down to the local shop, three times a week, with three or four, or half a dozen eggs, as the case may be, getting in exchange for them her small supplies. This system of minute retail is most ruinous to the people, as they are charged much more for their goods, and as regards tea, they are quite at the mercy of the local dealers.

The better-off farmer's wife takes her three or four dozen eggs once a week to the shop, or sells them to a man who comes round with tea and sugar in a cart, receiving the latter commodities in exchange for the eggs.

Butter is mainly used at home, and is of the worst possible quality.

Poultry are not sent out of the district, but are either used in the house or else disposed of locally: the only exceptions to this are geese, which are sold yearly to a man who sends them off to Liverpool and elsewhere; he gets them at from 1*s.* 3*d.* to 1*s.* 6*d.* each, sometimes however giving up to 1*s.* 8*d.* or 1*s.* 10*d.* The eggs are almost universally sold to the local dealers, except when used in the house; they generally pass through two or three hands before reaching the consumer.

In some cases, as I have already mentioned, the eggs are taken down two or three times a week, and sometimes only once a week, to the local shop. Let us take the extreme cases. The hen lays an egg on Saturday: this egg is brought down the following Friday to the central shop, or, if sold to a local dealer, it will in all probability be a week older before it gets to the man who exports them. The eggs are sent off to Carrick on Friday: they leave Carrick on Tuesday by cart for Donegal, where they arrive on Wednesday, and are then forwarded to Derry, where they are probably disposed of at the Saturday market. Thus, for a woman who sends her eggs once a week to a central dealer, the age would range from 14 days to 9 days, 9 days being the least; if sold to local shops, as most of them are, they will in all probability be at least a week older; so that I should say the average age of an egg is from three weeks to a fortnight.

Not many eggs are sent out of Ireland; those that are would have another 4 days added to their age. About 739,080 eggs leave the district yearly; they are not preserved in any way, and often carelessly packed.

(9.) Rail, steamer, sailing boat, road, postal and telegraph facilities.

The nearest Railway station at present by land is Donegal, distant from thirty-seven to twenty-six miles. In another year the line to Killybegs will be open, reducing the distance proportionately. Also the Glenties Railway in another two years will bring the railway within ten miles of those townlands to the north of the district. By water the nearest is Ballyshannon or Bundoran and Sligo. A steamer calls at Malinbeg and Killybegs and takes off goods for Sligo, Derry, Liverpool, etc.; she also brings goods, as meal, &c. The service is only monthly. A new steamer has recently been put on for the Donegal coasting trade, which will give increased facilities for goods. There are five smacks which sail weekly between Sligo and Teelin: they are the main means of supply to the district.

Road facilities are on the whole good; in this district lie three of the 1891 Relief roads – viz., road down Cashel Hill; completion of Glen Ardara road and bridge, and new road round Lougheraherk and bridges, a continuation of this latter to Port would be of great and material benefit to the community, as it would enable those townlands of the "hinterland" to get an unlimited supply of seaweed. The townlands it would benefit are Meenasillagh, Glenlough, Kiltyfanned, Lougheraherk, Croaghacullion, Straboy, Stranagartan, Owenteskiny, Stravally, Meenacurrin, Lagunna, Lergynasearhagh, Leamagowra, Meenaboll, Meenagolan, Meenacross, and Largybrack, or over one hundred and twenty families would be benefited. In the north-east of the district lies another of the 1891 Relief roads, viz., the road to Laconnell; a continuation of this to Maghera and a bridge over the river (the original intention of the work) is very much needed.

There are two Post Offices in the district: one at Glencolumbkille, and the other three miles distant in Malinmore. There is a Post Office at Meenaneary on the outskirts of the district which serves it also. In the two former there is a daily post, in the latter a tri-weekly. The Post Offices of Carrick and Ardara also serve the district, but between Ardara and Meenaneary (the nearest Post Office on that side) the distance is twelve statute miles.

The nearest telegraph stations are Carrick and Ardara. Carrick is four miles away from the nearest point, six miles from Cashel, and nine from Lougheraherk. Ardara is two miles from Scaddaman and twelve from Lougheraherk.

(10.) Employment for labourers in the district, whether temporary or constant, and rate of wage.

From the month of March till October, or from March to March, a very few hire themselves to local farmers at wages from £9 to £11 a year for boys, and £5 to £6 a year for girls, or £5 to £6 for half a year for boys, and £2 10*s.* to £3 for girls for same period. The higher payment to men is to those who mow and harvest, in the season; in all cases it includes feeding and lodging. There is no other employment for labourers in the district.

(11.) Migratory labour, average earnings per head, and where earned.

Only two or three labourers from the district go to Scotland or the Laggan for harvest work: their wages average about £8 or £9.

(12.) Weaving, spinning, knitting, and sewing, whether used locally or sold, and where.

Weaving and spinning combined form the principal industry of the district – viz., tweed or "flannel" making.

Spinning with its attendant industry carding, are essentially cottage industries. Weaving is more of the nature of a trade. The wool is first carded or combed to clean if from dirt and impurities. This is a most important matter, as on the cleanliness of the wool and its freedom from dirt and heather twigs depends the uniformity of the yarn and the quality of the tweed or "flannel" in the web.

When carded the wool is rolled into small cylinders about nine inches long, and an inch in diameter. The spinner then takes one of these rolls and fixing it to the spindle begins spinning. As each roll is finished another is worked in, and so on until a large ball is spun, when it is taken away and generally hung up or put in some safe place, until there are enough of them to send away to the weaver, who converts them into the tweed or "flannel." There are altogether about 410 wheels in the district, and 34 weavers. The present winter output of webs of "flannel" or tweed is about 370 webs of lengths, varying from thirty to sixty yards, and some pieces of twenty to thirty yards. The approximate number of yards would be 17,000.

The foregoing is I should say an understatement, if anything, as it is based on statistics acquired from the people themselves. I calculated about 400 webs would be about the gross total, from the numbers at each fair for the six winter months. These numbers do not unfortunately represent the total number of webs manufactured, as at least 25 per cent. of the total number are not sold owing to their inferior quality.

There are several reasons for this, and also for the falling off in the quality from the "flannel" or tweed produced five or six years ago, which keep the price of the tweed down, in spite of the good demand, to from 11*d.* to 1*s.* 2*d.* a yard for plain, to 1*s.* 4*d.* and 1*s.* 8*d.* a yard for checks. As this is a very important matter I should like to refer to it more particularly.

Since the introduction of the McKinley Tariff the sprigging industry, at one time a source of good income to the district, has been gradually failing, as for example:– the orders for February, 1890, of one large agent amounted to £88, and for the same month of 1892, to £9. His gross receipts for six months, ending March, 1891, were £451 5*s.* 10*d.*; for six months, ending March, 1892, were £138 11*s.* 9*d.* Other sprigging agents tell a similar story. This being the case, and one great means of revenue being taken from them, they had to turn to something else, and the making of "flannel" or tweed has suggested itself as being the quickest and best way of making money: consequently, they devoted all their attention to getting as large a quantity of "flannel" on the market in as short a time as possible.

Owing to this haste in preparation, many faults and blemishes crept into the manufacture of the tweed or "flannel." The first of these, in many cases, is buying inferior wool, as many do now, the home supply not being sufficient, and they buy the wool as cheaply as possible in order to make the largest profit on the tweed. This wool is very dirty and coarse, and is carelessly carded or cleaned, and is sent up for spinning in an unprepared state, with little grits and heather twigs not all taken out. Then, the spinning is done too fast, and is uneven and lumpy. The weavers, under the same high pressure, do their work too loosely and too fast, trying to cover the greatest space in the shortest possible time, and with the minimum of stuff. The oil, too, used, is of an inferior quality, and is injurious to the tweed: another reason for inferior weaving is the number of boy weavers at present learning the trade: they lack the experience of the older men. All these reasons combine to lower the quality of much of the flannel or tweed, though, of course, there is still a great deal of good work turned out. Another thing that effects the sale is the unequal width of many of the webs, varying as much as two or three inches. Then, again, they sometimes soak the webs in water coloured with the ordinary washing blue; this comes out often in patches, and spoils the appearance of the web.

The last two defects often affect the local dealer, who, perhaps has not examined the web carefully when buying, and as soon as it is opened in London or elsewhere, and the defects found in it, it is returned to him at once, and the dealers often have a number of such returned webs on their hands. In fact, so common was this becoming that now the dealers have to measure the width of every yard as well as the length. The loss to the producers on these accounts is very great, as, with a superior article, they might get from 3*d.* a yard for plain to 6*d.* a yard for checks of an increase in price on their goods.

As a means towards this end, I would beg to suggest the following plan:–

> Let a depôt be established at Ardara (the great tweed or "flannel" market) for the reception of all webs that come to the fair, these webs should be in the depôt at least three days beforehand to enable the webs to be examined (it takes about an hour to examine and measure ten webs), and every web should have the owners' and weavers' names attached for identification, and a registered receipt be furnished for every web so lodged. At this depôt have three men skilled in judging the quality of the flannel or tweed.
>
> Let the flannel or tweed be divided into three classes. First, the check; second, the herring-bone and twill; third, the plain greys or browns. Each Inspector to take up one of these classes. Every web that is presented at the depôt shall be received, care being taken to ticket it, and to give a receipt to the man who brings it.
>
> Every web, so presented, shall be examined, each in its own class by the Inspector, and if the quality be satisfactory shall be pronounced passed, and shall be marked across the end with the single edges up with some indelible substance in order to prevent its being re-presented for examination. The tweed is always rolled double.
>
> In addition to this cross, it shall have a label attached, having the Inspector's name and the Board's seal affixed. The number of such labels issued to dealers to be carefully checked, and to be returned as soon as the web is finished. This precaution is to prevent dealers from marking the webs with the cross, and selling them as having passed the Board's Examiners.
>
> For every web that passes the Inspectors a bonus shall be paid, half to the weaver and half to the spinner and carder, the bonus to vary with the class of the tweed:–
>
> For third class, a bonus of 2*d.* per yard.
> For second „ „ 3*d.* „
> For first „ „ 4*d.* „
>
> Every web shall have the weaver's and spinner's name attached (spinning and carding being nearly always done in the same house).
>
> It would not, I think, be well to have Inspectors from the neighbourhood.

This is in outline the plan I would suggest; of course it might be altered in detail, and by its means the flannel or tweed might be raised to a very high degree of excellence, as it would be in the interest of all parties to turn out as good an article as possible.

The knitting industry through the district is very small indeed, almost the only work being done is for home use and wear. The girls know most of the ordinary stitches and knit fairly well. I shall deal with the knitting industry more particularly in my report on the Glenties district.

Sewing in the way of sprigging or embroidery is slowly dying out in consequence, as already stated, of the McKinley Tariff and also to a large degree, owing to the introduction of the machine-made embroidery which, although very inferior in quality to the handwork, still looks very well, and is liked as well by many, who do not know the difference.

The flannel (plain grey home woven) is used for shirts and drawers and jerseys for the men, and for petticoats and vests for the women: sometimes the men's trousers are made of it and their waistcoats, but these are more generally corduroys or other bought material.

The Sunday shirts are all bought. It seems a strange thing that with enormous Irish influence in America, something could not be done to do away with the McKinley Tariff in the case of Irish Home Industries.

(13.) Kelp-burning, and sale of seaweed.

There is almost no kelp burnt at present in the district. There is plenty of seaweed at Port, but the industry has quite died out in consequence of want of demand and smallness of price failing to pay cost of making and getting it out of the district.

Seaweed is free to all who wish to get it, but there is no means except at Glen for getting it into the district.

(14.) Sale of turf, nature and extent of bogs.

The sale of turf is prohibited but is carried on to a very small extent, except in the cases of the townlands of Gannew and Curreen, Cashel, Contycro, Straid, Garveross, Faugher, Kilgoly, Dooey, Doonalt, Kilaned, Farranmacbride, Cloghan, Ballard, and Bangort turf is easily got at, all through the district. The people of the townlands above mentioned, have to creel down the turf on their backs every day, occupying from one to three hours in the operation. It is a most disastrous custom, as it makes them lose so much time every day, at a most important time when they are putting in the crop, to say nothing of every day through the winter.

(15.) Lobster fishing, number of men and boats employed.

In this district seventeen men are employed in lobster fishing, and three boats, one boat having only a crew of four. The chief fishing ground is from Glen Bay to Glenlough, and there are, I believe, plenty of lobsters, but a rocky dangerous coast. The Glenlough lobsters are particularly fine, going up to four and five pounds weight. There is no harbour all along the coast for the boats to put into, if it comes on rough, except Port, and it, at present, is not particularly safe.

The lobsters fetch about 6*s.* a dozen, and, at present, must be rowed from Port or Glen to Malinbeg, as that is the only place where the steamer will stop. From Port to Malinbeg is about eight miles. The steamer could easily lie off Port or Glen Bay and take in the fish there.

(16.) Sea fishing. Facilities for sale of fish, and number of boats and men solely employed in fishing.

This district has a coast-line of, roughly speaking, 28 statute miles. Along this entire coast-line the sea is accessible at only four places – Malinmore, Doonalt, Glen Bay, and Port, so that it could never become a centre for fishing. None of those places mentioned are safe for keeping boats. Any fishing that is done in the district, and it is of a very desultory character, is done off Malinbeg and Rathlin O'Birne. There are no men and boats solely employed in fishing.

(17.) Number of boats and men employed in carrying turf or seaweed or in fishing. Classification of boats.

There are eight boats in the district used sometimes for fishing, sometimes for carrying seaweed; three of these are used for lobster fishing in the season. They are all open, undecked boats – No. 3 rating. There are two other boats in Malinmore not used for fishing. There is a boat in Maghera engaged in carrying seaweed. The number of men who fish sometimes in the following townlands are:–

In Malinmore . . . . .21 men.
In Doonalt, ...14 „
In Dooey, ...16 „
In Kilanned, ...8 „
In Garveross, ...5 „
In Port, ...2 „
In Meenasillagh . . . . .2 „

Altogether about 68 men. Of these only about 14, or two boat-crews, are fishing constantly.

(18.) Fish; whether consumed at home or sold.

Any fish that are caught in the district are sold to itinerant vendors. Some haddock and whiting (there being no sale for them) are used at home, also some cod and ling are dried.

(19.) Extent of fish-curing.

There is no regular fish-curing in the district. Some fish are salted for home use.

(20.) Piers and Harbours, existing and suggested, and how far those existing are adapted to wants of district.

There is in the district one small boat-slip at Malinmore. A boat-slip is suggested at Doonalt and one at Port; of the former I think unfavourably, as the south and south-westerly gales blow right in on it, and it is rocky and dangerous to boot. At Port a slip might be made, but there is at present only one boat there.

(21.) Extent of salmon and freshwater fisheries. Number of men earning their livelihood therefrom.

There are no salmon or freshwater fisheries in the district.

(22.) Banks and Loan Funds.

The Ulster Bank have a branch at Killybegs permanently, and at Carrick and Kilcar on fair days, and at Ardara once a week.

There are no Banks nor Loan Funds in the district.

(23.) Mineral and other resources.

There is a good deal of bog ore in the district, but it is generally too far away to pay cost of procuring it.

There is a fair quantity of limestone in Kinakillew, Altclogh, and Lougheraherk. In Kilgoly townland there is a very good rich limestone. There is probably limestone in Cashel and also in the townland of Kiltyfanned.

Limestone is also found in Meenacorha and Meentashesk, but of a poor quality.

(24.) Relative prevalence of cash or credit dealings, length of credit, interest charged, extent of barter, etc., etc.

All goods which can be bought in comparatively large quantities as meal, flour, and oatmeal, are got on credit. Tea, sugar, tobacco, snuff, and retailed food stuffs, are either bartered for eggs or paid for. For the poorer classes flour is got in retail and sometimes oatmeal, as they cannot afford to buy as much as seven stone of flour at a time.

The length of credit varies with the year, the price of stock, the expectation of rise or fall in price of stock, and the value of the buyer. For some (in fact for all) in a good year, they will get, as they say themselves, too much credit. It may run to twelve months, but if a bad year follows, unless last year's books are paid up, credit is stopped.

From numerous inquiries, I find that, on an average, credit lasts for from six to twelve months for most, but in a poor or bad year from one month to four or five.

The interest charged varies largely – for a bag of meal for a month to three months, 3*d.*; from three to six months, 6*d.*; and over that 1*s.*, that is, I think, the usual charge; sometimes it is more. A bag of meal varies from 12*s.* to 15*s.* Some shopkeepers are said to charge no interest, but they always add on to the price on that account. I should think that the average interest would be from 9 to 10 per cent.

As regards the extent of barter, it goes on mainly in eggs and sometimes butter for tea, sugar, tobacco, and snuff, &c. Sometimes corn is given in barter, they get from 6*d.* to 7½*d.* a stone in value for it.

The extent of credit varies also, but is, on an average, about five months supply for a fairly well-off farmer, and two or three months for a poorer farmer.

(25.) Estimated *cash* receipts and expenditure of a family in ordinary circumstances.

The estimated *cash* receipts and expenditure of a family consisting of 6 persons, man and wife, 2 boys, 2 girls, having 12 hens, 4 ducks, 2 geese, 10 sheep, 2 cows, 1 calf, are as follows:–

Receipts		£ s. d.	Expenditure		£ s. d.
Sale of 4 doz. eggs for 12 weeks, Sale of 2 doz. eggs for 12 weeks, Sale of 2 doz. eggs for 8 weeks,	80 doz. at 5½*d.*,	1 16 8	11 bags meal at 14*s.*,		7 14 0
			6 bags flour at 12*s.* 6*d.*,		3 15 0
			Rent,		2 10 0
			County Cess,		0 7 6
			Dog license,		0 2 6
			Tea, ¾ lb. a week at 3*s.*,		5 17 0
Do., 9 doz. ducks' eggs, at 7*d.* per dozen,		0 5 3	Sugar, 4 lbs. to 1 lb. tea at 3*d.*,		1 19 0
			Oil, 6 gallons at 10*d.*,		0 5 0
Do., 10 geese at 1*s.* 4*d.*,		0 13 4	Salt, &c.,		0 2 6
Do., pig,		4 0 0	Spades, &c.,		0 4 0
Do., cow (beast),		5 0 0		£ s. d.	
Do., 5 sheep at 14*s.*,		3 10 0	Dress, 3 women,	3 0 0	
Do., 1 web at 1*s.* per yard,		3 0 0	Shawls, 3 women,	0 15 0	2 8 9
Do., 1 piece, 20 yards at 1*s.* 4*d.*,		1 6 8	Boots and soles,	1 2 6	
Do., 20 stone corn at 7*d.*,		0 11 8		4 17 6	
Do., 50 lbs. butter at 6*d.*,		1 5 0		2 years.	
American money,		2 0 0		£ s. d.	
			Dress, 1 man, 2 boys	4 0 0	
		23 9 3	Boots and soles,	1 14 6	
If stock improved £3 more on beast sold,		3 0 0	Hats, 3 at 2*s.*, ties, 3 at 1*s.*,	0 9 0	3 1 9
4*s.* each on sheep,		1 0 0		6 3 6	
				2 years.	
			Tobacco and snuff, 1*s.* 4*d.* per week,		3 9 4
			Sucking pig in March,		0 14 0
					£32 10 4
			If don't buy flour,		3 15 0
		£27 9 3			£28 15 4

(26.) Estimated value of home-grown food consumed, and period during which it lasts.

As the result of many inquiries I find that potatoes in an average year last from September till April in the inland townlands or a period of, say, thirty-two weeks.

	£	s.	d.
A family of six persons will consume 12 stone weekly, or 384 stone at 3*d.* per stone =	4	16	0
From the corn there will perhaps be 5 cwt. of meal at 13*s.* per cwt., lasting 2 months,	3	5	0
Total,	£8	1	0

For poorer families and those towards the sea-shore (with some exceptions), potatoes last till February, or, say, twenty-six weeks at ten stone weekly –

	£	s.	d.
3*d.* per stone =	3	5	0
The poor people will not have corn to make meal, but will sell the corn unground, say 20 stone at 7*d.* per stone,	0	11	8
Total,	£3	16	8

Both these estimates are for those who save both potatoes and corn seed.

(27.) Dietary of people, number of meals daily, and kinds of food throughout the year.

The dietary of the people in the district is very simple, consisting almost altogether of meal and potatoes, with perhaps a little fish.

There are three meals every day.

Breakfast. – At about eight o'clock consisting of home-made bread of flour and Indian meal, tea, and if they have it, butter. Sometimes potatoes, oatmeal stirabout is also taken. The poorer people, Indian meal stirabout, tea, and bread.

Dinner. – At two o'clock, potatoes while they last, and a bit of fish, tea, and home-made bread, after potatoes are finished tea and home-made bread. The poorer people often have to get stirabout again as they cannot afford always to have flour for bread.

Tea. – At about eight o'clock is just the same as breakfast.

If there is plenty of fish they may take a little at all meals.

The kind of food only varies from potatoes to meal, when the former are run out. Flour is much preferred to oatmeal, and is largely used; the people say they do not need to drink so much with flour bread.

Tea is drunk to excess three times a day by most, and by all once or twice. In nearly every instance 3*s.* a pound is paid for tea, 10*d.* a quarter, or 5½*d.* for 2 ozs. The people are quite at the mercy of dealers as regards their tea, paying three or four times its value.

(28.) Clothing, whether home-made or bought, etc., etc.

As regards the clothing of the people in this district – the underclothing, as vests, drawers, shirts, petticoats, &c., are all home-made, as also are socks and stockings. Trousers are generally corduroys or discarded Sunday trousers. The Sunday clothes of the younger men are all bought, either from itinerant vendors or in the shop, by the yard. The women all wear one or two shawls – the older women always two; for these they give from 7*s.* 6*d.* to 15*s.* each. Girls buy their Sunday dresses in the shops by the yard, and get them made up, costing from 15*s.* to £1 10*s.* for stuff, and making, and trimmings. Many of the older men and women wear home spuns.

(29.) Dwellings: kind of houses, home-life and customs, etc., etc.

The average dwelling in the district is of a very inferior description, usually consisting of two rooms, but in the very poor houses only one. The houses are, as a rule, very dirty inside, no effort being made to keep them clean, the farm stock having admittance at all times. The outside is generally better than the inside, often they are whitewashed, but the manure heap and cesspool are always up close to the door, and in summer this cannot but be most injurious. The houses are all thatched, and roped down to prevent the thatch being blown away. The girls are generally clean, but the men are not, as a rule, except on Sundays. The home life is very simple. In summer they get up at about half-past six or seven, milk and put out the cows, and see to the stock generally, have breakfast at about eight, and then go to their farm work, the girls going to assist them or else work at spinning or knitting indoors. At two o'clock they have dinner which occupies them nearly an hour, after which they go to work again. At seven or eight the cows are brought in and milked, and if it is summer time turned out again, if winter kept in. A fire is kept in all day in the winter, in the summer it is revived at the approach of each meal. In winter they do not get up until about eight o'clock, milk the cows, then turf has to be carried, and perhaps they do a little fencing or draining, but not often. They are without occupation a great part of the winter.

A typical Donegal hamlet of several whitewashed, thatched, two-roomed houses grouped together. (Note the car and driver of the photographer, Robert Welch, to the right, behind the wall.)

(30.) Character of the people for industry, etc., etc.

In this district the people are not, as a rule, industrious, and though one cannot but blame it as a fault, it is to a certain extent their misfortune, for, until lately, they had no interest to better themselves as they feared an addition to their rent in consequence, and even to the present day, though the fear of the rent being raised is a thing of the past, yet they have the same feeling over them still, and until they get some violent stirring up will remain so.

(31.) Whether any organized effort has been made to develop the resources or improve the condition of the people. If so, by what means.

No organized effort has been made in this district to develop the resources or improve the condition of the people.

(32.) Suggestions as to any possible method for improving the condition of the people in future.

The first possible means in my opinion would be to improve the stock of the district. The cattle are poor and weak; the sheep are a poor breed very liable to disease; the horses are small and weak; the pigs large and coarse. I have already referred to the introduction of a breed of donkeys.

The poultry might be improved by better care and feeding; better breeds might thrive, but should be experimented on carefully and on a small scale.

The next means that occurs to me would be to increase the farm produce, as on this to a great measure the farmer's solvency depends. With a larger farm produce, he has better food for himself and his stock, thus increasing the value of the latter.

A winter green crop is very much needed, at present there is none. Turnips grow well in many places, but because of the sheep they cannot be cultivated. One drawback to an increase of land under cultivation is the want of manure. Here I think something might be done showing them how to save their manure properly and how to save their refuse and anything else that might be made into a compost heap. Some approved system of rotation to be introduced. At present the land lies fallow all through the winter. Lime I have dealt with elsewhere.

The flannel industry I have dealt with under that heading.

In order to increase their knowledge of these various matters, I would suggest that pamphlets be issued free, each pamphlet bearing on one particular subject, such as – Poultry; Dairy and butter; Reclamation, drainage, and making of bog drains; Manures, and compost heaps; Management of cattle, sheep, pigs; Proper use of lime, and methods of burning, &c., &c.

The townland of Maghera would be much improved by having the river channel straightened and banked, and the adjacent land reclaimed. At present the river floods the meadows and destroys the hay.

There is one suggestion I should like to make with regard to a migration scheme. It is so large that I make it with diffidence, but am pressed to it by the deep sense of necessity.

In the townlands of Straid, Garveross, Beefan, Ballard, Bangort, Drum (part of), and Cloghan, in the Electoral Division of Kilgoly, all situated along the base of Glen Mountain, there are forty-nine families, who are very poor and never could possibly be anything else, living where they do on the side of a rocky precipitous mountain. Their united stock is 19½ score sheep, and 86 cattle including cows and calves. I would venture to suggest that these people be migrated by degrees (experimentally) to the lands in Cashel, and those in Meenavean and Creenvean, referred to in my report on the Teelin district, page 2. It is in my opinion the only means of the people ever being able to better themselves. They are now in a chronic state of debt and misery.

When sending in my final report there are some suggestions of a general nature which might be made, and which I reserve till then.

F. G. TOWNSEND GAHAN,
Inspector.

11th May, 1892.

To

The Congested Districts Board for Ireland.

CONGESTED DISTRICTS BOARD FOR IRELAND

COUNTY OF DONEGAL – UNION OF DONEGAL

REPORT OF MR. GAHAN, *Inspector*

DISTRICT

OF

LOUGH EASK

STATISTICAL TABLE

ELECTORAL DIVISION.	Area in Statute Acres.	Poor Law Valuation.	Number of Ratings at and under £10 and above £4 Valuation.	Number of Ratings at and under £4 Valuation.	Population in 1891.	Number of Families in 1891.	Number of Families on Holdings exceeding £2 and under £4 Valuation.	Number of Families on Holdings at and under £2 Valuation.	Number of Families in very poor circumstances.	Number of Families which have no Cattle.
		£								
Clogher,	8,738	1,439	91	104	1,059	215	88	16	8	6
Grousehall,	6,300	877	44	30	589	117	27	3	4	–
Haugh,	3,912	696	26	48	494	96	33	15	2	–
Laghy,	10,800	2,128	109	128	1,474	319	65	63	20	18
Lough Eask,	15,061	981	43	34	450	89	30	4	4	–
Tawnawully,	7,919	647	46	107	710	142	75	32	16	12
Templecarn,	18,516	891	26	70	747	138	54	16	5	9
TOTALS,	71,246	£7,659	385	521	5,523	1,116	372	139	59	46

(1.) Whether inland or maritime.

The district is inland.

(2.) Average quantity of land cultivated on holdings at and under £4 valuation, under (*a*) oats, (*b*) potatoes, (*c*) meadow, (*d*) green crops.

The quantity of land cultivated on holdings at and under £4 valuation varies in different localities. In some portions of the district, viz.: Tawnawully, Lough Eask (part of), Clogher (part of) Electoral Divisions, there is more land under potatoes than under corn, while in other parts of the same Electoral Divisions, and in Haugh, Laghy (part of), and Templecarn (part of) Electoral Divisions corn and potatoes cover equal areas, and in the lower portions of Haugh, Lough Eask, Laghy, Clogher, and Templecarn Electoral Divisions, and generally through Grousehall Electoral Division, the area under corn exceeds that under potatoes, being in these cases about a ratio of 2 to 1 or 1½ to 1.

On an average holding in Tawnawully and the more mountainous portions of Lough Eask and Clogher Electoral Divisions on holdings under £4 valuation about 1½ to 2 acres would be under potatoes, an acre under oats, and a rood or so under cabbages, 2 acres of meadow, and 2 of grazing. Turnips or other green crops are hardly ever grown on these holdings.

In the lower and better farms 2 acres corn, 1½ potatoes, a rood or two of turnips, and a rood of cabbages, three acres of meadow, and two or three of grazing, may be taken as near the general average of the remainder of the district.

(3.) Extent of mountain or moor grazing, and rights possessed by tenants, whether in common or otherwise.

The extent of mountain or moor grazing in this district, and rights possessed by tenants, is as follows:–

Electoral Division	Extent in Area	How held
Clogher,	2,000	Common for sheep.
Grousehall,	2,500	Divided. Sheep run common.
Haugh,	1,500	Divided.
Laghy,	5,000	Common generally.
Lough Eask,	10,000	" "
Templecarn,	15,000	" "
Tawnawully,	4,500	" "
Total,	40,500	

(4.) Extent and description of land, if any, which could be profitably reclaimed and added to existing adjoining holdings.

In the Electoral Division of Clogher, on many of the mountain farms, are lands (bog) which might be reclaimed and added to existing holdings.

In Grousehall Electoral Division, on that side facing Lough Derg at Golirk, the farms might be greatly improved by adding reclaimed portions of the bog to them.

In Laghy, Lough Eask, Templecarn, and Tawnawully Electoral Divisions on nearly all the mountain holdings are bog lands which could advantageously be reclaimed.

All through the district the drainage is imperfect; even on better farms, where such matters should be carefully attended to, the drainage is very faulty as a rule. The people do not understand or appreciate the benefits to be derived from thorough drainage, and until they do they will not practise it.

(5.) Particulars as to any suitable land in district which could be obtained, and to which families could be migrated with a reasonable prospect of success.

In the Electoral Division of Templecarn there are immense tracts of bog land to the South-west of Lough Derg and others to the North of Breecy Mountain, which might be reclaimed and drained. The tract round Lough Derg is at an elevation of some 400 or 500 feet above sea-level, and would, perhaps, be too high for profitable reclamations with a view to migration, but it could, I think, be profitably planted with Austrian firs, and perhaps after the course of some years the land might be profitably cultivated. The tracts of bog to the North and North-east of Breecy are not so high and might more easily be cultivated. In many places the bog is not deep, and in all the slope for drainage is good. If this land were reclaimed it would be necessary to make a road through the centre of the tract of about two miles or two and a half miles in length; portions of this land also might be afforested. Trees planted near Belleek on Cliff Estate have done very well. I was able to get no reliable information as to probable price of land, but a farm from the neighbourhood of £3 rent went for £60 which was not considered a large sum; area of farm about 12 acres with grazing.

(6.) Method of cultivation, manures, rotation of crops, etc., etc.

The methods of cultivation in this district are very similar to those employed in the Inver District. Potatoes cultivated in "lazy beds" and corn broadcasted, turnips and cabbages in small separate plots, where cultivated at all. Very few farmers employ the drill for the cultivation of potatoes, even large farmers stick to the "lazy beds" in preference. About the end of March the ground is dug or ploughed over, and last year's corn land is lined for potato ridges, and last year's potato land levelled for corn this year. The potatoes are cultivated in two ways – some "kib" or "dibble" the seed in first, and after a period of three weeks cover with manure and earth to a depth of about two inches; while others lay the seed first on the manure and cover with earth, then re-cover the plant in about three weeks, and give it a final moulding about six weeks after setting. Almost no weeding is done, and consequently there is quite as good a crop of weeds as of potatoes, and the weeds are let die down into the ground, preparing thus for a better crop of them the next year. The people do not seem to see any reason why they should weed the ridges, nor do they understand that the weeds eat up at least half the productive strength of the soil. Turnips and cabbages, except by big farmers, are cultivated in small patches, varying from one to two roods in extent. The manure used is almost invariably farm-yard manure, and until some better and more intelligent method of preserving it than the people at present have, is found, it will be very difficult to increase the size of their holdings. None of them seem to have the slightest idea of keeping the manure heap in a place where the good liquid manure will not escape; as often as not a way is made for it to overflow; none of them have any idea of making a compost heap, and they would laugh at you if you told them that the manure heap would be better under cover, and until these and many other prejudices are removed, it will be extremely difficult to improve their methods of farm culture.

Through the greater part of this district, the principle of rotation is understood, but in many places it is not practised.

The general rotation is potatoes to oats, oats to potatoes; turnips and cabbage, generally cover such small areas that they can hardly be included in a regular rotation. Though as a rule the land the potatoes and cabbages and turnips are in this year will be corn next year, and the year after that potatoes will be where the cabbages and turnips have been, and *vice versa.*

(7.) General information with regard to stock, and suggestions as to improvement of breeds – (*a*) cattle, (*b*) sheep, (*c*) horses and donkeys, (*d*) pigs, (*e*) poultry, etc., etc.

The stock of this district varies in different Electoral Divisions: in some, as Lough Eask, Laghy, Templecarn, Tawnawully, a number of sheep are kept. In others, as Haugh, Grousehall, and part of Clogher, cattle are kept in greater numbers.

Cattle.– These are for the most part of the small mountain breed, for which it is at present impossible to get any price in the market. In the lower portions of Haugh, Clogher, Laghy, Grousehall, better cattle are seen; but all through the district there is a great need of improvement. In Haugh, and portions of Clogher, Laghy, and Grousehall, a Shorthorn would be a great benefit to the breed. In the mountainous portions of Lough Eask, Clogher, and Templecarn, and in Tawnawully Electoral Divisions, a Galloway or Polled Angus. The housing and feeding of the cattle is quite similar to that in other districts in Donegal.

Sheep.– In Lough Eask, Tawnawully, mountainous portions of Clogher, in Templecarn and the mountainous portions of Laghy Electoral Divisions, sheep are a good deal kept – in Lough Eask, Tawnawully, and Clogher being generally blackfaced Scotch. In the other divisions some whitefaced Irish sheep, and some a cross between them and blackfaces; but all are, as a rule, small and poor from constant inbreeding. In Lough Eask, Tawnawully, and Clogher it has been suggested to improve with Scotch rams. In the other portions Cheviots seem to be preferred. The sheep are generally shorn twice every year, and the wool sent away to factories to be exchanged for cloth. In the winter time the sheep are generally taken down off the hills and kept in the vicinity of the houses.

Horses.– There are very few horses in the mountainous portions of the district, but in the lower-lying portions of it they are kept by nearly all the farmers, some of them of a very fair quality, but the majority poor and small. In the mountainous portions of Laghy, Templecarn, and Grousehall, any that have means keep a horse and cart for purposes of selling turf. The stabling is poor and bad as a rule. Improve breed, and methods of keep and stabling.

If a Stallion could be placed at Lough Eask it would be a good central point for that portion of the district, and Pettigo or Ballintra for the Electoral Divisions of Templecarn, Laghy, and Cliff.

Donkeys.– A fair number of donkeys are kept, generally by widow women with sons not grown up, who drive the donkey to different towns and villages with loads of turf and bogwood. In Lough Eask and Tawnawully they are not kept except by very few.

Pigs.– These are generally kept through the district. The better off farmers generally keeping two and sometimes three. The breed is a large white breed, probably an inbred Yorkshire. They fetch however good prices, and at present pigs are the only stock which pays the farmer. A few Yorkshire three-quarter bred boars through the country would be of great benefit to the breed.

Poultry.– The poultry are, as a rule, the usual small cottage type; occasionally one sees a cross of Plymouth Rock or some other good breed, but they are very exceptional. Improve breed, and also try to get the people to understand the rudimentary outlines of poultry farming.

(8.) Markets and fairs for cattle and produce of district; also statement as to where the people obtain food and other supplies, and the prevailing custom with regard to the disposal of butter, eggs, and poultry; to what extent are they sold in the first instance to local shopkeepers and dealers, and, generally speaking, how old are the eggs when sold to the first buyer, and about how old when they reach their ultimate destination in Great Britain.

The principal fairs for this district are:– For Haugh, Lough Eask, and part of Clogher Electoral Divisions – Mountcharles, Donegal, and sometimes Ballintra.

For Tawnawully, Clogher, and Laghy – Donegal is the most important fair, also Ballintra. For Templecarn and Grousehall – Pettigo and Kesh are the principal.

Donegal is the chief market for the district for produce of all kinds; less important markets are held in Pettigo, Belleek, and Irvingstown. The two latter are in County Fermanagh. For portions of Lough Eask Electoral Division, Mountcharles or Frosses is the chief source of food supply. For Haugh, the remaining portions of Lough Eask and Clogher, Donegal is the centre. For Laghy, Donegal generally, though sometimes Ballintra or Laghy.

For Templecarn Electoral Division, Pettigo and Ballintra are the chief sources of supply, and for Grousehall, Pettigo or Kesh, generally the former. In addition to these main centres there are everywhere scattered through the district small shops where eggs and butter are changed for groceries, such as tea, sugar, tobacco, etc. Some of these small shops sell meal, but it is generally obtained in the towns.

Eggs and butter are disposed of to local dealers, who give in exchange so much tea and sugar, or other articles as desired. Of course this means a system of small retail, as disastrous to the consumer as beneficial to the man who supplies the goods. Poultry are rarely bought, and if bought at all, generally by itinerant vendors who call from house to house, sometimes giving tea and sugar, and sometimes cash, for the birds.

The age of an egg depends very much on the person into whose hands it falls. If sold to a man who deals direct with the market, its age before it is placed on that market will vary from three to ten days. If sold to a country shop, who again supplies one of the town dealers, the age will vary from five to seventeen days, and if again they are sold to one of the itinerant vendors above referred to, it may be two or three weeks before they are despatched. Eggs vary from a day to a week old before being sold to the first dealer.

(9.) Rail, steamer, sailing boat, road, postal and telegraph facilities.

There are at present no railways, properly speaking, in the district, but it is well served by the West Donegal Railway, which runs along the margin of Clogher Electoral Division to Stranorlar; and also by the Bundoran and Enniskillen line which touches Templecarn and Grousehall Electoral Divisions.

Of steamer service there is none, except an occasional cargo of Indian meal that comes to Donegal. The same remark applies to sailing boat facilities.

Road facilities are on the whole fair, except in Templecarn Electoral Division, where they are imperfect, and except the main road to Pettigo, those roads which do exist are bad. Postal facilities are good as a rule, as also are the Telegraph facilities, there being offices in Donegal, Mountcharles, Ballintra, Belleek, and Pettigo.

(10.) Employment for labourers in the district, whether temporary or constant, and rate of wage.

A good number of the young men and young women hire themselves to farmers in different localities for the half year; as they can go on from half year to half year, this employment may properly be considered constant. The rate of wage varies of course with the individual – from the little boy of 9 or 10 years of age who can only herd cattle, to the man who can plough and mow – the former getting from 30*s.* to £2, the latter from £6 to £7 10*s.*, all "found." Girls' wages vary also from £2 to £5 according to size and capacity for work. A few in Lough Eask Electoral Division obtain employment on the Lough Eask estate, and a few at present are employed on the Killybegs Railway.

(11.) Migratory labour, average earnings per head, and where earned.

There is very little migratory labour such as is found in "The Rosses," and elsewhere through that district; but I have found several instances of young men going to Scotland in October, or beginning of November, and returning to their homes the following April or May. I found this frequently occurring in Tawnawully or Lough Eask Electoral Divisions. They go to work in factories or on railways, or other similar employment, and generally bring home from £5 to £7.

(12.) Weaving, spinning, knitting, and sewing, whether used locally or sold, and where.

There is very little either weaving or spinning in the district; any that is done is solely for home use and consumption. The wool off the sheep is generally sent to Convoy or Lisbellaw, or some other factory, to be exchanged for cloth, 4½*d.* or 5*d.* per lb. being given for the wool.

The home hosiery is generally home knitted (though many of the girls buy their Sunday stockings); but with very few exceptions no stockings or socks are knit for the market. This is much to be regretted, as the women are in great want of some occupation, and the younger generation are not at all the same adepts with the knitting-needle as their parents were. Mr. Dunlevey of Donegal used to do a rather expensive trade in woollen goods; but latterly it has completely died out, the people thinking that it is not worth their while to knit at the prices paid for the work.

In the Electoral Divisions of Haugh and Lough Eask, there is still a good deal of "sprigging" done, Mr. Hugh Gallagher of Donegal being the principal agent. In Laghy, Templecarn, and Grousehall a good deal of similar work is done, but not at all to the same extent as formerly. Some cottage industry is much needed in these divisions, as since the collapse of the embroidery the women are for the most part idle. If shirt sewing, as is already started by Messrs. McIntyre and Hogg in Fanad and Rosguill Districts, could be started and set well going, I am sure it would be taken up by the people. Or if a small branch factory could be set on foot in Pettigo, where the girls might come in to be taught to work, it would be a great matter. When taught the use of the machine they could get one on loan, and begin work at home with it. That is the system pursued in the Northern portions of the county, where the industry is already on foot.

(13.) Kelp-burning, and sale of seaweed.

The district is inland.

(14.) Sale of turf, nature and extent of bogs.

Except in Haugh, the lower portions of Clogher, Laghy, and Grousehall Electoral Divisions, turf is very plenty in the district. This is specially the case in Templecarn and Laghy Electoral Divisions, where the supply is practically inexhaustible. A large number from these districts sell turf at from 2*s.* 6*d.* to 3*s.* 6*d.* a load, varying with the season and the year. Not much is sold from Lough Eask or Clogher Electoral Divisions, and in Haugh they have to buy their turf or cart it a long way.

(15.) Lobster fishing, number of men and boats employed.

The district is inland.

(16.) Sea fishing. Facilities for sale of fish, and number of boats and men solely employed in fishing.

The district is inland.

(17.) Number of boats and men employed in carrying turf or seaweed or in fishing. Classification of boats.

The district is inland.

(18.) Fish; whether consumed at home or sold.

The district is inland.

(19.) Extent of fish-curing.

The district is inland.

(20.) Piers and Harbours, existing and suggested, and how far those existing are adapted to wants of district.

The district is inland.

(21.) Extent of salmon and freshwater fisheries. Number of men earning their livelihood therefrom.

There are no salmon or freshwater fisheries in the district, but there is capital angling for trout on all the lakes, and for salmon in Lough Eask and in the Eask river.

(22.) Banks and Loan Funds.

There are Banks in Donegal and Pettigo, and fair-day branches in Mountcharles (for Haugh Electoral Division), and Ballintra.

There is a Loan Fund in Donegal, and one in Pettigo. In the Donegal fund, 7½*d.* is charged on every pound borrowed, and in addition there are 5½*d.* of various charges. A £1 loan costs a 1*s.* to borrow; £2 loan, 1*s.* 8*d.*; £3 loan, 2*s.* 3½*d.*; and so on; £5 (the usual amount) costs 3*s.* 7*d.* The loan has to be repaid in £1 (for £5) instalments every four weeks, so the whole amount is repaid in twenty weeks; if instalments not up to date, 1*d.* in the pound fine is imposed. The interest to each individual is about 18 per cent.; 450 have already borrowed from that in Donegal.

(23.) Mineral and other resources.

The principal geological formations in the district are granite, Griffith's sandstones, mountain limestone, and a highly fossiliferous limestone. Bog ore is found in small quantities, and in the townland of Druminnin a boring was sunk many years ago for coal; but I believe nothing was found, though the formation is carboniferous limestone, and it was generally thought that coal ought to have been forthcoming. There is a good deal of micaceous schist in Templecarn and Pettigo and Laghy Electoral Divisions. At Castlecaldwell in Co. Fermanagh, near Cliff and Templecarn Electoral Divisions, there is a good brick clay, but latterly the work has been given up.

(24.) Relative prevalence of cash or credit dealings, length of credit, interest charged, extent of barter, etc., etc.

In this district, as in others, it is customary to obtain meal, flour, &c., on credit, and to pay for tea, sugar, and household necessaries in cash, or its equivalent in eggs and butter. These last have, during the winter, to be obtained on credit also, at times when the eggs and butter are scarce. The length of credit varies very much, sometimes with the year; in a bad year many dealers do not press their debts if they think there is a chance of improvement; sometimes with the customer, if he is a constant customer, and has always paid up well, he will be let run on to eighteen months; on the other hand, if he is a casual or newcomer, they do not like letting an account run for more than six months.

The extent of credit – quite distinct from the length of credit – varies also with the year, and with the dealer's knowledge of his customer's circumstances. In a bad year, a dealer is much more chary of giving out goods to any extent than in a good year, and probably £4 or thereabouts would be about his average limit. On the other hand, on a good promise of harvest, or in a good year, he will go as high as £7 or £8 to the same man.

The interest charged depends very largely on the dealer, the people being, as a rule, completely at his mercy, and as far as they are concerned, he could make any charge almost he liked without their being aware of it, especially in cases of long credit. Many dealers state that they do not charge interest at all, but if they don't do it openly they put an equivalent for it on to the account. The interest charged also depends on the proximity of the customer to the dealer; if he lives far away, he will be charged more, if near at hand, less. The average rate would lie between ten and twenty per cent., in many cases I believe it is more.

In this district, as in others, eggs and butter are exchanged for tea, sugar, tobacco, snuff, &c., &c. There is no barter, strictly speaking, the nearest approach to it is where "sprigging" or sewn embroidery is changed for tea or sugar as is commonly done – but in this case, as in the case of the eggs and butter, a strict regard is paid to the monetary value of the articles.

Turf was plentiful in much of Donegal and, unlike in other parts of the congested districts where sale was prohibited, people could make up to 3s. 6d. on a load of turf. Donkeys, with creels or baskets strapped on either side, were invaluable in this work.

(25.) Estimated *cash* receipts and expenditure of a family in ordinary circumstances.

The estimated *cash* receipts and expenditure of a family in ordinary circumstances are as follows:–

RECEIPTS

	£	s.	d.
1. Sale of 110 doz. eggs at 6*d.*,	2	15	0
2. " 20 doz. duck eggs at 7½*d.*,	0	12	6
3. " 6 young geese at 1*s.* 8*d.*,	0	10	0
4. " 2 cow beasts,	5	0	0
5. " 5 sheep at 12*s.*,	3	0	0
6. " pig at 40*s.* per cwt.,	3	10	0
7. " 50 lbs. of butter at 8*d.*,	1	13	4
8. " 30 carts of turf at 3*s.*,	4	10	0
9. " Sprigging,	5	0	0
10. Two members of family away on hire,	9	10	0
11. Sale of oats, 8 cwt. at 10*d.*,	2	13	4
12. If sell hay, 1 ton at 2*s.* a cwt.,	2	0	0
	£40	14	2

3. Templecarn is a great district for geese.
4. In Haugh and lower parts of Clogher, in Grousehall and lower portions of Laghy Electoral Divisions, 3 cattle will probably be sold.
7. In the above named Electoral Divisions from 75 to 100 lbs. of butter.
8. Sale of turf restricted to Templecarn and Laghy Electoral Divisions.
11. If corn not made into meal.
12. Not much hay sold.

EXPENDITURE

	£	s.	d.
Rent,	3	0	0
Taxes – County Cess 8*s.* 6*d.*, Dog, 2*s.* 6*d.*,	0	11	0
8 bags meal at 12*s.* 6*d.*,	5	0	0
10 bags flour at 12*s.* 6*d.*,	6	5	0
39 lbs. tea at 2*s.* 6*d.*,	5	4	0
156 lbs. sugar at 2½*d.*,	1	12	6
Tobacco and snuff per week at 1*s.* 3*d.*,	3	5	0
Whiskey and other luxuries,	2	12	0
Soap, paraffin oil, candles, etc.,	1	0	0
Farm implements,	0	10	0
Service of 3 cattle,	0	4	6
Purchase of young pig,	0	15	0
Purchase of one cow (beast),	1	10	0
Purchase of five lambs at 6*s.*,	1	10	0
Clothes – women and girls,	2	0	0
Hats,	0	10	0
Boots, 3 pair and soles £1 5*s.* 6*d.* / 2	0	12	9
Men's clothes, £2 10*s.* / 2	1	5	0
3 pair boots 7*s.* 6*d.*, 3 soles 2*s.* 6*d.*	1	10	0
Hats, 3 at 2*s.*, ties, 3 at 1*s.*,	0	9	0
Hair oil, sweets, etc., etc.,	0	10	0
Church dues,	1	0	0
	£40	15	9

The cattle districts of Haugh, Laghy (lower), Clogher (lower), and Grousehall probably buy two cow beasts and no sheep, or only a couple.

(26.) Estimated value of home-grown food consumed, and period during which it lasts.

The estimated value of home-grown food is as follows:–

	£	s.	d.
350 stones of potatoes (12 stones per week, for approx. 30 weeks), at 3*d.*	4	7	6
7 cwt. oatenmeal at 13*s.*	4	11	0
Milk, 1½ quarts per diem, incl. buttermilk, at 1*d.*,	2	5	7
15 tons manure at 2*s.* per cwt.,	1	10	0
Hay, 3 tons at 2*s.* per cwt.,	6	0	0
Straw, 1½ tons at 1*s.* per cwt.,	1	10	0
900 head cabbages at 1*d.* per head (less 10*s.* for purchase).	3	5	0
If they have turnips (about 10 per cent.) 60 cwt. at 10*d.* per cwt.,	2	10	0
Value of eggs and poultry eaten	0	12	6
Value of butter, 120 lbs. at 6*d.*	3	0	0
Total,	£29	11	7

The 40 or 50 carts of turf they get is not included in this estimate.

Potatoes last generally for Tawnawully and Lough Eask (part of) and Clogher (part of), till end of March; for Templecarn and Laghy (part of), till middle of April; and for the low lands of Lough Eask and Clogher, for Haugh, Grousehall, and the lower parts of Laghy, till May or June; in many cases in these last named divisions holding out for the year.

The corn is used either for meal or else it is sold. If used for meal, it is used sparingly as an article of diet, approximately at the rate of one cwt. per month, and an average farmer would have from six to eight hundredweight.

(27.) Dietary of people, number of meals daily, and kinds of food throughout the year.

The dietary of the people is quite similar to that in the adjoining district of Inver, and may be called a purely vegetarian diet. The general number of meals is three; but twice a year, at seed-time and harvest, when there is heavy work on hands, and when the men work late in the evenings, it is increased to four, the extra meal being partaken of at about five o'clock, p.m., often in the field, and sometimes in the house.

Breakfast.– Consists of generally oatmeal porridge (while it lasts), and tea and bread – butter if it is to spare. If potatoes are plenty, potatoes are taken instead of stirabout.

Dinner.– Consists mainly of potatoes and milk, with tea after, or when potatoes are finished, of stirabout and milk.

Extra Meal.– This meal consists of tea and bread and butter.

Supper.– This meal is taken at about eight o'clock in summer, and seven o'clock in winter; consists generally of Indian meal stirabout.

If they chance to be near the sea, or if they have the means, they sometimes have a bit of fish for their dinner, with the potatoes. Bacon is a rare luxury, and fresh meat of any kind quite unknown except on high days and holydays.

They have only the two main kinds of food throughout the year, viz.:– potatoes and Indian meal. When the former fail then they begin using the latter.

(28.) Clothing, whether home-made or bought, etc., etc.

The people's clothing is, as a rule, bought, with the exception, in Lough Eask, Tawnawully, upper parts of Clogher, Laghy, and Templecarn, of the underclothing, which is generally home-made. All the Sunday clothes are bought, and are generally of a wonderfully good quality. One of the most striking things about the peasantry is the contrast between their workday and their Sunday attire, the one dirty and slovenly, the other clean and neat and always brilliant. Girls pay for the stuff for their dresses from one and sixpence to three shillings a yard; these dresses last with care for a couple of years, and if any striking change in fashion comes in they are remodelled to suit the taste of the wearer. Boots and stockings are worn by the women on Sundays for going into chapel, but as a rule for the rest of the week they go barefooted. The older women are not at all so particular about their attire as the younger ones are, and may often be seen gathered about one of these itinerant clothes vendor's stalls on the look-out for a good shirt or a shawl, or such like.

The men's clothes, except their vests and drawers, are bought. Often the cloth comes from the factory to which they sent their sheep's wool, which cloth cost them 2*s.* 6*d.* to 3*s.* 6*d.* per yard less the price of the wool, eleven pounds being taken as equivalent to seven yards of cloth. The men always wear shoes and stockings, the latter are always home-made. In winter they wear two or three vests as a rule, and a couple of pairs of drawers. When an old vest gets too thin to be sufficient, but too good in their opinion for rags, they put another over it and wear both together for a time. Formerly by far the majority of the boots were hand and home-made, but latterly these have been given up, and shop boots are worn by all, as they consider they are better value for their money.

(29.) Dwellings: kind of houses, home-life and customs, etc., etc.

The houses in this district are quite similar to those in the adjoining district of Inver, and almost every graduation from comfort to wretchedness is to be found among them. The better class cottages have always two rooms and sometimes a loft, the outer room being the general family room where meals are taken, and where the women sit when in the house. Where there is no loft, there is generally a bed or beds in this room for the men of the house to sleep in. The inner room is kept for the girls of the house, and for any visitors, as priest or clergyman, to be shown into. It is kept very fairly clean as a rule, and usually has a boarded floor; the floor of the outer room is always of clay. In the inner room is generally kept the milk set for churning, and sometimes the potatoes are stored there. In poorer homes both these rooms are often dirty and untidy, the outer one always so.

In some of the poorer portions of Lough Eask and Tawnawully, and indeed in all the Electoral Divisions of this district, specimens of the poorest houses are to seen, where there is only one room for the family to live in, and probably no window – where everything is black and grimy. A wretched pallet in one corner, a broken stool or chair, an old rickety dresser with some delph, completes the furniture – the calf, or the pig, having free ingress and egress, the hens being in as a matter of course; outside the door, close up to it, the manure heap, on which all the refuse and ashes are thrown from the door – the whole making up a habitation so miserable and wretched that it is impossible to conceive how human beings can live there.

The home life is very simple, and is probably the same now as it was fifty years back. They rise at about half-past six in summer, and put out the cows and see to stock generally; sometimes they do a bit in the fields before breakfast. Breakfast comes about eight o'clock in summer, and after it they work in the fields till dinner, the women being engaged in household work or herding the cattle.

After dinner the same routine as before, broken by a meal at five o'clock. At about seven the cows are taken in and milked, and the stock made up for the night; then they have their supper, and at about nine o'clock or half-past nine they go to bed. In the winter time they do not go to bed till very late, and they get up very late. They are very fond of spending the evenings at one another's houses, gossiping or listening to a newspaper being read. The men make it a *sine qua non* to attend all fairs within their reach whether they have business there or not. Where they themselves are concerned they set no value on their time, but when it comes to hiring for a day's pay it is quite another matter. The men on the Killybegs railway are at present on strike because they are only getting 14*s.* per week.

(30.) Character of the people for industry, etc., etc.

The men are industrious during seed-time and harvest; but during the remainder of the year there is very little for them to do. They do not, as in "The Rosses," migrate to Scotland; numbers however go to America where, I understand, they turn out first-rate workmen. The women are industrious when they can be so; there is, however, unfortunately almost no outside occupation for them; sprigging is almost a dead letter – though I understand there is at present a slight increase in demand – and the knitting for the market is practically nil. Some winter occupation is sorely needed for both men and women.

'One of the most striking things about the peasantry is the contrast between their workday and Sunday attire, the one dirty and slovenly, the other clean and neat and always brilliant', noted Inspector Townsend Gahan.

(31.) Whether any organized effort has been made to develop the resources or improve the condition of the people. If so, by what means.

There has been, so far as I am aware, no effort made to develop or improve the condition of the people.

(32.) Suggestions as to any possible method for improving the condition of the people in future.

To make the people as nearly as possible self-supporting is the great end to be attained, and in order to have them so, their present system of farm cultivation must be as much as possible superseded by the more modern methods. The improvement of stock is also one of the great means to this end, and the increase of cultivated land, which also means an increased supply of manure for the land, an intelligent appreciation of rotation of crops even on a small scale, a knowledge of the rudimentary practice of thorough drainage and reclamation, these and many other lessons will have to be learned by the peasantry before they can be fairly set on the road to self-support. For the women, a knowledge of the rudiments of proper dairy management and also of poultry rearing. In this last, if the people could only be brought to see it, I believe a great deal of money is to be made, and there is no reason why in many cases three and four times as many fowl should not be kept as are kept at present.

Pamphlets dealing shortly and clearly with the various subjects connected with farm culture – manures, drainage, reclamation, &c. and with stock-rearing and management, with the dairy and poultry yard, would, I think, be of great use to the people, as at present their ideas on all these subjects are the same as those of their grandfathers fifty years ago. This district is, as a whole, not at all so poor as either Teelin, Glencolumbkille or Brockagh congested district.

F. G. TOWNSEND GAHAN,
Inspector.

2nd November, 1892.

To

The Congested Districts Board for Ireland.

CONGESTED DISTRICTS BOARD FOR IRELAND

COUNTY OF DONEGAL – UNION OF GLENTIES

REPORT OF MR. MICKS

DISTRICT
OF
"THE ROSSES"

STATISTICAL TABLE

ELECTORAL DIVISION.	Area in Statute Acres.	Poor Law Valuation.	Number of Ratings at and under £10 and above £4 Valuation.	Number of Ratings at and under £4 Valuation.	Population in 1891.	Number of Families in 1891.	Number of Families on Holdings exceeding £2 and under £4 Valuation.	Number of Families on Holdings at and under £2 Valuation.	Number of Families in very poor circumstances.	Number of Families which have no Cattle.
		£								
Annagary,	9,601	602	6	680	2,925	563	34	520	23	29
Rutland,*	7,970	758	10	478	2,354	432	40	397	30	24
Dungloe,	8,919	593	17	210	1,286	250	32	201	11	12
Maghery,†	10,246	766	5	430	2,017	408	72	321	17	10
Crovehy,	9,610	130	2	85	480	86	9	74	1	-
Lettermacaward,	9,628	804	15	382	1,900	400	90	288	8	8
Doochary,	10,660	143	3	87	415	87	20	62	4	1
TOTALS,	66,634	3,796	58	2,352	11,377	2,226	297	1,863	94	84

* Exclusive of inhabited islands, except *Cruit* which is regarded as part of the mainland.
† Exclusive of inhabited islands.

EXTENT OF DISTRICT.

(1.) Whether inland or maritime.

The district referred to in this report consists of "The Rosses" and the Electoral Divisions of Doochary and Lettermacaward, with the exception that the inhabited islands of the Rutland and Maghery Electoral Divisions are dealt with in a report on the western islands of Donegal. The local name of "The Rosses" has come to mean the parish of Templecrone, with special reference, however, to *the promontories* from which it originally took its name. The district has a large extent of sea-shore, but it is inhabited by very few fishermen.

(2.) Average quantity of land cultivated on holdings at and under £4 valuation, under potatoes, oats, green crops, and meadow.

An ordinary tenant grows about an acre (statute) of potatoes, or a little more; half an acre to an acre of oats; about a rood of green crops; and about a rood of meadow, that is about two and a half acres in all.

(3.) Extent of mountain or moor grazing.

The tenants living in a great many townlands along the sea-shore have hardly any run for cattle of which, therefore, they have very few. The people who live a couple of miles and more from the sea have ample grazing rights in common on the mountains and moors, and in a few instances tracts of unfenced moor or mountain are in the occupation of individual tenants.

(4.) Whether land could be reclaimed and added to adjoining holdings.

There is not any land that could be profitably reclaimed and added to *adjoining* holdings that are situate along the sea-shore; and the tenants of holdings remote from the sea-shore have never been prevented from reclaiming land adjoining their own farms. Many tenants however who live along the sea-shore have purchased the tenant-right of mountain "cuts," two, three, or four miles away, which they have reclaimed. I have ascertained that houses have been built on sixty-four new holdings in the townlands of Annagary Mountain, Meenbanid, and Meenabolligan, and the tenants live for part of the year at the sea and for the remainder on the moor or mountain side according to the nature of the work to be done. On the new holdings there are unrestricted grazing rights, and there is also an unlimited supply of turf, which, in the case of people by the sea, has to be brought from bogs a few miles away. The acquisition of detached additions to holdings seems to possess some advantages; and in this particular district, if a judiciously laid out road were made from Belcruit to Lough Anure, the erection of a second dwelling-house, with the accompanying danger of subdivision, might possibly be avoided. At the same time I think that the Board, with the assistance of the Executive Government, might succeed in preventing subdivision where private landlords would altogether fail. If a list of amalgamated or increased holdings were given with suitable particulars to the Constabulary, the earliest encroachment towards subdivision could be ascertained and reported at once, and the Board would be in a position to take action without loss of time.

(5.) Possibility of migration.

Many townlands, such as Cloghglass, Arlands, Keadue, Tullyillan and Cruickaghmore, are from an agricultural point of view greatly overcrowded. For instance in Keadue there are exactly 100 families, while the valuation of the townland is £103 4*s.* 0*d.* The population is 505, so that the valuation per head of the population amounts to four shillings and one penny! And yet, owing to the wages earned in migratory labour, the people of Keadue are in ordinary years well fed according to the standard of the district, and also comfortably clad and housed. In cases such as this it would be fallacious to regard the very small Poor Law Valuation as a sure test or indication of great poverty, while it undoubtedly does show that the rated occupiers and their families do not and could not subsist on the vegetation of the land. It would, however, add greatly to the comfort of the people in such townlands if some of the families could be provided with new holdings elsewhere, leaving the old holdings to be amalgamated with those of the occupiers remaining behind. There are two large tracts of land near Dungloe, one in the occupation of Mr. W. Hammond, J.P., of Burton Port, and the other of Mr. O'Donnell, whose agent is Mr. John Sweeney, of the Hotel, Dungloe. Either of these tracts might, I think, afford suitable unreclaimed land for an experiment in migrating families.

(6.) Method of cultivation, &c., &c.

There are not any ploughs in the district, for which indeed the rocky land or deep bog is unsuited; and the harrowing of corn land is done nearly altogether with a large wooden rake. Along the seashore during the winter many spread over their potato land the broad-belted sea-weed (locally known as *leagh*) that is washed ashore during stormy weather on exposed parts of the coast. Such spreading of sea-weed is almost the only agricultural work done during the winter, there being at that time of the year no turning-up of the land, draining, or fencing. Exceedingly few fences are proof against sheep which are therefore allowed to roam all over the country when the potatoes have been dug. I may here observe that just before the sowing of potatoes and oats all the sheep are driven off to the mountains or moors, to which uninviting pasturages they are restricted only by the unremitting vigilance of children and well-trained mongrel dogs; and very frequently the frontier patches of the cultivated land suffer severely from the incursions of sheep.

About the middle of March the digging of the land is commenced. Many people in "the Rosses" now plant their potatoes in drills, but ridges are more usual and they are about $3^{1}/_{2}$ feet in width. The burning of the land has been discontinued by comparatively few, but the practice is condemned by those in the district who are reputed to be good authorities. Seed potatoes are "kibbed" four across into the unmanured ridges about the 15th April, an operation that means the boring by a dibble of a hole a few inches deep into which the seed potato *cuts* are placed, the earth being at the same time pressed over by the finger or thumb.

In two or three weeks after the kibbing of the seed manure is spread on the drills or ridges, and on the following day, or soon after, the drills or ridges are "set up," that is covered with clay from the space which becomes the furrow. Both wrack (the sea-weed that is cut off rocks) and farm-yard manure together are used at this stage by those who can procure wrack, but people remote from the sea-shore have as a rule only farm-yard manure, the supply of which is lamentably deficient on every holding. I believe I do not exaggerate in saying that the failure to obtain a good and plentiful supply of home-grown food is to be attributed in this and most other congested districts, *not* as a rule to the small amount of land at the disposal of the occupiers, but to the deficiency of manure and to the absence of skilful management of land and live stock – or, in a word, to bad farming. I need only point out that the absence of sheep-proof fences precludes the growing of green crops to any extent, and that therefore house-feeding of cattle and the consequent accumulation of manure cannot be attempted to any considerable extent. As it is, the cattle roam over hill-sides and moors where the scanty vegetation is only sufficient to maintain their wretchedly lean and listless existence. When the potato stalks are being "shovelled," or earthed, a little more farm-yard manure, if procurable, is put on the land, after which the potatoes and weeds are on most holdings allowed to compete together without any weeding. About half the occupiers in the district use each season a bag of artificial manure, in addition to sea-weed and farm-yard manure. A *rotation* of crops is a misnomer here, the course being a see-saw between potatoes and oats, with an occasional rest. The oat crop, it need hardly be said, is not manured.

In no way, in my opinion, can so much good be done in this district as by the energetic imparting of practical instruction in good farming.

(7.) Information with regard to live stock and poultry.

Horned cattle are of a very poor small worn-out breed, but in some localities the introduction of a Polled Angus or Kerry bull has been followed by marked improvement.

The sheep of the district are small, lean, and unsightly. After their first shearing they are at times partially shorn, and, when they have passed out of the lamb stage, they nearly always present an unkempt and half-naked appearance. Their restless agility and capacity for trespass are also a drawback, and the introduction of an improved breed is most desirable, regard being had to the quality of the wool.

There are not any goats in this part of the county of Donegal.

The ponies of "the Rosses" were some years ago much sought after, and though they have become comparatively scarce, many pretty little ponies are yet to be met with. Few inhabitants of this district make anything by horse-breeding, but the recent introduction of hackney horses by the Board will, while improving the supply, also enable many families to make something yearly by selling a foal out of their working mare. In one neighbourhood of this district, namely, from Burton Port to Annagary, there are a great many donkeys, and a Spanish jackass lately stationed at Dungloe by the Board, will doubtless be most beneficial.

The breed of pigs requires improvement very badly, but there are hardly any sows in the district, the practice of the people being to purchase young pigs for fattening at fairs, such as Crossroads and Glenties, outside the district.

The poultry in "The Rosses" are good for laying, but the eggs are small. The breed of fowl, ducks, and geese is of the usual nondescript kind, and the birds are not good for the table.

(8.) Markets and fairs for sale of cattle and produce, and for the purchase of supplies.

There is a monthly fair in Dungloe which is tolerably well attended considering the remoteness of the village. There are also small fairs at Doochary, Ballynacarrick, and Meenalecky. From the southern part of this district people attend the fairs of Ardara, Glenties, and Brockagh, and from the north of the district people go to the fairs of Crossroads and Milford. At the principal fairs buyers of young stock attend, but the small local fairs are to a great extent used merely for the barter and exchange of cows and other live stock among the peasantry. Fat pigs are not sold at fairs, but are killed in the district and sent by cart to Ballybofey or Letterkenny where they are sold by weight to bacon merchants. Poultry are not sold. Eggs, as a rule, are exchanged with shopkeepers for tea, tobacco, &c., and in most localities eggs are brought to the shops before they are a week old. Itinerant egg-dealers are now almost extinct in the district. On an average, I should say it takes about three weeks for the eggs to reach the consumers in Great Britain. The tendency exists to some extent among the exporting shopkeepers of keeping back eggs when the market is rising, and similarly of losing no time when a fall in price is anticipated. From "the Rosses," eggs are generally sent by sea to Derry, and from Doochary and Lettermacaward they are sent by cart to Letterkenny and thence by rail to Derry. All the eggs of the district therefore have to bear the cost of the Derry merchants' commission, and harbour dues in Derry, as well as the profit of the local shopkeepers, before they reach Great Britain. Butter is not extensively made in the district, hardly any family making during the summer more than from 40 to 56 lbs., which is gathered and sold in one vessel at prices varying from 8*d.* to 1*s.* per lb., to the local shopkeepers who send it to Derry.

There are in the district numerous good shops at which meal, flour, groceries, and tobacco can be purchased. In addition to general "stores" here and there in the country, there are several clothing and hardware shops at Dungloe.

(9.) Rail, steamer, boat, road, postal and telegraph facilities.

The nearest existing railway stations are at Letterkenny and Stranorlar, each of which is about twenty-eight miles from Dungloe by Doochary Bridge. There will be a station at Fintown on the narrow-gauge railway from Stranorlar to Glenties that is now in progress of construction, and that station will be about twelve miles from Dungloe, but the approach road is incurably bad and hilly. It was the unanimous opinion of Major-General Hutchinson, R.E., and his three colleagues, who were commissioned in 1890 to inquire into and report upon the proposed railway extensions in Donegal, that the most desirable railway extension in the county would be from Stranorlar to Glenties, Dungloe, and Burton Port. *The carrying out of such a project seems to be so desirable as to be almost necessary for the opening-up and development of the district.*

Mr. Wm. Hammond, J.P., of Burton Port, and Mr. John Herdman, J.P., of Carricklee, Strabane, own two steamers, carrying about 200 and 300 tons respectively, that trade between Derry and Burton Port, Port Noo, Teelin, Killybegs, and sometimes Falcarragh (Ballyness), Mountcharles, and Ballyshannon. All the heavy traffic such as meal, flour, salt, oil, timber, slates, coal, &c., are carried by sea. Occasionally a small sailing ship is chartered with a cargo by a local merchant, but there is hardly any service of sailing boats or ships.

The roads in "The Rosses" are without doubt the worst in all Donegal, and this is very largely to be attributed to the fact that only one grand juror is a resident in the district. If a railway were made, very little need be done in road-making: otherwise a good approach road ought to be made from Dungloe to the railway at Fintown; and the road from Crolly Bridge to Dungloe by Lough Anure ought to be repaired and put into the condition of a main road. There are other minor roads of which the Board are sure to hear much, but for the present, I only refer to main roads. For the convenience of the people of Lettermacaward, a passage over the Gweebarra, by a work partly a causeway and partly a bridge, would be of the greatest service, as it would afford a ready access to the railway at Glenties, and also to Port Noo where Mr. Hammond's steamer discharges.

In the present state of development of the district the postal and telegraphic facilities are fairly good, though doubtless the extension of the telegraph to Kincaslough, Doochary, and Lettermacaward, would be desirable.

(10.) Employment for labourers in district.

Practically there is not any employment for labourers in the district, except in loading and unloading Mr. Hammond's steamers, and at this occasional work only a few men are employed. The repairing of the roads is done, or rather left undone, by the families of the road contractors as a rule.

(11.) Migratory labour and earnings.

Almost all the able-bodied men, girls, and children in the district are migratory labourers. The men go to Scotland, and the girls and children to farmers in East Donegal, Londonderry, and Tyrone. The district in Donegal, on the east shore of Lough Swilly, in the barony of Raphoe, to which migration first commenced, is known as "the Lagan," and taking service as migratory labourers in that or any of the neighbouring localities is spoken of as "going to the Lagan." A large number of men go to obtain general work in Scotland as soon as their own crops have been put in, and others go for the Scotch harvest only. The time of return also varies – some return in October, others at the end of the year, and others not until it is time for the spring work on their own holdings in Donegal. Those who go for the harvest bring home about £6. A man who works from May to October can in a fairly good year save £20. In addition to ordinary harvest work, men get employment in Scotland in hay-making and turnip-weeding. Great numbers also work in oil refineries and other miscellaneous occupations. From some families two or three and, very rarely, even four men go to Scotland to work. Boys and girls go in great numbers to the hiring-fairs of Letterkenny, Derry, Strabane, and Ballybofey for service in "the Lagan." The wages vary according to the strength and usefulness of the little boy, girl, or young woman from £2 to £5 10*s.*, or £6 *for a half year.* I observe that for the current half-year wages were as high as £7 10*s.* in some instances. The hiring-fairs are in May and November, and many get employment all the year round; but almost all of those remaining for the second half-year, even in cases where they are re-engaged, go for amusement to the hiring-fairs or "rabbles" as they are sometimes called. In my opinion, £16 a year is a moderate estimate of the earnings of an average family from migratory labour of all kinds. There is, however, no subject upon which more erroneous and misleading opinions are given. It is the main resource of the people of "the Rosses," and those who are inclined to represent the poverty of the district as very great are slow to believe or admit that migratory labour produces so much.

(12.) Weaving, spinning, knitting, and sewing.

There are only three or four weavers in the entire district, and there is hardly any spinning. Wool is sent to be made into cloth or tweed at some Scotch factory or at the Convoy factory, near Raphoe, or at Mrs. Ernest Hart's factory in Gweedore.

The women and girls knit most industriously, and their chief employers are the Messrs. McDevitt, of Glenties, but during the six months from May to November large numbers of the workers are absent as migratory labourers at "the Lagan." Besides, during the summer the women remaining in the country have many outdoor occupations, so that far more knitting is done in winter than in summer. I should say that a family earns on an average about 4*s.* a week during the winter six months, or a sum of about £5. During the remainder of the year I think it would not be safe to say that more than £2 10*s.* is earned. Towards the end of 1890 Mrs. James Sinclair, of Bonnyglen, Inver, started some industrial classes in "The Rosses" for teaching plain sewing, embroidery, drawn linen work, and superior knitting. She is hopeful of success, but it is in my opinion too soon to judge whether the instruction that is being imparted by her will enable girls to earn higher and more regular wages than they have hitherto obtained by knitting socks and stockings. A Miss Roberts, an English lady, has for some years done much useful work in conducting an agency for the sale of various knitted articles. In all plans for industrial development in "The Rosses," it should be borne in mind that young women and girls leave the district for six months of the year to go to "the Lagan," and that cessation from industrial work for half the year is likely to interrupt a trade connection that may require work to be done regularly all the year round. In the knitting of socks and stockings women in "The Rosses" can generally get regular and sufficient employment, when they want it, though at low wages but it yet remains to be proved that more remunerative work can be provided for them during the winter. It would undoubtedly be a great advantage for the girls from many points of view if employment at home could be provided for them all the year round, but such employment must produce at least as large an annual amount of earnings as "the Lagan" wages and the earnings for winter knitting combined.

(13.) Kelp and seaweed.

Kelp is not extensively made in the district, not more than half the families in a few townlands bordering the sea being engaged in its manufacture. In the islands off the coast the industry is important, and it is referred to in a report on the West Donegal Islands. The price of kelp in the district last year was £4 a ton on an average.

(14.) Sale of turf – and nature and extent of bogs.

All the habitual residents either possess or acquire a right to cut turf, so there is not any turf worth mentioning sold in the district, nor is any turf exported. The bogs are of good quality and of great extent, but the people living along the sea-shore have as a rule to cart their turf for long distances. As the bogs in this district are at a considerable distance from the harbour at Burton Port, the establishment of any peat industries is impracticable.

(15.) Lobster fishing; number of men and boats employed.

From the Gweebarra river to the Crolly river there are about 16 boats and about 48 men engaged in the lobster fishery. Sometimes the lobsters are put on board coasting steamers and sometimes they are sent by cart to Letterkenny and thence to Derry and Liverpool.

(16.) Sea fishing, etc.

There are practically no regular fishermen along the coast of the mainland in this district, and the islands off the shore are dealt with in a separate report. When mackerel, herring, or fry come close to the shore the mainland people engage vigorously in fishing for the time.

(17.) Number and class of boats employed in fishing or carrying turf, or seaweed.

There are about 170 boats on the mainland of the district employed in fishing occasionally, and in carrying seaweed and turf. Of this number only 12 boats are engaged in fishing, and 17 in carrying turf. The remaining 141 boats are used in getting seaweed. In sheltered bays, as at Dungloe, ordinary open boats of great beam are used; and on the more exposed parts of the coast the Greencastle yawl is preferred.

(18.) Fish, whether used at home or sold.

Whatever fish is caught is, as a rule, used at home, but when there is an exceptionally large take of herrings, some are sold to hawkers, and some are salted.

(19.) Fish-curing.

Except rough salting in a rude fashion during large takes, fish are not preserved, and the process cannot be called fish-curing in the technical sense of the phrase. There used to be a large fish-curing establishment on Rutland Island, near Burton Port, but it was closed about ninety years ago during the temporary absence of herrings from the coast, and it was not opened again. In my report on the West Donegal Islands, I suggest that a fish-curing station should be started at Burton Port, as the harbour appears to be suitable as a centre for developing fishing.

(20.) Piers and Harbours.

Burton Port is the only place where there is a pier in the district, and it requires to be extended for a few feet, at a trifling cost, to a rock that is bare at low water. There are also a couple of sand banks between the open sea and the pier, and they could probably be removed by a steam dredger, if one were hired. Some of the Donegal harbours would admit steamers at ordinary tides, or perhaps at half-tides, if dredging were done occasionally. I have spoken to owners of steamers, and in their opinion money could not be spent more usefully than in improving the depth of harbours, so that they could be approached as far as possible at any state of the tide. In addition to the small extension of Burton Port pier it is also proposed that the end of the pier should be faced with cut stone, so that it might be used as an additional berth, and it is suggested that the pier-space should include a rock that would require to be levelled. Great numbers of small open boats from Arranmore and other islands now come in at the back of the existing pier, and the making of a boatslip there would be a great convenience. The Board have already had before them, in connection with the working of projected granite quarries, a proposal that a small breakwater, a pier, a basin and a slip should be constructed at Gortnasate in Cruit Bay near Kincaslough. I shall refer to the granite quarries in another paragraph, but apart from the stating of a possible trade in granite, the construction of a sheltered deep-water harbour and pier at Gortnasate is, in my opinion, a project beyond the commercial requirements of the locality. Besides, the making of such a pier would be a diversion of traffic from the existing harbour of Burton Port, which could at a comparatively small expenditure be made adequate for the district. Another objection to a commercial pier at Gortnasate is that the district outside the immediate locality can only be approached by hilly rugged roads. As I have before stated there are hardly any regular fishermen on the mainland of "the Rosses," and boats from all the islands, with the exception of Owey, where there are only twenty-nine families, bring their fish almost invariably to Burton Port, where they also obtain their supplies. At the same time I think that the building of a boat-slip at Gortnasate would be very useful for the boats occasionally engaged in fishing and in getting sea-weed. The inhabitants of Owey would also use such a slip because they get their supplies at Kincaslough, where they also cash the money orders they receive for lobsters.

(21.) Salmon and fresh-water fisheries.

There is a salmon fishery in the Gweebarra River and also in the Crolly River, but they are fished by anglers only. Similarly there is an excellent sea-trout fishery at Dungloe late in the year.

(22.) Banks and Loan Funds.

The Northern Banking Company have a branch office at Dungloe; and the district is fortunate in not having any loan funds within or near its limits. Very few small loans are made by the Bank to the occupiers of land in the neighbourhood.

(23.) Mineral and other resources.

There is throughout "the Rosses" an unlimited quantity of good granite, but in most places it is at too great a distance from a deep-water pier to be profitably worked for export. Granite that is locally considered to be of good quality could be easily quarried in a ravine at Gortnasate, but the fact that all the able-bodied men of the district migrate every year to Scotland for employment raises a difficulty in the continuous working of the quarry on a large scale. It would be a dangerous experiment, I fear, to induce these men to remain at home during the summer to try their luck at quarrying. The men themselves would hesitate, and their prudent friends would hesitate to ask them, to sever a connection with employment in Scotland that they might not be able to resume if the working of the granite quarries were to fail. I have, however, for a long time had an idea that winter operations at granite quarrying might be tried with advantage. I should be disposed to commence on a small scale by paying two or three instructors to teach the men of "the Rosses" how to prepare granite for the market. The expenditure in plant and wages would not be large, and the local men, because many of them are completely without employment in winter, ought to be willing to work on the basis that the proceeds derived from the sale of the prepared granite should be divided among them, in proportion to the length of time spent by each man at the works. It might however be found more desirable to introduce some other system for dividing the proceeds. It is quite possible, I fear, that men might refuse to work on chance for what their work might bring, and in this case they would leave themselves open fairly enough to the imputation that they cannot be very anxious to increase their means and resources.

There is some bog-ore and soap-stone in the district, but neither of these are valuable minerals. Limestone is procurable throughout the district at a fair cost.

(24.) Dealings – whether cash, credit, or barter.

Credit dealing was almost universal some few years ago, but now, as far as I can judge, half of the purchases in the district are cash transactions, and both buyers and sellers are glad of the change. May, June, and July are the months in which credit is most largely given in ordinary years, but in a year in which the potato crop is bad, or in seasons when the rate of wages for migratory labourers is low, credit is sought for much earlier, often as early as January. There are different prices in cash and credit dealings, but interest for delay of payment in credit transactions is not charged – for instance, supposing that 12*s.* per bag is the cash price for meal, the credit price would be 13*s.* 6*d.*, payable in the following November, when most of the migratory labourers return home. But whether the meal was given in May, June or July, would be immaterial as regards the amount to be paid, which would be 13*s.* 6*d.*, as I said in the case that I took as an example. Many shopkeepers, when their customers fail to meet their obligations in November, take bills or promissory notes for the amount due, and I believe that in this way traders get accommodation from the Bank to meet their own liabilities. Eggs are nearly always exchanged at market prices for tea, sugar, or tobacco, and, as shopkeepers make a much larger profit on tea than on other commodities, they naturally prefer to give tea rather than any other commodity in exchange for eggs. I am informed that shopkeepers pay only 1*s.* or 1*s.* 3*d.* *per lb.* for the tea that they retail at 2*s.* 4*d.* or 2*s.* 6*d.* *per lb.*, and it is questionable whether people would consume as much tea as they do if they had to pay cash for it, while the shopkeepers know that they are sure of the trade in meal, flour, and the necessaries of life. Butter, of which comparatively little is made, is sometimes sold for cash and sometimes exchanged for goods. Some shopkeepers are buyers of kelp, and they take the kelp made by a family in reduction of an outstanding account for goods supplied.

(25.) Estimated cash receipts and expenditure of a family in ordinary circumstances.

CASH ACCOUNT.

For a year of an average family in "The Rosses."

RECEIPTS	£	s.	d.	PAYMENTS	£	s.	d.
Sale of cattle, . .	6	0	0	Flour, 208 stones at 3*s.* 6*d.* per 4 stones, or bakers' bread, .	9	2	0
Do., sheep, . .	2	10	0	Tea, 1 lb. per week, at 2*s.* 4*d.*,	6	1	4
Do., pigs, . .	3	0	0	Indian meal, 3/4 of cwt. per week for 15 weeks, at 7*s.* per cwt., .	3	18	9
Do., of eggs, . .	6	0	0	Sugar, 208 lbs. at 2½*d.* per lb.,	2	3	4
Scotch earnings, . .	10	0	0	Fish and bacon, . .	2	0	0
"Lagan" earnings, . .	6	0	0	Salt and soap, . .	0	10	0
Knitting and sewing, etc., .	7	10	0	Oil and candles, . .	0	15	0
Miscellaneous sales (kelp, butter, fish, foal, etc., on an average (say),	2	0	0	Clothing (exclusive of Scotch and Lagan purchases), .	6	0	0
				Rent, . .	1	10	0
				County cess, . .	0	5	0
				Church dues, &c., . .	1	0	0
				Tobacco, . .	3	0	0
				Furniture, delph, fishing gear, etc., . .	1	0	0
				Replacing (or exchange) of cattle,	2	0	0
				Young pig, . .	0	10	0
				Bran, . .	1	0	0
				Carts, harness, implements, etc., .	1	0	0
				Artificial manures, etc., etc., .	1	0	0
Total,	£43	0	0	Total,	£42	15	5

(26.) Estimated money value of the products of an average holding, with other local advantages.

The following is the respective money value of each of those farm products and local advantages which are, either entirely or in part, used or consumed on a holding, and which are not included in the foregoing statement and cash account:–

HOME CONSUMPTION ACCOUNT.

	£	s.	d.
Potatoes, 10 barrels (10 cwt. to barrel), at £1 a barrel,	10	0	0
Oats, 6 cwt. of meal at 12*s.* per cwt.,	3	12	0
Straw, 60 stooks at 5*d.*,	1	5	0
Grass and grazing rights and aftergrass,	1	10	0
Hay,	2	0	0
Turnips and cabbages,	4	0	0
Eggs and butter, home consumption, at 1*s.* a week,	2	12	0
Milk,	9	2	0
Wool,	1	2	6
Farm-yard manure,	2	10	0
Turf,	3	0	0
Seaweed for manure, in the case of those near the seashore,	2	0	0
Total,	£42	13	6

If, therefore, we add the amount of the Home Consumption Account to each side of the Cash Account, we find that, using the words in a wide sense, the total *income* of an average occupier is estimated at £85 13*s.* 6*d.*, and the total *expenditure* at £85 8*s.* 11*d.* a year.

This very close approximation between receipts and expenditure in the foregoing Cash Account is accidental, and I did not add up the figures in either column until I had completed the entries.

If it were to happen in a particular season, as has to some extent occurred at long intervals previously, that the earnings of migratory labourers were very small, and if at the same time there should be a serious failure of the crops in "The Rosses," no doubt the people who had not saved money would be unable to do more than struggle painfully through the spring and early summer unless they could obtain goods on credit, as they probably would, from the shopkeepers with whom they had been in the habit of dealing. In the not very numerous class in poorer circumstances than the average family the struggle would be still harder. I should add that in a few townlands along the coast, such as Keadue, very many families have not cows, and upon such families most of all "a bad year" presses severely. In the Cash and Home Consumption Accounts of these last mentioned families all entries relating to cows and their produce disappear, but most of such families make more than the average amount put down in the Account for the sale of kelp.

(27.) Dietary of the people.

The dietary of the people of the district is almost entirely vegetable, and there is very little change or variety in the articles of food. Notwithstanding the monotony of diet, the health of the people appears to be excellent and the appearance of physical strength among the young and middle-aged men and women is remarkable. The diet in autumn and winter, speaking roughly, is different to that used in spring and summer, and throughout the year there are four meals in each day. The following table shows the hours for meals and the kinds of food provided at each meal. There is not any deficiency in the amount of food in ordinary years:–

Period.	Breakfast at 8 o'clock.	Dinner at 12 o'clock.	Tea at 4 o'clock.	Supper at 8 o'clock.
15th August to 30th April.	Bread, tea, milk, sugar.	Potatoes, salt fish, followed by tea, milk and sugar.	Bread, tea, milk, sugar.	Potatoes and salt fish, or bread and tea with milk and sugar, or oatenmeal porridge and milk.
1st May to 15th August.	Do.,	Indian meal porridge and milk, also tea, milk, and sugar sometimes.	Do.,	Indian meal porridge and milk, or bread, tea, milk, and sugar.

N.B. – Tea is taken as a rule *three* times a day. During the spring and summer if tea is taken at dinner it will probably not be taken at supper and *vice versa.* Not infrequently eggs and butter are used at breakfast or dinner, chiefly when the men are engaged in farm work.

(28.) Clothing and bedding of the people.

Men buy much of their clothing in Scotland, and their costume on Sundays is practically the same as that of Lowland Scotch working-men. While they are working at home in the fields some wear Scotch clothes, "moleskin" trowsers being very common, but home-spun tweeds are worn by many. The people send away their wool to be spun and woven, as I explained under heading No. 12, and they get back in return cloth, tweed, flannel, or blankets as are required. The supply of home-grown wool is, I need hardly say, insufficient for the clothing of an average family in "The Rosses." Women and girls have not yet, with few exceptions, discarded their bright and pretty shawls for the cheap and unbecoming imitations of fashionable hats and jackets that doubtless make country girls feel as awkward and uncomfortable as they look. With shawls, on the contrary, the women seem to be thoroughly at their ease, but I fear that the "fashionable" hat and jacket are making way against the comfortable and graceful shawl. The material for women's gowns and also their shawls are bought at shops as a rule, but petticoats are made of home-spun flannel or tweed. Men wear boots invariably, but very many women wear their boots only when they go to Mass, to a fair, or to some social gathering. I may say, in conclusion, that the people in "The Rosses," with very few exceptions, are well and comfortably clad. Their bedding too is as a rule fairly good. There is a straw paliasse and a chaff tick over which is a sheet. A pair of blankets and a quilt, but no sheets, are used as overcovering.

(29 and 30.) Character, disposition, dwellings, home-life, and customs of the people.

With the exception of clergy and doctors there is only one resident gentleman in this large district extending from the Crolly river to the Gweebarra river, and the residence in "The Rosses" of Mr. William Hammond (the gentleman to whom I refer) is due to the fact that he became the land-agent for the Marquess Conyngham, who is the largest land-owner in West Donegal. It is a remarkable circumstance that throughout such a large area as "The Rosses" and Lettermacaward there does not reside even one family of landowners or gentry; so that the small occupiers of land do not in their own neighbourhood meet in everyday life persons of a social *status* above their own. Whether as a consequence of this, or because of a natural independence of character, one can observe that there is an almost complete absence of any conventional deference or politeness. The chief man in the locality is the parish priest, and, except the doctor, there is very rarely any other resident who has received a good education. The influence of the priest is exceedingly great, but in this district he is usually slow to exercise his power actively in matters that in his opinion are *indifferent* from a religious point of view. The people are law-abiding as regards common-place crime; and, even during the recent land agitation, no serious disturbance occurred, except in the village of Dungloe where there was some years ago considerable boycotting largely owing, it is believed, to trade jealousy. Debts for rent, or in respect of goods given on credit, and obligations in general are fairly well met and discharged. Habitual drinking to excess is unknown, except among a few village loafers, but on *fair* days there are some arrests for drunkenness, principally because the Constabulary enforce the law strictly by arresting anybody who is at all "under the influence" of liquor. The change in the habits of the people in this respect is to be attributed to the action of the Most Reverend Dr. O'Donnell, Bishop of Raphoe, who has almost entirely put an end to *shebeening* and the making of *poteen* throughout the diocese by the enforcement of a strict ecclesiastical discipline in this respect. The bishop and the clergy are also most active in promoting the movement for total abstinence from intoxicating drink, and in every parish very large numbers of men are total abstainers. As far as my observation goes I should not say that a large proportion of the people are thrifty in the sense of being frugal, saving, and strictly economical: their habit is rather to live in such comfort as their means permit, but I do know of many instances in which large sums of money have been saved. So far as the nature of their employment allows, nearly all the people, except in some very poor remote townlands, are clean and tidy; and I may here make a general observation, that an opposite opinion is often given by observers who forget that for those who are engaged in agricultural and other manual kinds of labour a relative standard of cleanliness and tidiness should be established. Similarly one bears very severe and hasty judgments as regards the industry, or I should say alleged want of industry, among Irish tenants in congested districts. No doubt, as much is not done as might be done. Until recent years it was possible that the result of hard work might be a proportionate increase of rent, and it would not be unreasonable to suppose that the fear of such a result may have deterred many tenants from improving their condition. If such a habit of thought had been formed, it would not vanish immediately on the passing of an Act of Parliament, and, as an illustration of the ignorance that still exists, I may mention that one of the most intelligent and improving tenants in West Donegal recently asked me whether it would not be prudent for him to allow his land to fall into a bad condition for these last few years of his fifteen years' judicial tenure, lest if the farm were found in good heart, an increased judicial rent might be fixed by the Land Commission. It is not denied by anybody that the Donegal people work most industriously for a money wage, but I admit that they require to be taught and convinced that certain agricultural and industrial methods outside and beyond their observation and experience will be remunerative in the comparatively near future. In the months of November, December, January, and February the men of the district now under consideration undoubtedly live an idle life while they are at home, but I believe that they will set to work readily and steadily if people, in whom they confide, recommend them to follow the advice of those who may be authorized by the Board to give instruction. As regards the dwellings of the people, which are usually well white-washed externally and internally, there are some very poor houses in which there is only one room without a partition, but most of the houses have one room, and some two rooms, in addition to the kitchen or day-room. Where there are only two rooms in a house the father and mother sleep near the fire in the day-room, and the rest of the family in the other room, the males being in one bed and the females in another. The males get up first in the morning and go out of the room when dressed. Where there is a large family there is almost invariably a second room, and therefore separate sleeping rooms for males and females. Cattle in many instances are housed at night at one end of the day-room, and the poultry often perch overhead. The building of detached houses for cattle and fowl is increasing largely.

During the long days people get up at six o'clock or earlier, and they return to rest at about eleven o'clock. In the short days few get up in the morning before eight or nine o'clock, and they do not go to bed earlier than in the summer. In "the Rosses" the young people are famed for their love of dancing and they prefer the modern "round" dances to the old country dances. Their dancing assemblies, which are held in the winter or early spring, are of three kinds – "*surrees*" (clearly a corruption of soirees); meetings for charitable or other *raffles*; and *parties* held after a benevolent or friendly labouring assemblage. A "*surrees*" is a profitable undertaking; it is notified that there will be a "*surrees*" at a particular house and for each couple (young man and girl), an entrance fee of (say) eighteen pence is charged, the fiddler also being paid often as much as a shilling by each of the young men. The owner of the house keeps the entrance money for himself, and the refreshment (if any) is of the lightest and most harmless description. *Raffles* for a sheep or some article are often got up by or for those in need of money. The proceedings begin with a dance and terminate with a draw for the prize. Dancing *parties* are also given after the gathering of a number of young men for the purpose of digging a friend's land, and in the evening the girls of the neighbourhood drop in for a dance. Drinking of intoxicating liquors is now hardly ever known at social gatherings of any kind, except perhaps occasionally at farewell parties before emigrants leave. On such occasions it is usual for people to sit up at night, and on the departure form what they call a "convoy" to escort the emigrants for some distance on their way. Apart from these formal gatherings there is an almost nightly practice in the winter

Children playing barefoot along the shoreline, their homes in the background.

called "kaleying," or the assembling by a few after nightfall at some friend's house to talk and pass the evening without refreshments. During the day "the word goes round" at whose house the meeting is to be, and occasionally the visitors contribute in providing some slight refreshment such as tea, and this arrangement is spoken of as "a join." People still assemble in numbers at *wakes*, but intoxicating drinks are not provided, only tea, tobacco, and snuff being supplied. The clergy are, I understand, in some localities discouraging the attendance at wakes of any persons except relatives of the deceased. There is not as a rule any dancing at weddings, nor are intoxicating drinks usually supplied. The parents of young couples before their marriage do not, as in some other parts of Ireland, "make matches" or get the assistance of professional match-makers. The young men and women, who marry early in life, as a rule, when they meet at some fair or other social gathering, come to an understanding themselves without any benevolent intervention from outsiders.

(31.) Organized efforts for improvement of the district.

Until recent years no systematic effort was made for the development of the district, but a few years ago Mr. William Hammond, of Burton Port, as a private enterprise of his own, bought (in conjunction with Mr. John Herdman, of Sion Mills) a steamer to trade between Derry and Burton Port. This steam service has proved of great value to the locality, as before the steamer ran, all heavy goods had to be carted to and from Letterkenny, between which place and Derry there is communication by rail. The following are the landlords of the several electoral divisions, and all of them, with two or three inconsiderable exceptions, are non-resident:–

Annagary,	The Marquess Conyngham, R.W. Peebles, and General Twigg.
Croveighy,	The Marquess Conyngham, Walter Charley.
Dungloe,	The Marquess Conyngham
Maghery,	Michael Houston, James Sweeney, The Marquess Conyngham, John O'Donnell.
Rutland,	The Marquess Conyngham, Walter Charley, James O'Donnell.

(32.) Suggestions for the improvement of the district.

The condition of the people of "the Rosses" and Lettermacaward appears to be capable of improvement by the following methods:–

I. Establishment of steam and other communication;
II. Agricultural development;
III. Introduction of good breeds of live stock and poultry;
IV. Development of fisheries;
V. Provision of industrial occupation for the male population during the months of November, December, January, and February;
VI. Technical instruction of girls in needlework, and kindred occupations;
VII. Development of tourist traffic;
VIII. Migration of population and reclamation of land;
IX. Promotion of minor miscellaneous occupations.

I shall now refer in detail to each of the foregoing headings –

I. – *Improvement of Communication.*

For the really satisfactory opening-up and improvement of the district, I must say that, in my opinion, railway extension appears to be necessary. As I have the advantage of having been a member of the Commission appointed to report on railway extension in the county Donegal in 1890, I have inquired into this subject minutely, and have heard all the arguments for and against the several routes proposed. The report of the Commission, to which I refer, was a unanimous expression of opinion that, of all projected railways in county Donegal, the line to Dungloe, with an extension to Burton Port, was the most desirable. There are two routes by which Burton Port might be reached, *one* by an *extension* of the Stranorlar to Glenties Railway *via* Maas, Lettermacaward and Dungloe, and *the other* by means of a *branch* line from Fintown *via* Doochary Bridge and Dungloe. Either route is good, and it does not seem to be desirable to enter here into details on the subject. It was also proposed that "the Rosses" should be indirectly served by an extension of the Letterkenny Railway to Gweedore, but I see little in favour of this project except what might be said in favour of the interests of the Letterkenny Railway Company.

Pending the extension of a railway to the district, the establishment of a regular steam service by sea is most desirable, and, even after railway extension, it seems probable that steam-ships would continue to run with advantage, because heavy traffic will always go by sea when practicable. A further advantage is that the marketing of fish might be adequately carried out by a coasting steamships service at fixed times, such as I have in view. There are at present three local irregular services. Mr. W. Hammond and Mr. John Herdman jointly own two steamers; the trustees of the late Earl of Leitrim also own two steamers; and Mr. Christy, of Derry, owns a steamer which is frequently chartered for Donegal ports. Mr. Hammond's steamers trade irregularly between Ballyshannon, Montcharles, Killybegs, Teelin, Port Noo, Burton Port, Ballyness, and Londonderry, with an occasional run to Glasgow or Liverpool. The Earl of Leitrim's service is perhaps more regular, and his steamers trade between three ports on Mulroy Bay, Port Salon, Malin Head, Glasgow, Portrush, and Londonderry. Mr. Christy's is only a chartered occasional service. I think it would be possible through the payment of moderate subsidies by the Board that the immense benefit of a regular steamships service should be established between the several ports on the Donegal coast and such other port or ports of destination as might be considered desirable after investigation and inquiry. The ports of destination that occur to my mind are Sligo, Buncrana, or Fahan on Lough Swilly, Londonderry, Portrush, and Ardrossan in Ayrshire. I mention Ardrossan as perhaps the nearest commercial port across the Channel, but I rather think while traffic to a British port may be a more desirable commercial arrangement, that such long runs would on the other hand involve a serious addition to the number of the existing fleet of steamships if, as seems most desirable, the sailings should be very frequent, and that the days and hours of sailings should be fixed and published some time before. I am inclined to think that Fahan and Sligo would be the best ports of destination. The benefits of a regular, and if possible, daily steamship service are that *fish could be brought to market*; that *the cost of the carriage of imported goods would be greatly reduced*; and that *facilities would be given for the transmission of eggs and other productions* that are exported – in short *people in the district would pay less for their imports and receive more for their exports.*

A very large number of roads, piers, and boatslips are suggested in the district – some for access to railways and others for access to turf-bogs, limestone, the seashore, or for other apparently good reasons. Unless the Board should ask for a further report on this subject, I refrain for the present from any comments on the numerous, and, no doubt, in some instances, excellent public works that are suggested, I believe, with the object of *a temporary gain in earning wages*, as well as a permanent advantage to the locality as regards improved communications. The income, and indeed the principal sum, placed at the disposal of the Board would, I should say, be entirely inadequate to satisfy one half of the apparently reasonable claims for projected roads, causeways, piers, boatslips, and bridges, with which at present the air is thick. I fear, if once the Board yield to the requests for small local works, that no ultimately beneficial and far-reaching projects for the permanent improvement of the general condition of the people will, unless accompanied by the payment of wages, be received by those concerned with that amount of sympathy and co-operation that is desirable, if not essential, to the success of any joint efforts. The payment of wages for work would, beyond all question, be the most *popular* mode of expenditure of the Board's income; but a concession to one locality also involves the causing of disappointment and jealousy in unsuccessfully competing localities, and much therefore can be said in favour of deferring the undertaking of execution of local public works until the merits of the numerous proposed works can be compared together.

II. – *Agricultural Development.*

I have already described the mode in which the lands are tilled and worked. All good local judges concur in believing that much better crops might be taken off the land if the method of cultivation were improved. If portions of holdings could be fenced against sheep, then green crops might be grown, and cattle might be house-fed. The supply of farm-yard manure would accordingly be much increased, and a much larger yield of crops would be the result.

III. – *Improvement of Live Stock and Poultry.*

In consequence of the recent distribution of sires by the Board it is unnecessary for me to say anything on this subject, except that more bulls might be supplied and also rams, boars, and an improved breed of poultry.

IV. – *Fishery Development.*

In my opinion Burton Port, or one of the neighbouring islands, would be the best centre for developing the fishing industry on the West Coast of Donegal. As I have mentioned in paragraph 20 of this report, with a comparatively small addition to the pier of Burton Port, together with some dredging operations, the harbour would be very greatly improved. Already, however, it admits a steamship of 300 tons at ordinary high tides, and there is a land-locked anchorage about 200 yards from the pier. Dredging is recommended for the purpose of clearing a passage through an intervening bank of hard sand that does not shift. At another place, called "the Narrows," some dredging and a little blasting would also be desirable. If, in addition to the steamship service that I have already recommended, a curing station were established, the prospects of successfully employing first-class fishing boats would, I think, be most hopeful. There are considerable numbers of fishermen in the neighbouring islands, but they only have open Greencastle yawls, which are unfit for winter fishing. Some men along the coast fish for lobsters and herrings, and they are tolerably skilful in the management of a boat. These men generally return from working in Scotland early in November, and if they were successful in fishing during November, December, January, and February, they might continue fishing and withdraw in part or altogether from the Scotch labour market, thus causing a demand for other labourers which could be supplied from some of the poor districts in the county where the men are not migratory labourers.

V. – *Industries for Men.*

In the preceding sentence I have indicated fishing as a means by which employment might be provided for some in the four idle months. Men might also be profitably employed in improving their farms when they have received, or while they are receiving, suitable instruction from the Board. A small sum might be spent, I would suggest, in the purchase of tools for quarrying and for preparing granite for sale. One or two trained workmen might also be engaged for a few months to teach this industry to the residents of the locality in which good granite is to be found in the best situation for exportation.

VI. – *Industries for Women.*

Women, as a rule, are fully occupied in "the Rosses" and Lettermacaward, but they might, I believe, earn good wages sooner, and eventually much higher wages, if they were given technical training early in life. Some efforts have been and are being made in this direction by Miss Roberts, an English lady, and by Mrs. Sinclair, of Bonnyglen, County Donegal.

VII. – *Tourist Traffic.*

There are not any public vehicles passing through this district to or from Gweedore and Glenties, and this want is a great obstacle to tourists who at present have to hire post horses at considerable expense. Although the inns and private hotels of the district are fairly adequate for present requirements, yet they are not suitable for any considerable number of tourists. The opening of good hotels is desirable, and the establishment of a cheap regular car-service would be most useful.

VIII. – *Migration and Reclamation.*

As far as my inquiries have gone, people would not migrate to lands at a distance, but they would, I believe, be willing to reclaim moor or bog land in their own neighbourhood. Mr. Wm. Hammond, J.P., of Burton Port, is reclaiming some bog land about a mile from Dungloe; and if portion of his mountain could be obtained by the Board, the reclaiming tenants would have the advantage of seeing well-managed reclamation being carried out on an example holding at their very doors.

IX. – *Miscellaneous Occupations.*

It is possible, when the Board have fewer pressing subjects awaiting their attention, that the kelp trade may be found capable of improvement; and the export of soap-stone and bog iron-ore, which are found in parts of the district, may also be worthy of assistance. In addition to the resources and trades expressly referred to, many subsidiary occupations will naturally follow close upon the successful development of the fishing industry; and, in my judgment, the Board may rely upon the industry and common sense of the people of "the Rosses" and Lettermacaward to take full advantage of any projects that are wisely conceived and honestly carried out in their interests.

William L. Micks.

Gweedore Hotel, Co. Donegal,
27th May, 1892.

To

The Congested Districts Board for Ireland.

Curraghs, or canvas-covered canoes, brushed with tar to make them waterproof, were popular all along the west coast of Ireland, not only for fishing but also for carrying turf and seaweed.

CONGESTED DISTRICTS BOARD FOR IRELAND

COUNTY OF SLIGO – UNION OF SLIGO

REPORT OF F. G. TOWNSEND GAHAN, *Inspector*

DISTRICT

OF

GRANGE

STATISTICAL TABLE

ELECTORAL DIVISION.	Area in Statute Acres.	Poor Law Valuation.	Number of Ratings at and under £10 and above £4 Valuation.	Number of Ratings at and under £4 Valuation.	Population in 1891.	Number of Families in 1891.	Number of Families on Holdings exceeding £2 and under £4 Valuation.	Number of Families on Holdings at and under £2 Valuation.	Number of Families in very poor circumstances.	Number of Families which have no Cattle.
		£								
Cliffony North,	4,732	2,062	122	228	1,783	339	154	74	40	*
Cliffony South,	4,663	1,705	115	99	1,317	229	75	24	10	
Lissadill North,	4,695	2,621	160	203	1,743	367	89	114	20	
Lissadill West,	4,043	2,229	99	238	1,830	344	107	131	25	
TOTALS,	18,133	8,617	496	768	6,673	1,279	425	343	95	*

* Varies from 5 per cent. in the inland districts to 20 per cent. of the population along the coast.

(1.) Whether inland or maritime.

The district is maritime and includes two small islands, one Dernish, situated in Milkhaven close to the land, the other Inishmurray, situated N.W. from Streedagh Point, some four or five miles out to sea.

(2.) Average quantity of land cultivated on holdings at and under £4 valuation, under (*a*) oats, (*b*) potatoes, (*c*) meadow, (*d*) green crops.

In this district the average farm at and under £4 valuation varies a little in size. In the northerly portions the area of a £4 farm would be about six acres, while in the southerly portions about four acres or £1 per acre.

Very little oats is grown comparatively speaking, in some places not equal to the area under potatoes. Generally speaking, however, corn and potatoes cover equal areas. On a six-acre farm the division would be somewhat as follows:– Potatoes and oats from three roods to one acre, cabbage half a rood (these are generally planted in the "brews" or sides of the potato ridges), turnips half a rood, from an acre to an acre and a-half of meadow, and the remainder grazing. In the little "gardens" or plots of land beside the dwelling-house cabbage is generally planted. Some few farmers sow a little wheat, and a few barley or rye, but only in small quantities.

(3.) Extent of mountain or moor grazing, and rights possessed by tenants, whether in common or otherwise.

There is practically no mountain grazing in the district.

(4.) Extent and description of land, if any, which could be profitably reclaimed and added to existing adjoining holdings.

With the exception of small isolated patches of "cut-away" bog there is no land suitable for reclamation in the district adjoining existing holdings. These portions of cut-away bog are, at present, let to the different tenants by the landlord at from 2*s.* 6*d.* to 5*s.* an acre, and are capable with care of producing very fair crops.

(5.) Particulars as to any suitable land in district which could be obtained, and to which families could be migrated with a reasonable prospect of success.

The only land which might be perhaps obtained for the purpose is that portion of Ballyconnell and Kilmacannon townlands, which lies east from Knocklane Castle. There is here a great waste tract of some 1,000 acres or more. A portion of this was once inhabited and cultivated, but I understand that a great many years ago the sand drove the people out. There is a certain depth of sand over the soil, but it has not the appearance of being very deep. The surface is now covered with short sweet grass and portions of it with bent grass. The greater portion belongs to a Captain Gethin, the remainder to Sir Henry Gore-Booth. I did not under the circumstances think it advisable to make any inquiries into the probable cost of the land, but I do not think it is at present worth very much.

(6.) Method of cultivation, manures, rotation of crops, etc., etc.

The methods of cultivation are somewhat similar to those employed in N.W. Donegal, except that the farmers have more horses and consequently more ploughs. The man who has not a plough lends his horse to the man who has a plough and only one horse, and in return gets the loan of the plough to work his land.

However, a great deal of labour is done with the spade. The potatoes are generally planted in ridges or lazy beds towards the end of March, the land having been previously dug over and set up. Some set the potatoes in drills, and this method of cultivation is, I understand, becoming more popular. Corn is broadcasted generally in the end of March or beginning of April. Cabbages are generally planted into the potato "brews" or else in a "garden" close to the house. Turnips are sown in the usual manner, and the land sometimes yields very good crops, but the amount sown is, as already stated, very small.

The potatoes are "moulded" about six weeks after their setting, or when they are some nine inches above the ground; after this moulding they are not interfered with until the time for digging. A few of the better class of farmers may weed and clear the ridges or drills, but as a general rule the strength of the weed crop exceeds that of the potato crop. The grass land is top-dressed with either farm manure or seaweed and shells, which are scraped off the rocks in spring time. The manure is left in heaps on the fields, and often not spread for weeks after it is put out.

The manures used are – 1, farmyard manure; 2, seaweed and shells; 3, guano. Owing to the smallness of the farms, and the consequently limited stock, the supply of farmyard manure is necessarily small; but even as it is, with a little care in keeping the manure heaps and saving the waste about the house, the supply could be almost doubled. The water from the manure heap is in most cases allowed to drain away, and a great deal of good manure-making material thus wasted.

This district is, perhaps, more dependent on seaweed for a manure than any district in Donegal, for the reason stated above, viz., that the quantity of farm manure is so small. In Cliffony South and the Lisadill Electoral Divisions a good deal of guano is bought, generally a bag going to every rood and a-half of potatoes. Lime is not much needed, as a great portion of the district is on limestone formation. The only rotation, properly speaking, is potatoes, oats, and lea land. Generally, two crops of potatoes are taken from the lea land, then oats, and, if they have land enough, grass or clover is sown with the oats, and a grass crop taken off. The light boggy soil sometimes gives good crops of rye, but the cultivation of rye is going out. The quantities of cabbage and turnips grown are too small to be considered in a rotation.

(7.) General information with regard to stock, and suggestions as to improvement of breeds – (*a*) cattle, (*b*) sheep, (*c*) horses and donkeys, (*d*) pigs, (*e*) poultry, etc., etc.

The stock in this district is, on the whole, superior to that in the Donegal districts. The cattle are a very fair class, and some fine beasts are to be found. The landlords, Sir H. Gore-Booth and the Hon. E. Ashleigh, both keep bulls for the benefit of their tenantry, the service of which they get at a low price.

I understand that the bulls at present kept by Mr. Ashleigh are not so good as those he kept formerly, and that consequently there is a deterioration in the stock got from them. The breed preferred in the district is the Shorthorn, and although opinions differ as to their suitability to the district, still with the tenantry they are much more in favour than the Polled Angus breed. The location of bulls at different centres in the district would undoubtedly be productive of great benefit, as, of course, all cannot take advantage of the bulls kept by the landlords, some on account of the distance and some for other reasons.

There are not many sheep in the district; probably about ten per cent. of the tenantry keep sheep. The breed is good, being a cross on the Roscommon breed; they produce from five to six pounds of wool, which is very fine in quality and much softer than that obtained from the black-faced sheep.

The horses in the district are small, but strong and fairly well formed. About 25 per cent. of the farmers have horses, and 70 per cent. of the remainder donkeys; these latter are very small, but are used for every conceivable purpose – carting turf, seaweed, manure, provisions, etc., etc. The Board have, I understand, a horse in the care of Major Eccles, at Moneygold; but in my opinion it would be wiser to place the horse in Grange Village (although the expense might be greater), as country farmers do not care, as a rule, to take their mares to a private house, and many who would apply for and get the service in Grange would not go to Moneygold. With private individuals, too, there may be local differences which would greatly impair the usefulness of the project. Three or four good jackasses placed at, say, Lisadill, Grange, Cliffony, and Bunduff, could not fail to be of the greatest benefit in improving the local breed.

The pigs in the district are, on the whole, good, and are really the staple stock of the smaller farmers, and on their good or bad sale largely depends their balance to profit or loss each year. Each farmer has two and very often three pigs; and, unlike the farmers in the pig districts of county Donegal, they sell two lots of pigs, as a rule, in the year. Two or three good boars in the district, at suitable centres, would be of great service, and I believe suitable men could be found to take them on the Board's terms. At present sows have to be taken some miles for service.

As regards the poultry, the hens are generally the ordinary barndoor breed, and in this class there is room for a great deal of improvement. Owing to the proximity of Sligo and Bundoran, the poultry trade in the district ought to be a very valuable one, but I understand that very little is done in it. All classes of poultry should be profitable here, more especially hens and turkeys. Geese are kept by a few, but not largely. The establishing of poultry farms in the district as distributing centres, and the distribution of some good geese and ganders and some bronze turkeys, would be of immense benefit. The neighbourhoods of Carney, Grange, Cliffony, Mullaghmore, and Bunduff would be good centres.

This district, owing to its proximity to what should be very good markets, could profit by an improvement in existing breeds. The number of poultry generally kept on the smaller farms is from twelve to sixteen, and on the larger from twenty to thirty; twice this number could be kept easily and profitably if a little care were exercised, and the fowl properly looked after, for the same cost. Here, however, as elsewhere, no attention is paid to the housing and feeding of the poultry; as a general rule they have to look after themselves; they are fed irregularly and housed badly. The usual quota of ducks is kept attached to each house, but as these are maintained rather for pleasure than profit, they call for no remark.

(8.) Markets and fairs for cattle and produce of district; also statement as to where the people obtain food and other supplies, and the prevailing custom with regard to the disposal of butter, eggs, and poultry; to what extent are they sold in the first instance to local shopkeepers and dealers, and, generally speaking, how old are the eggs when sold to the first buyer, and about how old when they reach their ultimate destination in Great Britain.

The principal fairs are Grange, in the district (thirteen fairs yearly), and Sligo, Ballyshannon, and Kinlough, outside. Grange is the principal fair, and Sligo the principal market, twice weekly. Meal and flour are sometimes obtained from Sligo and sometimes from local dealers; with these the price is generally 1*s.* to 1*s.* 6*d.* dearer than in Sligo. Sugar, tea, tobacco, and other groceries are generally obtained in small quantities from the local shops. Bakers' bread is bought from carts which make daily rounds; these come from Ballyshannon, Bundoran, and Sligo.

Eggs are sold to the local dealers, being paid for in tea or sugar, never in cash. Butter is often made into firkins of 70 lbs. and sold in Sligo, but it is also disposed of in a similar manner to the eggs. The poultry trade is small. There was a poultry market, I understand, in Sligo, but it is given up by the people in the district. The dealers who come round in "tea carts" often buy poultry in exchange for tea. There is a good market in Mullaghmore and Bundoran during the bathing season. Eggs vary in age from five days to three weeks before they reach the English market; how old they may be when they reach the consumer it is difficult to ascertain. In some cases local dealers, if they think there is any immediate prospect of a rise in the price of eggs, will often hold over a lot of eggs for a fortnight in order to take advantage of it.

(9.) Rail, steamer, sailing boat, road, postal and telegraph facilities.

Properly speaking, the district has no railway facilities. Sligo being the nearest railway station on one side, and Bundoran on the other, each being thirteen miles away from a central point in the district. The construction of a railway (1) from Bundoran to Sligo, connecting Sligo with the Great Northern Railway, or (2) from Sligo to Ballyshannon, connecting with the Donegal Railway Company (proposed line). This latter project would, I think, be the best for the district, although the more expensive, as it would connect the whole district at once with Derry and Glasgow, Liverpool, &c. The capital for either of these schemes could not, I fear, be subscribed locally, but if made by Government grant I believe the scheme would pay.

Steamer. A steamer plies between Sligo and Liverpool.

Sailing boat *nil.*

Roads very good.

Postal facilities sufficient for the district.

Telegraph good. There are two telegraph offices, Cliffony and Grange. In this latter place I understand there is a difficulty in getting a sufficiency of messages to cover the guarantee, an office is suggested at Ballinful, a local guarantee would be forthcoming if required. Ballinful is four miles from Grange.

(10.) Employment for labourers in the district, whether temporary or constant, and rate of wage.

There is no constant employment for labour in the district other than that given by the landlords (who employ some thirty to forty men) and the road contractors. There is, however, a fair share of irregular labour, and an ordinary family, with a man and a strong boy, may count on making about £4 per annum in wages. The general rate of wage is 1*s.* per day, with food, and 1*s.* 6*d.* per day without.

(11.) Migratory labour, average earnings per head, and where earned.

There is no migratory labour properly so called. Any of the young men who go to Scotland generally remain away for some time before coming home.

A number emigrate yearly to America.

(12.) Weaving, spinning, knitting, and sewing, whether used locally or sold, and where.

There is comparatively very little weaving and spinning carried on in the district. Some years ago there used to be a good deal of work done, but since the mills in Convoy, Lisbellaw, Galashiels, and other places have been established the farmers send their wool there to be made into cloth, and sell any surplus wool they may have either in Sligo or to the factory.

The district itself is not a wool-producing district, though immediately adjoining one. There are at present some three or four working weavers in the district. These weave linen almost more than frieze; petticoats for the women, towels, coarse sheets, and such like, but the demand, as well as the supply, is local and small.

There should be a good opening in the district for a profitable woollen industry, as the quality of the wool is good, and the supply, which could be obtained sufficient, but there does not appear to be any local interest in the matter. In this lies a demonstration of the great difference in position, financially, of the farmers on this side of Donegal Bay and those on the west side. There they must work in order to live at all, as their stock and their farms cannot support them, while here the industry would only be taken up as a means to better their position, and as, on the whole, they are without ambition, so there is no real anxiety shown in the development of an industry.

Knitting, there is practically none, except for home use, and that only sometimes.

Sewing, in the shape of "sprigging," has quite gone out, but quite recently a local industry of limited extent has been started, with Sligo as its headquarters, giving out work of different sorts to girls in the district. This, I fear, is not likely to be constant, although at present the number earning at it is considerable.

Mrs. Eccles of Moneygold, County Sligo, still employs girls at "sprigging" work and turns out some very beautiful work, which she disposes of privately to friends and others, but of course here too the supply and demand is limited.

(13.) Kelp-burning, and sale of seaweed.

A large quantity of kelp is manufactured along the coast of this district. This season, 1895, about 1,000 tons was shipped. Of this the Cliffony Electoral Division supplied about 400 ton, and the Lisadill Electoral Division about 600. All the kelp of the district is shipped from Mullaghmore in schooners. The price this year was from £3 10*s.* to £3 15*s.*

One great drawback to the manufacture of good kelp is that in the purchase of it by the dealers a premium is practically put on dishonesty, there being no proper discrimination exercised as to quality, and they will perhaps pay a man who has inferior kelp, but a specious tongue, more than the man who has honest kelp, but who cannot get into the dealer's good graces. Then again, the dealer can give what price he likes, especially to those who come long distances, as they sometimes do, ten or fifteen miles, sooner than take the kelp back they will take five shillings to ten shillings a ton less than they are entitled to. The price during the past two years has been on the decline, and those who live far away have to consider whether it is worth their while to spend so much time at it when the price is so low. The buying is nearly all in the hands of one man, who receives a commission of ten shillings a ton on all kelp bought. In the four Electoral Divisions about three hundred and fifty families are engaged in the manufacture of kelp.

Sale of Seaweed. – On the Hon. E. Ashleigh's estate a small amount is added to the rent of each tenant, and all have the right of gathering the weed. On Mr. Jones' estate the seaweed is in the landlord's hand, and is divided among the tenants, they paying so much; on Captain Gethins' estate a somewhat similar practice prevails, and on Sir H. Gore-Booth's estate the tenants along the shore have the seaweed rights, and if those inland want it they must pay at from 5*s.* to 7*s.* a cart.

(14.) Sale of turf, nature and extent of bogs.

The sale of turf on the estates is prohibited, but nevertheless all the tenants who have the opportunity sell it, and the money they make on it is a very large increase to their yearly receipts – getting from 1*s.* 6*d.* to 2*s.* for a small cart and 3*s.* to 5*s.* 6*d.* for a large one, according to the season, and, selling about fifty cart-loads in the year, the earnings would range from £3 15*s.* to £10.

This practice, combined with the large number who rightfully draw their fuel from the bogs is rapidly reducing their extent so that in another sixty to eighty years' time all the bog in the electoral divisions will be cut out, and the community will have to face the very serious problem of how to provide fuel. It is in the interest of the people themselves and their descendants that this indiscriminate sale of turf should be put a stop to.

Each tenant pays 2*s.* 6*d.* a year for 200 barrels, or about thirty-three cart-loads of turf, which is all they are supposed to cut. Tenants not on the estate pay from 10*s.* to 15*s.* for the same. The total extent of bog land in the district is about 1,000 acres and a good deal of that is partially cut. The turf is generally of an inferior quality. The lowest strata of the bog is generally worked with the hands. The turf are formed into round balls and squeezed very firmly together; these when dry burn somewhat like coals, with an intense heat.

(15.) Lobster fishing, number of men and boats employed.

There are some twenty boats fishing for lobsters during the season, and these make from 8*s.* to 10*s.* per week per man, three men generally in the boat. There is a good local market for lobsters in Bundoran and Sligo, and some are shipped to Liverpool in the steamer.

(16.) Sea fishing. Facilities for sale of fish, and number of boats and men solely employed in fishing.

The sea fishing in this district is considerable and the local market very good. The two principal centres are Raughley on the south and Mullaghmore to the north-east of the district, the latter being the most important centre and that at which the greatest quantity of fish is landed. Milkhaven, Streedagh, and Ballyconnell or Knocklane, are also minor fishing centres, but owing to the want of harbour accommodation at these points the large fishings all take place from the two first named places. On the sea itself the island of Inishmurray may develop into a good fishing centre as it is near the cod banks, but at present the men seem rather apathetic about it. Inishmurray is the only portion of the district where the fishermen have not an immediate market for their fish, and to meet this want the Board are opening a curing station on the island, which should be of immense benefit to the islanders, though there may be some doubt as to whether they could sell to the Board's station at 3*s.* to 3*s.* 6*d.*

per dozen when they could get from 5*s.* to 6*s.* on the mainland. At Mullaghmore, 8*s.* per dozen for cod and ling is considered a very low price, and 20*s.* for herring per 1,000. At Raughley, the market for white fish is also good, but comparatively few are landed there. Sligo at one side of the district and Ballyshannon and Bundoran at the other, give a constant market to the fishermen, and the fish hawkers who sell the fish make large profits on their sales. There are very few men solely engaged in fishing, the fisher families on Mullaghmore to the number of forty or fifty approach nearest to this, but even these have little patches of land and keep one or two pigs, and sometimes a cow. The number of boats solely engaged in fishing is hard to ascertain, as a number of them are used for seaweed gathering in the early spring, but probably about thirty boats on the Mullaghmore and Raughley guards are solely engaged in fishing. The average local prices for fish are somewhat as follows:– cod and ling, 7*s.* to 12*s.* per dozen; haddock, 2*s.* 6*d.* to 3*s.* per dozen; herring, 10*s.* to 30*s.* per 1,000; whiting, 10*d.* per dozen.

(17.) Number of boats and men employed in carrying turf or seaweed or in fishing. Classification of boats.

The number of boats on the Mullaghmore guards is about twenty-five, of which seven are trawlers, the crews number six to the boat, or total 150 men and boys. The number on the Raughley guards is thirty-five of which four are trawlers, the approximate crew is seven. A number of these boats on the Raughley guards are old indifferent craft, and the fishing done is limited – above figures include the Inishmurray boats. Boats in the spring are employed in carrying seaweed, but none exclusively. One or two boats in Milkhaven are employed occasionally in boating turf to Dernish Island.

(18.) Fish; whether consumed at home or sold.

The fish is, with a small exception, all sold. A few cod and ling and haddock are dried each year, and some herrings roughly cured by the fishermen, but the whole amount is small. A great deal of the fish is sold in the surrounding country, and the remainder in the towns of Sligo, Ballyshannon, and Bundoran.

(19.) Extent of fish-curing.

There has been no fish-curing of late years in the district until the Congested Districts Board opened their station at Raughley in 1894. Mullaghmore, possessing as it does a fine fresh fish market, is not suited for a curing station, unless the takes are very large. Raughley, being more out of the way, is not so frequented by hawkers, so that the fishermen are more disposed to take the Board's price for their fish. If a railway were constructed from Sligo to Bundoran or Ballyshannon a fresh fish trade might be established between Mullaghmore and Liverpool or Glasgow which would be advantageous to that portion of the district.

(20.) Piers and Harbours, existing and suggested, and how far those existing are adapted to wants of district.

There are three piers or artificial harbours in the district, namely, Mullaghmore, Milkhaven, and Raughley. The first of these was designed by Mr. Stephenson, the money being found by the late Lord Palmerston, who owned the property. It is an enclosed basin, with one main entrance and a small "scour" entrance, which is bridged over.

The area of the harbour at high water is about five acres. A great portion runs dry at low tide, when there is not more than two or three feet depth of water along the quay wall.

This is the principal harbour of all this district, and from it all the kelp – amounting this year to 1,000 tons – of the district is shipped and the coal of the district and all the fish is landed. The traffic is large, but the fine quay has, through neglect, been allowed to fall into a bad state of repairs. The harbour is the property of a private individual, but the Board, seeing that the whole surrounding congested area was largely dependent on the harbour, made a grant of £300 for the repair of the quay walls and breakwater and the re-making of the roadway. These improvements will, when complete, prove of great service to the locality, enabling them to cart their kelp along the quay, and to cart away fish, etc., from the vessels without danger.

Milkhaven is a natural harbour, lying immediately to the south-west of Mullaghmore, where, I understand, in "'47" a small pier was constructed. The harbour is very safe and sheltered, and accessible in calm weather; but in bad weather or when there is a ground sea, there is a nasty "bar." It is suggested to clear away a channel lying to S.W. of present channel, by which it is supposed a scour would be caused which would deepen the channel sufficiently to do away with the "bar," at least at one entrance. But owing to proximity of drifting sand the experiment would be probably unsuccessful, and, in any case, of doubtful utility.

The third harbour, Raughley, was constructed by the Board of Works a number of years ago. It is very judiciously situated as regards the prevailing winds and the heaviest seas; but unfortunately the water in the vicinity is very shallow, so much so that no boat of the larger class can, at low water, approach at all near the shore. The quay walls are in fairly good repair, and a number of small fishing boats make it their headquarters. The great drawback to the usefulness of this harbour is the want of a road to it. The public road approaches to within some 300 yards of the quay, and the remainder of the way lies across private grounds. The landlord does not, I understand, prevent foot passengers, but charges a royalty on all carts going through.

The construction of a road to this pier would supply a much felt want. The chief difficulty would lie in the obtaining of the land which, I understand, the landlord (Mr. Jones) is not willing to sell unless for very substantial remuneration.

The most serviceable road to the pier would be about three furlongs in length, constructed along the edge of the shore from the country road at Mr. Jones' gate. An alternative route – shorter, but not so serviceable – could be made from the road which passes the coastguard station. The length of this road would be about one and a-half furlongs.

It is difficult to understand a pier being constructed without an approach to it, except through private grounds, especially when the pier has been constructed with public money; but Mr. Jones (the landlord) states that no approach was ever made, nor was he made any offer for land for same.

A landing place is suggested in Ballyconnell townland, about two and a-half miles N.W. from Raughley, at a point called Knocklane. The place in question is situated at the end of a long strand, which at this point is boulder strewn, the boulders having evidently been torn by the sea from the sides of the "knock," or hill, on which the waves are year by year encroaching.

From the character of the boulders and the positions in which they are lying, it is evident that a heavy sea runs here at times, and it would further appear that if a boat could not land on the present strand it could not land on a slip. All that is required to make the landing place as safe as circumstances would permit is the clearing away of a sufficiently wide track through the boulders, and this is a work which I think the fishermen should carry out for themselves. The only hindrance to the landing place at present is that the men must get wet on entering and leaving their boats, as the water is shallow for some distance out. A remedy for this would be the construction of a landing stage similar to that the Board have constructed at Magheraroarty, Co. Donegal. A cheap paved slip from high-water line to the top of the bank would facilitate the pulling up and down of the boats, and the number of boats in the port would scarcely seem to justify a larger expenditure than this would entail – some £50 or so.

A landing place is suggested at Streedagh, a point situated about half-way between Mullaghmore and Raughley. A landing place here would be useful, as on this point the Inishmurray fishermen land, and from here all persons – doctor, clergy, police, &c. – going to Inishmurray embark.

There are also several fishing boats in the locality, and during the herring fishing a number of boats put in here, as the fish move round the coast. A stage somewhat similar to that constructed at Magheraroarty would be very useful here, and, in addition, the construction of a short length of sea wall connecting a gap between two ledges of rock, which would act as a breakwater, would be desirable to make the landing place more secure. If this were done, landing here would be very fairly safe under most conditions, northerly to north-easterly gales excepted, and with these no great height of wave can rise, as the "fetch" is limited.

A drawback to Streedagh as a public landing place is that, as at Raughley, there would be no public right of way to the shore at the place. In order to reach it, it is necessary to pass through fields belonging to a Mr. Jones (not the landlord of Raughley), and although he does not prevent traffic with the shore, still he closes and locks all his gates once a year to maintain his right. Of the two points, Knocklane and Streedagh, Streedagh is in my opinion the more important.

(21.) Extent of salmon and freshwater fisheries. Number of men earning their livelihood therefrom.

There is a salmon fishery in Bunduff river belonging to the Hon. E. Ashleigh, which gives employment to six men during the summer.

Also at Mullaghmore and Streedagh are fisheries which are leased to Mr. Petrie, of Liverpool. There are no men dependent on these fisheries for their livelihood. About fifteen men earn money from them for about ten weeks each year. There are no freshwater fisheries.

(22.) Banks and Loan Funds.

There are no banks in the district, the nearest being at Ballyshannon on one side and Sligo on the other. A branch from Sligo is open at Grange on fair days. There is a loan fund at Drumcliff and another in Bundoran. The very general opinion seems to be that the loan funds do a great deal of harm in the districts in which they are placed, and so far as I could gather about 50 per cent. of the farmers in the district have borrowed from them. The borrowing is a very costly process, for not only has the borrower to pay the interest on the loan, but he must also bring in and pay two securities, and if his loan is not paid to date he is fined.

The interest charged is very high, and it is difficult to see where the profits, which must be very great, go to.

(23.) Mineral and other resources.

With the exception of some bog ore and kelp there are no mineral or other resources of a similar nature in the district.

(24.) Relative prevalence of cash or credit dealings, length of credit, interest charged, extent of barter, etc., etc.

This district is placed similarly to congested districts in County Donegal, as regards its credit dealings with the local shopkeepers. A great deal of credit is given, indeed the greater number of families exist mainly on credit, all debts being cleared up as far as possible half-yearly. The only goods for which a present equivalent is given are tea and sugar, and they are generally paid for with eggs or butter. Meal and flour are always obtained on credit, but the same quantity of these commodities is not consumed here as in Donegal, for in this district the people live very largely on bakers' bread and do not make much home-made bread, and do not eat much "stirabout."

On the whole, there is far more business done on the credit than on the ready money system. The interest charged varies from ten per cent. to fifteen per cent. The general length of credit given is about six months, though sometimes a longer time is allowed to elapse before payment, and even then full payment is rarely, if ever made, as no dealer likes to have his customer clear in his books. Barter in the way of getting an equivalent in kind for eggs, butter, and poultry is common, indeed the two first named articles are never paid for in cash, with the one exception, when butter is sold in the firkin it is then generally paid for in cash, but in all cases of retail it is paid for in kind.

Harvesting fish and seaweed in a busy local port.

(25.) Estimated *cash* receipts and expenditure of a family in ordinary circumstances.

The cash receipts vary in different localities. There are those portions of the district where kelp is largely made, those where fishing is carried on, those where turf is largely sold, and those that have none of these advantages. They are all noted in the following table, those items which are not common to all are noted as such:–

Cash Receipts	£	*s.*	*d.*	Expenditure	£	*s.*	*d.*
* Sale of cows,	9	0	0	Rent and taxes,	4	10	0
Sale of 3 pigs,	8	0	0	* Tea,	4	10	0
* Sale of sheep,	2	0	0	Sugar,	1	10	0
Sale of eggs,	5	5	0	Bakers' bread,	4	0	0
Sale of poultry,	1	0	0	Meal and flour,	8	0	0
‡ Sale of butter,	6	2	6	Clothes,	7	10	0
‡ Sale of oats,	0	13	4	Tobacco, drink, &c.,	3	15	0
‡ Sale of hay,	2	0	0	Fishermen, £2 extra,	2	0	0
§ Sale of turf,	5	0	0	Church dues,	0	16	0
¥ Sale of kelp,	12	0	0	Farm implements,	0	15	0
¥ Sale of fish,	20	0	0	Artifical manure,	1	10	0
† Sale of wool,	1	0	0	Oil, candles, salt, &c.	1	10	0
Earnings in year,	5	0	0	Carting and saving turf,	2	0	0
				Buying 3 pigs,	2	5	0
				Replenishing stock,	2	0	0
				If keep horse,	8	0	0
				Interest on loans,	0	10	0
					£55	1	0
				Without horse,	£47	1	0

* Fishermen, perhaps only one, £3.
† Only inland.
‡ Only inland.
§ Only inland in certain districts.
¥ On coast.

* The tea purchased in this district is seldom under 3*s.* 6*d.* per pound.

(26.) Estimated value of home-grown food consumed, and period during which it lasts.

	£	*s.*	*d.*
Potatoes (10 barrels at 12*s.*),	6	0	0
Poultry,	0	5	0
Milk and butter,	5	0	0
Turnips (house consumed),	0	10	0
Total,	£11	15	0

Potatoes generally last until the middle of April, or beginning of May, in a very good year until June, in a bad year only until the new year. Turnips, hay, manure, &c., can hardly be looked on as assets by themselves, as they are consumed in the produce of stock, cultivation of land, &c.

(27.) Dietary of people, number of meals daily, and kinds of food throughout the year.

The dietary is, of course, very simple – here, as in Donegal, the people are almost complete vegetarians. The most marked difference in diet of the people in this district is the large amount of bakers' bread consumed. The amount made at home being very small in comparison. Bacon is the only animal food they eat, and that seldom, fish occasionally, and, perhaps, once or twice a year a fowl or two. Eggs are more eaten here than in Donegal – not so much in the winter as in the summer months, as in winter they are a more marketable commodity than in summer. Oatbread is sometimes eaten, but not largely. For dinner, cabbage and dripping is a very favourite dish. Breakfast is generally taken at eight o'clock, and consists of tea and bread, sometimes porridge. Dinner about one p.m., consisting of potatoes mainly, which they eat with buttermilk, and cabbage and dripping sometimes. When the potatoes are finished, bread and tea, and sometimes porridge are taken.

There is generally some sort of meal about four o'clock, consisting of dry bread or tea and bread. The regular "tea" is taken between seven and eight, and consists generally of stirabout or, if potatoes are plentiful, of potatoes and milk. Potatoes generally last from August until April, and between those dates form the staple food of the people; from April until August, stirabout and bakers' bread they principally live on. Tea is partaken of at least twice a day and most often thrice, it is make very strong and unwholesome, through the habit they have of stewing it. Stirabout is almost always made with Indian meal, very seldom with oatenmeal.

(28.) Clothing, whether home-made or bought, etc., etc.

The clothing is almost entirely bought – underclothing and all; formerly when weaving was common in the district, blankets and undershirts were made locally; but since the factories at Convoy, Lisbellaw, &c., have been established the farmers prefer to send their wool there, such as have it, getting in exchange a certain quantity of cloth, those who have no wool generally buy as much as will make all the clothes they will need, send it to the factory and get an equivalent in cloth or blankets, paying so much extra for the weaving.

The women still have their linen petticoats woven locally, as they wear so much better than those they buy, also, as a rule the men's socks and the women's everyday stockings are home made. A quantity of second hand clothes is purchased at the fairs in Grange from itinerant vendors. These are generally shawls and children's garments and men's overcoats.

One noticeable feature in this district is the small number of barefooted people one sees, with the exception of a few small boys and girls no one is ever seen barefooted.

On Sundays and holidays the young women dress up in remarkably fine clothes, indeed from what I could learn, the younger female portion of the community spent a great deal too much on dress.

(29.) Dwellings: kind of houses, home-life and customs, etc., etc.

On entering this district from the north-east side one is struck with the cleanliness and comfort of almost all the cottages, they are well built and have large good windows, a marked contrast to the tiny light holes one is accustomed to see in County Donegal. The reason for this is that the former landlord, Lord Palmerston, who took a very deep interest in his tenantry, used to give prizes for the best built and best kept houses, gardens, &c.; he also supplied windows to all his tenants. On the south side the houses are not so good, especially in the neighbourhood of the townlands of Ballyconnell and Cloonagh, where some very poor houses are found. There are other very poor townlands where the houses are in keeping with the poverty of the people, but on the whole the houses of the district betoken a much greater degree of prosperity and comfort than exists in the districts on the north side of the bay. It is said, however, that the poverty of the people should not be judged by the appearance of the houses. The home life is simple and quite similar to that in other districts. In summer they get up about six, in the winter seven, or perhaps later. The stock is

Traditional West of Ireland village from the 1890s.

attended to, the cows milked (sometimes this is not done till much later in the day, the cows being put on the grass for an hour or so). About eight o'clock breakfast, after breakfast they all go about their various avocations, the men to the farm or the bog, the women to churn, herd cattle, &c. (on account of the better fencing in this district cattle herding is not so much required as in Donegal) and the children to school. Dinner comes on about one o'clock, and after dinner the same routine till tea time. At night the cattle are housed (generally both winter and summer for the sake of the manure) and milked, the pigs put in and fed, and about ten o'clock they all retire. There is practically no such thing as a cottage with only one room in it in this district, they have all a sleeping room for the women and often one for the men – if not, the latter sleep in the kitchen or living room. There are, so far as I could gather, no distinctive customs, wakes of course are held, but not apparently to the same extent as formerly. In former days a good deal of smuggling was done on the coast, but that is entirely done away with.

(30.) Character of the people for industry, etc., etc.

The people are fairly industrious – they have as a rule only small farms, and work these to the best of their abilities and knowledge, which is in most cases limited. This of course does not keep them constantly employed, and some constant employment or any money-making employment in the winter months is much needed both for men and women.

(31.) Whether any organized effort has been made to develop the resources or improve the condition of the people. If so, by what means.

Lord Palmerston, in his day, seems to have done a great deal for the tenantry on his estate. He caused the Mullaghmore harbour to be constructed, he gave local prizes for the neatest houses, the neatest gardens, &c. He gave the tenants window sashes for their houses, so that they should have them well lighted, and took a deep general interest in their welfare. The fruits of this are still to be seen in the neatness and cleanliness of the houses. Beyond this there does not seem to have been any organized effort made to improve the condition of the people in any way or to develop the industrial resources of the district.

(32.) Suggestions as to any possible method for improving the condition of the people in future.

There are many internal evidences that this district is in many respects better off than the majority of the congested districts on the north side of the bay.

The chief of these are (1) the large price obtained for fish; (2) the character of their dwelling houses; (3) the fact that all the population (nearly) wear boots and shoes, and all the women on Sundays hats or bonnets; (4) the fact that there is no home industry; (5) the quantity of bakers' bread bought. Nevertheless there are many means which might be adopted to improve their condition. The first of these I would consider to be an improvement in their fishing methods; for the most part the boats are old and poor – new boats and modern methods are wanted. In Mullaghmore larger boats are required, and I understand crews could be obtained easily who would club together to purchase one of these boats. It would be wiser to begin with one or two. As they have the enclosed harbour, there would be no trouble about their safe-keeping. In my reply to query 20 I have referred to the landing places on the coast.

Secondly.– Railway development of the district. (See reply, *query* 9).

Thirdly.– Industrial development. In my reply to *query* 12 I have referred to the reason which seems to me at present opposed to the industrial development of the district – viz., the people have enough to live on, and are not, as a rule, ambitious to improve. It seemed to me, too, that the younger women of the district seemed to think that it was rather beneath them to spin (I refer now to the woollen industry). The Board have made a small grant to Mrs. Eccles, of Moneygold, for the purpose of the development of the industry, but the conditions appear to me very vague. The weaver and loom are there (the former having been instructed by an instructor sent by the Board from their depot at Ardara), but no one comes to learn unless Mrs. Eccles will pay them for it. This, it seems to me, is not a proper condition of things.

With a view to attempting the development of the industry, I would suggest the following scheme:–

1. That the instructor at Moneygold be paid the usual price per yard for the stuff he turns out, and that the Irish Industries Association take the webs as they are made (always providing the quality is good).

2. That the instructor be paid the sum of £1 for every pupil he turns out capable of weaving a web of thirty yards by himself, to pass one of the Board's Tweed inspectors.

3. That looms be supplied to those pupils who desire them on easy terms.

4. That until a local fair be established, the Irish Industries Association would take those webs of good quality for sale or to sell.

5. That prizes similar to those at Ardara be given for the weaving.

6. That an instructor be sent to instruct the women in dying wool and mixing the colours, a man similar to the Board's instructor in Glencolumbkille, who would move from house to house.

7. That prizes be given for spinning, apart from the weaving, the spinners to bring in their yarn on the day fixed for the examination of the webs, the prize to be at the rate of 1*d.* per pound of wool, the mixing of the colours to be taken into consideration also.

8. That the spinners receive also a prize for the web similar to that in Glencolumbkille district. The chief difficulty in the development of the industry will be the revival of the spinning, therefore I have suggested a separate prize for this branch of the industry. Prizes might also be given for the best 20 lbs. of raw wool raised in the district. The cost of this scheme to the Board would be comparatively small, and after a trial of two years, if the people took no interest in it, the scheme might be abandoned.

The improvement of the various stock has been referred to in reply to Query 7.

Improvement in agricultural methods is much needed; drainage is badly attended to; their land insufficiently laboured; their crops not properly attended to.

Bee-keeping should, I think, in this district, be attended with satisfactory results, as there would be a good market for honey in Sligo and Bundoran.

Osier-growing and basket-making might form an industry, as the soil seems suitable, but the difficulty is getting a market for the baskets, as the local market would be too limited.

There is one scheme of migration I would like to see effected for the benefit of the district, and that is the Inishmurray islanders. The island is a flat, barren, unsheltered rock of very limited extent, and under the present conditions the people on it must always live in wretchedness. If they could be migrated to spots on the mainland, such as that land referred to in reply to Query 5, it would be of immense benefit to themselves. There would, I think, be a great difficulty in inducing them to leave the island, and then there is always the danger of the migrated families saying "You have brought us here and must look after us." The matter is one I consider worthy of consideration.

The lack of ambition in the character of the Irish peasant is the greatest drawback to his improving his condition, and combined with this there is a feeling of false shame and fear of being laughed at by their less enlightened and unambitious neighbours, which keeps those who would gladly rise tied to the same position. The peasantry are keenly sensitive to ridicule, and it is this fear of being laughed at or thought to be trying to better his condition, and so raise himself above his neighbours, that keeps many a young man, who would otherwise rise, down in the old grooves. This feeling is one ingrained through long years, and one which cannot be all at once eradicated. However as time goes on and education progresses, no doubt the people will come eventually to see, each for themselves, what is clearly for their own interests and will act accordingly, without having regard to the gradually decreasing mocking of those who would live themselves on the lowest level and would keep others there if they could.

F. G. TOWNSEND GAHAN,
Inspector.

12th December, 1895.

To

The Congested Districts Board for Ireland.

CONGESTED DISTRICTS BOARD FOR IRELAND

COUNTY OF LEITRIM – UNION OF CARRICK-ON-SHANNON

REPORT OF HENRY DORAN, *Inspector*

DISTRICT

OF

KILTUBBRID

STATISTICAL TABLE

ELECTORAL DIVISION.	Area in Statute Acres.	Poor Law Valuation.	Number of Ratings at and under £10 and above £4 Valuation.	Number of Ratings at and under £4 Valuation.	Population in 1891.	Number of Families in 1891.	Number of Families on Holdings exceeding £2 and under £4 Valuation.	Number of Families on Holdings at and under £2 Valuation.	Number of Families in very poor circumstances.	Number of Families which have no Cattle.
		£								
Aughacashel,	2,522	483	20	90	387	69	36	18	12	
Barnameenagh,	5,889	1,117	70	171	759	143	55	24	16	
Drumreilly East,	4,627	436	38	116	476	85	35	7	5	
Drumreilly West,	5,987	907	56	258	719	143	44	50	20	60
Gortnagullion,	4,498	1,781	118	215	1,184	223	67	20	12	
Kiltubbrid,	3,022	952	62	180	721	142	65	23	20	
Moher,	4,175	1,440	121	222	965	197	63	23	15	
Yugan,	3,870	1,368	107	360	1,120	226	113	43	20	
TOTALS,	34,590	8,484	592	1,612	6,331	1,228	478	208	120	60

(1.) Whether inland or maritime.

The district is inland.

(2.) Average quantity of land cultivated on holdings at and under £4 valuation, under (*a*) oats, (*b*) potatoes, (*c*) meadow, (*d*) green crops.

There are about four statute acres, on an average, of permanent meadow land on holdings of about £4 valuation, and about 2¼ statute acres under cultivation, as follows:–

	A.	R.	P.
Oats,	0	3	0
Potatoes,	1	1	0
Green crops, including Cabbage,	0	0	30
Meadow grown from cultivated grass seeds,		Nil.	
	2	0	30

(3.) Extent of mountain or moor grazing, and rights possessed by tenants, whether in common or otherwise.

About 8,000 acres, or nearly one-fourth of the entire area of this district, is a mountainous tract, extending northwards from the outskirts of the town of Drumshambo, and comprising the greater part of the Leitrim mountains on the east side of Lough Allen, which attain an altitude of 1,700 feet over sea-level.

In most cases the tenants of every Townland which includes part of these mountains, have *rights* of grazing over the mountain in their respective Townlands. But there are no mearings; and, as a matter of fact, the mountains are all grazed upon in common during the summer half-year, by cattle and a small number of sheep, belonging to persons who occupy holdings comprising any part of the mountain.

(4.) Extent and description of land, if any, which could be profitably reclaimed and added to existing adjoining holdings.

About 1,000 acres of this mountain are capable of reclamation, but none of the tenants can exercise more than grazing rights over it.

The greater part of the land in the occupation of the landholders lies on the side slopes of the mountains at a lower elevation than the grazing, and most of it is only in a semi-reclaimed state. Its improvement and thorough reclamation would be much more reproductive than the reclamation of the grazing lands, and ought to be accomplished before attempting the reclamation of the latter.

(5.) Particulars as to any suitable land in district which could be obtained, and to which families could be migrated with a reasonable prospect of success.

There is no land which can be obtained at present to which families could be migrated from this district.

(6.) Method of cultivation, manures, rotation of crops, etc., etc.

The land is chiefly cultivated by manual labour. No rotation of crops is followed. The only crops grown are potatoes, oats, rye, and a plot of cabbage. Very few people grow even a small plot of turnips. Potatoes are grown in "lazy beds," made narrow to keep the seed bed dry. Artificial manure is not used. The only manure used is that made on the farm, which, in the case of small landholders having little or no stock, is largely composed of rushes, heath, and coarse grass placed in cesspools to rot and afterwards mixed with the manure of the live stock. The same plot of ground is frequently kept in cultivation for several years. No grass seeds are sown. The permanent meadow is old grassland in low-lying ground, or so situated on the side slopes of hilly ground that it can be irrigated by the surface water of the higher lands. As a rule, the hay is coarse, and of inferior quality.

(7.) General information with regard to stock, and suggestions as to improvement of breeds – (*a*) cattle, (*b*) sheep, (*c*) horses and donkeys, (*d*) pigs, (*e*) poultry, etc., etc.

The cattle are capable of much improvement, but they are much superior to those in most of the congested districts. The comparatively good quality of the cattle in this and the adjacent congested districts of Leitrim is, I think, accounted for by the fact that it is, and has been, the custom amongst a large proportion of the landholders to send their young stock to good grazing farms in the neighbourhood of Boyle and Carrick-on-Shannon for the summer half-year.

The bulls generally in use are those brought from the County Roscommon, and usually purchased at Boyle and Croghan Fairs. The common type of Roscommon bulls is too large to produce suitable stock for mountain districts, but if the smallest and most compactly formed animals of this breed obtainable were selected for such places they would beget useful stock.

I consider Polled Angus bulls would be suitable for the improvement of the cattle of this district.

In the selection of bulls for this mountainous district or, indeed, for all the congested districts, it should be borne in mind that highly pampered or overfed animals are quite unsuitable. Such sires invariably beget weakly offspring, which are difficult to rear up to yearlings. Bulls of any breed suitable for congested districts should be long, low, thick-set animals of robust constitutions. Those fed up for Show purposes or directly descended from parents that have been much confined in houses and very carefully hand fed, as the animals of most pedigree herds are, are quite unsuited for congested districts. There are very few sheep in the district, and I do not think it necessary to offer any suggestions for their improvement. The number of horses in the district is small. The small landholders do not keep horses, but all have donkeys, which would be much improved in size and strength by crossing with the smallest class of Spanish stallion asses. The pigs would be much improved, in a short time, by crossing with large Yorkshire boars, The poultry of the district can be easily improved by the distribution, of stock fowl or eggs, of hardy breeds.

(8.) Markets and fairs for cattle and produce of district; also statement as to where the people obtain food and other supplies, and the prevailing custom

At Ballinamore, Drumshambo, and Dowra markets and fairs, the live stock and produce of the district are mainly disposed of, and in these towns the people obtain the bulk of their food and other supplies.

with regard to the disposal of butter, eggs, and poultry; to what extent are they sold in the first instance to local shopkeepers and dealers, and, generally speaking, how old are the eggs when sold to the first buyer, and about how old when they reach their ultimate destination in Great Britain.

Ballinamore is the principal butter market. The greater part of the butter is sold in "cools" or "tubs"containing 75 lbs. of heavily salted butter. A good deal of butter is sold at the weekly markets in "lumps" of no particular shape or weight, and slightly salted. The average quality is bad and the prices, as a rule, are low and unremunerative, especially of late years.

Eggs are sold to local dealers in parts of the district most remote from the towns, but the greater part of them are sold to dealers or exporters in the towns on market days.

Generally speaking the eggs are about one week old when they reach the first buyer, and from a fortnight to three weeks old when they reach their destination in Great Britain.

There are good fowl markets in this district, especially in Ballinamore, where chickens commonly sell from 1*s.* to 2*s.* 6*d.* each.

(9.) Rail, steamer, sailing boat, road, postal and telegraph facilities.

The Cavan and Leitrim Light Railway, which connects the Northern Railway lines with the Midland Great Western at Dromod, passes Ballinamore, and branches from there to Drumshambo and Arigna, and affords ample facilities for the transport of the exports and imports of the district.

Steamers can come from Limerick *via* Carrick-on-Shannon to Drumshambo and Lough Allen, but this water-way is rarely used of late years. There is also a Canal from the Shannon near Leitrim town *via* Ballinamore to Lough Erne, but it is not navigable now.

The postal and telegraph facilities are sufficient for the requirements of the district. There are telegraph offices in each of the market towns.

(10.) Employment for labourers in the district, whether temporary or constant, and rate of wage.

There is employment for a limited number of labourers for a short time in spring and harvest in the adjacent non-congested districts. The usual rate of wages is one shilling per day with diet. Most of those who have very small holdings in the Electoral divisions of Drumreilly East, Drumreilly West, and Yugan, migrate to England and Scotland for three or four months of the year, or send one or two male members of their families there.

A large proportion of the young people (male and female) reared in this district emigrate to America before they reach twenty-five years of age.

(11.) Migratory labour, average earnings per head, and where earned.

The majority of those who migrate to England and Scotland leave home between April and June, and return in November. Their average earnings there, vary a good deal, ranging from 15*s.* to 25*s.* per week. They save, and send, or bring home, from £8 to £10 per man on an average.

(12.) Weaving, spinning, knitting, and sewing, whether used locally or sold, and where.

A very small number of the people who have sheep on the mountain make flannels, socks, stockings, and a small quantity of frieze for their own use, but not for sale.

Nearly all the socks and stockings worn are made at home, chiefly from purchased yarn.

(13.) Kelp-burning, and sale of seaweed.

The district is inland.

(14.) Sale of turf, nature and extent of bogs.

There is no turf sold except a small quantity in the market towns of the district. The quantity disposed of is so trifling that the sale of turf cannot be regarded as a source of income available for those in need.

Turf for fuel is abundant in the district and, as a rule, easily obtained.

(15.) Lobster fishing, number of men and boats employed.

The district is inland.

(16.) Sea fishing. Facilities for sale of fish, and number of boats and men solely employed in fishing.

The district is inland.

(17.) Number of boats and men employed in carrying turf or seaweed or in fishing. Classification of boats.

The district is inland.

(18.) Fish; whether consumed at home or sold.

The district is inland.

(19.) Extent of fish-curing.

The district is inland.

(20.) Piers and Harbours, existing and suggested, and how far those existing are adapted to wants of district.

The district is inland.

(21.) Extent of salmon and freshwater fisheries. Number of men earning their livelihood therefrom.

The district is inland.

(22.) Banks and Loan Funds.

There is an office of the Northern Bank in Ballinamore, and a sub-office of the same Bank, open on market days, in Drumshambo.

There is a Loan Fund office, open weekly on market days at Drumshambo. No borrower can get a larger loan than £10. The issue of £5 loans is common. The borrower has to provide two approved sureties, and for a loan of £5 he receives £4 16*s.* 6*d.*, the sum of 3*s.* 6*d.* being stopped for interest, and he has to repay the loan by monthly instalments of £1 each.

(23.) Mineral and other resources.

There is some coal, and also iron ore, in the mountainous portion of the district. The coal is reputed to be of very inferior quality. Attempts were made from time to time to raise the coal, but in every instance the work was abandoned after a short and unprofitable trial.

(24.) Relative prevalence of cash or credit dealings, length of credit, interest charged, extent of barter, etc., etc.

Credit is not given now to anything like the same extent as it was up to six or eight years ago; but owing to a large extent to the reckless trading of former years, the majority of the people are in debt to shop-keepers and banks. It is customary to have a running account, partly made up of the balance of an old debt, with provision merchants, who expect to receive substantial payments at least twice a year. Interest varying from eight to twenty per cent. is charged on overdue accounts. Some traders sell goods at a much lower price if cash be paid than when sold on credit. It is a common practice to sell Indian meal at a small profit for cash, but when sold on credit 3*d.* per sack is added to the first cost for every month the price remains unpaid. The present cost-price is 15*s.* per sack, and if not paid for twelve months the charge will have increased to 18*s.* Local dealers give flour, groceries, and other household requisites in exchange for eggs, and a few dealers also take butter.

(25.) Estimated *cash* receipts and expenditure of a family in ordinary circumstances.

The receipts and expenditure of a family of six persons, living on a holding of about £4 Poor Law Valuation, would be as follows:–

Receipts	£	*s.*	*d.*	Expenditure	£	*s.*	*d.*
Sale of cattle (2 animals on an average),	8	0	0	Indian meal (family), pigs, poultry,	5	0	0
Sale of pigs (3 animals on an average),	9	0	0	Flour for family,	5	0	0
Sale of butter,	4	0	0	Cost of grinding oats into meal,	0	10	0
Sale of eggs,	3	10	0	Tea and sugar,	2	10	0
Sale of chickens and geese,	0	15	0	American bacon,	1	10	0
Savings from earnings in England or Scotland, and money received from members of family who emigrated.	8	0	0	Tobacco,	1	8	0
				Grazing money for 2 yearlings,	2	10	0
				Cost of 3 young pigs,	2	2	0
				Candles, soap, &c.,	1	10	0
				Salt fish and sundries,	0	10	0
				Clothes: man, wife, 4 children,	7	0	0
				Rent and County Cess,	4	5	0
	£34	15	0		£33	15	0

(26.) Estimated value of home-grown food consumed, and period during which it lasts.

The estimated value of home-grown food consumed on a holding of about £4 valuation, and the period during which it lasts, is as follows:–

	£	s.	d.
Potatoes (August to May) when crop is average,	10	0	0
Eggs and Milk,	4	0	0
Butter,	1	0	0
Cabbage,	0	10	0
Oats ground into meal,	1	10	0
Total,	£17	0	0

The supply of turf when saved on holdings is worth £3.

(27.) Dietary of people, number of meals daily, and kinds of food throughout the year.

The dietary of the people – number of meals daily – and kinds of food throughout the years consists of –

From 1st April to 1st August.

Breakfast.– Stirabout and buttermilk. The majority use Indian meal; some use oatmeal, and others use stirabout made of oatmeal and Indian meal mixed.

Dinner.– Flour bread and tea and eggs occasionally.

Supper.– Same as for breakfast.

From 1st August to 1st April.

Breakfast.– Potatoes and milk (when potato crop is average), and frequently a little bread and some tea after.

Dinner.– Bread (flour, or flour and Indian meal mixed) with tea. Occasionally potatoes, with cabbage seasoned with the grease of a small quantity of fat American bacon. Salt herrings are sometimes used with potatoes for dinner.

Supper.– Same as for breakfast.

The above represents the dietary of the people in average circumstances. Those who have no milch cow or have no milk to use with their potatoes or stirabout, substitute for milk very thin oatmeal porridge for use with potatoes, and sugar for use with stirabout.

(28.) Clothing, whether home-made or bought, etc., etc.

Excepting the small number of persons who keep sheep and make flannel and friezes for their own use there is no other clothing made in the district but socks and stockings, which the people knit chiefly from purchased yarn. A large number of the poorer people get their outer clothing from pedlars who take van loads of second-hand clothing to the weekly markets and dispose of them there by a form of auction peculiar to the trade.

(29.) Dwellings: kind of houses, home-life and customs, etc., etc.

The dwellings as a rule are substantially built with stone walls (about seven feet high to eave) and mortar, and contain a kitchen and two rooms. The roofs are thatched, oats or rye straw being used for the outer covering by all who can provide it. Those who have not straw, use rushes or long heath. The great majority of the people have out-offices for their live stock, and very few keep cattle in their dwellings. There are few dairies, and the milk and butter are usually kept in one of the sleeping rooms.

(30.) Character of the people for industry, etc., etc.

The people work hard for three-fourths of the year, but they are practically idle from November to February. Even those who could employ their leisure time to great advantage in the drainage and improvement of their lands make no effort to do so during the winter months. This is to be deplored, but I fear there is little prospect of changing their habits in this respect unless they become purchasers of their holdings, in which event I have every hope that the people will, after a few years, bestow their best attention on the improvement of their lands.

(31.) Whether any organized effort has been made to develop the resources or improve the condition of the people. If so, by what means.

No organized effort has been made to develop the resources or improve the condition of the people.

(32.) Suggestions as to any possible method for improving the condition of the people in future.

There is some coal under the summit of that part of the Leitrim mountains included in this district, but any of it that has been raised was found to be of very inferior quality and not worth the cost of procuring. As far as I can form an opinion the district cannot be regarded as possessing any mineral resources capable of profitable development.

The people derive their principal means of subsistence from the land, supplemented in a large number of cases, by earnings obtained from migratory labour and money received from members of families who have emigrated to America.

The agricultural resources of the district are capable of immense development, and any methods adopted for permanently improving the condition of the people should be directed towards increasing the productiveness of the land and improving the live stock reared upon it.

The lands in the occupation of the people lie chiefly on the southern and western slopes of the Leitrim mountains east of Lough Allen. There is scarcely a vestige of planting or strong hedge rows to afford shelter to crops, houses, or beasts on those bleak hill sides.

The land is very wet, and could be greatly improved by drainage – covered stone drains to a limited extent – but, chiefly, by cutting up the holdings into small fields by judiciously laid out ditch and bank fences, run slightly downwards across the slope of ground, with the ditch or gripe on upper side to carry away the surface water, and the bank planted with thorn-quicks. These thorn-quicks would, with some slight care and attention, afford valuable shelter after about ten years to the growing crops, and to the live stock. Small plantations should be made in belts across the holdings, in waste corners, and around the houses.

After the land has been drained it would be greatly benefited by an application of lime, and facilities to procure it could be provided by Congested Districts Board, as explained hereafter.

A large number of householders, especially in the Electoral Divisions of Drumreilly East and Drumreilly West, are in extreme need of accommodation roads or passes, as a means of access from existing roads to their houses. Many of the houses are distant a quarter of a mile, and some half a mile, from the nearest point of public road, or laneway, and the occupants have no means of getting their provisions or saleable produce to or from the roads except on their backs across fields and fences, or over the same course on donkeys, when they have to knock down and build up every "gap" in fences made for the passage of the donkeys. The absence of suitable accommodation roads makes the daily life of the people, who are circumstanced as I described, dreadfully irksome, and renders it almost impossible for them to make any successful effort at the improvement of their land. There are ten families living in part of one townland near the summit of the mountain in Drumreilly East, who are so completely cut off from means of access to any road or pass that the district they live in is locally known as "Spike" from a fancied resemblance to the convict station of Spike Island, suggested by its inaccessibility.

I append to this Report a list of the roads, passes, and foot-bridges, which I consider are urgently required, and also an estimate of the cost.

Some of the roads would be useful public roads, and would probably be made by the County if the Congested Districts Board offered to contribute towards the cost, the sums I suggest.

The accommodation passes and foot-bridges referred to, would not be made at the expense of the County, and there is no hope that the landlords would even contribute towards their construction. They are, to my mind, precisely the class of works in the way of providing road accommodation which the Congested Districts Board ought to undertake. I do not think the Board should contribute the whole cost of construction of these private roads or passes. If they gave a grant of about one-half of the estimated cost of the unskilled work involved, two or three of the parties interested could present themselves as joint contractors for the execution of the work in accordance with a specification, it being privately arranged amongst all those concerned in a pass that they were to contribute equal labour towards its construction, and the nominal contractors could distribute the money equally amongst them when the work was performed.

The foot-bridges referred to are in connection with the accommodation passes. The whole cost of materials and providing skilled labour should be defrayed by the Board. These bridges should be made six feet wide, and strong enough to bear traffic with donkeys and cleaves, and riding-horses as well as foot passengers.

The cattle of this district are in need of improvement, but they are much better than the cattle of most of the congested districts. They can be readily improved by the introduction of suitable bulls, and by exercising care in the selection of breeding animals.

The hens of the district could be greatly improved by crossing with the Black Spanish, Plymouth Rock, or other breeds of medium size, and possessing hardy constitutions.

Ducks, geese, and turkeys could also be improved by crossing with larger breeds.

During the last few years, since oats became very cheap and the potato crop more precarious than formerly, the people are beginning to use oatmeal largely for food. This ought to be encouraged. There is a mill at Ballinamore, and another in Cloverhill Electoral Division and there is one much required in the Ballinagleera parish, for the Electoral Divisions of Drumreilly East, Drumreilly West, and Yugan, to replace a very defective mill which is now at work there. The owner of existing mill is a poor man, but could (the Parish Priest informed me) provide solvent sureties, for a loan not exceeding £100, to erect a mill with suitable machinery in a central part of the parish, to be used chiefly for the grinding of oats for home consumption. The water-power to present mill is not good and it may be considered advisable to remove to another place, in the event of the Board determining to grant a loan for this purpose, if application be made to them.

I may summarise the suggestions above offered for the permanent improvement of this district as follows:–

1. Promote the improvement of live stock by the introduction of suitable bulls, boars, donkeys, and poultry.

2. To assist the people to provide shelter for their crops, live stock, and buildings, by providing them with suitable trees at a low price; and, to exercise skilled supervision over the planting of them, to ensure their growth.

3. To induce the people to drain their lands, chiefly by cutting up their holdings into small fields, by forming ditch-and-bank fences across them, and planting the banks with thorn-quicks supplied by the Board at a small price.

4. To induce the people to drain, with covered stone drains, such portions of their holdings as can be most profitably improved by that means, by establishing a system of prizes or grants, which would cover one-fourth or one-half of the actual cost of the work done by the successful competitors, under the conditions of a scheme framed to meet the circumstances of the district.

5. To assist the people in providing accommodation passes and main roads, to facilitate the carriage of provisions and saleable produce, and to enable them to develop the latent capabilities of the lands they hold.

6. To assist the people to provide lime for application to the land drained by them, and for the making of compost matter as a topdressing of the permanent meadow land so general in the district, and which is the most valuable class of meadow land.

7. To promote improved systems of husbandry and the growth of a greater variety of crops. To convince the landholders of the advantage of frequent change of seed potatoes and seed oats by enabling them to obtain small quantities of new seed every year at prices current in the district for ordinary seed.

8. To promote improved systems of dairy management amongst the landholders in the district, but, especially, amongst those who have not more than three cows, which cannot produce sufficient butter to enable the owners to pack a 75 lb. "tub" or "cool" with butter of uniform quality, in consequence of the necessity of numerous churnings extending over months. This can best be done by organizing fresh butter markets in the towns of the district, and by providing an Instructor, who would visit the houses of the people and educate the housewives in the manipulation of butter and the conditions of cleanliness, etc., etc., so essential for the production of good butter. Facilities should be afforded for the purchase of churns best adapted for the churning of small quantities of cream.

9. By establishing a system of agricultural organization throughout the district which would educate and stimulate the people to produce butter, fowl, and eggs of as high a

standard of excellence as their resources permit; and to place this produce on the best markets obtainable, which, probably, could be readily effected through the agency of the Honorable Horace Plunkett's Agricultural Organization Society.

With reference to the above suggestions, I may remark that it is a comparatively easy matter to narrate the defective systems of agriculture prevailing in a district. But, it is extremely difficult to present a scheme for the correction of what is admittedly wrong which will appear practicable to persons who have no personal local knowledge of the district.

At the commencement of the operations of the Board the question of the improvement of live stock, including poultry, appeared to be considered a very simple matter, but the experience of the results of the Board's operations is decidedly conclusive in demonstrating that bulls obtained from pedigree herds, where they and their ancestors for many generations have been treated with all the care and attention that science could suggest or money procure, are not the class to beget offspring, possessing hardy constitutions and useful and thrifty characteristics when crossed with animals which must subsist on the worst of land. In dealing with the improvement of poultry the operations of the Board have operated in the same natural manner, and prove beyond doubt that fowl procured from persons who keep them for show purposes and bestow the greatest care on their feeding and treatment are much too delicate for congested districts.

In my former reports I have expressed the opinion that bulls, fowl, or other live stock suitable for the improvement of the live stock of any congested district, should be produced from stock possessing hardy constitutions and reared *in a natural manner* without any exceptional care or extra hand feeding. Pedigree stock or prize strains of poultry cannot be obtained in any number except from persons who *force* them by feeding, etc., in preparation for a fancy market and high prices. I am, therefore, of opinion, that the Congested Districts Board cannot obtain suitable sire animals nor poultry for the improvement of existing breeds unless they procure a few farms within the congested districts where such live stock can be reared with a view to the development of their most useful characteristics. The Board would have little difficulty in procuring such farms on lease or by purchase. Each farm should be placed in charge of an experienced agriculturist. Carefully selected herds of cattle and pigs would be kept, and fowl also; and the bulls, boars, sows, and fowl required for the congested districts could be obtained from these farms at much less expense than the market price of ordinary pedigree animals.

Where any of these farms was situate in a district where a stallion horse or ass was required these animals could be kept there at little expense.

A portion of each farm should be set apart for a nursery for forest trees and thorn-quicks, which, being thus procured at first cost, could be sold to residents of congested districts at a low price and at a minimum loss.

On the cultivated portion of each farm different varieties of potatoes, oats, and other crops most likely to be suitable for the district should be grown, and this part of the land could be made to serve the purpose of an experimental station for the surrounding district. By this means information of great value as to the relative merits of different potatoes would be gained. That such information would be of inestimable value is strongly brought home to the minds of farmers and others living in poor districts this year, after there has been a partial failure of the potato crop, and when there is not a Government Department in a position to give advice of any greater value than that of the most ignorant farmer as to the most suitable varieties of seed potatoes. It is the general opinion amongst farmers that the Champion potato is rapidly degenerating, and, as scarcely any other variety of potato has been extensively grown within the congested districts for many years, there is no satisfactory information forthcoming from any source to justify the people in substituting any other variety for it.

Considering that the frequent failure of the potato crop in this country, and especially in the congested districts, has always been associated with the cry of famine and an appeal for "relief works," and has often been the primary cause of violent social disorder, it is strange that no Government has adopted any means of providing reliable information upon the best methods of mitigating the disastrous effects of the disease.

There is a farm in this district which is suitable in every respect for the purposes above indicated. It is situate in Aughacashel Electoral Division. The house known as Aughacashel House is commodious and in good repair, and there are very extensive out-offices attached, which are also in good repair. The area of the land attached to the house is about 287 statute acres, and is owned in fee-simple (with the exception of 17a. 2r. and 8p. held under a statutory lease), by Mr. James Maguire, J.P., merchant, of Enniskillen, who is in very delicate health, and is anxious to dispose of the place.

The present owner acquired the place about fifteen years ago. It had been previously occupied by gentlemen farmers. The house and offices must have cost quite as much as the whole place is now worth. A large outlay has also been made in fencing the land and reclaiming bog.

A considerable part of the land is of fairly good quality, and is sound pasture over limestone rock. It is exceptionally well adapted for the rearing place of sire animals intended for the adjacent or other congested districts. The large garden which is enclosed by a high wall would form a suitable nursery for seedlings, which could be transplanted to more exposed ground preparatory to being planted out. Any extent of land required could be devoted to the growth of thorn-quicks, and for the growth of potatoes, oats, or other crops.

There is an inexhaustible supply of limestone on the land, and culm for the burning of it into lime is procurable in a mountain on another property about a mile distant. Lime for the district can be produced on the farm at a small cost.

I would recommend the Congested Districts Board to purchase this farm if they can do so at a reasonable price. Mr. Maguire's interest in the lands is, in my opinion, worth £2,500. He wrote to me that he expected £5,000. The gross Poor Law Valuation is £113 5*s.* 0*d.* If it is managed as I have pointed out it can be made a most powerful agency in the agricultural development of the County Leitrim congested districts, supplying them with suitable sire stock and poultry, forest trees, thorn-quicks, and lime. A small quantity of seed potatoes and seed oats could be distributed at ordinary market prices every year.

Considerable employment would be afforded in connection with the farming, stock raising, growth of forest trees and thorn-quicks, and the burning of lime. The agriculturist could do much useful work in laying out fences and drains, instructing the people in improved methods of cultivation, and in the general agricultural organization of the district.

HENRY DORAN,
Inspector.

31st January, 1895.

To

The Congested Districts Board for Ireland.

APPENDIX TO REPORT ON KILTUBBRID DISTRICT.

Parish in which proposed Work is.	Nature of Work.	Particulars of Work Suggested.	Estimated Total Cost.	Amount which Inspector suggests the Congested Districts Board might contribute.
			£ s. d.	£ s. d.
Ballinagleera	Public Road	To make a public road – 420 perches in length, 16 feet wide – in continuation of public road through Tullynahaia, through townlands of Aughrim and Slievenakilla, to join public road in latter townland, including bridges.	600 0 0	300 0 0
Do.,	do.,	To make a public road – 560 perches in length, 16 feet wide, between fences – from public road near Frazer's Bridge in Cortober, through the townlands of Cortober, Urbolber, Dereenageer, Farna, Muck'agh North, and Tullynapurtlin, joining public road to Dowra from Drumshambo at junction of old and new roads in Tullynapurtlin.	500 0 0	250 0 0
Drumshambo and Kiltubbrid,	do.,	To make a public road – 16 feet wide – from public road at Mrs. Booth's in Derryhallagh, through the townlands of Derryhallagh, Corloughlin, Aughagrania, Aghaginny, Aghakilbrack, and Moher, to join public road near Early's house in Gortnawaun, a distance of 840 perches, and bridges included.	1,000 0 0	400 0 0
Kiltubbrid,	do.,	To make a continuation of mountain road through Gortnawaun and Mullagharve, for a distance of 260 perches, to meet public road through Mullagharve.	200 0 0	100 0 0
Ballinagleera,	Accommodation road.	To make an accommodation road – paved and gravelled over, 12 feet in width – for a length of 144 statute perches from public road at Stony River Bridge to village of Sradrinagh.	57 0 0	30 0 0
Do.,	do.,	To make an accommodation road in continuation of above from village of Sradrinagh to the mountain, 9 feet wide, properly formed, paved and gravelled over, for a distance of 92 statute perches.	25 0 0	12 0 0
Do.,	do.,	To erect a timber bridge across river where marked on Ordnance Map, 41 feet in width, with centre pier built in solid masonry, to enable residents of part of Slievenakillagh to get to public road near shooting lodge, and including the making of accommodation road from bridge to road, a distance of 24 perches.	30 0 0	30 0 0
Do.,	do.,	To make an accommodation road, 352 perches in length, from Aughrim Pass to "Spike," part of the townland of Tullynahaia, and including a bridge over river.	100 0 0	60 0 0
Do.,	do.,	To improve Aughrim Pass, 288 perches in length, from its junction with public road near school-house on road to chapel, to junction with proposed new road at Tullynahaia, near Early's house, and including the erection of a timber bridge, 7 feet wide, over the Yellow River, having centre pier of solid masonry, and being sufficiently strong for traffic with donkeys and horses carrying loaded creels.	50 0 0	50 0 0
Drumshambo,	Public road,	To widen and re-make to a width of 16 feet 300 perches of the old road from the new bridge at Michael McGlynn's in townland of Greaghnagullion, and including branch road connecting new and old roads, and also the lowering of steep hills, filling of hollows, and erection of bridges and gullets.	250 0 0	120 0 0
Do.,	Timber bridge, 6 feet wide.	To erect a rough timber bridge, strong enough to carry traffic with donkeys and horses, with creels of turf, &c., over river at Drumcroman near O'Brien's house, to accommodate 12 families, including six who would use it only in connection with their turf supply. The bridge would have one span of 20 feet and another of 12 feet, and have a centre pier built of solid masonry. The side abutments and training walls might be built in dry work, carefully laid without mortar.	25 0 0	10 0 0
Kiltubbrid,	Public road,	To make a public road – 480 perches in length, 16 feet wide – from the public road at Thomas Gallagher's land at Cornaleck, through the townlands of Cornaleck, Currahagha, Edenavow, Drumany, and Aghaginry, to join main road leading from Drumshambo to Aughacashel.	300 0 0	150 0 0
Kiltubbrid and Drumshambo.	Accommodation road.	To make an accommodation road, 12 feet wide, in clear of fences, from railway crossing in townland of Roscunish, through the townlands of Roscunish and Drumcroman, to connect with bog road in Drumany, a distance of 288 perches.	144 0 0	60 0 0

CONGESTED DISTRICTS BOARD FOR IRELAND

COUNTY OF LEITRIM – UNION OF MANORHAMILTON

REPORT OF MAJOR GASKELL, *Inspector*

DISTRICT

OF

KILTYCLOGHER

STATISTICAL TABLE

ELECTORAL DIVISION.	Area in Statute Acres.	Poor Law Valuation.	Number of Ratings at and under £10 and above £4 Valuation.	Number of Ratings at and under £4 Valuation.	Population in 1891.	Number of Families in 1891.	Number of Families on Holdings exceeding £2 and under £4 Valuation.	Number of Families on Holdings at and under £2 Valuation.	Number of Families in very poor circumstances.	Number of Families which have no Cattle.
		£								
Glenanniff,	8,232	916	76	163	813	162	44	15	17	8
Kiltyclogher,	7,790	2,064	156	283	1,595	308	77	60	60	51
Glenfarne,	4,082	1,075	55	112	727	128	47	41	20	13
Cloonclare,	4,907	950	75	177	946	182	61	24	20	20
Killarga,	8,134	1,162	77	186	836	159	53	18	20	16
Mahanagh,	(*a*) 7,642	2,415	210	329	1,937	403	131	57	60	34
St. Patrick's,	(*b*) 4,312	1,129	76	164	870	154	45	32	40	38
Arigna,	4,411	440	32	121	459	82	29	13	20	20
Garvagh,	4,423	1,164	95	156	1,153	226	73	45	50	50
TOTALS,	53,933	11,315	852	1,691	9,336	1,804	*560	*305	307	250

(*a*) Excluding 226 acres of water. (*b*) Excluding 2,882 acres of water.
* See Appendix A – Table showing the aggregate assessments of individual ratepayers.

(1.) Whether inland or maritime.

The district is inland and mountainous, situate in the Parishes of Ross-Inver, Killasnet, Cloonclare, Killarga, Inishmagrath, and Killanummery. The formation is the millstone grit, except in a small portion of Kiltyclogher Electoral Division, where it is limestone. The rivers and streams, which are numerous, cut deep and very broken channels down the steep hillsides and through the alluvial bottoms, and much valuable soil is lost by floods and the slipping of banks.

(2.) Average quantity of land cultivated on holdings at and under £4 valuation, under (*a*) oats, (*b*) potatoes, (*c*) meadow, (*d*) green crops.

The average quantity of land cultivated on holdings at and under £4 valuation is as follows:–

Potatoes from 1/2 to 1 statute acre.
Oats from 1/2 to 3/4 statute acre, but this crop is rare.
Green crops – Turnips, 1/4 acre; cabbage, 1/4 acre.
Meadow from 1 1/2 acres to 3 acres.

The farms vary from 5 acres upwards, exclusive of "mountain"; 25 acres is considered a large farm.

(3.) Extent of mountain or moor grazing, and rights possessed by tenants, whether in common or otherwise.

Of a total of about 10,500 acres of "mountain," 2,500 acres are retained by the respective landlords; the remainder is assessed to tenants in proportion to their holdings, and grazed in common.

(4.) Extent and description of land, if any, which could be profitably reclaimed and added to existing adjoining holdings.

Much of the land has been reclaimed within living memory, and with good results. Speaking generally, there appears to be abundant room for profitable reclamation or re-reclamation, within the boundaries of existing holdings. In a few instances a good beginning has been made.

(5.) Particulars as to any suitable land in district which could be obtained, and to which families could be migrated with a reasonable prospect of success.

There is no land for sale in the district which would be suitable for the migration of families.

(6.) Method of cultivation, manures, rotation of crops, etc., etc.

The soil on the slopes of the hills is usually clay of a very retentive character, with a sub-soil consisting either of flag-rock, or of a close hard clay gravel, most difficult to drain. On the tops of the hills, bog, very broken and wet; in the valleys also bog, but of a better consistence, and more or less mixed with alluvial matter. Rushes abound. The tillage area is extremely small; and in very many instances there is practically no rotation of crops. Owing to the steepness, or wetness and softness, of the surface, the whole of the cultivation is done by hand, the implement used being the "loy," as better suited than the spade to deal with the clay sub-soil. Potatoes follow potatoes on the same ground year after year. Oats are quite an exceptional crop; a few turnips and cabbages only are sown and planted. The manure consists of refuse hay trodden under foot in the byres, and owing to the general absence of carts and by-roads it must be carried on to the land in baskets on donkeys' or men's backs. Artificial manures are also used, but not to a large extent. The custom of burning the surface soil used to prevail; and the surface growth is often burnt now in preparing ground for turnips, the ashes supplying the manure.

In a portion of the Glenanniff Electoral Division the people irrigate their meadow land in summer.

(7.) General information with regard to stock, and suggestions as to improvement of breeds – (*a*) cattle, (*b*) sheep, (*c*) horses and donkeys, (*d*) pigs, (*e*) poultry, etc., etc.

Cattle.– These are on the whole a very fair class both as to quality and condition, the majority being milch cows and calves under one year. Among the best are some remarkably good dairy cows, half-bred Shorthorn, or Shorthorn and "Irish." On the other hand, many poor specimens are found on the worst and most exposed holdings. Among these "cripple" often occurs; and "red water" is frequent throughout the district. Owners of cattle which most require improvement are least able to afford, and least inclined, to pay more than they are obliged, or to send long distances, for the service of a bull.

Inter-communication in this district is difficult, hills and rivers intervening awkwardly between Electoral Divisions and parts of divisions, and by-roads being scarce. So long as inferior bulls are within easy reach at a low price, they will be patronized, particularly by those who intend to sell their heifers in-calf. Well-bred bulls are found here and there throughout the best parts of the country round Manorhamilton, but are hardly accessible to the tenants of distant hill townlands, to whom the difference between the value of a good and a bad calf is of the utmost importance. This is a pastoral and dairy country, and it is or used to be the calves that pay the rent; any system which has for its object the ousting of bad bulls from the villages should have special regard to the situation, as well as to the suitability in other respects, of the farms on which the improving animals are placed; and the fee for service should be kept as low as possible. Calves are seldom allowed to suck; for ten days or a fortnight they get about a gallon of new milk a day, after that buttermilk only. Experienced opinions favour the view that imported "premium" bulls often deteriorate from the moment of their arrival in a poor district; and that their progeny are less robust and ultimately less valuable than that of good locally bred bulls. At Croghan, near Carrick-on-Shannon, there is an annual fair in October, where such bulls are largely bought and sold at farmers' prices.

The Polled Angus have been tried in this district to a limited extent only. They are liked by those who can feed their stock well; and the cross between the Polled Angus bull and the Shorthorn cow is found to mature quickly. But if the breed is growing, it has not as yet made much progress, in public favour, particularly among the smaller tenants whose preference for roan, here called "grey," Shorthorns is very decided, and with reason, as they are most readily saleable. The Polled Angus bull supplied by the Board to John Keaney of Clooncalre

E.D., fetched £10 10*s.* only when sold, as fat, at the expiration of his owner's agreement; whereas the Shorthorn supplied by the Board to D. McLaughlin of Glenfarne E.D., realised £18. The best and finest Shorthorn bull I have seen is that supplied by the Board to Mr. George Nixon, and by him kept in first-class condition. Mr. Nixon thinks he will be worth £30 when four years old.

Horses.– These are rarely kept by the small tenants, owing probably to the nature of the country, the wetness of the surface, and the scarcity of by-roads, also to the smallness of the holdings and the necessity of converting as much as possible of the produce of the land into butter. It is, nevertheless, a good horse and pony breeding country; and the horse fairs at Enniskillen, Sligo, and Carrignagat, near Collooney, are important, though less so than formerly, owing to the best young stock being now bought up privately. Notwithstanding the number of "registered", and other thoroughbred stallions, within a radius of twenty miles from Manorhamilton, breeders complain of the want of a really good horse, suitable for getting first-class hunters. There are two Arab stallions near Sligo and one near Enniskillen. Mr. George Nixon, above referred to, keeps two stallions – a horse and a pony; both of which are of known pedigree, have established a good reputation, and are much in request. They are not thoroughbred but have many good qualities.

A good many handsome jennets, in and about the district, were got by an excellent though somewhat plain pony bred in the County Galway and owned by William Eames, Killarga.

Donkeys.– These are numerous, and much used for carrying manure, turf, and produce. Some are of good size, but the majority are small, and improvement of the race is desirable, without, however, substituting mules for asses.

Sheep.– These are kept in a few townlands only, and on the driest of the hills. The country generally is too wet for them; and they are very subject to "fluke" on the clay soils. Some are Scotch Blackfaces, but most are half-bred Roscommon.

Goats.– These are seen everywhere; almost every family has at least one. The milk is much fancied with tea, and the kids are half-starved in order that the family may have it. Thus the cows' milk is spared and reserved for butter.

Pigs.– These are moderately good; some black, of Berkshire type, some white, some black and white. None of these approach in merit the pure Yorkshire, which are occasionally seen; but the people have a prejudice against the latter, because of the hair with which the young are covered.

Poultry.– In the outlying districts, poultry are not more than half as good or as numerous as they might be, although the people are fully alive to the value of the eggs, and depend much upon them to pay for their tea and sugar. Sufficient pains are not taken to provide clean laying places, and, in consequence, eggs come to market disfigured by dirt. Near the towns efforts to introduce improved breeds are apparent, and everywhere sittings of imported eggs are much appreciated.

(8.) Markets and fairs for cattle and produce of district; also statement as to where the people obtain food and other supplies, and the prevailing custom with regard to the disposal of butter, eggs, and poultry; to what extent are they sold in the first instance to local shopkeepers and dealers, and, generally speaking, how old are the eggs when sold to the first buyer, and about how old when they reach their ultimate destination in Great Britain.

Manorhamilton is the principal fair and market town, being centrally situated and close to a railway station. Weekly markets are held at Kiltyclogher, Black Lion, Drumkeeran, and Dromahair, and Sligo market is within reach by rail, with cheap market tickets. Fairs take place at all these towns, at Lurganboy near Manorhamilton, at Kinlough, Garrison, Dowra, Ballyfarnan, and Ballintogher. Boyle and Enniskillen fairs are also attended from this district. Enniskillen is the best horse fair. Eggs and butter are the chief market produce, both being brought by the farmers or their representatives to the market towns, except at Dromahair, where a baker, and a mill-owner, who employ several vans and carts on regular road circuits, collect a portion of the eggs which are exported weekly. Both eggs and butter are uniformly and well packed for export by the principal buyers – the eggs in crates specially made in Sligo of narrow board; the butter in cases, butts, and firkins made in the country. The egg crates will contain either six or twelve "hundreds" of eggs, weighing, when packed, one or two hundredweight respectively. The cases of butter are made to hold 56 pounds; the butts, from 40 to 60 pounds; and the firkins about 90 pounds. A ton of eggs will be twenty of the smaller or ten of the larger crates, containing 14,400 eggs. The weekly export of eggs from Manorhamilton averages seven tons; from Glenfarne and Belcoo stations, together, about the same; and from Dromahair, three tons. From the four places, therefore, seventeen tons of eggs, or 244,800 a week, or about thirteen millions a year. The price of eggs ranges from 5*d.* to 10*d.* a dozen, and if the average be taken as low as 6*d.*, the thirteen millions would represent about £27,000 a year. The butter sent out of this district is almost all put on the railway at Manorhamilton, and goes eastward, only a small proportion finding its way to Sligo. The majority of the small farmers require the money at once, and cannot afford to wait to fill butts or firkins; consequently much of the butter sold in Manorhamilton and Drumkeeran is in lumps or rolls, which, as soon as bought by the exporter, are wrapped in muslin and packed in 56-pound cases. Such butter realises to the producer 6½*d.* a pound all round, although it may be of several grades of quality. When the markets are glutted, and by some dealers at all seasons of the year, lump butter is mixed, salted, and repacked in butts. Butter in butts fetches at least 1*d.* a pound more than lump butter, as it keeps longer, is of more uniform, if not altogether better quality, and sells better ultimately – its average value is 8*d.* a pound. Firkin butter is worth more in Sligo market than even butt butter in Manorhamilton by about 1*d.* a pound. Every firkin is there tested by an Inspector appointed by the Town Council, and marked "first," "second," or "third." 300 firkins of about 90 pounds each passed through the market on the 2nd June, and the price was 9*d.* for "firsts," or 84*s.* a hundredweight; the quotation on the same date being a fraction lower for Cork, and for Dublin about 1*d.* a pound higher. Butts and firkins cost from 2*s.* to 3*s.* each, and are not returnable. The number of firkins of butter passing through Sligo market in summer is from 1,000 to 1,500 per week. All goes to Glasgow.

The above details are given because butter-making is the principal industry of this district. It is admitted by buyers on all hands that the rough mixed mountain pastures produce sweeter butter than rich land; but, coming from several classes of dwellings and through varieties of treatment, the butter varies much in sample when offered for sale in the market. The price paid is therefore low. Organization of the industry is much required. A creamery has been tried, but, so far, unsuccessfully. (See Appendix B.)

The amount of butter sent away from Manorhamilton averages 2½ tons weekly, or about 130 tons in the year. The value of a ton at 7*d.* per pound, which is the average price, is £65. A ton of eggs at the middle price of 7¼*d.* a dozen has the same value.

(9.) Rail, steamer, sailing boat, road, postal and telegraph facilities.

The Sligo, Leitrim, and Northern Counties Railway passes across Cloonclare and Glenfarne Electoral Divisions, and touches one extremity of Kiltyclogher Electoral Division, with stations at Glenfarne and Manorhamilton. Lisgorman and Dromahair stations are also used by the people of the southern half of the district. The old coach roads are good; and a road leading about nine miles along the hillsides through the Garvagh, Arigna, and St. Patrick's Electoral Divisions, is a model work as to levels. It is said to have been laid out by Mr. Nimmo. The poorest and most thickly populated portions of the district are the least fortunate in their means of communication. Two mails daily pass along the Sligo, Leitrim, and Northern Counties Railway from and to Dublin and the North. Glenfarne, Manorhamilton, and Dromahair get the benefit of these mails. Drumkeeran has one mail daily by car from Carrick-on-Shannon; and distributes letters in Killarga, Mahanagh, and St. Patrick's Electoral Divisions, through branch offices in Tawnylea and Dowra, by foot messengers only. There are branch offices also at Belhavel for Killarga village, and at Tarmon; the former receiving letters from Dromahair by foot messenger, and the latter by car from Carrick-on-Shannon. There is no distribution in Arigna Electoral Division. Kiltyclogher gets letters once a day by foot messenger from Glenfarne station; Glenanniff once daily from Manorhamilton. Garvagh Electoral Division is but partially served by foot messenger from Dromahair. There are telegraph stations at Manorhamilton, Dromahair, Drumkeeran, and Kiltyclogher.

(10.) Employment for labourers in the district, whether temporary or constant, and rate of wage.

A small amount of employment is given to labourers by resident proprietors, but the chief reliance of the former is on their neighbours, who may be only slightly better off than themselves, and who hire help by the day or year. The wages are 1*s.* a day and support, or about £8 a year with board and lodgings.

(11.) Migratory labour, average earnings per head, and where earned.

Including migrants or emigrants, 200 special tickets were issued last year – from 1st April 1893 to 31st March 1894 – from Manorhamilton for Londonderry and Sligo. Of these, about 150 would be men going to Scotland or England for harvest work. The earnings may average about £7 a head. Besides the migration to Scotland and England, there is a considerable movement of labourers to the counties around Dublin at mowing and harvest time.

(12.) Weaving, spinning, knitting, and sewing, whether used locally or sold, and where.

Weaving is dying out, except in a part of the district adjoining Glenanniff Electoral Division; spinning and knitting are confined to the making of stockings for the family. There is no sewing industry.

(13.) Kelp-burning, and sale of seaweed.

The district is inland.

(14.) Sale of turf, nature and extent of bogs.

The sale of turf is confined to a few donkey loads and cart loads occasionally brought into the towns and is altogether inconsiderable.

(15.) Lobster fishing, number of men and boats employed.

The district is inland.

(16.) Sea fishing. Facilities for sale of fish, and number of boats and men solely employed in fishing.

The district is inland.

(17.) Number of boats and men employed in carrying turf or seaweed or in fishing. Classification of boats.

The district is inland.

(18.) Fish; whether consumed at home or sold.

The district is inland.

(19.) Extent of fish-curing.

The district is inland.

(20.) Piers and Harbours, existing and suggested, and how far those existing are adapted to wants of district.

Spencer Harbour on the N.W. shore of Lough Allen, where the remains of a wharf and pier exist, and called after Earl Spencer, who, in 1882, inaugurated the Brick, Tile, and Sanitary Pipe Factory, for which the wharf and pier were constructed, is a sheltered bay. It is well suited for a terminus of water communication between this district and Drumshambo, and thence southwards by Lough Allen and Canals.

(21.) Extent of salmon and freshwater fisheries. Number of men earning their livelihood therefrom.

Salmon are seldom if ever taken within the boundaries of this district. Small trout are numerous in the rivers; but there are no men earning a livelihood by the freshwater fisheries.

(22.) Banks and Loan Funds.

The Ulster Bank, Limited, has a branch at Manorhamilton and from it attendance is given once a fortnight at Drumkeeran.

(23.) Mineral and other resources.

There are coal mines, employing six or seven hewers, in St. Patrick's Electoral Division. The seam is only about twenty inches thick and the miners work under difficulties (it is said lying on one side, and often on boards to keep themselves as dry as possible), and earn from 12*s.* to 15*s.* a week only. The coal is of a useful quality, making a good and long-lasting fire when mixed with Scotch coal or turf. The culm or small coal when mixed by the people with clay, makes good fuel for the cabins. "Irish coal" is contracted for by the Manorhamilton Board of Guardians at 18*s.* 6*d.* a ton, and used half and half with Scotch coal. The mines referred to, Layden's and Lyons' Pits, are about four miles from Drumkeeran, southwards. Cartage is costly. From the pits to Dromahair would be thirteen miles; to Manorhamilton sixteen miles, and to Dowra twelve miles.

In Killarga Electoral Division, at Creevalea, in 1852, iron mines were opened, and a great deal of money was spent by the purchaser of the two adjoining townlands in erecting buildings and plant. The engine house, boilers, two blast furnaces, hot blast stoves, roasting kilns, and coking stove, still remain in charge of a Scotch caretaker, and are kept by him in good order. There are also several houses for manager and workmen, and good stabling for horses. The iron was smelted with coal, carted six or seven miles from Layden's Pits; and pig-iron of excellent quality was produced with the best of the coal; but the coal was much broken in transit over rough roads, and the refuse choked the fires. There is hope of the works being re-opened for the manufacture of charcoal iron, with peat charcoal produced on the spot. All the manufactured iron had formerly to be carted twenty miles to Sligo.

Besides coal, ironstone, and fireclay, flagstone for paving and building, cement shale, and black shale containing a small quantity of combustible oil, are found at Creevalea; and coal has been discovered one mile to the north.

At Monesk Mountain which bounds Clooncläre Electoral Division on the south, two lines of borings, to a depth of about 100 feet, three borings in each line at intervals of from a quarter to half a mile, were made about fifteen years ago by a Mr. Manning with the object of discovering coal. There is no authentic record in the district of the results; but one of the men employed in the work, Peter Cullen of Cloonaghmore, Clooncale E.D., survives. One line was taken about due south from the townland of Cloonaghmore; the other about half a mile eastward, and ending at Tents Lake.

Also at Monesk Mountain, on the property of the Earl of Morley, flagstone quarries are open, valuable fireclay in large quantities is close to the surface, and a coal mine was opened last year, a tramway being laid for half a mile or more, as a beginning of communication with the Sligo, Leitrim, and Northern Counties Railway near Glenfarne. The tramway would have passed through Glenfarne Electoral Division; but it appears that the lessee of the minerals, after an expenditure of about £1,500, decided that he had not sufficient capital to carry out the enterprise. The work was stopped in November 1893, and all the plant sold off. Since then, in April last, Mr. Hilton, a Mining Engineer, has visited the mine, and made a survey of the mountain. Flagstone occurs frequently throughout the district; many of the streams and rivers flow over flagstone beds, forming continuous cascades between steep and richly clothed banks.

There are limekilns in Killarga village not far from the boundary of Killarga Electoral Division. Barytes is found in the hill of which Glenanniff Electoral Division forms part. Mr. Conscadden, of Glenboy, talks of opening a mine for this mineral in or near Glenanniff, and endeavouring to carry on the manufacture in Manorhamilton by water-power.

Peat is found in large tracts throughout the district.

(24.) Relative prevalence of cash or credit dealings, length of credit, interest charged, extent of barter, etc., etc.

Credit is universal, though shopkeepers exercise as much caution as competition allows. Accounts appear to run on from year to year, and never to be settled. Tradesmen say they have great difficulty in getting money, and commercial travellers seem despondent. But the bank manager does not complain. No doubt interest is charged by some on long overdue accounts; but there is no reason to think that it is oppressive. If exaction is practised it is on the prices first charged or booked. Buyers on credit, particularly in the drapery shops, are not careful to ascertain the price of what they desire, but cannot pay for at the moment. To a small extent eggs and butter are exchanged for groceries; but they are generally sold for cash to an exporter. It is to be feared that the small, but not inconsiderable sums so obtained are spent as soon as received.

The building of roads and walls were works frequently funded by the Congested Districts Board. Road-building was an essential element in opening up communications between the outside world and many backward areas.

(25.) Estimated *cash* receipts and expenditure of a family in ordinary circumstances.

The estimated *cash* receipts and expenditure of a family in ordinary circumstances are as follows:–

INCOME	£	s.	d.	EXPENDITURE	£	s.	d.
POULTRY:–				12 bags of flour, at 8*s.* 6*d.*,	5	2	0
16 hundreds of eggs sold,	5	0	0	12 cwts. Indian meal, at 5*s.* 3*d.*,	3	3	0
20 hens or chickens,	0	15	0	2 cwts. bran, at 7*s.* 4*d.*,	0	11	8
5 geese, at 2*s.* 6*d.*,	0	12	6	6 oz. of tea per week, say 20 lbs. at 2*s.* 6*d.*,	2	10	0
PIGS:–				4 lbs. sugar per week, at 2½*d.*,	2	3	1
4 cwts. bacon, at 45*s.*,	9	0	0	Salt fish, bacon, or other relish, at 1*s.* 6*d.* per week,	3	18	0
CATTLE:–				Tobacco, 2 oz. a week, at 2*d.*,	1	6	0
3 calves, sold at £2 7*s.* 6*d.*,	7	2	6	Oil, 5*s.*; lime, soda, baking powder, &c.,	0	10	0
BUTTER:–				Clothing,	6	0	0
210 lbs. of roll butter, at 6½*d.*,	5	13	9	Rent, rates, and taxes,	5	15	0
				Church fees,	0	19	0
Harvest or American money,	7	0	0	Artifical manure, 2 cwts. at 8*s.* 6*d.*,	0	17	0
				Turnip seed, 1*s.* 6*d.*; cabbage plants, 1*s.* 6*d.*,	0	3	0
				2 bonhams, bought in May or June,	2	0	0
				Service of bull for 3 cows,	0	4	6
				Refreshment at markets and fairs,	2	0	0
	£35	3	9		£36	16	6
				Extra items:– Railway Market Tickets, £2.			

(26.) Estimated value of home-grown food consumed, and period during which it lasts.

The estimated value of the home-grown food consumed is as follows:–

	£	s.	d.
5 tons of potatoes, at £2,	10	0	0
4 tons of rough hay, at 15*s.*,	3	0	0
Turnips, £2; 600 cabbage, £2	4	0	0
	£17	0	0

The potatoes usually last till about the first of April.

In addition to the above food, milk, butter, eggs, and buttermilk are consumed by the people.

(27.) Dietary of people, number of meals daily, and kinds of food throughout the year.

The number of meals is nominally three. Potatoes are the staple of one, if not of two. Flour and meal in the forms of home-made bread, and stirabout, are the other staples. Tea with sugar and goats' milk, butter and buttermilk are additions. Bacon is less used than herrings, as a relish. There is no doubt that Indian meal stirabout forms a large item in the dietary of this district.

(28.) Clothing, whether home-made or bought, etc., etc.

Clothing is almost entirely derived from the shops, and new fashions seem to be rapidly circulated from Belfast. It is said that industrious fathers of families have sometimes to complain of the extravagance of their wives and daughters who are led by the temptations of the shops to run up bills, of which the man knows nothing at the time; but which he must ultimately meet as best he can, to the prejudice of his farm. I have not found any tradesman to admit the charge implied by this statement; but the County Courts could furnish evidence of its truth.

(29.) Dwellings: kind of houses, home-life and customs, etc., etc.

The large majority of the dwellings are comfortable, and sufficiently supplied with rough furniture, most of them thatched, with good doors and windows, others well-built and slated. The "cabins" have all level flagstone floors. Poultry and other members of the farm stock occasionally pass in or out of the open doors, but are not domiciled with the family. The manure heap is generally too near at hand, but whitewash is freely used inside and outside the houses, and often the doors and window frames are painted; and creepers are planted round the walls. Trees are also planted round the house in not a few instances.

The custom which prevails in some of the villages of the men carrying heavy baskets of manure, knapsack fashion, up the steep hillsides, gives them a flatness of back and general physical development which are remarkable. Turf is carried long distances, to and from the bog in the same way, by the men.

(30.) Character of the people for industry, etc., etc.

The people are said to be industrious, and it may be said that the men would work if they had the inducement of wages, or the stimulus of seeing returns for their labour. Hard work is done on the hillsides in spring, and in the mowing season. But the condition of the meadows thickly overgrown with rushes, of watercourses not cleared out, of banks unrepaired, of yards and drainage about houses unattended to, above all the extremely small amount of tillage, produce the impression that work is here reduced almost to a minimum. This may be due to natural causes. The soil where it is not bog, is exceedingly retentive and wet; the climate owing to the high hills and nearness to the sea is stormy; and the seasons are late. Up to the middle of May this year, to step off a road or bank was to sink almost to the ankles in moss, clay, or bog; neither the bog nor the clay will grow oats well, and "as the oats fell in price tillage died out." It does perhaps pay better to leave as much as possible of the small holdings in pasture; and drainage may be difficult: but in the few places where a shopkeeper, for instance, has expended capital and labour on his land, its appearance is in marked contrast to that which has been less well treated.

(31.) Whether any organized effort has been made to develop the resources or improve the condition of the people. If so, by what means.

Some forty-five years ago there was on the borders of the Killarga Electoral Division a linen factory employing seventy or eighty hand looms. It has long ceased to exist.

In 1852 many thousands of pounds were spent in starting Iron Works at Creevalea in Killarga Electoral Division. The work was discontinued after a few years owing to the difficulties of transport; partly also from want of coal of good quality. (See also Appendix C.) Coal pits opened at the same time in St. Patrick's Electoral Division still continue to supply and distribute a useful fuel.

In 1882, extensive Brick and Tile Clay Works were established at Strandhill, or Spencer Harbour, also in St. Patrick's Electoral Division, and these were continued for twelve years on a costly scale with small steamers and barges on Lough Allen. It is said that they failed through bad and extravagant management. Coal mining in Monesk Mountain, bordering Clooncl are Electoral Division, gave promise of success last year, but was suddenly stopped for want of capital.

With reference to Layden's and Lyons' Coalpits, to the Clay Works at Spencer Harbour, and to the Creevalea Iron Works, it should be stated that about two years after the Sligo, Leitrim, and Northern Counties Railway was opened, a scheme was also proposed to connect Drumshambo with Dromahair by a line sixteen miles long, which would touch Spencer Harbour, Drumkeeran, and Creevalea. Such a line would present no engineering difficulties and would pass through a very populous country.

In 1887, a small Creamery was started by a small Company at Manorhamilton. No profit was looked for: on the contrary higher prices were at first paid to the farmers than the Company realised in the market. The Company lost all its capital in five months, and was wound up for want of sufficient support. (See also Appendix B.)

(32.) Suggestions as to any possible method for improving the condition of the people in future.

Industries.

As directly affecting the welfare of this district the re-establishment of the Clay Works at Spencer Harbour, the re-opening of the Iron Works at Creevalea, and the renewal of coal-mining and fireclay manufacture in Monesk Mountain, deserve the consideration of the Board.

There is also a water-mill at Manorhamilton in working order, close to the Manorhamilton Railway Station, which would be available in case the Board should require it for industrial or other purposes.

Agriculture.

This being a pastoral country and butter the chief product, the improvement of the pasture, the cattle, and the butter-making are the chief points which force themselves on the attention. Whether or not the growth of corn can be agriculturally and economically desirable, drainage would appear to be urgently required on almost every farm throughout the district. It would be difficult in many localities. Perhaps the necessary labour is not available. The small tenants find it hard to meet the new mode of living on the shops. If they could revert to the former custom of growing, grinding, and eating their own oatmeal, with their milk, butter, and eggs, they would be better off. But the water-mills throughout the country which used to grind the oats brought down to them on the back of asses, stand roofless and disused. If they could be restored, it is hoped in some quarters that the people would grow oats, and keep the mills employed. On the other hand it is more often said that the drinking of tea has weakened the stomachs of the present generation so that they cannot digest oatmeal porridge. American flour is cheaper than oatmeal, and no move appears to be likely in the direction of repairing the water-mills.

The people are most anxious to increase their supply of eggs. The establishment of a poultry farm or farms in the district would be welcomed. But instruction in poultry management would also be necessary.

The supply of good seed, suitable to the various soils, is also urgently required. The Board of Guardians have established a small home farm round the Union Workhouse, and the Master of the Workhouse is an enthusiastic agriculturist. The crops at present on the farm are very promising. No doubt the Board would be willing to assist in carrying out agricultural improvements in the Union. It will be found in many cases that the able-bodied son of a family is obliged to hire out his labour, which, with his board, would represent at least £1 a month. If about that sum could be earned by reclamation at home, reclamation would be gladly undertaken.

Planting would be an advantage to the country, which is much exposed to storms. In the townland of Drumafaughnan, on the borders of St. Patrick's Electoral Division, there is a farm of about 100 acres, which has been bought by the tenant under the Land Purchase Acts, and is paying a rent charge of £14. "It consists of whinny bad land, and would make an

New dwellings were built with the assistance of the Congested Districts Board.

excellent larch plantation. The soil was partly burnt some years ago. There is reason to believe that the tenant's interest could be bought cheap at the end of the grazing season of this year." The words between inverted commas are quoted from Mr. George Hewson, of Dromahair, who is the agent of the adjoining property.

Miscellaneous.

In the Glenanniff Electoral Division a road leads through the division from Ballynameehan to Kinlough along one side of the glen. Across the river on the other side of the glen, another road, constructed in 1886, at a cost of £800, runs through the holdings nearly three miles to a quarter of a mile of the first road, which it was intended to join. The making of the quarter mile to complete the connection would save a number of families the long detour which they must now make to get their cattle to Kinlough.

In the Mahanagh Electoral Division, the school in Greaghnaglogh Townland, which serves six townlands, is one and a half miles distant from the nearest road. If an 8-foot road could be made from the north side of Geaglom Bridge in the townland of that name, towards Greaghnaglogh School, but carried round the hill, so as to meet the Dowra Road at Kellegher's Mill, Alteen Acres, Glebe Townland, it would be an immense boon to many families.

Arterial drainage is required on the northern boundary of this district.

W. P. GASKELL,
Inspector.

11th June, 1894.

To

The Congested Districts Board for Ireland.

APPENDICES TO KILTYCLOGHER REPORT

APPENDIX A

TABLE showing the Aggregate Assessments of Individual Ratepayers.

ELECTORAL DIVISIONS.	£2 and under			£4 and over £2			£10 and over £4			£20 and over £10			Over £20			Total Assessments	REMARKS
	No.	Amount	Average	No.	Amount	Average	No.	Amount	Average	No.	Amount	Average	No.	Amount	Average		
		£ s. d.	£ s. d.		£ s. d.	£ s. d.		£ s. d.	£ s. d.		£ s. d.	£ s. d.		£ s. d.	£ s. d.		
Glenanniff,	15	28 8 0	1 11 2	45	138 10 0	3 1 6	74	480 4 0	6 9 9	16	231 5 0	14 9 0	1	64 15 0	—	151	One ratepayer on a valuation of £3 5s. in this E.D. pays also on £5 5s. on another, unscheduled; one of £6 pays on £15 elsewhere, unscheduled.
Kiltyclogher,	60	74 13 0	1 4 10	77	48 14 0	3 4 7	143	930 19 0	6 10 2	46	760 18 0	16 10 10	1	60 15 0	—	327	
Glenfarne,	41	49 5 0	1 4 0	48	153 15 0	3 4 0	48	304 5 0	6 6 9	15	199 13 0	13 6 2	{ 1 5	112 15 0 228 10 0	— 45 14 0	} 158	
Clooncläre	24	24 15 0	1 0 7	61	194 16 6	3 3 10	72	466 12 0	6 9 7	19	265 2 6	13 18 0	2	53 0 0	26 10 0	178	
Killarga,	18	21 2 0	1 3 5	53	172 12 0	3 5 0	75	489 15 0	6 10 7	22	282 9 0	12 16 9	4	163 10 0	40 17 6	172	
Mahanagh,	57	62 17 0	1 2 0	131	423 19 0	3 4 9	192	1,250 19 0	6 10 4	36	445 7 0	12 7 5	{ 1 5	133 0 0 135 5 0	— 27 1 0	} 422	
St. Patrick's,	32	40 0 0	1 5 0	45	135 10 0	3 0 0	75	491 0 0	6 11 0	15	203 4 0	13 10 11	{ 2 5	133 5 0 129 15 0	66 18 0 25 19 0	} 174	
Arigna,	13	21 12 0	1 13 3	29	82 3 0	2 16 8	31	202 16 0	6 10 10	8	106 19 0	13 7 4	1	25 5 0	—	82	
Garvagh,	45	52 14 0	1 3 5	73	225 7 0	3 1 9	83	516 17 0	6 4 6	18	272 10 0	15 2 9	{ 1 3	43 0 0 72 11 0	— 24 3 8	} 223	
Total,	305	370 6 0	1 4 3	502	1,775 6 6	3 3 2	793	5,133 7 0	6 9 0	195	2,767 7 6	14 3 10	32	1,355 6 0	42 6 2	1,887	

APPENDIX B

THE MANORHAMILTON DAIRY.

This Dairy was carried on by a registered Company, whose paid up capital amounted to £126. A convenient cottage, close to a river which runs through Manorhamilton, was lent and specially fitted for the purpose.

Dairy work commenced on 3rd October, and continued till 5th December, 1887; began again on the 2nd May, 1888, and continued till the 16th August of that year; when the Dairy was finally closed, and a decision was taken to wind up the Company.

Expenses had been kept as low as possible from the outset, but the loss on the five and a half months' trading was £46, owing chiefly to the fact that, in order to encourage the farmers, from 1*d.* to 1½*d.* per lb. in excess of the market price had been paid to them for their butter. Cream only was accepted by the Company; each lot being separately churned, and credit given to the sender for the amount of butter produced. The average weekly quantity of butter made by the Company was 2 cwts. Churning was done entirely by hand labour. The dairymaid employed to make up the butter belonged to the neighbourhood, and had been trained at the Glasnevin Model Farm. The prices obtained for the butter ranged from 9*d.* to 1*s.* a lb. The Dairy was closed owing to the failure of the supply of cream; the townspeople would have continued to bring in theirs, but farmers living in the country complained of the trouble and loss of time involved in the journeys to and fro, as well as of the poor feeding quality of skim milk as compared with buttermilk. The highest number of cream contributors was 26.

The whole of the paid up capital was lost, and is thus accounted for – repairs to premises, £25; apparatus, cost £48 but realized £25 when sold, £23; wages, £32; loss on the five and a half months' trading, £46; total, £126. The apparatus consisted of two Holstein churns, and two butter workers, with the necessary utensils.

APPENDIX C

CREEVALEA IRON WORKS.

In 1880-1 a report was made, "after careful examination of the ground and of the Mines themselves," by Mr. Edward T. Hardman, M.E.F.C.S., of Her Majesty's Geological Survey, to the owner of the land and works, Nathaniel Bridges, Esq., 23 Red Lion square, London. The report is detailed, technical, and specific; giving sections of the ground, and estimates of the cost of working the minerals; a copy of it fills 15 closely written pages of foolscap.

The Mines are situate in the townlands of Tullynamoyle and Gowlaun (in the Electoral Division of Killarga). The minerals are Clay Ironstone, in numerous bands and nodules, sometimes very rich; Fireclay; Argillaceous Limestone, which might be useful for cement stones; and extensive beds of Flagstones, which would afford excellent building material should facility of carriage be provided at any future time. The Ironstone exists in three principal zones, first, middle, and third. The middle zone is the most important; it has been opened up in one place, where the ore is very abundant, and of very excellent quality. The main level was driven 1,000 feet to the East, with cross-cuts; a considerable quantity of ore was extracted, and there are now at the very least from 1,000 to 1,500 tons of ore massed on the hill above the mine. There is no doubt that the main seam extends quite across the property; and it has in fact been seen in a ravine more than three miles from the mine. The Third Ironstone contains numerous bands of very good quality; and the same ore has been found 600 yards from the works; a level was driven, and a good deal of ore extracted. From the entire workings there have been accumulated several thousand tons of good iron ore, which, if there were cheap means of transport, would be worth a considerable sum of money. Fireclay, and Cement Shales, are found close to the Ironworks, in beds eighteen inches and two feet thick. Coal has not been discovered, and there is not the slightest likelihood of its being discovered, on the property; but one mile to the North of the northern boundary of Gowlaun coal has been found, and worked to some extent. It is what is known as the First Coal, or lowest level of the Lough Allen district; and is of poor quality. It doubtless extends into Lackagh townland, but is worthless for smelting purposes. It is possible, however, that the middle seam may occur in the northern portion of Lackagh; and, if so, that it would be worth working.

The latter half of the report contains specific suggestions and estimates for the manufacture of the iron with peat charcoal prepared on the spot. The upper portion of the estate is covered with peat of excellent quality. The greater portion is very thick, from 8 to 12 feet; and it is for the most part a good heavy black turf, with but little fibre. An attempt was formerly made to utilize this great turbary for smelting the ore at the Ironworks, but the expensive nature of the process of preparation prevented any profitable result. Two methods are suggested, either of which might probably be worked economically, viz.: hot air drying of the turf, and the making of peat charcoal. The heating value of charcoal made in the way suggested would be much higher than that of coal, and the cost of the fuel would be less than 2*s.* 6*d.* per ton. A trial of the peat charcoal process is strongly recommended in the event of the works being re-opened; and a net profit per week is shown of £28 17*s.* on an output of 50 tons of manufactured iron delivered in Glasgow; two and a half tons of ore being allowed for one ton of iron, and cartage being relied upon as the only means of carriage from the works to the nearest station, Dromahair. But if the prospects of the undertaking should improve, a small tramway is recommended; and in this connection it is stated that a very superior style of tramway had then recently been laid down at Sligo, for the purposes of a water contract, at a cost of £350 per mile. The cost of a similar line from Creevalea to the railway, with the necessary plant and wagons, would be under £3,000.

The report concludes with a paragraph in high praise of the caretaker at the Works, Charles McGlashan.

CONGESTED DISTRICTS BOARD FOR IRELAND

COUNTY OF MAYO – UNION OF WESTPORT

REPORT OF MAJOR ROBERT RUTTLEDGE-FAIR, *Inspector*

DISTRICT
OF
ACHILL

STATISTICAL TABLE

ELECTORAL DIVISION.	Area in Statute Acres.	Poor Law Valuation.	Number of Ratings at and under £10 and above £4 Valuation.	Number of Ratings at and under £4 Valuation.	Population in 1891.	Number of Families in 1891.	Number of Families on Holdings exceeding £2 and under £4 Valuation.	Number of Families on Holdings at and under £2 Valuation.	Number of Families in very poor circumstances.	Number of Families which have no Cattle.
		£								
Achill,	8,861	432	5	273	1,417	276	26	209	73	about 100 (all four divisions)
Corraun Achill,	18,288	557	21	289	1,602	290	37	219	75	
Dooega,	10,249	713	11	449	1,698	310	23	294	110	
Slievemore,	17,143	849	18	510	1,810	373	33	282	88	
TOTALS,	54,541	£2,551	55	1,521	6,527	1,249	119	1,004	346	about 100

(1.) Whether inland or maritime.

The district is maritime.

(2.) Average quantity of land cultivated on holdings at and under £4 valuation, under (*a*) oats, (*b*) potatoes, (*c*) meadow, (*d*) green crops.

There are about four acres on an average cultivated on a holding at and under £4 valuation in the following way:–

Under potatoes	2 acres.	
„ oats or rye	2 „	generally the latter.
Total,	4 acres.	

There may be said to be practically no meadow or other green crops grown.

(3.) Extent of mountain or moor grazing, and rights possessed by tenants, whether in common or otherwise.

In the Achill and Dooega Electoral Divisions tenants on the Pike Estate are granted grazing by the Trustees on 9,000 acres of mountain lands at the following annual charges:– Cattle, 3*s.*, horses, 6*s.*, and sheep, 1*s.* each. In Corraun Achill Electoral Division the Trustees of the late S. Dickens give grazing on some 5,000 acres to their tenants for cattle at 5*s.* per "sum," horses, 5*s.* each, and sheep, 5*s.* per eight. The Trustees of the Achill Mission who own land in all four Electoral Divisions charge their tenants the following amounts for grazing over 10,000 acres of mountain and moor, – cattle, 2*s.* 6*d.*, horses, 3*s.*, and sheep, 6*d.* each. On the three above-mentioned Estates the grazing rights are vested in the owners by the adoption of this custom, and the charges which I have quoted could at any time be increased. There are four other landlords in the district who own smaller tracts of mountain, on which their tenants enjoy the right of free grazing as part of their holdings.

(4.) Extent and description of land, if any, which could be profitably reclaimed and added to existing adjoining holdings.

There is sufficient mountain and moor-land round most of the villages which could be profitably reclaimed and added to existing adjoining holdings. The owners are always willing to allow their tenants to cultivate such land, and no rent is charged for several years. Where seaweed can be obtained bog-land is being gradually reclaimed.

(5.) Particulars as to any suitable land in district which could be obtained, and to which families could be migrated with a reasonable prospect of success.

I cannot hear of any suitable land in this district being for sale to which families could be migrated with a reasonable prospect of success.

(6.) Method of cultivation, manures, rotation of crops, etc., etc.

Spade cultivation is carried on in this district.

The Manures in use are dung or seaweed spread on ridges over which seed potatoes are laid about a foot apart. After this sowing, seaweed (or sods impregnated with smoke and soot, generally taken from the roofs of the houses and cut into small pieces with spades) is used as a sort of top-dressing, the potatoes being afterwards moulded. In fine weather the land is also burned. In some of the villages there is a scarcity of seaweed, especially on the south side of the Achill Island. Shell-fish scraped from the rocks are also used as manure.

The rotation of crops is as follows:– Rye or oats – where the latter will grow – then potatoes, and potatoes follow rye, until the soil is worn out. The land is then allowed to lie idle for a few years when the same rotation of crops is again commenced. Grass seeds are rarely sown.

(7.) General information with regard to stock, and suggestions as to improvement of breeds – (*a*) cattle, (*b*) sheep, (*c*) horses and donkeys, (*d*) pigs, (*e*) poultry, etc., etc.

Cattle and sheep are of the most inferior description that can be imagined; ponies are rough but hardy and capable of great endurance; pigs are very bad and not much bred by the people – I am told those bred on the Achill Island nearly always die. Pigs are generally brought from Newport and sold at Achill Sound Fair; these thrive fairly well.

Poultry are small, especially ducks and geese; the hens are splendid layers, the people deriving more profit from the sale of eggs than from any other industry, except migratory labour; many tenants told me that they would rather lose their cattle than part with their hens.

Kyloe and Galloway bulls and black-faced rams might be tried, but "soft" breeds of all kinds of stock should be carefully avoided, as the land is altogether too poor to rear a really good class of animal.

A few cockerels of a hardy breed might also be sent to this district, Andalusians for choice, as I hear they throve well formerly. West Mayo seems to have been altogether omitted from the recent distribution of cockerels.

(8.) Markets and fairs for cattle and produce of district; also statement as to where the people obtain food and other supplies, and the prevailing custom with regard to the disposal of butter, eggs, and poultry; to what extent are they sold in the first instance to local shopkeepers and dealers, and, generally speaking, how old are the eggs when sold to the first buyer, and about how old when they reach their ultimate destination in Great Britain.

Monthly fairs are held at Achill Sound and Mulrany; some people also go to Westport and Newport fairs. Food and other supplies are obtained from local dealers, except clothes which are generally bought in England and Scotland by the migratory labourers; any clothes purchased in the district are bought at Westport.

No butter or poultry is exported – very little is sold for local consumption. Eggs are exported in thousands by the local dealers who purchase them from the people. They are generally kept a fortnight and are then sent by boat to Westport. Sometimes they have to be retained three weeks owing to bad weather. They are always nearly three weeks old before reaching their final destination in Great Britain.

(9.) Rail, steamer, sailing boat, road, postal and telegraph facilities.

Westport is at present the nearest railway station for this district, being twenty-eight miles from Achill Sound; but a line to Achill is now in course of construction. No steamers call to any part of the district. Sailing boats trade with Wesport and convey all goods purchased there to Achill Sound. There is very little cart traffic from Westport. The postal arrangements are good: letters are delivered daily, except on Sundays, at three post offices in the district.

A telegraph office was opened last year at Achill Sound.

(10.) Employment for labourers in the district, whether temporary or constant, and rate of wage.

The employment for labourers is temporary – just a little at spring and harvest time – wages being 2*s.* per day.

(11.) Migratory labour, average earnings per head, and where earned.

The migratory labourers probably number 1,318 persons in this district. They leave between March 20th and June 20th, returning from September 20th up to Christmas. All females and a few men go to Scotland, working in Lanark, Ayr, and Mid Lothian. The great majority of the male labourers proceed to Lancashire, Cheshire, and Yorkshire. The average earnings for men are from £9 to £10 cash, and £1 10*s.* value of clothes purchased. The average earnings for women are from £5 to £7 cash, and £1 10*s.* value of clothes purchased.

(12.) Weaving, spinning, knitting, and sewing, whether used locally or sold, and where.

There are very few weavers in the district; this industry being almost entirely confined to making a little flannel for men's shirts, etc., etc. The women spin and knit for their own families. Nothing is ever sold. I understand the girls bring home from Scotland large quantities of thread for knitting socks and small shawls.

(13.) Kelp-burning, and sale of seaweed.

There is no kelp-burning carried on in the district. A little kelp was formerly made on one of the north-east headlands (Ridge Point), but for some years the price was so low that the people abandoned the industry for migratory labour and emigration. It has never since been revived though the price now given for kelp is fairly remunerative. Some £15 is paid annually to the Achill Mission Trustees for seaweed on Inishbiggle Island (which forms part of the Achill Electoral Division) by the people of the adjoining district of Ballycroy. No other seaweed is sold.

(14.) Sale of turf, nature and extent of bogs.

There is no turf sold. The bogs are practically inexhaustible, and the turf is of excellent quality.

(15.) Lobster fishing, number of men and boats employed.

There are numbers of lobsters all round the coast of the district, but the people do not fish for them – although the Connemara and Inishkea fishermen take them in hundreds almost from the very doors of the people.

(16.) Sea fishing. Facilities for sale of fish, and number of boats and men solely employed in fishing.

Very few of the people can be called fishermen. I doubt much if there are half a dozen *bona fide* fishermen in the entire district. Up to the present time no facilities for the sale of fresh fish existed and the consumption was confined to local wants and a little salt fish which was taken to Westport and sold. The Westport Mulrany and Achill Railway ought to alter matters in this respect.

(17.) Number of boats and men employed in carrying turf or seaweed or in fishing. Classification of boats.

The number of boats employed in fishing, or carrying turf or seaweed, and their classification, are as follows:–

3	Hookers, 2nd class.
11	Hookers, 3rd class.
226	Yawls and rowing boats.
35	Curraghs.
Total, 275	Boats.

(18.) Fish; whether consumed at home or sold.

Fish is generally consumed in the district, salmon is sent to the English markets, and a little salt fish is sold at Westport.

(19.) Extent of fish-curing.

Fish are salted in a very inferior manner: otherwise the people of the district know nothing of fish-curing.

(20.) Piers and Harbours, existing and suggested, and how far those existing are adapted to wants of district.

On the north of Achill there is only one pier which was built by the Board of Works in 1880-81, a proportion of the expenditure being defrayed by the Earl of Cavan. This pier is made almost entirely of solid concrete. It has stood well and is now vested in the Grand Jury of the County. The site selected is unfortunately very much exposed, and the pier affords no shelter in stormy weather. It is therefore not much used by fishing boats.

Another pier has been suggested at Doogort, about four miles west of Lord Cavan's pier. There are a considerable number of families in the locality and the proposed site has been well chosen, having regard to the difficulty of obtaining sheltered places anywhere on the coast. On the south side of the district, piers or slips have been made at Kildavnet (2), Dooega, and Keel.

The pier at Kildavnet, built many years ago by the Grand Jury, a substantial structure, is still in good repair. A boat-slip (a very useful little work) made last year under the Relief of Distress Act already requires some slight repairs.

The small pier built at Dooega, in 1886, by the Piers and Roads Commission has been washed away. £1,200 was expended by the same Commission at Keel in making a harbour for fishing boats. The place chosen is perhaps the most sheltered on the north side of Achill, and if sufficient funds had been provided the project in all probability would have been successful. The present state of this harbour may be briefly described as follows:– All solid concrete work built on a rocky foundation, has stood the force of many severe storms without the slightest apparent damage. The inner works, which seem to have been made of slight stones and faced with concrete, are now little better than a heap of ruins.

At Dooagh, a village two miles further west, a landing place for curraghs was made by cutting away the solid rock. This landing place might be much improved, but it could never be used by large boats.

There are several small piers on the east side of Achill, most of which are used for landing goods brought from Westport by sailing boats. That at Bunacurry is the most useful, and I hear fish are sometimes landed there. The road leading to this pier is in very bad repair.

(21.) Extent of salmon and freshwater fisheries. Number of men earning their livelihood therefrom.

There are no freshwater fisheries in the district. There are fifteen bag nets and four drift nets at various points round the coast. Thirty-five men are employed at wages averaging 10*s.* weekly. Seven carts at £1 each per week and two hookers at £4 10*s.* per week each, are also engaged: each hooker carries a crew of three men. Salmon fishing is carried on from April to August, but the bulk of the fish are taken in June and July, and it is during this latter period that the carts and hookers are employed.

(22.) Banks and Loan Funds.

There are no Banks or Loan Funds in the district.

(23.) Mineral and other resources.

A copper mine was worked in the Corraun Achill Electoral Division by two companies, both of which, I hear, failed. Iron ore and sulphur are also found there. Soapstone in large quantities and very easily worked can be obtained in the Dooega Electoral Division.

(24.) Relative prevalence of cash or credit dealings, length of credit, interest charged, extent of barter, etc., etc.

During spring and summer, credit dealings prevail. All debts are expected to be discharged when the migratory labourers return from England and Scotland, 15 per cent. is generally charged for long credit. Should the potato crop be deficient, credit has to be obtained at Christmas or in some cases even earlier.

Barter is carried on extensively in eggs and corn, which are exchanged for tea, sugar, and tobacco. Enquiries lead me to believe that while the people are still deeply indebted to the local shopkeepers, their debts have not materially increased of recent years.

Nets drying on the pier at Clare Island, with Mayo's holy mountain of Croagh Patrick in the background.

(25.) Estimated *cash* receipts and expenditure of a family in ordinary circumstances.

The *cash* receipts and expenditure of a family in fairly comfortable circumstances (husband, wife, two sons, aged 19, and 12, and two daughters, 17 and 14), are, on an average, as follows:–

RECEIPTS	£	s.	d.	EXPENDITURE	£	s.	d.
Father's migratory earnings (with clothes), . .	9	0	0	Rent of holding, . .	1	0	0
				Grazing for cattle and sheep, .	1	0	0
Son's do., (with clothes),	9	0	0	County Cess, . .	0	2	6
Daughter's do., (with clothes),	6	0	0	Clerical charges, . .	0	10	0
Sale of eggs (1,800),. .	4	10	0	Meal, 4 bags, . .	3	0	0
Sale of pig (profit), . .	1	10	0	Flour, 6 bags, . .	3	12	6
Sale of one bullock, . .	3	0	0	Groceries, ½lb. tea, and 1 st. sugar per week, . .	7	10	0
				Tobacco, 8 ozs. per week, .	5	14	0
				Clothing for those at home (say),	3	0	0
				Household, etc., . .	2	10	0
	£33	0	0		£27	19	0

Estimate for a family in poor circumstances (husband, wife, and five children; eldest a boy, 13 years of age):–

RECEIPTS	£	s.	d.	EXPENDITURE	£	s.	d.
Father's migratory earnings, with clothes, . .	10	0	0	Rent of holding, . .	1	0	0
				Grazing of cattle, .	0	10	0
Sale of eggs, . .	4	0	0	County Cess, . .	0	2	6
Sale of pig, . .	1	10	0	Clerical charges, . .	0	5	0
Sale of bullock (one sold every two years), . .	1	10	0	Meal and flour, . .	4	4	0
				Groceries, . .	3	15	0
				Tobacco, . .	2	12	0
				Clothes (say), . .	3	10	0
				Household, . .	1	10	0
	£17	0	0		£17	8	6

(26.) Estimated value of home-grown food consumed, and period during which it lasts.

The estimated value of home-grown food consumed is as follows:–

	£	s.	d.
Potatoes, 4 tons, at £2 per ton,	8	0	0
Corn, 30 cwt., at 5*s.* per cwt.,	7	10	0
Straw, 2 tons, at 30*s.* per ton,	3	0	0
Total,	£18	10	0

(27.) Dietary of people, number of meals daily, and kinds of food throughout the year.

The dietary of the people consists of three meals daily each person; the custom of taking four meals in some instances (especially during spring work) is now creeping in.

Breakfast. – Tea and flour bread; *very* poor people, potatoes and tea.
Dinner. – Potatoes and fish or eggs; in many cases tea also.
Supper. – Potatoes and milk or eggs.

In summer Indian meal stirabout is substituted for potatoes, and eggs and milk are also then more used.

(28.) Clothing, whether home-made or bought, etc., etc.

The clothing of the people in this district is principally bought in England and Scotland. Money is also sent home by the migratory labourers to purchase wool for flannel and making stockings.

(29.) Dwellings: kind of houses, home-life and customs, etc., etc.

The houses are nearly all built of stone, though a few sod huts may also be seen. The houses generally contain a kitchen and one room – better class houses having two rooms. The cattle occupy one end of the kitchen, and the family take their meals and some members sleep in the other end. The fowl roost on the rafters. I am told pigs are often kept in the same apartment.

(30.) Character of the people for industry, etc., etc.

In spring, a good deal of work is carried out very energetically to enable the migratory labourers to leave for England and Scotland; but at other periods of the year the people do not exert themselves to improve their holdings, very little work being done in winter.

(31.) Whether any organized effort has been made to develop the resources or improve the condition of the people. If so, by what means.

A considerable number of families were assisted to emigrate in 1883-84 by the Tuke Fund Committee. Most of these families resided in the north-eastern corner of the Island, and an improvement in the general circumstances of the people in this part of Achill is plainly to be seen. In the remaining portion of the district the number of families leaving was so small that little appreciable effect could be expected.

(32.) Suggestions as to any possible method for improving the condition of the people in future.

I see no reason why cottage industries, which flourish in Donegal, should not fare equally well in Achill. An effort might be made next winter to teach the women a better system of knitting and supply them with materials in the same manner as has been so successfully carried out in County Donegal. Skilled instructors would have to be employed, and a Local Committee could, I have no doubt, be easily formed to supervise the necessary details. There are several buildings now vacant which I hear could be obtained at a mere nominal cost for such a purpose.

The extension of the Railway System to Achill ought, in addition to the many other benefits which it will confer, largely to assist in the development of fishing – an industry which would, with proper encouragement, afford ample means of subsistence to many families who are now struggling under adverse circumstances. To enable fishing to be thoroughly developed, it will be necessary to provide places of refuge or shelters for boats. The entire coast of Achill is singularly deficient in this respect, and doubtless to this cause must be mainly attributed the neglect of the islanders to make use of this important means of bettering their condition.

Turf was plentiful on Achill Island and cut solely for home use.

The following places seem to me most suitable for these shelters or refuges:– On the south – the small harbour at Keel already commenced by the Piers and Roads Commission in 1886; Camport in Dooega Bay; and Achillbeg. On the north shore – a pier built at Doogort would be very useful. At the same time it is right to mention that the construction of any of these works must necessarily entail a large expenditure of money, but without them I fail to see how fishing can be safely carried on.

ROBERT RUTTLEDGE-FAIR,
Inspector.

27th April, 1892.

To

The Congested Districts Board for Ireland.

CONGESTED DISTRICTS BOARD FOR IRELAND

COUNTY OF MAYO – UNION OF BELMULLET

REPORT OF MAJOR ROBERT RUTTLEDGE-FAIR, *Inspector*

DISTRICT

OF

BELMULLET

STATISTICAL TABLE

ELECTORAL DIVISION.	Area in Statute Acres.	Poor Law Valuation.	Number of Ratings at and under £10 and above £4 Valuation.	Number of Ratings at and under £4 Valuation.	Population in 1891.	Number of Families in 1891.	Number of Families on Holdings exceeding £2 and under £4 Valuation.	Number of Families on Holdings at and under £2 Valuation.	Number of Families in very poor circumstances.	Number of Families which have no Cattle.
		£								
Belmullet,	10,949	1,832	70	238	2,294	380	108	130	91	35
Binghamstown, North.	10,273	1,582	67	152	1,389	233	91	59	56	46
Binghamstown, South.	9,869	1,741	73	169	1,656	289	106	63	91	80
TOTALS,	31,091	£5,155	210	559	5,339	902	305	252	238	161

(1.) Whether inland or maritime.

The district is maritime.

(2.) Average quantity of land cultivated on holdings at and under £4 valuation, under (*a*) oats, (*b*) potatoes, (*c*) meadow, (*d*) green crops.

There are about four and a half acres of land on an average cultivated on holdings at and under £4 valuation in the following way:–

2 acres of oats.
2 acres of potatoes.
¼ acre meadow.
¼ acre other green crops.

Total, 4½ acres.

(3.) Extent of mountain or moor grazing, and rights possessed by tenants, whether in common or otherwise.

There is very little mountain or moor grazing in most of this district – the tenants being principally confined to their holdings. In a portion of the Belmullet Electoral Division there is a fairly large tract of mountain, upon most of which the tenants adjoining possess the right of free grazing. In two instances, however, the owners hold some fifteen or sixteen hundred acres in their own possession, and either take in grazing stock at a fixed price per head or let the land to graziers upon eleven months tenancies.

(4.) Extent and description of land, if any, which could be profitably reclaimed and added to existing adjoining holdings.

Excluding grazing farms, there does not appear to be any great extent of land that could be profitably reclaimed, and added to existing adjoining holdings. In some of the villages almost every acre of reclaimable land is either at present under cultivation, or from years of continuous crop growing has become so exhausted that it is nearly useless for any purpose. Round other villages there are considerable tracts of "cut-away" bog lands which the tenants are gradually reclaiming.

(5.) Particulars as to any suitable land in district which could be obtained, and to which families could be migrated with a reasonable prospect of success.

I have enquired whether any suitable land could be obtained to which families could be migrated with a reasonable prospect of success, and I cannot hear of any such lands being now for sale.

(6.) Method of cultivation, manures, rotation of crops, etc., etc.

The method of cultivation is, as might indeed be expected in a district so remote, of the most primitive nature; potatoes, oats, barley, and rye being the principal crops. The soil varies from a sandy loam in Binghamstown South to light clay in Binghamstown North, and peat in Belmullet. The quality of the land is generally of a superior nature in the southern part of the district. Potatoes are sown by spade labour in lazy beds of a much greater width than I have seen in other parts of Ireland, sometimes quite seven feet wide. In places, too, the ridges exposed to south-westerly winds are raised nearly a foot higher on the south-west side and sloped gradually towards the north-east to afford shelter for the young stalks. In some parts of this district potatoes are sown in January and February, and owing to the sandy nature of the soil become fit for use early in June. *This industry might, I think, be further developed.*

Sea-weed mixed with a small quantity of farm-yard manure is generally used. Artificial manures are almost unknown. Oats, barley, or rye follow the potato crop. In very small holdings this rotation is carried on year after year until the land becomes thoroughly worn out. On the larger holdings attempts are made to lay down small plots in grass, but either from bad cultivation, neglect of keeping weeds down, inferior grass seeds, or very likely a combination of all three, a really good plot of rye grass and clover is hardly ever seen.

(7.) General information with regard to stock, and suggestions as to improvement of breeds – (*a*) cattle, (*b*) sheep, (*c*) horses and donkeys, (*d*) pigs, (*e*) poultry, etc., etc.

The permanent pasture being of good quality, cattle of a better class are kept. Large numbers of yearling calves bred in Roscommon, Sligo, and Fermanagh are sold at the monthly fairs of Belmullet and Binghamstown. These calves are kept for twelve, or in some cases, eighteen months, during which time they *grow* well but do not *fatten*, and are then sold to County Meath and English buyers. Good bulls are much required, as the cattle bred in the district are distinctly inferior to those purchased in other counties for feeding purposes. Every person to whom I have spoken advocates the introduction of a few good Shorthorn or Polled-Angus bulls. I feel sure a marked improvement would soon be noticeable if this suggestion was adopted.

Sheep are of a very inferior quality; the introduction of Shrop rams would I believe be productive of much good. The cross of Shrop rams with the mountain ewes of this district has already been tried with excellent results by some of the larger farmers. Horses are of a very poor class; but this question is already being dealt with by the Board.

Several of the better class tenants have asked me to represent that pig breeding has been altogether neglected for years past, and it is thought that a few Berkshire or Yorkshire boars should be distributed here and there through the district.

In the recent distribution of cockerels through the western districts, Belmullet was apparently forgotten. There is no district where the breed of fowls (particularly ducks and geese) could be so much improved.

(8.) Markets and fairs for cattle and produce of district; also statement as to where the people obtain food and other supplies, and the prevailing custom with regard to the disposal of butter, eggs, and poultry; to what extent are they sold in the first instance to local shopkeepers and dealers, and, generally speaking, how old are the eggs when sold to the first buyer, and about how old when they reach their ultimate destination in Great Britain.

There is a weekly market at Belmullet and fairs are held once every month at Belmullet and Binghamstown, the latter place a little hamlet two and a half miles west of Belmullet. All supplies are obtained from the local merchants at Belmullet, who purchase their goods at Westport and Sligo, so far as meal and flour are concerned. Sugar, tea, hardware, drapery, etc., etc. are obtained direct by local traders from Manchester, Glasgow, and Liverpool.

There is a small export trade in butter during the summer and autumn months. Hardly any butter is sold in winter and spring. The average price is from fourpence to eightpence per pound according to quality.

A very large export trade is carried on in eggs, *thousands* being weekly purchased at Belmullet; the price generally paid is about sixpence per dozen. The eggs in the first instance are three, four, and even six days old before they are brought for sale to Belmullet.

The local buyers at Belmullet keep these eggs for a week in summer, and for a fortnight in winter, before sending them to Ballina, from whence they are transmitted to the large English and Scotch cities. It may safely be assumed that the eggs from this district are always a fortnight, and often three weeks, old before they reach their final destination in Great Britain.

(9.) Rail, steamer, sailing boat, road, postal and telegraph facilities.

Ballina is at present the nearest railway station (forty-one miles from Belmullet). The railway now in course of construction from Westport to Achill will not much benefit Belmullet, as the nearest station – Mulrany – is by road thirty-five miles distant. A branch line from either Cleggan (nineteen miles), or from Mulrany (twenty-two miles), as the railway would run, would afford Belmullet ample railway facilities.

Steamers seldom come to Belmullet. Now and again small steamers are chartered by one of the local traders to convey flour, meal, and timber from Sligo.

Large-sized sailing boats trade in summer between Westport and Belmullet, bringing flour and other heavy goods. They pass through Achill Sound – the narrow channel which divides Achill Island from the mainland – and so avoid rounding the dangerous western headlands of Achill. There is a fairly good main road to Ballina (forty-one miles). A considerable quantity of heavy goods are conveyed by cart on this road, particularly in winter, when sea communication with Westport is often for weeks impracticable. The mails are conveyed from Ballina every morning by a well-appointed two-horse car, and are sent to Blacksod, ten miles further west, *twice* every week. There is telegraphic communication between Ballina and Ballycroy.

(10.) Employment for labourers in the district, whether temporary or constant, and rate of wage.

The employment for labourers in this district is generally temporary. A little permanent employment is given by a few (three or four) of the resident gentry and by some of the Belmullet shopkeepers. Temporary employment is limited to spring and harvest work. Nine or ten shillings per week is the general rate of wage for temporary employment, and seven shillings for constant labour.

(11.) Migratory labour, average earnings per head, and where earned.

There may be said to be practically no migratory labourers in this district.

(12.) Weaving, spinning, knitting, and sewing, whether used locally or sold, and where.

The weaving, spinning, knitting, and sewing that are carried on are altogether for home use. Small quantities of flannel , frieze, and socks are sold at Belmullet by the country people on fair and market days. The purchasers live in the locality, and buy because they have no wool of their own to convert into material. So far as I can learn nothing is exported.

(13.) Kelp-burning, and sale of seaweed.

I learn from the local agent that he purchased 250 tons of kelp in this district last year, price averaging £3 10*s.* per ton. Most of the landlords levy a *royalty* of 33 per cent. on all kelp made on their respective properties. This is paid by the landlord either receiving one-third of the kelp and selling that portion himself, or else the tenants remit a third of the amount received from the local kelp agent. *One* landlord charges only 25 per cent., but 33 per cent. is the general charge made.

There is no sale of seaweed.

(14.) Sale of turf, nature and extent of bogs.

A little turf is sold in the town of Belmullet, but otherwise there is no sale of turf from this district. There are extensive bogs containing turf of excellent quality in the Belmullet Electoral Division, and there is also plenty of turf in the Binghamstown North Electoral Division; but in Binghamstown South, the bogs for many years have been cut away, and turf is obtained from Achill and Ballycroy, being conveyed in boats across Blacksod Bay.

(15.) Lobster fishing, number of men and boats employed.

The lobster fishing in this district is confined to the Inishkea islanders, and the villagers of Fallmore and Blacksod. This fishing generally commences about 1st April. Some fifty boats, large and small, and about one hundred men are employed "off and on" till the rough weather sets in (generally about the middle of September). The lobsters are sold at Belmullet, priced five to six shillings per dozen. They are sent by mail car to Ballina, thence by rail to England.

(16.) Sea fishing. Facilities for sale of fish, and number of boats and men solely employed in fishing.

There is excellent sea fishing in this district, but owing to the want of facilities for the sale of fish, there is little encouragement to induce the further development of this very important industry. A considerable number of boats are engaged from time to time, but I cannot ascertain that there is *one* really *bona fide* fishing boat in the district. This would not be so if a ready sale for fish was always available.

(17.) Number of boats and men employed in carrying turf or seaweed or in fishing. Classification of boats.

In this district there are no first-class boats; there are three second-class boats; twenty-nine third-class boats; and one hundred and forty-two curraghs.

(18.) Fish; whether consumed at home or sold.

The fish caught are mostly consumed at home or sold to neighbours for consumption in the district. Small quantities of superior fish such as turbot, &c., are sometimes sent for sale to Dublin. The facilities for the sale of fish are so defective that any export trade is almost impossible.

(19.) Extent of fish-curing.

Fish-curing in this district is entirely confined to salting cod, ling, and herrings, which are sold in the Belmullet market for local consumption during the winter months. The people have not the slightest idea of fish-curing in the proper acceptance of the term.

(20.) Piers and Harbours, existing and suggested, and how far those existing are adapted to wants of district.

There are two piers at Belmullet, one at Blacksod, and one on the South Island of Inishkea. A boat-slip was last year partially constructed on the North Island of Inishkea. It has been much damaged by the recent storms, and unless speedily repaired, will soon be washed away.

A boat-slip was also constructed at Glenlara by the Board of Works at a very considerable cost, and was since several times repaired by the Grand Jury: it has now been completely washed away. The place seems to me to be totally unsuitable for the erection of any such work, as it is exposed to the full force of northerly gales, and, I believe no building, however substantial, could be maintained in such an exposed situation.

A nice harbour of refuge, and one much required for fishing boats could be constructed at the Inishkea Islands. It would also have the great advantage of being close to the fishing banks. I have been informed that years ago capable Manx and Skerry fishermen stated that if there was a place of safety at the Inishkea Islands for their boats they would always come there during the fishing season.

(21.) Extent of salmon and freshwater fisheries. Number of men earning their livelihood therefrom.

There are no salmon or freshwater fisheries in this district.

(22.) Banks and Loan Funds.

There are no Banks or Loan Funds in this district.

(23.) Mineral and other resources.

With the exception of a granite quarry at Blacksod, which is not at present worked, there are no mineral or other resources in this district.

(24.) Relative prevalence of cash or credit dealings, length of credit, interest charged, extent of barter, etc., etc.

Credit is not given to the same extent as it was ten years ago. Cash is oftener paid for meal and flour than for other commodities, but a shopkeeper would not refuse credit to customers. Clothes are mostly given on credit, and payment is never demanded for at least twelve months, and in numerous instances for a much longer period. Fifteen per cent. at least is charged for credit; when the old accounts are paid up fresh ones are almost immediately afterwards opened. It may safely be assumed that a large number of the people are hardly ever out of the shopkeepers' power. At the same time I think most of the Belmullet traders deal leniently with them, and are not by any means exacting in their demands.

Barter is not carried on at Belmullet, but in some of the villages further west *very poor* people exchange eggs for tobacco, tea, and sugar, with the village hucksters. The extent of this dealing is I think very small.

(25.) Estimated *cash* receipts and expenditure of a family in ordinary circumstances.

Estimated *cash* receipts and expenditure of a family in ordinary circumstances in an average year. Family: four children – one being an adult. Holding: eight acres of land, with small mountain run:–

Receipts

	£	*s.*	*d.*
Sale of –			
20 cwt. of oats at 4*s.* 6*d.*, .	4	10	0
4 tons potatoes at 33*s.* 4*d.*, .	6	13	4
2 two-year old cattle, .	12	0	0
3 pigs (profit), .	4	10	0
A foal, ...	5	0	0
Eggs, 20 hens at 150 eggs each,	7	10	0
Surplus butter, . .	1	0	0
10 lambs at 8*s.* each, . .	4	0	0
Surplus fish, say, . .	3	0	0
	£48	3	4
Deduct Expenditure,	37	2	0
Net Profit, . . .	£11	1	4

Expenditure

	£	*s.*	*d.*
Rent, . .	4	0	0
County Cess, . .	0	8	0
Clerical charges, . .	1	0	0
Clothes at £2 per head, .	12	0	0
Meal (June and July) 4 bags at 17*s.* 6*d.*, . .	3	10	0
Flour for year, 8 bags at 12*s.*, .	4	16	0
52 weeks groceries and "kitchen,"	6	11	0
Tobacco at 1*s.* per week, .	2	12	0
Spades, shovels, forks, .	0	10	0
Pots, pans, delph, tubs, .	0	15	0
Lamp and candle light, .	1	0	0
	£37	2	0

N.B. – In a bad year the following deductions from the receipts would have to be made – £6 13*s.* 4*d.* potatoes, as none could be sold, and £4 10*s.* profit on pigs, and £1 surplus butter. Total, £12 3*s.* 4*d.* The total receipts being, therefore, £36. The expenditure would also be largely increased, as a much greater quantity of meal and flour (certainly twice as much as in an ordinary year) must be purchased. On the other hand, a saving of (say) £4 11*s.* 6*d.* might be effected in the items set down for clothing, groceries, tobacco. In such a year either previous savings would have to be expended, or debts to the extent of at least £6 13*s.* 2*d.* must be incurred.

Receipts and expenditure of a *poor* family in an average year may be estimated as follows:–

Receipts

	£	*s.*	*d.*
Sale of –			
5 cwt. oats at 4*s.*, . .	1	0	0
Profit on sale of pig, . .	1	10	0
1,500 eggs at 6*s.* . .	3	15	0
Profit on sale of kelp, . .	2	10	0
Fishing, 5 months (off and on), at £2 per month,	10	0	0
	£18	15	0
Net profit, . . .	£ 0	15	0

Expenditure

	£	*s.*	*d.*
Rent of holding, . .	1	0	0
County Cess, . .	0	2	0
Clerical charges, . .	0	6	0
Clothes (at least), . .	4	0	0
Meal (June and July), .	3	10	0
Flour, 3 bags, . .	1	16	0
Groceries, 52 weeks, . .	3	12	0
Tobacco at 1*s.* per week, .	2	12	0
Household and farm implements	0	12	0
Lamp and candle light, .	0	10	0
	£18	0	0

(26.) Estimated value of home-grown food consumed, and period during which it lasts.

The home-grown food consumed is principally confined to potatoes and straw, the latter being consumed by the cattle. A family in fairly ordinary circumstances would consume about five tons of potatoes (selling price £8 6*s.* 8*d.*, at 2½*d.* per stone); £1 10*s.* might be added for straw; and 10*s.* for cabbages. Total, £10 6*s.* 8*d.* Potatoes in a good year would last from nine to ten months. Cattle are housed at night from November to the following April, during which time they are fed on straw.

(27.) Dietary of people, number of meals daily, and kinds of food throughout the year.

The dietary of the people is as follows:–

Breakfast, Potatoes, and fish or milk or eggs. In summer – porridge, and milk or sugar.

Dinner, Tea, and flour or meal bread.

Supper, Potatoes, and fish or milk. In summer – porridge and milk.

The dietary of very poor families is as follows:–

Breakfast, Potatoes, and sometimes a little fish. In summer – Indian meal stirabout.

Dinner, Tea sometimes, but more often potatoes with "kitchen."

Supper, Potatoes. In summer – Indian meal stirabout.

(28.) Clothing, whether home-made or bought, etc., etc.

In this district stockings, shirts and drawers are generally of home manufacture. Everything else is bought. Poor families purchase very little, most of their clothing being made of rough flannel – either white or blue.

(29.) Dwellings: kind of houses, home-life and customs, etc., etc.

Houses are now nearly all built of stone, roofed with "scraws" and straw or rough mountain sedge. There are some places where a few houses are still built of sods, but since the Tuke Fund emigration they are dying out. The houses generally consist of one room and a kitchen. In the latter, the family principally reside, and the female members sleep in the room. The cattle are housed at the lower end of the kitchen near the door. The fowls roost overhead on the rafters. The beds and bedding are mostly of the roughest material (the latter, straw-covered with coarse sacking). Sheets are not often used, and when the blankets are worn out the people are often too poor to replace them.

Early rising is a general custom and the people retire to rest before nine o'clock, P.M. During the winter months little farm work is done, except that along the sea coast some drift weed may be collected.

(30.) Character of the people for industry, etc., etc.

With regard to the character of the people for industry, etc., etc., I cannot say much in their favour; but it should be remembered that there is very little inducement to encourage them in industrious habits.

(31.) Whether any organized effort has been made to develop the resources or improve the condition of the people. If so, by what means.

Owing to the success of an emigration scheme, carried out under the auspices of the Tuke Fund Committee in 1882 - 83 - 84, the condition of the people has very perceptibly improved during the last ten years. During those years a number of families (nearly 250) – most of whom were steeped in abject poverty and misery – were assisted to emigrate to Australia, Canada, and the United States. The removal of those families has been attended with very happy results, for not only were they placed in other countries in what was to them comparative affluence, but the land which they occupied was generally purchased by their neighbours to increase the size of their own holdings which were too small to afford them means of subsistence.

(32.) Suggestions as to any possible method for improving the condition of the people in future.

The chief reasons which impoverish the people of this district are:–

1. The total absence of proper facilities for the sale of farm produce and fish.
2. The want of employment for the male population, especially in the winter months.
3. The overcrowded state of a large number of small holdings and the deterioration of the land by continuous cropping.

I believe much of this poverty could be successfully overcome by an extension of the Westport and Mulrany Railway to Belmullet, a distance of some twenty-two statute miles, and by encouragement of the fisheries.

Efforts might also be made to improve the breed of cattle, horses, sheep, poultry, etc. But the extension of the railway system to Belmullet is of vital and paramount importance. I am clearly of opinion that until this want is effectually remedied little permanent good can be effected.

ROBERT RUTTLEDGE-FAIR,
Inspector.

29th March, 1892.

To

The Congested Districts Board for Ireland.

CONGESTED DISTRICTS BOARD FOR IRELAND

COUNTY OF MAYO – UNIONS OF SWINFORD AND CLAREMORRIS

REPORT OF MR. DORAN, *Inspector*

DISTRICT

OF

KILTAMAGH

STATISTICAL TABLE

ELECTORAL DIVISION.	Area in Statute Acres.	Poor Law Valuation.	Number of Ratings at and under £10 and above £4 Valuation.	Number of Ratings at and under £4 Valuation.	Population in 1891.	Number of Families in 1891.	Number of Families on Holdings exceeding £2 and under £4 Valuation.	Number of Families on Holdings at and under £2 Valuation.	Number of Families in very poor circumstances.	Number of Families which have no Cattle.
		£							about	about
Kiltamagh,	4,673	1,633	126	521	2,518	496	109	209	120	100 (both divisions)
Knock, North,	6,627	1,436	117	181	1,774	309	106	41	50	
TOTALS,	11,300	£3,069	243	702	4,292	805	215	250	170	100

(1.) Whether inland or maritime.

The district is inland.

(2.) Average quantity of land cultivated on holdings at and under £4 valuation, under (*a*) oats, (*b*) potatoes, (*c*) meadow, (*d*) green crops.

There are about 4 statute acres on an average cultivated on holdings of about £4 valuation in the following way:–

Oats,	$1\frac{3}{4}$ acres,
Potatoes,	$1\frac{5}{8}$ „
Meadow,	$\frac{1}{2}$ „
Green crops,	$\frac{1}{8}$ „
Total,	4 acres.

(3.) Extent of mountain or moor grazing, and rights possessed by tenants, whether in common or otherwise.

There are no extensive tracts of rough or mountain grazing in this district. What land there is of this description is held by tenants in connection with their arable land, and grazed in common.

(4.) Extent and description of land, if any, which could be profitably reclaimed and added to existing adjoining holdings.

On the greater number of the holdings in this district there is some land capable of profitable improvement by reclamation and drainage. There would be 1,500 or perhaps 2,000 acres of such land. It consists of wet land much in need of drainage, cut-away bog, partially reclaimed moor, and unreclaimed bog adjoining arable land and offering facilities for profitable improvement.

(5.) Particulars as to any suitable land in district which could be obtained, and to which families could be migrated with a reasonable prospect of success.

There is no suitable land in this district to which families could be migrated with any prospect of success, unless a number of the larger occupiers of land migrated to another district, leaving their farms available for the enlargement of the remaining holdings.

(6.) Method of cultivation, manures, rotation of crops, etc., etc.

The land is very badly cultivated and rotation of crops is not followed. The only crops grown in this district are potatoes, oats, a little cabbage, and occasionally a small plot of turnips.

A large number of the people have not sufficient live stock for their holdings, and they rarely have sufficient manure even for the potato crop. All use artificial manure and it has had a most exhaustive effect upon the land. Every one grows from three roods to one and a half acres (Irish) of potatoes, and those who have little or perhaps no cattle have to depend almost altogether on artificial manure. In some of the poorest parts of the Kiltamagh Electoral Division the land is held in *rundale*, and in some "villages" the tenants have only two or three acres each of land. Without removing a large proportion of these people, and *striping* the land amongst the remainder, no improvement in their condition, or system of cultivation can be effected.

(7.) General information with regard to stock, and suggestions as to improvement of breeds – (*a*) cattle, (*b*) sheep, (*c*) horses and donkeys, (*d*) pigs, (*e*) poultry, etc., etc.

All classes of live stock in the district are of an inferior description, and are much in need of improvement.

Cattle.– To improve the breed of cattle I would suggest Roscommon bulls, and Polled Angus. In the better part of the district the Pedigree Shorthorn would be suitable.

Horses.– These would be improved by the introduction of cob stallions with a good dash of breeding and good action and bone.

Donkeys.– These are very numerous in the district and would be much improved by crossing with Spanish asses.

Pigs.– The pigs can be improved by crossing with large Yorkshire boars.

Fowl.– By introducing new breeds of hens, geese, ducks, and turkeys to cross with existing breeds.

Sheep.– These are not so much in need of improvement as other stock, but can be improved by care in breeding. A good class of sheep can be obtained at the neighbouring fairs.

(8.) Markets and fairs for cattle and produce of district; also statement as to where the people obtain food and other supplies, and the prevailing custom with regard to the disposal of butter, eggs, and poultry; to what extent are they sold in the first instance to local shopkeepers and dealers, and, generally speaking, how old are the eggs when sold to the first buyer, and about how old when they reach their ultimate destination in Great Britain.

Fairs are held regularly at Kiltamagh, and a weekly market also. Persons in part of Knock Electoral Division go to Ballyhaunis market.

Butter is usually sold at the market by the producer. Eggs are sold at market and to local dealers. As a rule they are not more than a week old when they are despatched from this district to England and Scotland.

(9.) Rail, steamer, sailing boat, road, postal and telegraph facilities.

Ballyhaunis is the nearest railway station for this district.

There is telegraphic communication to Kiltamagh and Ballyhaunis.

(10.) Employment for labourers in the district, whether temporary or constant, and rate of wage.

There is no employment for labourers in this district.

(11.) Migratory labour, average earnings per head, and where earned.

Most of the small occupiers of land go to England as migratory labourers every year.

The amount saved by each one depends on the length of time he remains there, and on his frugal habits. The savings vary from £5 to £20, and would average about £8.

(12.) Weaving, spinning, knitting, and sewing, whether used locally or sold, and where.

Most of the socks and stockings worn by the people of this district are knitted at home. They make most of their flannel underclothing, and a little frieze. No work of this description is done for sale.

(13.) Kelp-burning, and sale of seaweed.

The district is inland.

(14.) Sale of turf, nature and extent of bogs.

Turf is not sold, except a very small quantity in the town. As a rule turf for fuel is easily procured.

(15.) Lobster fishing, number of men and boats employed.

The district is inland.

(16.) Sea fishing. Facilities for sale of fish, and number of boats and men solely employed in fishing.

The district is inland.

(17.) Number of boats and men employed in carrying turf or seaweed or in fishing. Classification of boats.

The district is inland.

(18.) Fish; whether consumed at home or sold.

The district is inland.

(19.) Extent of fish-curing.

The district is inland.

(20.) Piers and Harbours, existing and suggested, and how far those existing are adapted to wants of district.

The district is inland.

(21.) Extent of salmon and freshwater fisheries. Number of men earning their livelihood therefrom.

There are no salmon nor freshwater fisheries in the district.

(22.) Banks and Loan Funds.

There are no Loan Funds in the district. Banking accommodation is sufficient. There is a weekly sub-office of the Hibernian Bank in Kiltamagh.

(23.) Mineral and other resources.

There are no mineral nor other resources.

(24.) Relative prevalence of cash or credit dealings, length of credit, interest charged, extent of barter, etc., etc.

Most of the people are in debt to shop-keepers and Banks. Shop-keepers give usually a year's credit and they expect their accounts to be paid when the labourer returns from England, or at least a substantial payment to be made. The credit allowed is decreasing every year. The interest charged is from 6 to 10 per cent.

(25.) Estimated *cash* receipts and expenditure of a family in ordinary circumstances.

The estimated *cash* receipts and expenditure of a family of 6 persons living on a holding of £2 valuation are as follow:–

Receipts	£	*s.*	*d.*	Expenditure	£	*s.*	*d.*
Sale of two pigs, . .	6	0	0	Indian meal for family, .			
Do. butter, . .	2	0	0	" " pigs, .	6	0	0
Do. livestock (average), some				" " poultry, .			
years none, . .	3	0	0	Flour, 4 bags at 12*s*., .	2	8	0
Do. oats, . .	3	0	0	Shop bread, . .	0	10	0
Do. straw, . . .		–		Tea and sugar, . .	3	0	0
Do. potatoes (if crop is good), .	1	0	0	Tobacco for man, . .	1	10	0
Do. eggs (15 hens), . .	2	5	0	Clothing for man, wife and			
Do. chickens, . .	0	2	0	children, . .	5	0	0
Savings of man from his earnings				Candles, soap, oil, . .	0	15	0
in England, ...	8	0	0	2 young pigs purchased, .	1	5	0
				3 bags artifical manure, .	1	10	0
				Salt fish and sundries, .	1	0	0
				Rent of holding, . .	2	5	0
Total, . .	£25	7	0	Total, . .	£25	3	0

N.B. – The estimated receipts as shown here could only be realized by one who has sufficient stock for holding. The failure of the potato crop, the death of a cow or pig, would largely affect the receipts, and under such circumstances the expenses are kept down by spending less on clothes and meat, and substituting Indian meal to a large extent for flour in the dietary of the family.

In stating receipts from sales of pigs and cattle no allowance is made for casualties, which are of frequent occurrence.

Persons who keep the worst description of the cattle of the district do not realize from them much more than half the amount set forth above, and can not live in the manner indicated without going into debt, unless by remaining a considerable portion of the year in England

and sending home their savings, or when they receive remittances from members of their families who had emigrated to America or other foreign country. The majority of the people receive material aid in this way.

The estimated *cash* receipts and expenditure of a family of six persons living on a holding of about £4 valuation are as follow:–

RECEIPTS	£	s.	d.	EXPENDITURE	£	s.	d.
Sale of 2 pigs,	6	0	0	Indian meal for family, ,, ,, pigs, ,, ,, poultry,	5	10	0
Do. butter from 2 cows,	3	10	0	Oatmeal for family,	0	10	0
Do. oats, 10 cwt.,	3	10	0	Flour, six 7 st. bags at 12*s*. each, or a lesser quantity, when shop bread is available,	3	12	0
Do. straw or hay,	0	10	0	Shop bread,	0	10	0
Do. potatoes when crop is good,	2	0	0	Tea and sugar,	3	0	0
Do. eggs from 20 hens,	3	0	0	American bacon,	1	0	0
Do. chickens, 1 doz. at 4*d*. each,	0	4	0	Tobacco for man,	1	10	0
Savings of man for time working in England,	8	0	0	Clothing man, 50*s*. wife, 40*s*. children, 50*s*.,	7	0	0
Sale of live stock (average value),	6	0	0	2 young pigs purchased,	1	5	0
				2 bags artifical manure,	1	10	0
				Rent and County Cess,	4	5	0
				Salt fish and sundry requirements,	1	0	0
				Candles, soap, oil, etc.,	0	15	0
	£32	14	0		£31	7	0

N.B. – The same note as above applies to this estimate.

(26.) Estimated value of home-grown food consumed, and period during which it lasts.

The estimated value of home-grown food consumed is as follows:–

	£	s.	d.
Potatoes, 6 tons,	12	0	0
Eggs and milk,	2	10	0
Cabbage,	0	10	0
Total,	£15	0	0

(27.) Dietary of people, number of meals daily, and kinds of food throughout the year.

The dietary of the people in this district in ordinary circumstances living on holdings below £2 valuation is as follows:–

From April to August –

Breakfast.– Indian meal stirabout, frequently without milk; sometimes bread (made of meal and flour) and tea.

Dinner.– Bread (meal, or meal and flour), and tea, with eggs occasionally.

Supper.– Indian meal porridge.

From August to April –

Breakfast.– Potatoes and milk, or potatoes and salt fish.

Dinner.– Potatoes and salt fish, sometimes a little American bacon.

Supper.– Potatoes and milk, or potatoes and fish.

The dietary of people living on holdings of about £4 valuation is similar to that described for neighbouring districts.

(28.) Clothing, whether home-made or bought, etc., etc.

A small quantity of frieze is home-made, and used for coats. Flannels, socks, and stockings are made at home. A few people make linen sheeting and blankets; underclothes are made up at home. All other clothing is purchased in the shops.

These things are made only for home requirements and not for sale.

(29.) Dwellings: kind of houses, home-life and customs, etc., etc.

The dwellings of the people of the district have stone walls, about 8 feet high to the eaves, and usually about 30 feet long, and a thatched roof. The interior is divided into two apartments, one used as a living room, and at one end of it the cattle are usually kept. In it, also, there is a recess in the side wall, near the fire place, in which a rude bedstead is fixed, which is occupied by the husband and wife. The children of both sexes sleep in the second apartment, and the milk and butter are kept there.

Cattle are kept in most of the houses in all the congested districts in Mayo. Fortunately it is the universal custom with these people to use large quantities of turf-mould (they call it "black mud") for bedding their cattle and for increasing their manure heaps, and to this practice must be assigned the reason why fever epidemics are not of frequent occurrence amongst them. Reflecting on the habits of the people of this and neighbouring districts, who are born and reared in the same room as their cattle; where brothers and sisters occupy the same sleeping apartment, insensible of any violation of human decency; living in such foul surroundings, in such close association with the brutes of the field, I have often marvelled how they are so moral, so well disposed, and so good in many ways as they generally are.

(30.) Character of the people for industry, etc., etc.

When employed off their holdings, the people of this district are excellent labourers, but very few of them make any systematic attempt to improve their land or their homes. They work hard for a few weeks in springtime to put down "the crop." After that work is done most of the small occupiers go to England, and work hard there to save what they can, and when they return they seem to think they deserve a *holiday*, and they remain practically idle from November to February. When the men are absent, the women do the field labour, and cut and save the turf.

(31.) Whether any organized effort has been made to develop the resources or improve the condition of the people. If so, by what means.

No effort has been made to develop the resources or improve the condition of the people in this district.

(32.) Suggestions as to any possible method for improving the condition of the people in future.

In some of the most congested parts of the district the land is held in "rundale," and very little can be done for such people until a great many are removed, and the land *striped* amongst those who remain. The following methods, as fully set forth in my general report, dated April 30, 1892, I would suggest for permanently improving the condition of the people:–

Thatched cottage and outhouses in a typical family farmstead of the period.

Promoting better systems of agriculture through the agency of District Agriculturists.

Draining and reclaiming such portions of the holdings as would be capable of profitable improvement.

Deepening and improving the main drains and water-courses of the district.

Enforcing the sanitary laws, and afterwards educating the people how to make good butter.

Establishing Technical Schools to educate the people in classes of industrial work that would afford them remunerative employment as a home industry.

Affording facilities for the erection of factories by giving loans at a low rate of interest for providing buildings and plant, to private persons who could offer reasonable security.

Improving the breeds of cattle, horses, pigs, donkeys, and fowl by the introduction of good sires and good fowl.

Migrating the larger occupiers of land who desire to leave the district, and who have some capital wherewith to work better land, and apportioning their holdings among the small land-holders.

Planting trees for shelter, and osiers for basket-making, etc., on waste corners and other suitable places on their holdings.

Cottage gardening can be promoted by the District Agriculturist. The proper cooking of the vegetables grown in the garden can best be taught by an instructor who would visit the houses of the growers.

HENRY DORAN,
Inspector.

6th May, 1892.

To

The Congested Districts Board for Ireland.

CONGESTED DISTRICTS BOARD FOR IRELAND

COUNTY OF ROSCOMMON – UNION OF STROKESTOWN

REPORT OF HENRY DORAN, *Inspector*

DISTRICT

OF

ROOSKY

STATISTICAL TABLE

ELECTORAL DIVISION.	Area in Statute Acres.	Poor Law Valuation.	Number of Ratings at and under £10 and above £4 Valuation.	Number of Ratings at and under £4 Valuation.	Population in 1891.	Number of Families in 1891.	Number of Families on Holdings exceeding £2 and under £4 Valuation.	Number of Families on Holdings at and under £2 Valuation.	Number of Families in very poor circumstances.	Number of Families which have no Cattle.
		£								
Roosky,	4,612	1,203	70	328	1,167	240	68	78	32	50
TOTALS,	4,612	1,203	70	328	1,167	240	68	78	32	50

(1.) Whether inland or maritime.

The district is inland.

(2.) Average quantity of land cultivated on holdings at and under £4 valuation, under (*a*) oats, (*b*) potatoes, (*c*) meadow, (*d*) green crops.

On holdings of about £4 valuation there are usually about 2 statute acres under permanent meadow, and 2½ statute acres under cultivation, as follows:–

	Statute Measure.					
	A.	R.	P.	A.	R	P.
Potatoes,	1	0	20			
Oats or rye,	0	3	0	2	2	0
Meadow (1st crop),	0	2	0			
Turnips, cabbage,	0	0	20			
Permanent meadow,	2	0	0	2	0	0

(3.) Extent of mountain or moor grazing, and rights possessed by tenants, whether in common or otherwise.

There is no mountain or moor grazing in the district.

There are 2,482 acres of bog having a Poor Law Valuation of £20 on the Tredenick Estate, and in possession of the landlord's representative.

The tenants get permission to cut turf for their own use on applying for a bog ticket and paying 6*d.* or 1*s.*

(4.) Extent and description of land, if any, which could be profitably reclaimed and added to existing adjoining holdings.

If the tracts of bog above referred to were included in the tenants' holdings, or stripes of it, of from five to ten acres each, added to all holdings under £5 valuation, about 1,000 acres could be cultivated by the small landholders with profit to themselves.

The wild bog, when drained and properly treated, gives good crops in ordinary seasons when there are no spring frosts. The parts from which the turf would be cut off every year could be permanently improved and reclaimed.

(5.) Particulars as to any suitable land in district which could be obtained, and to which families could be migrated with a reasonable prospect of success.

There are no lands in the district suitable for migration.

There is some land near the village of Roosky, lying along the Shannon, from which tenants were evicted, and it has since been in the hands of the Receiver. Most of it is low-lying, and subject to flooding, and it is not suitable for resident agricultural tenants, but it would be of considerable value to some of the people in Roosky if parcelled out in stripes of sufficient extent to feed a cow the year round.

The farm of Ballykilcline, about four miles from Roosky Electoral Division, has been offered for sale. It is on the estate of Mr. Edward D. Beaumont Nesbitt, and contains about 150 Irish acres. It is held in fee-simple. The price asked is £2,400. The land is suitable for the purposes of migration, if it can be obtained at a reasonable price.

(6.) Method of cultivation, manures, rotation of crops, etc., etc.

A great part of the Electoral Division of Roosky is reclaimed bog, and one-third of the families live on holdings rated at and under £2. A great many small occupiers have no horned stock, and some of them never had any. They have succeeded in raising crops year after year by burning the bog soil, and adding to it as manure bog-mould, heath and rushes collected into cesspools or low places round the dwellings, and allowed to remain there to sour and decompose. Artificial manure is not much used. Clay is sometimes applied to the bog ground with very good results.

Lime when applied on dry bog land, produces very beneficial effect, but its use is not as general as it ought to be.

The crops grown are potatoes, oats or rye, turnips, cabbage, and rye grass. No rotation of crops is followed.

The cultivation is done almost entirely by manual labour.

(7.) General information with regard to stock, and suggestions as to improvement of breeds – (*a*) cattle, (*b*) sheep, (*c*) horses and donkeys, (*d*) pigs, (*e*) poultry, etc., etc.

The cattle kept are of very fair quality. Many of the young stock are sent to grazing farms outside the district for summer grazing. The bulls in use are of the Roscommon breed. The smaller classes of the Roscommon bulls obtainable would be suitable for the district, or bulls raised from pedigree Shorthorn bulls crossed with selected cows of the district.

There are no sheep kept, and there are very few horses.

There are a good many donkeys, the breed of which would be improved by crossing with Spanish stallion asses.

The people feed a good many pigs – in fact, pigs are the principal resource of the small occupiers, who have no cattle. They would be much improved by crossing with large Yorkshire boars.

The poultry are of the usual nondescript kind, and would be greatly improved if crossed with large but hardy poultry of good laying breeds.

(8.) Markets and fairs for cattle and produce of district; also statement as to where the people obtain food and other supplies, and the prevailing custom with regard to the disposal of butter, eggs, and poultry; to what extent are they sold in the first instance to local shopkeepers and dealers, and, generally speaking, how old are the eggs when sold to the first buyer, and about how old when they reach their ultimate destination in Great Britain.

The fairs and markets for this district are good. Longford is the principal market town. Some of the people go to Mohill markets. There is a weekly market at Roosky. The people obtain the greater part of their food supplies from shopkeepers in the village of Roosky, and they sell most of their eggs there. The poultry are sold in Longford and Mohill where there are very good fowl markets. The butter is sold in the Longford and Mohill markets. Eggs are usually about a week old when they reach their first buyer and about a fortnight old when they reach their destination in Great Britain.

(9.) Rail, steamer, sailing boat, road, postal and telegraph facilities.

The Shannon, which is navigable, forms the eastern boundary of this district. A steam boat passes twice weekly from Limerick to Carrick-on-Shannon.

Dromod railway station is only four miles distant. There is a telegraph office in the village of Dromod, and a post office in Roosky.

(10.) Employment for labourers in the district, whether temporary or constant, and rate of wage.

There is no employment for labourers in the district. A great many of the young people emigrate to America.

The population chiefly consists of elderly people and young persons under eighteen years of age. The proportion of able-bodied men and women is small.

Some persons get employment as farm servants in the adjoining county of Longford, and a small number get temporary employment in spring and harvest seasons in the adjacent non-congested Electoral Divisions. The rate of daily wages in hurried times is 1*s*. per day with diet. Strong boys from 15 to 18 years of age, get from £6 to £8 for spring and summer half-year as farm servants.

(11.) Migratory labour, average earnings per head, and where earned.

There are very few migratory labourers in the district. The best of the young people go to America. Sometimes young men who are anxious to emigrate and have not the necessary expenses, go to England for a few years and work there until they save sufficient to pay their passage to America.

(12.) Weaving, spinning, knitting, and sewing, whether used locally or sold, and where.

There is no weaving, spinning, knitting, or sewing done for sale. Most of the socks and stockings worn are made at home with purchased yarn. The underclothing worn is sewn at home. The people do not weave or spin.

(13.) Kelp-burning, and sale of seaweed.

The district is inland.

(14.) Sale of turf, nature and extent of bogs.

More than half the entire area of the district is bog in the hands of the representative of the landlord. The turf obtained from this bog is of excellent quality. Very few people sell turf, as the demand is limited, and the landlord's agent does not allow the tenants to cut turbary for sale unless they pay an extra price for it.

(15.) Lobster fishing, number of men and boats employed.

The district is inland.

(16.) Sea fishing. Facilities for sale of fish, and number of boats and men solely employed in fishing.

The district is inland.

(17.) Number of boats and men employed in carrying turf or seaweed or in fishing. Classification of boats.

The district is inland.

(18.) Fish; whether consumed at home or sold.

The district is inland.

(19.) Extent of fish-curing.

The district is inland.

(20.) Piers and Harbours, existing and suggested, and how far those existing are adapted to wants of district.

The district is inland.

(21.) Extent of salmon and freshwater fisheries. Number of men earning their livelihood therefrom.

There are no salmon or freshwater fisheries in this district.

(22.) Banks and Loan Funds.

There are branches of the Bank of Ireland, National, and Ulster Banks in Longford, and of the Hibernian and Northern Banks in Mohill.

There is a Loan Fund office in Mohill.

(23.) Mineral and other resources.

There are no mineral resources. Agriculture is the sole resource of the district.

(24.) Relative prevalence of cash or credit dealings, length of credit, interest charged, extent of barter, etc., etc.

Food supplies are generally obtained on credit. It is the prevailing custom to have a running account with the local shop-keepers, and to make substantial payments in reduction of account at least twice a year or after the sale of pigs, cattle, or farm produce. Credit is not given to as large an amount as was customary some years ago, and, as a rule, the shop-keepers are careful not to allow the indebtedness of a customer to exceed what they consider a safe limit. There is no uniform practice as regards the rate of interest charged on overdue accounts. It varies from five or six to twenty per cent. per annum.

Eggs are taken by local shop-keepers in exchange for groceries, flour, &c., but the sellers have the option of taking money for them if they so desire.

(25.) Estimated *cash* receipts and expenditure of a family in ordinary circumstances.

The receipts and expenditure of a family of six persons living on a holding of about £4, fully stocked, would be as follows:–

RECEIPTS	£	s.	d.	EXPENDITURE	£	s.	d.
Sale of cattle, . .	7	0	0	Indian meal for family, pigs and fowl, . .	5	0	0
„ pigs, . . .	6	0	0	Fowl, . .	3	10	0
„ butter,. . .	3	0	0	Oatmeal, . .	0	10	0
„ oats, . . .	2	10	0	Tea and sugar, . .	2	10	0
„ eggs and about 1 dozen chickens . .	4	10	0	American bacon, . .	1	10	0
Balance to be met by savings from wages earned or money received from members of family who have emigrated . .	4	16	0	Tobacco for man, . .	1	6	0
				Young pigs (generally two, sometimes three), average .	1	10	0
				Candles, soap, oil, blue, starch, etc.,	1	10	0
				Salt fish and sundries, .	0	10	0
				Clothes and boots – Man, ... 2 5 0; Wife, ... 1 10 0; Children, . . 2 0 0	5	15	0
				Rent and Country Cess,	4	5	0
	£27	16	0		£27	16	0

The receipts and expenditure of a family of six persons living on a holding of about £2 valuation would be as follows:–

RECEIPTS	£	s.	d.	EXPENDITURE	£	s.	d.
Sale of pigs, . .	6	0	0	Indian meal, . .	4	10	0
„ oats, . . .	1	10	0	Flour, . .	2	0	0
„ straw, . . .	1	10	0	Oatmeal, . .	0	10	0
„ eggs and poultry, .	4	10	0	Tea and sugar, . .	2	0	0
Deficiency to be met by savings from wages earned or money received from members of family who have emigrated . .	6	2	0	Bacon, . .	1	0	0
				Clothes – man, wife and children,	3	0	0
				Tobacco for man, . .	1	5	0
				Candles, soap, etc., . .	0	10	0
				Salt fish, salt, etc., . .	0	10	0
				2 young pigs, . .	1	10	0
				Rent and County Cess, .	2	2	0
	£19	12	0		£19	12	0

N.B. – It will be observed that no allowances are made for casualities, or casual expenses, such as doctor's fees, priest's dues, &c. The failure of the potato crop or the absence of sufficient live stock, would very considerably reduce the receipts as stated above.

(26.) Estimated value of home-grown food consumed, and period during which it lasts.

The estimated value of home-grown food on a holding valued at about £4 is as follows:–

	£	s.	d.
Potatoes (when crop is average), last from August to April,	10	0	0
Milk and eggs, and some butter,	4	0	0
Cabbage,	0	10	0
	£14	10	0

(27.) Dietary of people, number of meals daily, and kinds of food throughout the year.

The dietary of the people, number of meals daily, and kinds of food throughout the year, may be summarised as follows:–

From April to August –

Breakfast.– Potatoes and milk.

Dinner.– Potatoes and milk, sometimes bread and tea after. Occasionally potatoes and cabbage seasoned with the fried fat of a small piece of American bacon. Salt herrings are sometimes used with potatoes.

Supper.– Indianmeal stirabout and milk, or potatoes and milk.

From August to April –

Breakfast.– Indianmeal stirabout and milk; sometimes bread and tea.

Dinner.– Bread and tea; the man occasionally has a couple of eggs when working hard.

Supper.– Same as for breakfast.

A great many of the small landholders in this district have not a milch cow, and their dietary is very much poorer than stated above.

They sometimes eat their stirabout with sugar alone, or they substitute for milk thin oatmeal porridge, or a thin sauce made with boiled flour. Their dinner frequently consists of potatoes and salt herrings, or potatoes and flour-sauce seasoned with a small piece of American bacon boiled in it.

(28.) Clothing, whether home-made or bought, etc., etc.

Excepting socks and stockings, all their clothing is bought.

(29.) Dwellings: kind of houses, home-life and customs, etc., etc.

The houses are built of stone and mortar, and thatched. They usually contain two rooms and a kitchen, and are comparatively well kept. The old couple generally sleep in one of the rooms, the girls in another, and the boys in a settle-bed in the kitchen.

There are very few dairies, and those who have milk and butter keep them in one of the sleeping rooms.

The live stock are rarely kept in the dwelling-houses.

(30.) Character of the people for industry, etc., etc.

The people are industrious, and the majority of them make the most of the limited resources at their command.

(31.) Whether any organized effort has been made to develop the resources or improve the condition of the people. If so, by what means.

No organized effort has been made to develop the resources or improve the condition of the people.

(32.) Suggestions as to any possible method for improving the condition of the people in future.

Of the 240 families in this district, 146 occupy holdings valued at, and under £4.

Unless a considerable number of these small landholders leave the district or get their holdings enlarged, no substantial improvement in their condition can be effected, as there does not appear to be any reasonable hope of the possibility of establishing remunerative industrial work.

If suitable lands were available, about eighty families ought to be migrated from Roosky in order to give those who remained a chance of living in decent comfort. Excepting the lands of Ballykilcline, etc., referred to in this report, there is no land likely to be available within reasonable distance, and these lands would only accommodate a few families.

Homes were clustered together throughout congested districts, occupied by families who were usually interrelated.

The area of the district is 4,612 acres. Of this, about 2,482 acres are bog land in the landlord's possession, in the undermentioned townlands:–

—	Area.			Poor Law Valuation.		
	A.	R.	P.	£	*s.*	*d.*
Ballymagrine,	91	1	2	1	0	0
Cloonaufill,	99	3	22	1	0	0
Cloonfad,	200	0	26	3	0	0
Cloonfower,	160	3	14	2	0	0
Cloonshannagh,	486	1	21	2	0	0
Cuilbeg,	265	2	10	1	5	0
Derrymoylin,	366	3	10	2	5	0
Kilbarry,	602	2	28	5	15	0
Meelick,	208	0	15	1	15	0
	2,481	2	28	£20	0	0

If the tenants on the Tredenick estate, on which the bogs above referred to are situate, purchased their holdings under the Land Purchase Acts, and that these bogs were bought from the landlord by the Congested Districts Board and apportioned amongst the tenants, giving those who have the smallest holdings the best division of bog, it would then be possible to improve the resources of all the very small landholders. This "wild bog," when drained, limed, and well cultivated, yields good crops except in years when there are late spring frosts, and I consider that the most feasible means of improving the condition of the poorer people in Roosky would be to enlarge their present holdings by the addition of stripes of this bog, and to promote the improvement and cultivation of it by giving small grants for the making of drains; and to erect and work a lime-kiln in the district from which lime would be supplied at a low price.

It is possible that the landlord may be willing to sell the bog at any time to the Congested Districts Board for the enlargement of the tenants' holdings, but I did not feel justified in making enquiries relative to this, not knowing if the suggestion would meet with the approval of the Congested Districts Board.

The turbary on this large area is of good quality. The river Shannon forms the eastern boundary of the district, and I am of opinion that, owing to the special facilities for the cheap transport of the turf afforded by the proximity of this extensive bog to the Shannon, which is navigable, that remunerative employment could be afforded for many years to all the small landholders in cutting and saving turf; if arrangements for the transport and sale of it, at various centres on the Shannon, were put into operation by the Congested Districts Board.

The cut-away bog could be permanently reclaimed and made very good land; and, if all the turf the people could cut and save every year, could be disposed of at a price that would return from 6*d.* to 1*s.* per day for the young and able-bodied persons respectively employed at it, the condition of the people and their resources would be immensely improved in a few years.

HENRY DORAN,
Inspector.

31st January, 1895.

To

The Congested Districts Board for Ireland.

CONGESTED DISTRICTS BOARD FOR IRELAND

COUNTIES OF MAYO, GALWAY, ROSCOMMON, AND SLIGO

GENERAL REPORT OF MR. DORAN, *Inspector*

ON

THE UNDERMENTIONED DISTRICTS

STATISTICAL TABLE

DISTRICTS DEALT WITH IN SEPARATE REPORTS.	Area in Statute Acres.	Poor Law Valuation.	Number of Ratings at and under £10 and above £4 Valuation.	Number of Ratings at and under £4 Valuation.	Population in 1891.	Number of Families in 1891.	Number of Families on Holdings exceeding £2 and under £4 Valuation.	Number of Families on Holdings at and under £2 Valuation.	Number of Families in very poor circumstances.	Number of Families which have no Cattle.
		£							* about	about
Ballaghaderreen,	62,767	20,934	1,343	2,468	20,039	3,842	1,129	1,119	605	350
Tobercurry,	72,127	18,348	1,214	2,217	17,663	3,388	900	676	560	300
Foxford,	26,436	8,125	473	815	7,351	1,414	471	267	230	120
Swinford,	80,384	21,364	1,353	3,478	26,998	5,017	1,660	887	900	300
Kiltamagh,	11,300	3,069	243	702	4,292	805	215	250	170	100
Ballyhaunis,	53,879	16,186	1,042	1,785	14,935	2,654	839	385	415	300
Dunmore,	26,952	9,833	615	833	7,854	1,458	379	352	230	100
Glennamaddy,	38,236	10,843	771	1,354	9,509	1,803	508	360	305	200
Castlerea,	52,098	12,751	901	1,861	12,007	2,329	935	842	400	200
Claremorris,	9,027	4,605	266	507	3,776	686	138	220	60	50
Ardnaree,	50,496	12,030	698	1,520	11,097	1,975	605	468	300	200
TOTALS,	483,702	138,088	8,919	17,540	135,521	25,371	7,779	5,826	4,175	2,220

* These summarised figures have been revised, and they differ somewhat from the detailed figures given in the separate Reports on these districts.

Migratory labour.

In the above-mentioned districts, the habits of life, circumstances and resources of the people, are practically identical. These districts, covering some hundreds of square miles of poor land, are, I think, the most thickly populated in Ireland; and, supply the greater number of the migratory labourers who proceed to England every year.

From the Ballaghaderreen Railway Station, and the stations along the line, from Ballina to Castlerea, about 14,000 "harvest-men" go annually to England. They remain there from three to nine months; and the average amount of money saved out of their earnings, and brought, or sent home, would be about £8 per head, or £112,000 annually. An agent of the London North Western Railway Company informed me that from 20,000 to 22,000 "harvest-men" go to England from the west of Ireland.

Many objections are urged against the conditions of life here, which have made the people migratory labourers; but it is apparent that such a change in their resources and habits of life at home, as would enable them to earn what they draw from the English labour market, would have to be very great indeed.

Agriculture – method of cultivation, manures, crops, etc., etc.

The lands in the occupation of the small farmers in these districts may be aptly compared to a valuable mine, worked with the most antiquated machinery by an owner, possessing neither sufficient capital, nor skill to develop its resources.

Agriculture – method of cultivation, manures, crops, etc., etc.

Without assuming a high standard of skill, or requiring any additional labour beyond that now available, the gross produce derived from these small farms could be doubled.

This result would be accomplished if the people could be got to till the land already in cultivation in a husbandlike manner, keep it free from weeds, give it adequate manuring, sow good seeds; grow a variety of crops, especially soilage crops for feeding their cattle largely in houses in summer, so as to make manure, and supplement the inferior food obtained from their poor pastures; grow root crops for feeding their cattle in winter; drain, reclaim, or otherwise improve the bad land on their holdings; exercise care in the selection of breeding stock, keeping only those animals for breeding purposes that are well shaped, sound, and best adapted to the holding; pay special attention to the production of poultry and eggs; and, in fact, learn to make the most of everything their lands can produce.

One of the most frequent primary causes of their poverty is want of sufficient manure to grow good crops, and keep their lands in a productive state. Good tillage farming is impossible without a means of making manure. Bad land cannot be permanently improved without good cultivation and high manuring. The manure heap is the *backbone* of the farm.

The small farmer here rarely tries to grow any crops, except about one Irish acre of potatoes, the same extent of oats, a plot of cabbage, and occasionally a small plot of turnips. The cow or two he keeps are allowed to live as best they can in summer on the poor pastures of worn out land, and in winter they are barely kept alive with the bad fare they get, consisting of straw or hay, without roots. His cattle are seldom thrifty or profitable, and those he sells are disposed of at low prices. Very few keep sufficient stock to make manure enough for the land under potatoes, and all use artificial manure largely. As all grow much about the same extent of potatoes, the poorer the man is, the more artificial manure he uses; and the systematic use, in large quantities, of those stimulating manures has had a most exhaustive effect on the soil.

The manure made on the small holdings is largely composed of bog-mould or "black-mud" which is brought from the bogs in harvest time and placed to *sour* in an excavated pit, which is generally located in front of the dwelling-houses. The excrements of the live stock are also put into this pit and mixed with the "black-mud." Persons who have sufficient live stock make good manure in this way; but there are a great many, especially in the very poor districts, who have few or no cattle, and who, year after year, plant three roods or an Irish acre of potatoes and have no better manure than the *soured* "black-mud" and a couple of bags of artificial manure. With such treatment the potato will always be an exceptionally precarious crop for those people in poor circumstances, and by whom it is most keenly felt. In ordinary tillage-farming the manured root-crop is nearly all consumed on the farm by stock, and there is mud manure made to improve the land; but in these Congested Districts where manure is so essential for the permanent improvement of the land almost the only root-crop grown is potatoes, and they are chiefly consumed by the people.

Anyone knowing these districts cannot fail to be struck with the primitive and slovenly manner in which the cultivation of the land is attempted, and the thriftless appearance of the people, the live stock, and the houses and their surroundings.

I was hopeful after the passing of the Act of 1881, that the small farmers would set about working and improving their holdings, and gradually alter their systems of agriculture; but speaking generally, there is no improvement perceptible. However, since the passing of the Land Act, excepting the last two years, this part of the country has been in a state of violent agrarian agitation, which prevented the people from settling down.

I have often pictured to myself what a different appearance the country would present in a few years, if every landholder could be got to interest himself in his holding; and, knowing that any improvements he now made were secured to him by Law, that he would aim at making a "garden" of his farm, and that each one would vie with his neighbour to see who would do his work best.

In considering any scheme of agricultural development, the most formidable difficulties that present themselves, arise from the peculiarities of the people. Their migratory habits make them careless and improvident, and when they return home, after some months of hard work in England, they are more disposed to rest than to turn their attention to the improvement of their land.

Agriculture – method of cultivation, manures, crops, etc., etc.

It requires a powerful influence to induce them to change a custom, or to do anything for themselves in a different manner to that in which they always saw it done. But if a *modus operandi* can be applied to them, which will create a general desire to work to improve their position, give them hope in their own efforts, and engender such a spirit of emulation as will cause them to vie with each other in the improvement of their land and their homes, general poverty or periodic famine would be unheard of in these districts.

It will not be sufficient to enumerate their faults and failings and point out the remedies. All their failings do not arise from ignorance. Thousands of migratory labourers work year after year with farmers in England, on perhaps the best farmed land in the world, and yet they do not try to imitate the English system of culture. What then is to be done with them?

They must be both *driven* and *led* to do what is for their benefit, and once they can be got to move on the road to progress, successful results are insured.

As to the methods which would be likely to incite the farmers into adopting better systems of agriculture, I would suggest, that a number of intelligent, successful small farmers, or the better class of the men who fill the position of land-stewards on gentlemen's farms be employed at a salary of about £150 a year, and that each one be placed in charge of a Parish, or of a district covering as many cases as it would be found, after some experience, he could exercise efficient supervision over.

That these men, who shall be called Agriculturists, make themselves intimately acquainted with the people and circumstances of their district.

That the Board shall invite, by public announcement, the landholders of the districts to avail themselves of the advice and direction of the Agriculturists in the management of their land.

To engender a spirit of emulation, and attract the people to follow the advice of the Agriculturist, two or more prizes should be offered to the small occupiers of land in each townland, to be competed for by those in the townland, who, at the beginning of the year or other stated time, made application to the Board to enter into competition against each other, on the understanding that the competitor who followed most carefully and successfully the teachings of the Agriculturist would be accorded the prize.

The person who won, say, three prizes in his own townland could not again compete in the same way; but he could compete for a more valuable prize offered to all those in an Electoral Division, who had previously carried off their townland prizes; and to maintain the spirit of rivalry, I would have, say, one valuable prize – such as a bull, for each county or union, to be competed for by all prizemen in that district.

To teach them the advantage of sowing good seed the Agriculturist could order for his competitors, or advise them to get, every year, from respectable merchants, small quantities of seed such as half a cwt. of imported oats, and same weight of potatoes, besides other seeds. The amount paid for these small quantities would not be much, but the farmer would find that by buying a few stones of seed every year, and preserving the yield of the first two years, he would be able to sow his main crop the third year with the produce of the new seed.

It would be desirable that the Agriculturist should reside in a central place in his district, and, if convenient, the sires supplied by the Board should be placed under his charge, so as to bring him in every way in close contact with the people.

To give an idea of the probable expense of working a prize scheme such as I suggest, I would say it would be from £3 to £5 for each townland. There are in the Swinford Union 401 townlands, of which 384 are in scheduled Electoral Divisions. It would require about £2,000 a year to work actively such a prize scheme as I have outlined throughout the entire Swinford Union. It would be desirable to hold annual agricultural shows in a few convenient centres.

The Board is no doubt aware that a scheme of agricultural improvement has been inaugurated by the Royal Dublin Society in the Swinford district. The Society has placed a "Practical Instructor" there, whose duty is to go amongst the people and advise them how they ought to cultivate their lands. To afford practical demonstration of his teaching, he has got a few of the farmers in different districts to set apart about one statute acre of their land upon which they carry out a rotation of crops. The Society supplies the seeds and artificial

Agriculture – method of cultivation, manures, crops, etc., etc.

manures for these example plots, and the farmer gets the produce and a prize for carrying out the directions of the Instructor. The seeds and manure of each plot costs about £5. I visited all the example holdings (eleven) with the Practical Instructor, and was pleased to see how carefully his instructions had been carried out. I do not think, however, this will be found an effective method of introducing better systems of Agriculture. The expense of maintaining an example plot is too great to make them numerous, and the fact of seeing a man working a small patch of his farm in a certain manner, for which he is well paid, and the remainder of his land in the same way as his neighbours, is not calculated to induce outsiders to apply the example plot system of culture to their holdings. No doubt, if in time, the owners of these plots became convinced of the advantages of the new method of cultivation, and extended it to the whole of their farms, their neighbours would rapidly follow their example.

If, in connection with the Prize Scheme, which I suggest, the Board's resources permitted them to give loans to tenants at a low rate of interest, for the drainage and reclamation of their lands, such work to be carried out under the direct supervision of the Board's Agriculturist, no more effective means could be adopted to stimulate the people to improve their lands.

At present, tenants of holdings at and over £7 valuation can borrow money from the Board of Works for land improvement, the smallest sum advanced being £50, and the largest five times the gross Poor Law Valuation of farm. The loan is repaid in 22 years by half-yearly instalments at rate of 6½ per cent.

The Board of Works advance money for road making, house building, fencing, and many other works, which although often desirable, are seldom remunerative. The rate of interest is high and there is no attempt at efficient supervision. For these reasons the Board of Works loans have been more of an injury than a benefit to many of the small farmers who got them.

The results would be very different if the work were laid out and superintended by an experienced Agriculturist, and nothing attempted except what was certain to prove remunerative. Ten or fifteen pounds worth of labour judiciously expended on a small holding in drainage would make a marked improvement in it, and the money earned would help the tenant to purchase additional live stock.

Dwellings – kind of houses, home life and customs, etc., etc.

The home life and customs, etc., of the peasantry, as described in my separate reports on these districts, indicate the necessity of compelling the people to improve the character and surroundings of their homes.

The Government should make the Police the Sanitary Officers, and require them to enforce the Sanitary laws, viz.:– No person should be allowed to keep cattle, pigs, or fowl in their dwellings; a manure heap should not be kept within 20 yards of a dwelling; the houses should be whitewashed inside and out at least once a year; it should be illegal to keep milk or butter in a sleeping apartment.

There is no use attempting to teach the people to make good butter while they keep the milk in bedrooms, and make the butter in a dirty house.

General information with regard to stock – cattle, and poultry.

I have already explained that these lands cannot be properly cultivated in the absence of sufficient live stock.

A Law should be passed making it illegal for the owner of a sire of any description to offer him for service to the public, without having previously obtained a certificate as to soundness and suitability from some Government Officer.

It should also be declared to be illegal to breed from any animal possessing hereditary disease.

Cattle.– One of the greatest obstacles to agricultural development in these districts will be the large number of persons who are too poor to keep sufficient cattle on their holdings, while many have none. When a cow dies with one of the poorer people the loss so cripples their resources, that they often "can't get into stock" again, for years.

General information with regard to stock – cattle, and poultry.

If the Board would be disposed to help the really needy to obtain cattle, they could, I think, do so without loss, in the following way:–

To ascertain how much the person requiring aid could contribute towards the purchase of a cow, and oblige him to lodge that amount with the Board. The Board would then add what was necessary to procure one.

The Board's district Agriculturist would afterwards attend a fair accompanied by the person for whom the cow was intended, and having got a suitable one, would get the letters C.D.B. branded with a flesh brand on the hip or loin and burn a number on the horn for registration purposes.

Anyone getting a cow in this way would enter into an agreement to pay for her by instalments, and she would not become his property until all instalments were paid.

To prevent the cattle from being disposed of dishonestly, a public notice should be posted throughout the country stating that all those branded C.D.B. were the property of the Congested Districts Board, and warning all persons against purchasing them, unless the individual offering such for sale produced an official certificate stating that the animal having register No.– on horn had been purchased from the Congested Districts Board. The certificate would be issued by the Board after the loan was paid, and it should afterwards pass with the animal on changing ownership.

Poultry.– The circumstances of the small farmers give them exceptional advantages for carrying on poultry farming extensively and successfully. I am unable to discover any cause, beyond their own control, why they cannot compete with foreign countries in the production of fowl and eggs. If poultry farming could be established as an industry, it would be a great boon to the occupiers of small patches of land who could give it special attention.

The average small farmer keeps about twenty hens from which he sells about £3 worth of eggs yearly. The chickens are sold at from 3*d.* to 6*d.* each; ducks from 6*d.* to 8*d.* each; geese 1*s.* 8*d.* to 2*s.* 6*d.* each; turkeys 2*s.* to 3*s.* each. Only a small proportion of the people keep other fowl than hens.

As an example of what might be done, I would refer you to the Report on "Cottagers' Poultry in the West of Ireland" – [Appendix A] – prepared for me by the Rev. J. C. Smith, a Presbyterian clergyman who lives near Ballaghaderreen, and who has for over twenty years taken a special interest in poultry. He keeps all the well-known breeds, and is a successful exhibitor at Shows.

He quotes the case of a neighbouring woman, living on a farm at £4 5*s.* rent, who used to keep about forty of the common hens, and made about £9 a year out of their produce. She got some good fowl from him, which she found so profitable, that she increased her stock from forty to sixty and her sales from £9 to £18 a year.

The Rev. J. C. Smith is the best authority I know of on poultry, and I would direct your special attention to the suggestions contained in his notes. They are useful and practical.

The eggs sold from these districts bring the lowest price in the English markets, and yet the value of the eggs annually exported from Swinford, Ballaghaderreen, and Ballyhaunis amounts to about £70,000.

An improvement in quality, and increase in quantity, of even 20 per cent. would represent a substantial addition to the resources of the people.

Suggestions as to any possible method for improving the conditions of the people in future.

The means herein indicated of permanently improving the condition of the people would be within the reach of all land-holders in the Congested Districts; but the increased profits arising therefrom would not be sufficient to bring about a material improvement in the circumstances of persons having only a few acres of land, or those whose Poor Law Valuation did not exceed £3 or £4. The conditions of the latter cannot be substantially improved except by

(*a*) Migration.
(*b*) The establishment of home industries.
(*c*) The establishment of factories.

Migration. – In these districts there is little land suitable for migration purposes; and in

Suggestions as to any possible method for improving the conditions of the people in future.

some of the adjoining districts, where there are large tracts of grazing land, I failed to discover any instance in which it would be sold on reasonable terms.

If the Board desired to promote migration they could readily ascertain if land were available by issuing an advertisement inviting offers. There are many large grazing farms let by owners on eleven months' letting, which have been paying very badly for the last four or five years, and which, perhaps, could be purchased on favourable terms, as only one party (the landlord) would have to be dealt with.

If such lands were secured, the only way, to my mind, in which migration could be successfully worked, would be to offer allotments of the acquired land on conditions which would attract the *largest* land-holders from the Congested Districts, leaving their farms available for the enlargement of the adjacent small holdings. In this way several families may be benefitted by the removal of one family.

The land-holder who has had sufficient land to enable him to live upon it without leaving home, is a much more desirable person to transfer to better land, than the migratory labourer, who has no capital, and who is unsettled in his habits.

Furthermore, the man possessing some means, who has lived as a *farmer* in a Congested District, will be much more anxious to change to better land than the migratory labourer; and the latter will prefer having his old holding enlarged, or to get a new one similar to his own, in the same district, where he would be near his friends to help him in times of adversity or in hurried seasons.

The reclamation of waste lands for migratory purposes is impracticable under ordinary conditions. The fencing, levelling, and draining would almost amount to as much as the purchase money of medium arable land. Crops cannot be grown on waste land without manure, and as it could not support cattle to make manure before it was reclaimed and cropped, people could not live upon it.

The lands most suitable for migration are indifferent grazing which are in need of tillage, and paying very little in grass. Large tracts of this character are to be found everywhere in the West of Ireland outside the Congested Districts. It would be for the benefit of the country and State to have such lands in the occupation of working farmers, who would cultivate them, and get from them produce worth at least four times what they yield under grass. The present occupiers cannot till with profit, but working farmers having the labour in their own families can do so.

Where migration is not carried out, the most effectual means of improving the condition of the people would be in the establishment of home industries. I cannot write with authority on this matter, but in pursuing my enquiries, I have been much disappointed at the few industries that could be named as likely to prove suitable and successful.

Home Industries. – The wonderful state of perfection to which machinery has been brought of late years seems to have left little remunerative work for the idle hands of the cottage homes.

I do not know that there is a rural district in Ireland so thickly populated as the portion of the country I write of, or one where there are so many persons idle for four months of the year. If any home industries could be promoted, which would enable the mothers and daughters to employ themselves, when not engaged at household duties, at work that would bring 3*s.* or 4*s.* a week for each of their homes, they need have no dread of famine.

The only industries I can name are – knitting by machines, hand-made underclothing and such needlework, and handloom weaving.

The Nuns of the Convent of Ballaghaderreen are making a great effort to establish a knitting factory, and, as far as I can judge, with every prospect of success.

In October, 1891, they purchased some knitting machines and got from the North of Ireland a skilled person as instructor to teach the workers. They commenced with a few girls, they have now fifty-six employed, and most of these have become so skilful that their work will compare favourably with any in the trade, and the nuns are at present unable to meet the demands for their goods. One or two English firms have taken up the sale of the goods, and are ready to take more than they can at present be supplied with.

Suggestions as to any possible method for improving the conditions of the people in future.

The Nuns cannot extend the business very rapidly, as every additional worker put on has to be taught. I have no doubt they will succeed in establishing a large factory, if they so desire.

If supported by the Congested Districts Board, they would be desirous to make their workroom a Technical School to educate the girls from the country to become skilful in the use of the machine, and when they had learned to turn out good work, the Nuns hope to be able to help those girls to purchase knitting machines, which they would work in their own homes.

What a desirable change would be wrought in the home life of the people if the cattle were all evicted from the dwelling houses and the part of the kitchen they occupy fitted up as a workroom, and with a good big window in the gable to admit plenty of light and air!

I believe it would be easy to extend this industry to cottage homes, and the Ballaghaderreen Congested District may yet become famous for the production of socks, stockings, and other hosiery goods. Attached hereto is a sheet containing some statistical information bearing on the matter. [See Appendix B].

At the Ballaghaderreen Convent the Nuns are also trying to establish a hand-sewing industry, but it would appear that it takes a considerable time for a person to become sufficiently skilful to earn remunerative wages, and many girls can never be made really good needle women.

The Nuns of Swinford Convent have an old schoolroom about 40 feet by 18 which they would be anxious to convert into a Technical School for teaching handloom weaving.

It is a small room to use for this purpose, but it might be large enough to make a beginning in. The Nuns here would desire to work on the same lines as at Ballaghaderreen, using their school as a place were the girls from the country districts would learn to produce good marketable work, and when they had become skilful workers, they would return to their homes and be provided with a handloom, which they would become owners of by small weekly or monthly payments.

If an expert on Industrial work visited those places, I have no doubt many other suitable industries, besides those referred to, would be found feasible. But I do not see how any industry can be established without Technical Schools, which should be under the control of the Board. The Nuns of the Convents named are most anxious to assist in promoting home industries, but they cannot be good teachers, as they do not possess technical knowledge. Placing the supervision and control of the workers under the care of the Nuns in these districts, by locating the Technical Schools on the Convent premises might be very desirable, and could be open to no objection, as the entire of the poor people are Roman Catholics. The Board might see their way to provide good teachers in the Schools and organisers to visit the cottages and direct the work.

The land about Foxford is very bad, and little of it capable of profitable improvement.

The Electoral Division of Sraheen, Ballina Union, and convenient to Foxford, is exceptionally bad, better adapted for afforesting than agricultural purposes. Unless a great many persons be removed from that Electoral Division, the condition of the small occupiers of land cannot be improved, except by the establishment of home industries.

Factories. – In Foxford the Nuns have expended several thousand pounds in the erection of buildings and machinery for a woollen factory. (As several members of the Board have recently visited this establishment I need not enter into details with reference to it.)

The woollen factory, if successfully worked, will give employment to a considerable number convenient to the above town. The Nuns would also be glad to start a Technical School as proposed for Swinford and Ballaghaderreen Convents.

In Ballyhaunis there is a small boot factory carried on very successfully by men named McNamara. They employ about twenty hands. They informed me that, if they had capital to erect a large workroom, they could immediately enlarge their business, and rapidly increase the number of employees. They built a very good shop and dwelling house last year out of profits made from their business.

If the Board could assist enterprising persons in the establishment of industries such as boot-making, etc., etc., by giving loans on easy terms for the erection of workshops, and providing of machinery, when reasonable safe security is forthcoming, I believe such help would be the means of starting many industries.

HENRY DORAN,
Inspector.

30th April, 1892.

To

The Congested Districts Board for Ireland.

APPENDICES TO GENERAL REPORT OF
MR. DORAN, DATED APRIL 30, 1892.

APPENDIX A

REPORT BY THE REV. J. C. SMITH

ON

COTTAGERS' POULTRY IN THE WEST OF IRELAND.

Hens. – The ordinary fowls in the hands of the cottagers and small farmers in the greater parts of Mayo, Sligo, Leitrim, and Roscommon, are a small nondescript class of birds, which have been in-bred for generations, and reduced in both size and vitality. They are something like what one would expect from a cross of moderate barndoor fowls and a bantam. They are fairly good layers of small eggs, which, as a rule, are white in colour. These fowls have been, in many instances, bred for several years from the same stock, without any infusion of fresh blood. This poor, short-sighted system of breeding has reduced the birds in every respect. They are worse layers, their eggs are reduced in size, and they are less hardy, and very much more subject to disease.

When I first saw these fowls, fourteen years ago, when I had the opportunity of visiting a number of places all over the West, they were a much better class than they are now, owing to the bad effects of continuous in-breeding. Disease broke out in the majority of yards, which in a few weeks carried off ninety per cent. of the poultry. I examined several for people who sent them to me for the purpose. The majority died of Enteritis (inflammation of the bowels) which was brought on by tubercular disease, the result of in-breeding. As I had all the leading varieties, I was able to give eggs in exchange for others, to all who would accept them. I have given Brahmas of both varieties, Langshans, Plymouth Rocks, Wyandottes, Minorcas, Leghorns, Dorkings, Houdans, and Hamburgs, to all who came for them. The result of the cross of any of these breeds in the common fowl was very noticeable. In many cases the result of the cross would give an ordinary observer the idea that they were pure bred. I think the best way I can explain is to give a few cases.

Mrs. C. had in 1884 about forty hens of the small breed; they laid so far as I could find out, about 110 eggs each in a year, which she sold at about ½*d.* each. The rent of the farm was £4 5*s.* 0*d.*, and she was well pleased to think she could make double the rent on her forty hens. The eggs went to supply groceries, &c., for her family. The eggs were small, but as all the eggs in the country were small, she got them sold. The profit on this flock of hens would be about £9 a year. They were not very good winter layers, so she did not realize much when eggs were scarce and dear. In 1886 she lost about thirty hens; as well as I can remember the disease left her only seven hens; I gave her two sittings of Brown Leghorns, which, being a small, easily fed breed, she thought most suitable. She reared sixteen birds, only six of which were pullets. She bred in 1887 from the cockerels, and her old breed, and the result in 1888 was that her hens laid about 140 eggs each, and they were fairly good winter layers. She told me the Leghorns were "warm little hens, the cold does not go through them," meaning that Leghorns and Leghorn crosses would lay in severe weather, when her own small, in-bred lot ceased to lay. Finding the merits of the Leghorns, she increased her stock to about sixty hens, and was able to make about £18 a year, about double what she did formerly. Leghorns have since become very popular.

Mr. G. one day came to me and asked a few eggs from the breed which "crowed so well." This was a hard matter to settle, as I could not tell whether King Brahma, or the noble-looking Langshan excelled in this respect. He wanted a cock to crow, like those he could hear so plainly at his own house, over a mile off. I gave him two sittings, made up of Brahmas, Langshans, Dorkings, and Plymouth Rocks. The last time I passed his place, he showed me about sixty splendid fowls, bred from his own stock, and Plymouth Rocks and Langshan Cocks. There were a number of pure Plymouth Rocks, and a couple of Brahmas. He was proud of a nice Plymouth Rock Cock, which satisfied him in the line of crowing, but he found that he got more than he expected, for his hens laid more than double the number of eggs last winter that he usually got from the original stock. He was pleased with them in every way. "They were twice as good for killing, and far better than the small breed for laying, and the eggs were better and larger." This man did not sell many chickens, he was a good feeder, and had much taste, and like most people who take an interest in their stock, he was pretty well-to-do. He did not like the idea of selling fine large cockerels at a low price, so he sent none to market, but when it was known that he had good fowls, people from town sent to him, and gave him 1*s.* each for chickens when his neighbours sold theirs at 4*d.* each. From this I conclude that if the people would rear good fowls, there would be no trouble in getting up good markets.

Diseases. – The so-called "plague" is merely Enteritis, or inflammation of the bowels in every case I have investigated, and I have examined scores of fowls from different parts of Ireland. In the majority of cases I found tubercule, and the Enteritis was merely the result of tubercule. In all these birds I found Indian meal and potatoes where death occurred in a few hours after the attack, and on enquiry I found almost all were fed on this food. In-breeding tends to bring on tubercule, so do small, crowded, ill-ventilated poultry houses. In short, anything which tends to lower vitality increases the liability to contract this frightful disease, which is not only transmitted to the progeny, but to those who use the affected fowls or their eggs, in the same way as the milk of diseased cows will bring on consumption. The only way to remedy this is to clear out the whole stock, and start anew, taking, of course, precautions that the new stock will have a clean, healthy, well-ventilated apartment, and that good food only shall be used, and plenty of grit given. I need not recommend a lot of valuable foods to poor people, such as barley meal, buckwheat, &c., &c.; such feeding stuffs are beyond their reach. But there is an excellent food within the reach of all – good sound oats. Every man who has a little farm can take a sack of oats to the mill, get it dried and ground (without sifting or taking off any dust). This is far ahead of Indian meal, and it is cheaper. If potatoes are abundant, let them be boiled every morning and some ground oats mixed into them for the first feed. At mid-day some table scraps may be given, and in the evening a full feed of oats; not small; but good, heavy oats. On such feeding all fowls worth having will do well, and those which will not thrive on the food of the country have nothing valuable about them for peasants.

I think your method of distributing pure bred birds an excellent one, but I think something might be done in the way of giving practical instruction, such as lectures. At present little can be done in the way of distributing cockerels. Those who breed fancy fowls usually dispose of all their cockerels before the month of March. All that can now be done is to supply sittings of eggs, which can be very easily and cheaply done. They can be sent by Parcels Post for 6*d.* per sitting to any part of the country. Where a sitting of eggs is given, it might be arranged that all the cockerels, except one or two, could be bought at 1*s.* or 2*s.* each and given to others. The larger breeds should be set as soon as possible, but such as Leghorns can be hatched any time up to the 1st of July, and they will be good for breeding the following season. I would not advise goose or turkey eggs to be supplied in this way. These are fowls which only lay a sitting of eggs each, and breeders will not part with their best eggs. Those who merely keep geese and turkeys to sell their eggs rarely keep a good article; it is only from breeders that good geese or turkeys can be got, and they will not part with their best eggs. But ducks and hens lay an immense number of eggs, and all the breeders I know will give their best hen and duck eggs. I have got turkeys' eggs three times from England from the leading breeders, and none of them produced even moderate birds. Last year I got eggs from a bird which won 32 First Prizes and 6 Cups. The result was one bird – a small pullet, only 10 lbs. weight. I would therefore advise you to avoid supplying either goose or turkey eggs.

Perhaps it might be wise to try and get school teachers, who have accommodation, to breed a few fowls, that their pupils might have practical instruction, or at least see them and know their merits. Ten years ago I urged the National Board to print a book on the subject for use in Schools, instead of the ridiculous nonsense they have before the public (teaching, for instance, that a goose will lay 100 eggs in a year). I still hold that the National Board should publish a useful annual on fowls, and have the subject taught in connection with Agriculture.

The breeds I consider best suited for peasants, are Wyandottes (gold and silver), Orpingtons, Langshans, Plymouth Rocks, Leghorns, Andalusians, Minorcas. The three last names are merely egg producers, and should not be reared for table; but the others will be found to combine good table qualities with good laying. I have named them in their order of merit, according to my own experience of them. Those varieties most famous for table use, such as Dorkings and Indian Game, would not be suitable. I have found Wyandottes to be the best of all general fowls; I have a cock of this breed 11 lbs., and a Justice of the Peace reported that a pullet supplied to him laid 315 eggs in one year. This was very exceptional, but I found a pen of six pullets laid 160 eggs each in a year. I have found Orpingtons excellent layers and good table fowls. All the breeds I have named are hardy.

Ducks. – The common duck is a small bird, but a pretty good layer. If you want to improve the ducks of peasants for laying, I would suggest the Indian Runner and Cayuga as the most suitable. If you wish to have good layers with increased size, I think the Pekin is the best breed to cross the common ducks.

Geese. – The Western peasants rear geese in large numbers, which they sell in harvest from 1*s.* 8*d.* to 2*s.* 4*d.* each to dealers who send them to England. The common goose is a small bird from 6 lbs. to 9 lbs. weight. I think you would do a great deal of good by distributing a number of Embden and Toulouse Ganders for stock purposes. These are very large birds and would increase the value of the stock by half. There are other varieties of geese, such as Italians and Chinese, which have great merits, but I consider them too small to breed geese for market. The peasant needs a big fowl that will realize the highest price, and I therefore recommend the Embden and Toulouse.

Turkeys. – These, after geese, may be called the only variety of table birds the ordinary peasant takes up. Many peasants keep a turkey hen, and as one visit to the male bird suffices for her batch of eggs, she is sent at the proper time to some neighbour who has a "Gobbler." The hen lays from twelve to eighteen eggs, all of which are set, and if the season be fine, very little trouble is experienced in rearing them. They are usually fed on boiled nettles and Indian Meal till September or October, when they are sold at about 2*s.* each; some people keep them till Christmas when they get about 3*s.* each. I do not believe you can so easily improve any variety of fowls as turkeys. In hens, ducks, and geese, the male birds you supply must be mated with only a few birds, but not so with the turkey cock. The number of hens *brought* to him may be almost unlimited. A young bird could safely be mated with fifty hens if they are brought to him. I would not allow him to walk with more than twelve hens, as some might be neglected; but when the owner brings the bird to him, and leaves her an hour or so, there is no need for bringing her back again. I allowed a few to bring hens to one of my American "Gobblers"; one had fourteen birds after a single visit and none had a complete failure. The turkeys in the West are very poor; hens weigh from 6 lbs. to 8 lbs., and cocks from 8 lbs. to 11 lbs. when fat at Christmas.

I cannot better show the importance of introducing good blood than mentioning a case. In 1889 I allowed Mrs. C. (above named) to bring a hen to my imported American "Gobbler," which was a very grand bird of the highest merit. (He won First Prize at Doncaster Royal Show, and first at East Birmingham Show.) He was then a young bird; the hen weighs 7 lbs. Her last flock had been sold the previous Christmas at 3*s.* each. From this mating eleven birds were reared (six cocks and five pullets), which were sold to the person who bought the previous year, at 8*s.* each, which meant a clear profit of £2 15*s.* by using a first-class male bird. The cockerels in this case were 18 lbs., and the pullets 11 lbs. For crossing or breeding pure, there is no turkey so good as the pure American Bronze. Here I would advise care to be taken to avoid spurious imitations, of which there are thousands. I have had the Black Norfolk, the Cambridge, and the pure Wild Turkey. The Bronze is to the pure Wild what the English race-horse is to the Arab. The Wild is the original, the Bronze is the result of a century. By good feeding and careful selection of the best birds, the size has been increased without losing the hardiness of the Wild breed. The best weights of Wild "Gobblers" are 35 lbs. The bird I gave the use of to Mrs. C. weighed 48 lbs., and his sire weighed 50 lbs., and was the champion prize winner of America. If a good bird of the pure breed were placed in each parish, I believe the results would abundantly repay the cost. In my opinion each flock reared from a really good bird would sell £2 higher than if they were from the ordinary male bird.

The common Turkey is small, has a thin poor breast, and is hard to fatten. The American Bronze has a breast almost as good as a pheasant's, with immensely better quality of flesh than that of the common breed. The Wild Turkey is game of the finest kind, equal to a pheasant for eating. And the Bronze being nearly Wild bred – large, stands above all tame turkeys for quality of flesh. It is also the hardiest Turkey living. It grows rapidly, and thrives quite as well if allowed to roost in trees as if kept indoors. Turkeys are usually sold by weight in the large towns; if not actually weighed, the dealer will guess the weight to a few ounces. The small birds are not only unprofitable because there is little of them, but that little is bought at a lower price per lb. Cockerels from 24 lbs. to 30 lbs. at Christmas time will sell for 1*s.* 6*d.* per lb., whereas birds of 10 lbs. will not pass 8*d.* per lb.

Why? Many business houses send presents to good customers, and when a turkey is sent a big price is not grudged for a very fine one. Some like to have very large turkeys for their dinner parties, particularly when the good old style of bringing the bird uncarved to the table is observed: and they are willing to give good prices.

These are all the hints I can think of just now, but I shall be happy to assist in this matter in any way in my power. If I have omitted anything you would like to know, I shall have much pleasure in giving what information I can.

Yours, &c.,

J. C. SMITH.

To HENRY DORAN, Esq.,
Inspector.

CONGESTED DISTRICTS BOARD FOR IRELAND

COUNTIES OF MAYO, GALWAY, ROSCOMMON, AND SLIGO

SUPPLEMENTARY GENERAL REPORT OF MR. DORAN, *Inspector*

ON THE

INLAND DISTRICTS OF THE ABOVE-MENTIONED COUNTIES

At the Board meeting held on March 10th, 1893, I drew attention to the fact, that, while considerable sums of money had been allocated to some districts for the construction of roads, &c., &c., very little had been done for the Inland Congested Districts I had reported upon.

I was then directed to prepare a report, which I beg to submit herewith, offering specific suggestions as to the works, or other means, I would recommend for the permanent improvement of the inland districts referred to.

The members of the Board have been furnished with so many reports during the past year it is scarcely possible they could have read them all carefully, and I trust I will be excused for directing their special attention to my General Report of 30th April, 1892, as it contains, in a general way, all the suggestions I can offer for the improvement of these districts.

The statistical table on front page of that report shows:–

(*a*.) The area dealt with therein to be 483,702 acres, or, in round numbers, one-seventh of the total area of the Congested Districts.

(*b*.) The population on this area is 135,521, or one-fourth of the total population of the Congested Districts.

(*c*.) The Poor Law valuation is set out at £138,088, or one-fourth of the total Poor Law valuation of the Congested Districts.

It is important to bear in mind that these Inland Congested Districts contain one-fourth of the entire population the Board has to deal with, and that this quarter of the population occupy only one-seventh of the area of land. These figures prove that the inland districts are really the most congested, and a perusal of my General Report describing the habits of life and resources of inhabitants will show that the land is incapable of maintaining its population, and that the majority of the able-bodied men are compelled to spend from one-third to one-half of their lives engaged as migratory labourers, absent from their homes and unable to attend to the proper cultivation of their land. They have no resources at home beyond what they derive from the land they occupy. There is no employment obtainable, and they must migrate or become paupers. The districts are solely agricultural and will continue so, and through the land alone must be sought the means of permanently improving their condition.

I do not desire to make any comparisons that would appear to minimise the admittedly poor condition of the people along the sea-board, but it cannot be denied that they have many advantages over the poor people of the Inland Districts. They can have, as a rule, abundance of sea-weed for manure and can procure fish for food, and although there is only a small circulation of money amongst them, they live in a primitive manner, and the necessaries of life which they have to purchase are few.

The conditions of life of the migratory labourer are not conducive to the moral or social advancement of the individuals or to the welfare of the country.

The more labour expended in a country the richer the general community must become. This country being purely agricultural the application of labour must be mainly devoted to the land, and the more labour judicially applied to it the greater will be the value of the produce. There being no hope of industrial work springing up at home which would employ the superfluous labour, the fundamental remedy for the permanent relief of congestion is *migration*, attended with the most stringent conditions for the prevention of the future sub-division of the land.

My General Report deals in detail with the question of migration, and as there does not appear to be any immediate prospect of acquiring land for this purpose on reasonable terms, I pass to the consideration of the means immediately available, by which, I believe, the condition of the people could be most effectively improved in the absence of migration, viz.:– Agricultural development.

The most casual observer cannot fail to notice that throughout the Congested Districts the land is cultivated in a very primitive and slovenly manner; a great extent of the land is capable of profitable improvement by drainage and good husbandry; and the live stock of all classes are of a very inferior description. A scheme of agricultural development should be put into operation to remedy this state of things, by the following means:–

(*a.*) Promoting better systems of agriculture.
(*b.*) Drainage and reclamation of holdings.
(*c.*) Improvement of live stock and poultry.
(*d.*) Main and arterial drainage.
(*e.*) Construction of accommodation roads in exceptional circumstances.
(*f.*) Erection of lime-kilns, and the burning and sale of lime for agricultural purposes.

If a district is to be permanently and materially improved by the means indicated, any efficient scheme of agricultural development must embrace the entire of the above classification in its operation. Very little good will result from anything like a *piece-meal* organization at this development. Improving road accommodation in one district; promoting better systems of agriculture in another; improving live stock in a third; making main or arterial drains in a fourth, will be slow in effecting any appreciable improvement in the condition of the mass of the inhabitants.

Badly farmed and impoverished land will not maintain good cattle. Making a drain which dries the wettest portion of a holding of which the best and driest parts are so badly worked as to be almost valueless, will not do much good unless the assistance given by the Board stimulates the occupier to improve his methods of farming. The funds at the disposal of the Board are too small to yield *directly* any large results, no matter how carefully and judiciously administered; but if they can be applied in a manner that will stimulate into active co-operation the persons intended to be served, then striking results may be secured.

The agricultural development of these districts should be approached as a skilled agriculturist would attempt the improvement of an impoverished and neglected farm – placing good stock on it will not do; neither will draining the worst portion of it. His first efforts would probably be directed towards restoring the fertility of the parts that were naturally the best, as he will expect from them the quickest and best return for his outlay. And no matter how sanguine of ultimate success he may be, his experience convinces him that permanent improvement can only be brought about by a slow and gradual process and persistent efforts. As the land improves, the live stock can be improved and increased in number; the farmer can feed them better and make more manure, which, in turn, enables him to cultivate more of the land, and still further increase his facilities for its improvement.

The different phases of improvement must go hand in hand, and, in my opinion, the best way to bring about the agricultural development of a district would be through the agency of district agriculturists as explained in my General Report.

A skilled agriculturist should be placed in charge of a district, and be provided with a suitable house, offices, and a small farm – say, from 20 to 50 acres. Farms could be obtained on a twenty years' lease, or by purchase of the tenancy. Arrangements could be made with the agriculturists by giving the farms rent free in lieu of portion of salary, and let them work for their own account, or they could manage them for the Board under the direction of the Agricultural Department of the Land Commission. On this farm should be kept a bull, stallion, boar, stock of fowl, &c., and the allowance made for the maintenance of these animals would pay the greater part, if not the entire rent and expenses. The farms need not be expensively managed, and they should be self-supporting. On the larger farms a small herd of pure bred animals could be kept to supply sires for the district, and the animals so reared would be more suitable than imported ones, and they would cost far less.

Liberal prizes should be offered every year to the land-holders of the district who entered into competition and agreed to follow the advice of the agriculturist in the management of their lands. Prizes would be offered for certain crops, for best managed farm, for cleanliness of house, etc., for dairy management, for different classes of stock, fowl, butter, etc., etc., and an annual show should be held in each district, which should be made as attractive as possible.

The agriculturist could make himself very useful in organizing a speedy despatch of eggs and poultry and of butter to the best markets.

Persons managing their farms under the direction of the agriculturist might be assisted to procure good seed every year, and, in cases where drainage of holdings was necessary, loans might be advanced on the same terms as they are given to fishermen; or, if the Board objected to lend money, perhaps they would approve of giving grants, say to the value of one-fourth of the work done under the supervision of the agriculturist. The latter plan would be devoid of complication and the Board would have the satisfaction of knowing that, for a grant of, say £1,000 to a district, £4,000 worth of work would be done, which would be a source of immediate and permanent gain to the land-owners.

In any district where the people were actively co-operating in the scheme of agricultural development, and that the execution of arterial or main drainage, or the construction of a road or such works appeared very desirable, they should be undertaken by the Board. Thorough drainage on holdings, executed under a loan or grant, should be carried out under the supervision of the agriculturist and would be likely to be well done.

I would recommend that all the money which the Board can allocate to these districts should be reserved for migration and agricultural development, as explained above.

I have no faith in itinerant instructors. The agricultural instructor should be resident in the district and be in daily communication with the people and have some land which should be managed in a manner that would demonstrate the advantage of his skill and knowledge. If he cannot practise what he preaches, who can have faith in him? The hotel and travelling expenses of an itinerant instructor would pay the rent of a good farm.

These farms could also be made to serve the same purposes as the "Experimental Stations," which are maintained by the Agricultural Societies of England and Scotland, where experiments are conducted on the growth of different crops, the effects of the application of manures, etc.

I will not believe in an agricultural instructor who cannot take his neighbours over his farm and show them his crops – superior to theirs – his neat clean dairy, his good fowl, his good live stock, and tell them how they can follow his example.

By keeping the sires of all classes for the district at the farm, the neighbouring farmers would be constantly coming about the place and seeing the live stock and the general management of the farm.

If the Board do not approve of either of the foregoing means for the development of the Inland Districts, then, I would recommend that they should undertake drainage works and set aside the greater part of the available funds for that purpose. Money cannot be expended in these districts in any work which, *per se*, will yield such beneficial results as drainage. In other districts large sums are about being expended on roads and a corresponding expenditure on drainage could be made with advantage in these Inland Districts where there is such urgent need for main and arterial drainage. Any efforts, however, made by the Board in this direction must be very partial in its results, as only comparatively small projects can be undertaken, and the complete accomplishment of the work would involve an expenditure far in excess of the resources of the Board.

I have, within the past ten days, gone over several flooded districts with the object of seeing what could be done to improve the drainage, but, in most cases, sufficient fall cannot be obtained without deepening and improving the natural water-courses for several miles. I find it would take some weeks to find out the most desirable works to undertake, and, for that reason, I would suggest that, in the event of the Board deciding to undertake drainage-works, that they agree on the sum of money to be expended, and that this amount should be apportioned amongst the separate districts referred to in my General Report, and that I would then get some time to inspect the several water-courses of the flooded districts and select the most desirable works and supply plans and estimates of cost.

A short list of the drainage works I have had time to examine and an approximate estimate of the cost accompanies this Report.

HENRY DORAN,
Inspector.

30th March, 1893.

To

The Congested Districts Board for Ireland.

APPENDIX B

THE BALLAGHADERREEN HOSIERY FACTORY, BALLAGHADERREEN, CO. MAYO.

STATISTICS OF THE FACTORY

No.	Queries by H. Doran.	Hosiery Factory.	Shirt and Underclothing Department.
1.	When was the Knitting Industry started?	October, 1891.	July, 1889.
2.	How many workers now employed?	56	39
3.	What was the average cost incurred per worker in starting the work?	This item includes machinery, furniture and materials. £20 6*s.* 9*d.* A worker could be started at home for £10, if material were supplied by the employer.	This includes machinery, furniture and material. £9 6*s.* 2*d.* A girl could be started at home for £7, if material were supplied by the employer.
4.	What is the average wages account of workers employed?	£36 19*s.* 9½*d.* (per month).	£25 15*s.* 2½*d.* (per month).
5.	What degree of skill have they attained?	Many are proficient in both departments, as can be proved from the satisfaction which the work has given, while the skill of others is according to the time they have been employed.	
6.	How many pairs of socks per day can they knit?	1½ dozen each on average.	———
7.	How many is it expected they can knit when they become skilled at the work?	2 dozen per day. This some have already attained.	Workers in this department vary as to proficiency. Many are adepts at shirtmaking and underclothing, and send out work which gives the fullest satisfaction.
8.	What wages can they now earn?	According to the amount of work they do, some earn as much as 1*s.* 8*d.* per day, other less. 10*d.* per dozen is the rate of payment to skilled workers.	In this department, though not paid by piece work, their earnings are in the same proportion as in the Hosiery Factory. (See answers to No. 3.)
9.	If a large number of hands were employed at the work, would there be a market?	Yes. The factory is at present working for some of the largest firms in England, as well as in Dublin and Belfast, &c.	Yes. The employment of this department has been very much increased, and work disposed of at fairly remunerative prices.

CONGESTED DISTRICTS BOARD FOR IRELAND

COUNTY OF GALWAY – UNION OF CLIFDEN

REPORT OF MAJOR ROBERT RUTTLEDGE-FAIR, *Inspector*

DISTRICT

OF

CARNA

STATISTICAL TABLE

ELECTORAL DIVISION.	Area in Statute Acres.	Poor Law Valuation.	Number of Ratings at and under £10 and above £4 Valuation.	Number of Ratings at and under £4 Valuation.	Population in 1891.	Number of Families in 1891.	Number of Families on Holdings exceeding £2 and under £4 Valuation.	Number of Families on Holdings at and under £2 Valuation.	Number of Families in very poor circumstances.	Number of Families which have no Cattle.
		£								
Knockboy,	8,774	1,195	113	328	2,259	382	89	232	140	94
Owengowla,	13,408	378	29	218	837	162	48	65	40	
Skannive,	10,200	668	19	385	1,457	276	180	178	100	
Moyrus,	21,688	887	29	202	1,066	182	74	36	35	
Illion,	8,988	166	4	89	344	57	17	40	5	
TOTALS,	63,058	£3,244	194	1,222	5,963	1,059	408	551	320	94 *

* Principally in Knockboy, Owengowla, and Skannive.

(1.) Whether inland or maritime.

This is a mixed district, chiefly maritime but partly inland. The coast-line extends southward from the head of Bertraghboy Bay to the Avally River which flows into Kilkieran Bay a distance of some twenty-four miles. Quite nine-tenths of the population live along the sea-coast, the inland part of the district being very thinly populated.

(2.) Average quantity of land cultivated on holdings at and under £4 valuation, under (*a*) oats, (*b*) potatoes, (*c*) meadow, (*d*) green crops.

There are about 2¼ acres on an average cultivated on holdings at and under £4 valuation in the following way:–

Oats,	¾ acre.
Potatoes,	1½ acres.
Total,	2¼ acres.

Meadow may be said to be practically *nil* except in the Electoral Divisions of Moyrus and Illion, where families average about half an acre each. Other green crops are practically *nil*. The want of sheep-proof fencing renders the growth of turnips, &c., &c., very difficult. Here and there small plots of cabbage are grown, but the total area of such crops is inappreciable.

(3.) Extent of mountain or moor grazing, and rights possessed by tenants, whether in common or otherwise.

The Berridge estate comprises nearly three-fourths of the total area of this district, and the tenants on that property enjoy free grazing over very extensive mountain and bog lands as a right inseparable from their holdings. The same right also exists on the properties of most of the small proprietors. I am informed that the tenants on Colonel Nolan's and Mr. D.B. Leonard's estates have no grazing commonage attached to their holdings.

(4.) Extent and description of land, if any, which could be profitably reclaimed and added to existing adjoining holdings.

There does not appear to be any great estate of land in this district suitable for reclamation purposes. The townlands adjoining the coast are very rocky, exceptionally so, and the soil is of a very poor quality. In the inland portion of the district the few families residing there generally have as much land as they can conveniently manure available for cultivation.

In Finish Island there is a small grazing farm, about 60 acres, which would be a great boon to the islanders if let to them for grazing, as they have no commonage, and are obliged to graze their cattle on their own holdings.

The owner of the Island is Mr. D.B. Leonard; the farm is in the occupation of Mr. Thomas Hazell of Cashel, who lives nearly twelve miles away. The property is for sale in the Landed Estates Court, and a portion situated near Tuam has been already sold.

If the Island could be acquired by the Board, the tenants would, I understand, be willing to purchase their holdings, and this grazing farm could be then also sold to them.

(5.) Particulars as to any suitable land in district which could be obtained, and to which families could be migrated with a reasonable prospect of success.

The area of land suitable for migration purposes is very small, and it seems to me very doubtful whether it would be expedient to convert the few grazing farms in the district which are suitable for migration into tillage. There are large tracts of rough mountain which no doubt might be obtained for this purpose, but I think migration to such lands would not be successful. The cost of reclamation would be too expensive owing to the difficulties of obtaining manure.

(6.) Method of cultivation, manures, rotation of crops, etc., etc.

The method of cultivation is exactly similar to that described in previous reports. The land is dug up in March and April, and potatoes sown in lazy beds as soon as the weather permits. Oats is sown in "lands" and trenched to provide drainage.

In the islands of Mweenish, Finish, and Mason, where the soil is sandy, potatoes are planted in February. Seaweed is the chief manure, and better-off people mix it with farm-yard manure. Potatoes followed by oats is the only rotation, but in many instances potatoes are sown in the same plots year after year, the holdings being so small that no other ground is available. The holdings are so unprotected that green crops are seldom sown, except immediately round the houses where they are under close observation and can be easily watched; grass seeds are never sown except by a few, a very few, of the better class farmers.

(7.) General information with regard to stock, and suggestions as to improvement of breeds – (*a*) cattle, (*b*) sheep, (*c*) horses and donkeys, (*d*) pigs, (*e*) poultry, etc., etc.

Both cattle and sheep in this district are small, stunted, and difficult to fatten. A considerable improvement could be effected by crossing the country breeds with Kyloe or Galloway bulls and black-faced rams; but all soft bred pedigree bulls or rams should be carefully avoided, the land being too poor to maintain really good class animals.

There are a good many mares in this district, and I think the village of Kilkieran would be a good centre to place a Hackney sire next season. It is seventeen miles from Cashel where a Barb stallion stood this season.

A few Yorkshire boars should also be distributed to (say) half a dozen well-to-do farmers at a mere nominal price, all irksome conditions being carefully avoided.

This is the first district where I have met with the cockerels which were distributed by the Board last winter. I regret to say that as far as I can learn the experiment has not been very successful. Some of the birds are said to have died and others do not appear to thrive. This perhaps may be accounted for by climatic influences, difference of feeding, &c., &c. It might perhaps be well next year to distribute *eggs* instead of cockerels to a few carefully selected persons who could be depended upon. Such a course would, I think, be far more likely to succeed, as the birds would from the outset be accustomed to the climate and method of feeding. Andalusians and Leghorns are, I imagine, the best breeds for the West of Ireland, as they are excellent egg-producers, and "table" fowls do not, at present at least, count for much with the country people.

(8.) Markets and fairs for cattle and produce of district; also statement as to where the people obtain food and other supplies, and the prevailing custom with regard to the disposal of butter, eggs, and poultry;

There are four small fairs held at Kilkieran, a little village six miles east of Carna; this is the only place in the district where fairs are held; there are no markets. Cattle, &c., are generally sold at Clifden, twenty-five miles from Carna, the centre of the Knockboy, Owengowla, and Skannive Electoral Divisions, and about thirteen miles from Recess and to what extent are they sold in the first instance to local shopkeepers and dealers, and, generally speaking, how old are the eggs when sold to the first buyer, and about how old when they reach their ultimate destination in Great Britain.

Cashel, central places in the remaining Electoral Divisions. Large farmers sell their cattle in Galway.

Food and other supplies are generally brought by sailing boats from Galway to Kilkieran, Carna, Cashel, and other points along the coast. Hardly any butter is sold, and the same remark also applies to poultry, but eggs are disposed of by thousands. It is estimated that at least fourteen eggs are sold on an average by each family every week for ten months, or considerably over 600,000 eggs yearly. Owing to the difficulties of transit, eggs would be at least three weeks old before reaching their final destination in Great Britain, but the weekly steamer service between Galway and Kilkieran may, I think, improve matters in this respect.

(9.) Rail, steamer, sailing boat, road, postal and telegraph facilities.

Railway communication at present is almost *nil.* Galway, forty-seven miles from Carna, is the nearest station. The Galway and Clifden Railway, now in course of construction, runs through the northern portion of the district; but the thickly populated Electoral Divisions will be at least sixteen miles from the nearest proposed station.

The Galway Steamship Company have a weekly service to Kilkieran under conditions with which the Board are acquainted. Sailing boats bring most of the goods and other supplies from Galway. In winter this is a very uncertain means of communication, and I have known numerous instances of vexatious but unavoidable delays.

Roads.– The district is now fairly well off in this respect, a fact which may be attributed to the untiring energy of the late Rev. T. Flannery, P.P., who never ceased bringing under notice the wants of the district. (See paragraph 32).

Postal Facilities.– The post is despatched from Recess every morning (Sundays excepted) on the arrival of the mail from Galway to Cashel and Carna. From the latter place it is sent by a foot messenger to Kilkieran. I cannot see why this populous district should not be given a Sunday delivery; it is loudly called for by every person to whom I have spoken. Further, the transit of letters from Carna to Kilkieran is especially bad. Instead of the messenger starting from Carna on the arrival of the car and returning in time for the outgoing afternoon post, he is sent from Kilkieran in the morning and returns with the letters during the day. Hence, letters received at Kilkieran cannot be answered till the following day. This difficulty would require very little re-arrangement so far as the foot messenger is concerned; but a better arrangement still would be to send the mails by car from Carna. It is right I should mention that Ardmore, where I understand the Board contemplate establishing a fishing and fish-curing station, is on the road between Carna and Kilkieran, so that it is important that the postal arrangements should be as complete as possible.

I have previously reported on the necessity of establishing a telegraph office at Carna.

(10.) Employment for labourers in the district, whether temporary or constant, and rate of wage.

The permanent employment for labourers in the district is so small that it is not worth alluding to it.

(11.) Migratory labour, average earnings per head, and where earned.

There are no migratory labourers in this district.

(12.) Weaving, spinning, knitting, and sewing, whether used locally or sold, and where.

Much the same system as I have described in my report on the Letterfrack district is also carried on at Carna, so far as weaving and spinning are concerned; almost all the clothing worn in the district is made by the people. It is estimated that about three stone of wool is required to clothe a family of six persons, and those who have not sheep are often hard-pinched to obtain sufficient money to purchase wool; the price generally charged is 1*s.* per lb. Almost every article woven or spun is made for local use.

Knitting is on altogether a different footing in this district owing to the efforts of the Connemara Industries Company who, some three years ago, introduced skilled teachers from Donegal and trained a large number of girls. Vests, underclothing, and jerseys are now knit by these girls, of whom some 200 are employed from time to time, and the improvement which has been effected in a short time in knitting is something wonderful. They earn from 6*d.* to 8*d.* per day without interfering with their usual employment. A proposal as to the establishment of a central depot for the sale of work from this as well as from other districts will be laid before your Board. (See paragraph 32).

(13.) Kelp-burning, and sale of seaweed.

Carna is the great centre for the kelp industry; 360 families, or more than a third of the population of the entire district, are employed, and it is estimated that more than 1,800 tons will be made this season. Prices are better than for many years past owing to competition among buyers; three companies are purchasing now as against one in 1890. The price has risen to £5 per ton, being 10*s.* dearer than last year, and 30*s.* in advance of that price in 1890. I think, however, £4 10*s.* might be taken as an average price, and this would show that over £8,000 will be paid for kelp in the Carna district during this season.

(14.) Sale of turf, nature and extent of bogs.

As a general rule the people of this district have an adequate supply of excellent turf within easy reach of their dwellings, and the bogs will last for many years. On the Finish, Mweenish, and Mason Islands there is no turf, and the people have to purchase "banks" on the mainland, and cut it there. They are generally charged from 10*s.* to 15*s.* for a year's supply. In Glinsk, where the bog lies close along the sea-shore, a very thinly populated townland, two or three families cut large quantities of turf, and sell it in the following spring in County Clare, at Ballyvaughan, and other places. I understand they obtain from 30*s.* to 40*s.* per hooker load. The distance to Ballyvaughan is about twenty-six miles, and two headlands (Golan and Mace), where heavy seas break in bad weather, have to be rounded. In several places I observed that the people are cutting turf on land which had been reclaimed, a practice which should be checked if possible, as the soil is generally so shallow that when one or two "spits" of turf are cut there is nothing left for cultivation, and the place is then little but bare rock.

(15.) Lobster fishing, number of men and boats employed.

There are 186 men and 62 boats employed in lobster fishing; it is estimated that the men in average years can earn £8 each, or £24 per boat. Lobsters are principally sold at Roundstone; the prices average from 5*s.* to 6*s.* per dozen; this year they are rather lower owing to want of competition. The industry is an important one, and might be developed by establishing a depot at Roundstone, where some trustworthy person might be engaged to purchase lobsters at a fixed price, and send them to approved Liverpool or Manchester fish merchants for sale. There is a retired Chief Officer of Coast Guards living at Roundstone named Allen, who would be an excellent man for such a post.

(16.) Sea fishing. Facilities for sale of fish, and number of boats and men solely employed in fishing.

The number of *bona-fide* fisherman in the district are few, but on the other hand a large number of families fish "off and on," especially during the autumn months when fish are plenty. The people living on the islands and promontories running far seaward, such as Mace, are I think the most experienced fishermen, at least they fish more continuously than the people who live further off up the numerous bays and recesses which intersect the coast. The success of sea-fishing seems to me to depend on the establishment of a market, where the people can always count on their disposing of their fish at a reasonable price. If that difficulty was once overcome, I believe fishing in this district will become a chief factor in the circumstances of the people. At present when the small local demand is satisfied, there is no other market available.

(17.) Number of boats and men employed in carrying turf or seaweed or in fishing. Classification of boats.

There are 458 boats in the district, almost all third class, a few only being large hookers which bring goods from Galway. There are, practically, no curraghs.

(18.) Fish; whether consumed at home or sold.

The fish caught off this district is all consumed locally.

(19.) Extent of fish-curing.

In this district fish are roughly salted for local consumption. A curing station is, I understand, about to be established at Ardmore under the auspices of the Board.

(20.) Piers and Harbours, existing and suggested, and how far those existing are adapted to wants of district.

There are piers at Cloonisle, Lettercamp, Cashel, Mason Island, Ard West, Carna, Ardmore, and Kilkieran. Most of these piers are capable of considerable improvement and I would especially mention those at Ardmore and Mason Island. The pier at Ardmore was built by the Fishery Piers and Harbours Commissioners, and so I believe was the pier at Mason Island. The Ardmore Pier ought to be extended 60 feet, and the storm wall raised at least four feet. On the opposite shore of the little inlet a low shelter wall ought to be run out till in a line with the end of the present pier. One or two small rocks at the entrance to the channel should be also removed. The road leading to the pier also requires to be repaired and widened. It is at this pier the Board have resolved to open a fish-curing station. The Mason Island Pier – a most useful work – runs nearly due east and west, with a turn south-west. Opposite the narrow entrance, south-west, is a low shelter pier and wall not cemented, built of rough stones. This shelter pier is falling down. It should be repaired and raised about four feet, grouted and pointed with cement. The storm wall, on the south-west corner of the shelter pier, ought also to be raised a few feet; ample shelter would then be afforded. The pier at Ard West is in bad repair, and should be looked to at once if it is to be maintained; it was also built by the Piers and Harbours Commissioners.

(21.) Extent of salmon and freshwater fisheries. Number of men earning their livelihood therefrom.

There are two salmon and white trout fisheries in the districts – Ballinahinch and Gowla. Some 86 men are engaged as water bailiffs and watchers at salaries of £4 during the close season. Most of these men are also employed during the fishing season as boatmen, &c., &c., and are paid 3*s.* daily when so employed.

(22.) Banks and Loan Funds.

There are neither Banks nor Loan Funds in the district.

(23.) Mineral and other resources.

There is a marble quarry in the townland of Lissoughter. Several efforts have been made to work it; but, so far, they have all failed owing to the difficulties of transit. The quarry is about ten miles from the sea-coast. The Galway and Clifden Railway will pass within half a mile of it, and when it is completed some further effort might perhaps be then made to work the quarry with a better prospect of success.

(24.) Relative prevalence of cash or credit dealings, length of credit, interest charged, extent of barter, etc., etc.

Credit is extensively given by the local shop-keepers. No specified length of time can be stated; it varies according to the circumstances and requirements of the people. Generally, families commence to get credit at Christmas, and the accounts gradually rise till the following June, when some of the kelp is ready for sale, and lobsters too can be disposed of; some of the bills are then discharged. From August to December the people generally pay in cash for what they purchase, as cattle and sheep are then fit for sale. In bad seasons, credit commences in November, and it takes two or three good years to discharge the liabilities incurred in such periods. As a rule, I think the shop-keepers are not too exacting in their demands, so long as they see the people are honestly endeavouring to meet their liabilities. Interest varies from 10 to 20 per cent. Barter is principally carried on in eggs, which are exchanged for tea, sugar, and tobacco.

(25.) Estimated *cash* receipts and expenditure of a family in ordinary circumstances.

The estimated *cash* receipts and expenditure of a family (six persons) in fair circumstances on a holding of about £4 valuation are as follows:–

RECEIPTS	£	*s.*	*d.*	EXPENDITURE	£	*s.*	*d.*
Sale of 5 tons kelp, at £4 10*s.* per ton,	22	10	0	Rent of holding,	6	0	0
„ 2 pigs (profit),	3	0	0	County Cess,	0	16	0
„ 2 cattle,	10	0	0	Clerical dues,	0	10	0
„ 1 foal,	5	0	0	Flour at 14*s.* per cwt.,	15	12	0
„ 5 sheep at 6*s.*,	1	10	0	Groceries at 4s. 3*d.* per week,	10	9	6
„ 12 cwt. oats at 5*s.* 6*d.*,	3	6	0	Tobacco,	2	12	0
„ eggs,	1	10	0	Clothes and shoes, the former principally home-made,	5	14	0
				Household goods, &c.,	2	0	0
Total,	£46	16	0	Total,	£43	13	6
Surplus,	£3	2	6				

The estimated *cash* receipts and expenditure of a family of six persons in poor circumstances on a holding of about £2 valuation are as follows:–

Receipts	£	s.	d.	Expenditure	£	s.	d.
Sale of lobsters,	8	0	0	Rent of holding,	1	10	0
„ 4 tons kelp at £4,	16	0	0	County Cess,	0	5	4
„ pig (profit),	1	10	0	Meal at 7*s.* per cwt.,	4	4	4
„ * bullock,	2	10	0	Flour at 14*s.* per cwt.,	9	16	0
„ oats 6 cwt. at 5*s.* 0*d.*,	1	13	0	Groceries,	6	19	8
„ eggs,	2	0	0	Tobacco,	2	12	0
				Clothes and shoes,	4	10	0
				Household goods,	1	10	0
				Clerical dues,	0	6	0
Total,	£31	13	0	Total,	£31	13	0

* A Bullock is sold by such families about every two years.

(26.) Estimated value of home-grown food consumed, and period during which it lasts.

The estimated value of home-grown food consumed is as follows:–

	£	s.	d.
About 6 tons potatoes,	12	0	0
„ $1^1/_2$ „ straw,	2	5	0
Total,	14	5	0

For the Electoral Divisions of Illion and Moyrus one ton of hay must be added, bringing the total to £16 5*s.*

(27.) Dietary of people, number of meals daily, and kinds of food throughout the year.

The people of the district take three meals daily:–

Breakfast. – Home-made flour bread and tea.

Dinner. – At about 1 o'clock, consists of potatoes and eggs; milk also is taken when available, but tea is often used instead of milk.

Supper. – At 8 o'clock, potatoes with "kitchen" are taken; tea and bread by families in fairly good circumstances.

Indian meal is used by very poor families instead of potatoes when the latter are exhausted, but the use of Indian meal is gradually dying out.

(28.) Clothing, whether home-made or bought, etc., etc.

For information regarding the clothing of the people of the district, see paragraph (12).

(29.) Dwellings: kind of houses, home-life and customs, etc., etc.

The great majority of the dwelling-houses in this district are thatched buildings, very roughly built of loose stones without mortar. They generally consist of two apartments, a kitchen and one other room. In the winter cattle and horses are kept at one end of the kitchen, and in the other is the fire place, round which the people principally sit and take their meals. The houses are seldom whitewashed, except after an epidemic of contagious disease, when lime is provided for that purpose by the Sanitary Authority.

(30.) Character of the people for industry, etc., etc.

The people in this district are, I consider, hardworking and industrious. The making of kelp provides a profitable occupation during the summer months, and in spring and harvest the people are busy cultivating their little holdings.

(31.) Whether any organized effort has been made to develop the resources or improve the condition of the people. If so, by what means.

Some three organized efforts have been made to improve the condition of the people of the district:–

1. By emigration under Mr. Tuke's scheme in 1882-3-4, when a number of wretchedly poor families were assisted to proceed to the United States and Canada.

2. By the introduction of cottage industries, knitting, &c., &c., some four years ago by the Connemara Industries Company, principally at the instigation of the late Rev. T. Flannery, P.P.

3. By the recent attempt made by Miss Mansfield to aid poor fishermen by providing them with large fishing boats and proper gear for fishing.

(32.) Suggestions as to any possible method for improving the condition of the people in future.

One of the principal means by which the condition of the people in this district might be improved seems to me to lie in aiding and developing the fishing industry by – (1). Providing easy and constant means of communication by steamer with Galway, subsiding a buyer to purchase fish at a fixed price at certain places in the district, and establishing two fish-curing stations, one at Ardmore, and the other either in the townland of Mace or at Mason Island; and (2). Improving as far as possible some of the small piers in the district and connecting them with existing public roads.

Hitherto, owing to the want of these facilities, this industry has been totally neglected, and the people eke out a precarious existence by kelp making. There is, I think, very little doubt that large quantities of fish habitually frequent the coast in the immediate vicinity, and if a certain market was provided for the sale of fish, I think the profits derived would render many families, comparatively speaking, independent.

The knitting industry, which was introduced into this district three years ago, also seems to offer a field for further development.

Connemara Industries Company, and the Carna Industrial Fund.

I beg to submit for the consideration of the Board a memorandum prepared by Mr. Fred. Scott, Hon. Sec. of the Connemara Industries Company, and of the Carna Industrial Fund.

From Mr. Scott's statement it would appear that the industry is at present in danger of collapsing, partly owing to the interest taken by some members of the Company becoming lukewarm, owing to the death of the Rev. T. Flannery, P.P., and also to the fact that so far the business has not been a financial success. Mr. Scott attributes the latter reason to the Company having as yet been unable to secure the services of a suitable permanent agent to push the sale of the work, and bring its merit under public notice. He is of opinion that this difficulty can be overcome by establishing a central depot in a prominent position at Manchester with a skilled manager in charge, who would be under the observation of the Company. The cost of such a depot is estimated by Mr. Scott at £800 per annum, and he proposes that the Congested Districts Board should aid the Company in this scheme by either guaranteeing them against possible loss for two years, or paying half the cost of the depot, or fixing a maximum sum for which the Board would be responsible.

A father and his two sons outside their farmhouse, with 'the woman of the house' standing at the front door.

In the event of the Board assisting in the establishment of the depot, the Company would undertake, *unaided*, the training of hands for knitting in Achill, the Aran Islands, and other places.

Any scheme which would develop the knitting industry, not only in Carna, but also in Carraroe, Achill, and other densely populated localities, seems to be worthy of very careful consideration.

Technical Instruction at Cashel National School.

A proposition has also been made by Mr. Joseph D. Kelly, National School teacher at Cashel, to give Manual Instruction in carpentry to some twelve boys whom he would form into a class for that purpose. Mr. Kelly stated that he would erect a wooden hut covered with corrugated iron at a cost of £13 15*s.* 9*d.* as a class-room, and that about £4 10*s.* worth of tools would be required. He would also expect to be paid a small salary for giving instruction for two hours daily.

Technical instruction of any kind should be, I think, encouraged, and the assistance asked for in this instance is very trivial.

I have asked Mr. Kelly to let me have a short memorandum of his proposal, which I shall forward to the Board in due course.

I have already alluded to the necessity of connecting the existing piers at Ardmore and Ard West with the public roads; and I also think the relief road, commenced in 1890-91 to Mace, should be completed to the sea-shore where there is a small fishing village. The distance to be completed is only a few hundred yards.

Further, there is no road to the large and thickly populated townlands of Letterard, Glinsk, and Letterdeskert. One was commenced in 1890-91; this road ought to be finished through these townlands. It is impossible to expect people to improve who are cut off from communication with the rest of the district. There are more than 100 families living in these three townlands, and the completion of a road through the villages would enable them to bring fish, &c., &c., to Mace and Ardmore.

ROBERT RUTTLEDGE-FAIR,
Inspector.

15th August, 1892.

To

The Congested Districts Board for Ireland.

To accompany Major Ruttledge-Fair's Report on the Carna District.

CONGESTED DISTRICTS BOARD FOR IRELAND

I. – CARNA INDUSTRIES

Memorandum of proposals to the Congested Districts Board on behalf of the Connemara Industries Company (Limited) and the Carna Industrial Fund, by Fred. Scott, Hon. Sec. to both.

The work hitherto carried on by the Industrial Fund and the Company, is in danger of being discontinued, unless it receives such encouragement at this crisis as the Congested Districts Board alone can give.

The death of Father Flannery terminated the interest in both organizations of several subscribers who had been influenced by him on his first visit to Manchester; and the inability of Miss May Southern to remain at Kilkieran deprived the Fund and the Company of an honorary superintendent. Owing to circumstances over which the Company had no control, the business done has been insufficient to show a profit; on the contrary there has been an increasing loss for three years. With such a small capital as the Company required for its purpose this has been discouraging, but the active workers are by no means disheartened, and recognising the fact that the adverse conditions under which the work has been hitherto conducted may be removed, they desire to continue their efforts until success is achieved, and permanence thus secured for the industries. To carry the shareholders with them, however, it is desirable to show a fair prospect of developing the business very considerably.

On the retirement of Miss May Southern, and the consequent absence of a technical representative to superintend the making of goods, it became necessary to make arrangements whereby the Company's fixed expenses should cease, and they accordingly effected a transfer of their Industrial House, at Kilkieran, to Mr. Pattison, the London hosiery manufacturer introduced to Carna by the Industrial Fund in 1888. The conditions of the transfer are:–

1. That Mr. Pattison gives employment to all the Company's workers.
2. That the Company shall sell a given value of Mr. Pattison's goods per annum.

So far the Company has been unable to secure suitable permanent agents to enable them to carry out their contract with Mr. Pattison. The only plan that, in the opinion of the directors, is likely to ensure success is the establishment of a depot in England, for the distribution wholesale and sale retail of the goods produced.

There could be no better centre for such a depot than Manchester, and the Company could exercise direct control over it there. Such a depot might include not only the productions of the Company and their colleague, Mr. Pattison, but also those of the machine knitting industry at Carraroe, now being introduced by the Industrial Fund, the work of Mrs. Ernest Hart, in Donegal, the baskets made by Miss Sturge's workers at Letterfrack, etc.

With a view to securing a wider base of supply for the depot which would be a distributing centre for the whole of Great Britain, the Committee of the Industrial Fund would be glad to undertake unaided the training of "hands" for knitting, etc., in other districts, such as Achill Island, the Aran Islands, etc.

The Company has at present under consideration the establishment of a depot, but that would have to be at some distance from the centre of the city, owing to the high rents charged there, and thus the chances of success would be minimised. The writer is firmly convinced that a bold course is the wise one to take, and if such a course be simply tried as an experiment no very serious risk need be run. Such an enterprise, however, is not likely to be undertaken by the Directors unaided.

My proposal is that the Congested Districts Board should guarantee the Company against the possible loss, on conducting the depot for, say, two years, or, as an alternative, that the Board should guarantee, say, half the cost of the depot, or fix a maximum sum for which they would hold themselves responsible in case of loss.

I estimate the expenses of the proposed depot, as follows:–

	£
Rent, rates, &c.,	150
Wages,	250
Advertising,	300
Sundries,	100
Total,	£800

The accounts of the Company are audited by a well-known firm of Chartered Accountants, and the Directors would only be too glad to have systematic inspection on behalf of the Congested Districts Board of the books, &c., of the depot.

If the Board desire any further information, I would be glad to attend one of their meetings, or would wait on any of the members by appointment, or arrange a special meeting of the Directors to meet one or more members of the Board.

FRED. SCOTT.

Visitors from outside the village were reluctant to enter dwellings in deference to the occupants. Note the woman of the house (right), with the basket on her back for carrying turf and other items.

To accompany Major RUTTLEDGE-FAIR'S REPORT on the CARNA DISTRICT.

CONGESTED DISTRICTS BOARD FOR IRELAND

II. – CARNA INDUSTRIES

Clifden, County Galway,
21st August, 1892.

GENTLEMEN, – Referring to my report upon the Carna District, I have the honour to forward a further letter which I have received from Mr. Frederick Scott, Hon. Secretary of the Carna Industrial Fund, and of the Connemara Industries Company, Limited, relative to the proposed establishment in Manchester of a depot for the sale of goods made in the Congested Districts.

I also forward the reports referred to in Mr. Scott's letter.

It will be observed that while Mr. Scott's Directors have, subject to the Congested Districts Board co-operating with them in the establishment of a depot at Manchester, authorized him to proceed with the training of "hands" in Achill and the Aran Islands, no reference is made to their undertaking any part of the expenses connected with the establishment of the proposed depot. And the paragraph marked "A" in Mr. Scott"s letter would seem to imply that raising funds for that purpose would be difficult.

I have the honour to be, Gentlemen,
Your obedient servant,
ROBERT RUTTLEDGE-FAIR.

To the Congested Districts Board,
Dublin.

(Copy.)
CARNA INDUSTRIAL FUND.

Secretary's Office,
De Quincey Chambers,
44, John Dalton Street, Manchester,
August 18th, 1892.

DEAR SIR, – I beg to acquaint you that, agreeably with my undertaking at our interview at Carna, I reported at the Annual Meeting of this Fund, held to-day, the proposals I submitted to the Congested Districts Board through you, and they were approved. I further applied for authority to train "hands" in knitting, &c., at Achill and Aran Islands, and the following resolution was passed, viz.:–

> That conditionally upon the Congested Districts Boards co-operating with the Connemara Industries Co. (Limited), in establishing a Depot in Manchester, the training of "hands" in Achill and Aran Islands in the production of such goods as can be sold at or distributed from the Depot, be forthwith undertaken, and that the Secretary be empowered to take the necessary steps to give effect to this resolution, without further reference to the Committee.

The Annual Meeting of the Connemara Industries Co. (Limited) followed, and the shareholders also confirmed my proposal.

A: In order that you may understand exactly our position, I send you copies of the Reports of the Committee of this Fund and of the Directors of the Company. You will observe that we called up only small amounts of Capital – it was more than we thought we would need for some time; but, in order to establish a depot, it would be necessary to raise a great deal more to do the work in a sufficiently spirited way to command success. This, however, after showing a continuous loss for three years, would be difficult, although the causes of the losses are obvious and could not be helped.

I am convinced that the Depot would enable us to do such a trade as would ensure permanence for the industries already started, and enable us to extend our work in Ireland very extensively. If, as I hope, the Congested Districts Board view the experiment with favour, I shall be able to raise as much money as we require for the voluntary Fund for training purposes.

Yours faithfully,

FRED. SCOTT, Hon. Sec.

Major Ruttledge-Fair,
Congested Districts Board,
23, Rutland Square, Dublin.

Carna Industrial Fund.

Report for the two years ending June 30th, 1892.

The last Report from the Committee to their subscribers was for the year ended June 30th, 1890. No report was deemed necessary for the following year, because the operations of the Fund were practically suspended, owing to causes beyond the Committee's control. The chief of these was the threatened famine in the autumn of 1890, owing to the failure of the potato crop. Under ordinary circumstances, such a danger might be expected to have the effect of giving an impetus to the operations of this Fund and of the Connemara Industries Company, Limited, as affording independent means of support; but such industries as have been introduced by this Fund, and by Mrs. Ernest Hart in Donegal, being confined to very circumscribed districts, the responsibility rested with the authorities of affording succour to the larger areas which had no such remunerative occupations. Accordingly voluntary funds were started by the Chief Secretary (Mr. Balfour) and the Lady Lieutenant (Countess of Zetland), and subscriptions, which amounted in the aggregate to a very large sum, were received. These efforts, praiseworthy as they were, and absolutely necessary, perhaps, in the particular emergency, must of necessity share with all such spasmodic relief in the past the discredit of some evil consequences. The more general of these is the moral effect upon the people. Each experience of the kind naturally leaves with them a conviction that in the event of any serious danger, outside help may be counted upon, and thus their self-reliance is undermined. In a more limited sense, the evil of having to resort to tentative measures of relief is illustrated by the effect of the operations of the Relief Funds upon the cottage industries at Carna. It is at once conceded that those Funds were admirably administered, and so far as it is possible to avoid the demoralising influence of charitable contributions, that object was effected by distributing the funds in the form of wages for labour on useful public works. But the result was to attract the men in large numbers to the sources of employment offered, and the women and girls, who would otherwise have been free to work for the Industries Company, had to attend to duties such as preparing for the ensuing seed-time, ordinarily performed by the men. Of course, continuous employment for the men is very much to be desired. The effect would be that less female labour would be available for cottage industries, but this would render more feasible the cultivation of industries for the women and girls over a much wider area. The committee note with satisfaction, that since they last reported to their subscribers, a Congested Districts Board has been formed by Government, and provided with considerable funds for the purpose of encouraging fisheries, improvement of horses and cattle, and several other objects, calculated to afford remunerative occupation of a permanent kind to the male population; but the Board do not engage in industrial work themselves, and do not obviate the necessity for such undertakings as this Fund and the Connemara Industries Company.

As explained in a former report, one of the first acts of the Committee of the Fund was to introduce to Carna, as an employer of labour, a London hosiery manufacturer, who for about two years continued to provide steady employment for a large number of knitters. Almost coincidentally with the hindrance just referred to, the demand for the staple article made by this manufacturer at Carna practically ceased, and he had to cultivate some new production. These two causes were alone sufficient to render the further training of hands unnecessary for the time being. The industries were slowly recovering from these checks, when a great calamity occurred, viz., the death of the Rev. Father Flannery ("Father Tom"), the devoted parish priest of Carna, who had been the backbone of the movement for the promotion of industrial prosperity in his parish, and without whose co-operation the organization of this Fund, and the Connemara Industries Company, would not have been attempted. In recognition of the remarkable influence exerted by their late colleague, the Committee have deemed it wise to subscribe £5 5*s.* towards the fund which is being raised to defray the cost of erecting a simple monument to perpetuate the memory of a career which, though very short, was nevertheless a great object-lesson in such qualities as industry, perseverance, and self-sacrifice. Father

Flannery's successor, the Rev. Father McHugh, is deeply interested in the work of the Fund and Company, and will, it is believed, well sustain the influence exerted by "Father Tom." Previous to his appointment, the Company decided to alter their mode of working. By an arrangement with the manufacturer already referred to, he takes charge of production entirely, and in consideration of his employing all the Company's trained hands, he is guaranteed the purchase by the Company of a fixed value of goods per annum. The Company thus becomes a distributing medium only, and in proportion to their success in selling goods, employment at Carna will be increased. Another desirable result of the arrangement is that the resources of this Fund become available for the extension of its work to other districts. Early in the past year, preliminaries were arranged for extending operations to Carraroe, an adjoining parish. Arrangements have now been completed for establishing there a machine-knitting industry. In Father Conway, the parish priest of Carraroe, the Committee recognise an able and enthusiastic colleague, and they entertain great expectations from this new departure. For the past few months, three girls from Carraroe have been at Horwich, near Bolton, learning the use of the machines, with a view to instructing other workers on their return home. Probably it will be necessary to supplement this instruction by sending an experienced superintendent for some time to Carraroe, in order that the results of the native teachers' work may be observed, and more particularly for the important purpose of familiarising new hands with the mechanism of these delicate machines. It is likely, therefore, that the funds in hand will soon be exhausted, and the results so far achieved having been most encouraging, the Committee have no hesitation in asking for further contributions to extend their operations.

It ought to be added that a member of the Committee of this Fund (Mr. R. Newton) tried to afford some employment at Carna in the occupation of sorting bristles, but the experiment was not successful, owing apparently to the peculiarly tedious character of the work, for which children or grown persons unaccustomed to sedentary employment are unfitted.

Carna Industrial Fund.

Statement of Receipts and Payments for the year ended June 30th, 1891.

Dr.	£	s.	d.	£	s.	d.	Cr.	£	s.	d.
1890.							1891			
June 30.							June 30.			
To Balance, viz.:							By Sundry Payments,	0	15	6
In Bank,	109	7	11				„ Expenses of Instruction,	21	0	0
In hands of Father Flannery,	14	10	9				„ Balance in Bank,	112	6	4
				123	18	8				
1891							Examined and found correct,			
June 30.							Wm. Aldred & Co.,			
To Subscriptions,	4	3	6				Chartered Accountants,			
„ Bank Interest,	5	19	8				*Essex-street Manchester.* Hon. Auditors.			
				10	3	2				
				£134	1	10		£134	1	10

THE CONNEMARA INDUSTRIES COMPANY, LIMITED.

Directors. – J. W. SOUTHERN, Chairman; W. J. HADFIELD, T. HODGSON, ROSE HYLAND, MARCUS LYNCH, R. NEWTON, C. T. REDINGTON, F. SMALLMAN. *Secretary.*– FRED. SCOTT, F.C.A., 41, John Dalton Street, Manchester.

DIRECTORS' REPORT.

The Directors regret that, owing to a series of untoward events, the year's operations of the Company have been very meagre, and the largest loss yet recorded, viz., £171 11*s.* 1*d.*, has unavoidably been incurred. In the last report reference was made to the operation of the Fund raised by the Chief Secretary of State for Ireland when famine was threatened in the autumn of 1890. The disturbing effects of that Fund continued to be felt in the early part of the past financial year. Then came the lamented death of Father Flannery, and about the same time the necessity arose for the return home of Miss May Southern, the Company's Honorary Superintendent. These occurrences virtually put a stop for some time to the Company's operations, whilst fixed charges, such as rent, &c., could not be discontinued for several months. As soon as possible, arrangements were made to transfer the Company's "Industrial House" at Kilkerrin to Mr. Pattison, the London manufacturer introduced by the Carna Industrial Fund in 1888, the conditions being that he should employ all the Company's workers in consideration of the Company selling an agreed quantity of his goods per annum. The terms upon which the Company is supplied, permit of a profit being made. Thus the primary object of the Company to secure employment for a large number of persons at Carna (which embraces Kilkerrin) has been secured, whilst the responsibility of maintaining an establishment and superintending the work is no longer incurred. To carry out the contract with Mr. Pattison, however, a steady sale for the goods must be found, but so far the Directors have been unable to obtain suitable permanent agents. There is a good prospect at present of an arrangement being made with the Congested Districts Board, whereby a depot will be established in Manchester. This arrangement would enable the Company to develop very largely their business, and secure permanence for the industries established by the Industrial Fund. In any case the standing expenses of the Company having now terminated, there can be no further loss of any considerable amount pending further developments.

For the Directors,

FRED. SCOTT, *Secretary.*

The Connemara Industries Company, Limited.

Profit and Loss Account for 12 Months ended March 31st, 1892.

Dr.	£	s.	d.
1891, March 31,			
To Stock-in-Trade,	103	18	2½
1892, March 31,			
„ Woollen Goods,.	204	10	8½
„ Wages,	141	5	9½
„ Household Expenses,	69	12	10
„ Printing, Advertising, Stationery, &c.,	11	11	8½
„ Travelling Expenses,	2	12	6
„ Carriage,	11	2	4
„ General Expenses,	54	4	9
„ Postages and Petty Cash,	14	5	4
„ Proportion of Preliminary Expenses written off this year,	5	0	0
„ Returns,	22	10	9
„ Depreciation on Fishing Apparatus,	3	12	0
„ Rent of Kilkerrin House (3 years),	39	0	0
„ Bad Debts,	1	10	1½
	£684	17	0½

Cr.	£	s.	d.
1892, March 31,			
By Sales,	264	9	1
„ Bank Interest, Discounts, &c.,	5	5	1½
„ Stock-in-Trade,	243	11	9
	513	5	11½
„ Balance, being Loss,	171	11	1
	£684	17	0½

Balance Sheet, March 31st, 1892.

Dr.	£	s.	d.	£	s.	d.
To Nominal Capital, viz.:-						
5,000 Shares at £1,	5,000	0	0			
„ Subscribed Capital:-						
1,034 shares at £1,.	1,034	0	0			
Less Arrears,	55	0	0			
	979	0	0			
Less Loss in 1889-90 £67 17 3						
„ 1890-91 70 12 10						
„ 1891-92 171 11 1						
	310	1	2	668	18	10
Accounts owing by the Company,				28	16	9½
				£697	15	7½

Cr.	£	s.	d.	£	s.	d.
By Accounts owing to he Company:–						
The late Father Flannery – Balance of Loans for advances to Fishermen and others,.	16	0	11			
Trading Accounts,	92	4	9	108	5	8
„ Fishing Apparatus – Barrels,	18	0	0			
Less Depreciation at 20 per cent.,	3	12	0	14	8	0
„ Stock-in-Trade,				243	11	9
„ Furniture, as per last Account,	46	1	5			
„ „ Additions during year,	0	4	4	46	5	9
„ Preliminary Expenses, as per last Account,	45	0	0			
„ *Less* proportion written off this year,	5	0	0	40	0	0
„ Manchester and Salford Bank,.				213	3	11
„ Cash in hand,				32	0	6½
				£697	15	7½

Audited and found correct,

William Aldred & Co.,

Chartered Accountants

Essex-street, Manchester,

August 8th, 1892.

To accompany Major RUTTLEDGE-FAIR'S REPORT on the CARNA DISTRICT.

CONGESTED DISTRICTS BOARD FOR IRELAND

III. – CARNA INDUSTRIES

Clifden, Co. Galway,
21st August, 1892.

Sir, – Referring to my report on the Carna District in this Union, I beg to enclose, to be attached to the report, a memorandum which I have since received from Mr. Joseph D. Kelly, National School teacher, relative to a scheme of Manual Instruction in connection with the Cashel National School.

I am, Sir, your obedient servant,
ROBERT RUTTLEDGE-FAIR.

The Secretary,
Congested Districts Board, Dublin.

(Copy).

National School, Cashel, Galway,
16th August, 1892.

To Major RUTTLEDGE-FAIR.

Sir, – I beg to state for you, as requested, the plan which I propose as a scheme of Manual Instruction in connection with this school, and which I had some time ago forwarded to Mr. Tuke.

I have had a special aptitude for handicraft, and much practice in several handicrafts arts, and believing firmly in the very great usefulness of Manual Instruction for the youth attending our schools, and especially for those among whom I live, I took the earliest opportunity of making myself a qualified instructor by attending at the Central Model Schools training department for examination six years ago, on the Education Board first recognising handicraft as an "extra" subject which might be taught in National Schools.

I soon felt that the subject could be only very ineffectually taught through the want of anything in the way of a special workshop, and so, on Mr. Tuke's mentioning the matter to me, my most anxious concern to bring under that gentleman's notice was the serious want of a workshop.

So that one might be got up with as little delay as possible, I made out a plan for a wooden one, to be covered entirely with corrugated iron, being 16½ feet long, 12 feet wide, 7 feet high to eave, and 10 feet to the ridge of the roof. This being properly ventilated, would be, in my opinion, sufficient for instructing 10 or 12 boys, which number I considered enough to begin with; and getting prices of material from Galway merchants, Messrs. Cloherty and Semple, I found that such a workshop could be put up, the work being done entirely by myself and the boys, for the moderate sum of £13 15*s.* 9*d.*, and a grant for this sum I requested from Mr. Tuke.

This being done, my plan is to conduct my class nearly in accord with the National Board's programme of handicraft, but modified or influenced by the circumstances of the locality, and so improved on, that items of household and agricultural utility could be turned out by the boys in a moderately good workmanlike manner, and that the repairs of boats at their own homes might also be satisfactorily done.

But the National Board requires that boys qualified to be examined for Results Fees in this subject should have attained the standard of Fifth Class, and I consider it would be most useful to admit good boys of a lower literary standard, and for this reason, as also for the reason that longer time should be employed and a fuller programme gone into. I would request that Mr. Tuke and the other gentlemen might award me some pay for my own services. I would say £10 a year or so, as the Education Board's grant for handicraft is only five shillings a year for two years, for each boy of Fifth Class or higher, who passes the examination.

There would also be required some tools, in addition to a supply which I have, so as to put a class of 10 or 12 boys into working order. An ample supply would cost about £4 10*s*., but I should be most happy to put the class into working order on my own efforts, on having the workshop for them to work in.

With regard to the working hours, I would consider that a morning lesson of an hour on three days of the week, and an evening lesson of an hour or two on three days, with a longer time, say of two or three hours, on Saturday would be sufficient.

I am Sir, your obedient servant,

JOSEPH D. KELLY.

Generations of Connemara families saw great changes over the years, such as this new pier constructed with funding from the Congested Districts Board.

CONGESTED DISTRICTS BOARD FOR IRELAND

COUNTY OF GALWAY – UNION OF CLIFDEN

REPORT OF MAJOR RUTTLEDGE-FAIR, *Inspector*

DISTRICT

OF

CLIFDEN

STATISTICAL TABLE

ELECTORAL DIVISION.	Area in Statute Acres.	Poor Law Valuation.	Number of Ratings at and under £10 and above £4 Valuation.	Number of Ratings at and under £4 Valuation.	Population in 1891.	Number of Families in 1891.	Number of Families on Holdings exceeding £2 and under £4 Valuation.	Number of Families on Holdings at and under £2 Valuation.	Number of Families in very poor circumstances.	Number of Families which have no Cattle.
		£								
Inishbofin,	3,152	572	9	549	997	215	96	36	60	46
Sillerna,	5,792	916	38	576	1,588	307	133	110	75	56
Clifden,	8,544	2,955	127	920	2,905	524	106	134	60*	35†
Errislannan,	5,046	681	34	303	839	171	63	34	30	20
Bunowen,	7,430	1,112	46	374	1,374	266	82	102	60	42
Doonloughan,	3,544	646	27	223	504	97	26	17	14	12
Derrylea,	10,386	398	11	78	283	53	28	18	5	2
Roundstone,	6,838	1,104	52	369	1,366	275	83	91	70	40
TOTALS,	50,732	8,384	344	3,392	9,856	1,908	617	542	374	253

* Not including really poor families in the Town of Clifden.
† Town of Clifden excluded.

(1.) Whether inland or maritime.

This district is chiefly maritime, extending southward from Inishbofin to Inishmee Island in Bertraghboy Bay.

(2.) Average quantity of land cultivated on holdings at and under £4 valuation, under (*a*) oats, (*b*) potatoes, (*c*) meadow, (*d*) green crops.

There are on an average about three-quarters of an acre of oats, one acre of potatoes, and a few perches of green crops cultivated on a holding at and under £4 valuation. There is a considerable quantity of meadow grown, about half an acre to each family.

(3.) Extent of mountain or moor grazing, and rights possessed by tenants, whether in common or otherwise.

Most of the tenants in this district have free grazing rights on the mountain and moorland adjoining their holdings. In some instances a small charge is made for this privilege (notably on the estates of Mrs. Sophia Kendell and Mr. William Young), 5*s.* being paid by each tenant in the former case, and a charge of 2*s.* for each beast grazed in the latter. In the Doonloughan Electoral Division there is no mountain, but the tenants have free grazing over a large extent of sand-banks which are more valuable. On the Berridge estate the tenants in former years had free grazing but limited to a number of live stock proportionate to the rent paid for each holding. Of recent years this limitation has not been adhered to, and the people now graze any quantity of stock they think fit. There are some townlands scattered through the district to which no mountain grazing is attached, and in such cases grazing is purchased by the tenants in other localities.

(4.) Extent and description of land, if any, which could be profitably reclaimed and added to existing adjoining holdings.

In most of the Electoral Divisions in this district, bog or moor might be obtained, which could be profitably reclaimed and added to existing adjoining holdings, but it would seem to me that wherever reclamation is feasible and *pays*, the tenants are gradually bringing such land into cultivation. As a general rule the owners now make no objection to the reclamation of mountain or bog land by the tenants of adjoining holdings. Of course there are hundreds of acres of bog which, apparently reclaimable, are really not so owing to the difficulty of obtaining manure, a plentiful supply of which is absolutely essential for reclamation purposes.

(5.) Particulars as to any suitable land in district which could be obtained, and to which families could be migrated with a reasonable prospect of success.

Although the district is very extensive, I cannot hear that much land suitable for migration purposes is for sale. In Clifden and Sillerna Electoral Divisions there are two farms, "Doon" containing 554 acres, and "Maw" 424 acres, the property of the late Rev. A. McGee, which I understand his executors are anxious to sell; some of the land is fairly good, but there is a very large proportion of rough mountain. The valuation of "Doon" is £51, that of "Maw" £6 13*s*. Neither of these farms are as suitable for migration as those recommended in the adjoining Letterfrack district. In Bunowen Electoral Division, a large farm owned by the late Mr. John Burke, in the townland of Ballyconneely, would I understand be sold by his administrators. This is a fairly good farm, and seaweed can also be obtained close by. The area is 270 acres, and the valuation £17.

(6.) Method of cultivation, manures, rotation of crops, etc., etc.

There is more clay-land in this district than in Carna, and a slightly different rotation of crops is followed. Potatoes are generally sown for two years in succession, and then followed by oats. More turnips and mangolds are sown, particularly round the town of Clifden and village of Ballyconneely. Spade labour is generally followed, the surface being too rocky and uneven for ploughs and harrows. Seaweed is generally used as manure, and in Sillerna and Bunowen Electoral Divisions, where the weed is exceptionally good, dung is hardly ever used; in the remaining Electoral Divisions it is mixed with seaweed.

In the part of the district know as Errismore, lying to the south-west of Clifden, in the Slyne Head peninsula, early potatoes are largely sown, the land being of a sandy nature, with a southern aspect. There, potatoes are sown in January and February, and are ready for use in June and July, when they are sold in the Clifden market; the main crop in other parts of this district is not available till towards the end of August. Rye, and sometimes barley, is sown in the sandy parts of the district instead of oats.

There is a good deal of meadow grown in small patches, and much of it is cut with reaping hooks, the spaces between the stones being too small to allow scythes to be used.

(7.) General information with regard to stock, and suggestions as to improvement of breeds – (*a*) cattle, (*b*) sheep, (*c*) horses and donkeys, (*d*) pigs, (*e*) poultry, etc., etc.

As a general rule, the people of this district depend mainly on live stock, and keep a better class than in the Carna district.

Cattle.– So far as these are concerned, it is generally urged that Galloway bulls should be introduced, and crossed with the local breeds. In places, however, such as Ballyconneely, Roundstone, Doonloughan, and Clifden, I think the land is good enough to try a cross with Polled Angus cattle. In the Sillerna Electoral Division, and in Inishbofin Island, Galloways would probably be more suitable.

Sheep.– A good many sheep are kept, and nearly all farmers concur in recommending a cross with Scotch black-faced rams; some, however, urge the advisability of trying a Cheviot cross, basing their recommendation on the ground that Cheviot is superior to black-faced wool for local use. I think the mountains in this district are too wet for Cheviot rams, except, perhaps, in Doonloughan Electoral Division, which is all sand.

Horses.– A small Hackney sire, about 14½ hands, with good bone and action, should, next year, be sent to Ballyconneely. There are a large number of mares, quite 300, in that part of the district, and if another good Barb sire could be purchased, he, too, might be sent there.

Pigs.– The breed of pigs is most inferior, great bony long legged beasts, and very difficult to fatten. Some Yorkshire boars should be distributed here and there through the district.

Poultry.– Nothing has yet been done to improve the breed of poultry. Next year I think sittings of eggs might be given to the better-off farmers, and by this means an improvement will soon be effected. Leghorns and Andalusians are probably the breeds best suited for this district.

(8.) Markets and fairs for cattle and produce of district; also statement as ~~to~~ where the people obtain food and other supplies, and the prevailing custom with regard to the disposal of butter, eggs, and poultry; to what extent are they sold in the first instance to local shopkeepers and dealers, and, generally speaking, how old are the eggs when sold to the first buyer, and about how old when they reach their ultimate destination in Great Britain.

There are eight fairs at Clifden, six at Roundstone, and three at Ballyconneely every year. A weekly market is also held at Clifden. Food and other supplies are obtained at Clifden and Roundstone, being brought by sailing boats from Galway. The supplies for Inishbofin are often got from Westport, where the fishermen go to sell fish; but one of the Clifden shopkeepers has opened a branch establishment at Inishbofin, and sends cargoes there direct from Galway. There are also a large number of country shops scattered through the district. Much the same custom as in the Letterfrack and Carna districts prevails as to the disposal of eggs, butter and poultry, and the prices obtained are somewhat similar. I understand the Inishbofin egglers keep eggs four weeks before sending them to Westport.

(9.) Rail, steamer, sailing boat, road, postal and telegraph facilities.

Galway and Clifden are the railway stations for this district, distant 52 and 44 miles respectively. The Galway and Clifden railway is now being constructed. There is no steamer traffic, but goods are brought from Galway to Clifden, Roundstone, and other points along the coast in large sailing boats. The roads are good, and much has recently been done to open up the district. Letters are sent twice daily from Galway to Clifden, and once to Roundstone. From Clifden they are forwarded to Cleggan daily by car, and thence three times a week, weather permitting, to Inishbofin Island. Letters are also sent daily from Clifden to Ballyconneely by car, and by a foot messenger to Errislannan. There are telegraph stations at Clifden and Roundstone, and another will shortly be opened at Ballyconneely with telephonic communication to Bunowen Coastguard Station, five miles further west.

(10.) Employment for labourers in the district, whether temporary or constant, and rate of wage.

There is very little employment for labourers in this district except in spring and harvest. The rate of wages at such periods is 1*s.* 6*d.* per day and food.

(11.) Migratory labour, average earnings per head, and where earned.

About seventeen labourers proceed from Inishbofin Electoral Division to Scotland, remaining there about six months. They are said to earn £1 per week during this period. No migratory labourers, it is said, leave the other Electoral Divisions.

(12.) Weaving, spinning, knitting, and sewing, whether used locally or sold, and where.

Weaving, spinning, knitting, and sewing are carried on in this district solely for home use. A good deal of rough flannel and frieze is spun and woven, and socks are knitted. Some of the better-off farmers have tweeds made from their own wool, which they send to Athlone or Glasgow for that purpose. The poorer classes who have not sufficient wool purchase it at about 1*s.* per lb., and others buy home-made flannel and frieze at the Clifden fairs, which is brought there from Joyce Country, a part of Oughterard Union, where large quantities are made by the country people. Good flannel can be bought for 1*s.* 10*d.*, and frieze from 2*s.* 2*d.* to 2*s.* 6*d.* per yard. Tweed suits are now largely purchased in the local shops for Sunday use; frieze and flannel being worn for rough work.

(13.) Kelp-burning, and sale of seaweed.

Kelp is extensively made in the Roundstone, Bunowen, and Doonloughan Electoral Divisions, also to a lesser degree on the islands of Turbot, Inishshark, and Inishbofin, and in the townlands of Gannoughs, Rossadillisk, Aughrus Beg, Aughrus More, and Rusheen, in Sillerna Electoral Division. It is estimated that in the first three Electoral Divisions I have mentioned, more than 400 tons will be sold this year at prices averaging £4 10*s.* per ton. About 200 tons will be sold in the other places mentioned at £4 per ton. Seaweed is sold to families living further inland for manure. I cannot furnish an estimate of the quantity sold, but the price obtained is about 10*s.* per ton.

(14.) Sale of turf, nature and extent of bogs.

An extensive sale of turf is carried on in the Derrylea and Bunowen Electoral Divisions, the former supplying the town of Clifden, and the latter the Electoral Division of Doonloughan. Turf is sold in Clifden for 1*s.* 6*d.* to 1*s.* 9*d.* per box. The people of Doonloughan generally buy turf banks in Bunowen and save the fuel themselves, paying from 12*s.* to 15*s.* for a year's supply.

The bogs in the district are practically inexhaustible and of very good quality.

In some townlands in the other Electoral Divisions the people have to purchase turf from their neighbours. Here and there I observed many instances where the people, too lazy to cut turf elsewhere, were cutting away land which had been previously reclaimed, and were thus depreciating the value of their holdings.

In other cases, too, especially on Inishbofin and Inishshark Islands, half clay half peat sods are cut from the mountain commonage and used as fuel. Acres upon acres of these islands have been rendered useless for any purpose by this process.

(15.) Lobster fishing, number of men and boats employed.

Lobster fishing is extensively carried on; over 300 men and 100 boats are employed. In an average year each man would earn £10 or £30 per boat. These men stay away from their homes for several weeks. I have constantly seen Connemara lobster boats north of Achill Head, quite fifty miles from the Galway coast. Six shillings per dozen seems the general price obtained for lobsters from six to eight inches in length. I have had numerous complaints of the low price given in places where there is no competition among the buyers. The establishment of depots along the coast where lobsters could be sold would be a great boon.

(16.) Sea fishing. Facilities for sale of fish, and number of boats and men solely employed in fishing.

The number of boats solely employed in fishing is practically *nil*, except in Inishbofin and Inishshark Islands. See also paragraph (18) below.

(17.) Number of boats and men employed in carrying turf or seaweed or in fishing. Classification of boats.

There are in this district 252 boats and 7 curraghs employed in fishing, and carrying turf and seaweed. All the boats are third-class sailing and rowing boats, except a few large hookers, which are used in bringing goods from Galway.

(18.) Fish; whether consumed at home or sold.

Fishing is mainly confined to Inishbofin Electoral Division, the townlands of Rossadillisk, Aughrus Beg, Gannoughs, and Aughrus More, in Sillerna Electoral Division; Turbot and Inishturk Islands, in Clifden Electoral Division; Leaghcarrick in Doonloughan Electoral Division; Doohulla, Dolan, and Foorglass in Bunowen Electoral Division, and Inishlackan Island in Roundstone Electoral Division. Most of the fish caught is sold at Clifden and in the surrounding districts. The Inishbofin people generally sell their fish at Westport.

The Inishbofin and Inishshark islanders are the best and most practical fishermen on the west coast. I have little doubt that if some encouragement is given by the Board, in the way of providing an easy and certain market for the sale of fish in this portion of the district, the resources of the people will be immeasurably strengthened in a very short time.

(19.) Extent of fish-curing.

There is no fish curing attempted in the district, except salting fish in a very rough manner. A curing station has recently been established at Inishbofin Island, under the auspices of the Board.

(20.) Piers and Harbours, existing and suggested, and how far those existing are adapted to wants of district.

Ardbear, two miles from Clifden, and Bertraghboy Bay, the southern boundary of the district, are naturally sheltered harbours. Ardbear, owing to the want of lights, cannot be entered at night, and Bertraghboy Bay has neither lights nor leading marks.

At Inishbofin Island there is a small harbour well sheltered for fishing boats, but the deep water portion is exposed to south-westerly gales. A nasty rock makes the entrance rather difficult; this obstacle ought certainly to be removed. Piers or shelters exist at Inishbofin (east end), Inishshark Island, Aughrus Beg, Turbot Island, Inishturk Island, Clifden, Errislannan (2), Slackport, Bunowen, Dolan, Doohulla, Roundstone (2), Bealatragh, and Inishlackan Island.

The causeway and the pier at Inishbofin (east end) have only been recently constructed. The breakwater at Shark Island was commenced in 1886 by the Piers and Roads Commission; it was continued in 1891 under the Relief of Distress Act, and about £250 is still required to complete the works. I doubt whether any shelter on the west coast was so much required, or better carried out so far.

A large rock at the entrance ought to be removed, an easy task, as it is only covered for about two hours of flood tide. The rocks on which the pier-breakwater is built should be cut straighter to allow boats to come alongside at any time, and a rough patch of rocky ground over which boats have to be hauled up for safety should be grouted with concrete.

At Aughrus Beg, a nice shelter for small boats was made by the Piers and Roads Commission in 1886, but the entrance was not sufficiently deepened and widened; this defect might now be remedied, it would not be an expensive work.

I cannot recommend further expenditure at present on the Turbot, Inishturk, and Fahy boat-slips, or on the Clifden pier, although the Rev. Father Lynskey urges the extension of the latter – a work which he admits would cost between £5,000 and £10,000. An alternative proposal also mentioned by him, viz.:– placing dock gates across the channel near the existing pier, would not, I think, affect any improvement. The same remark applies to the piers at Errislannan (2) and Slackport.

At Bunowen is the only pier where deep water at all states of the tide can be got. It seems a sheltered place, but I have been informed by many boatmen that it is dangerous for boats in south-west and southerly winds. I understand the shelter wall on the north side requires to be extended till in a line slightly north-north-east with the end of the south pier, and curved towards it to narrow the existing entrance. This would be, I fear, an expensive undertaking, as most of the proposed work is in deep water and would require to be built in the most substantial manner.

The shelters at Dolan and Doohulla are not valuable works. At Roundstone there are two piers which together form a small harbour. There is a reef of rocks close by the point of the north pier which ought to be removed, or the pier extended to cover them, the latter, though more expensive, would be the best arrangement.

Beelatragh pier, near Roundstone, is another useful work made by the Piers and Roads Commission. I did not see the place at low water and am not, therefore, in a position to make any suggestions as to its improvement. I hear there are some rocks at the entrance which ought to be removed.

On Inishlackan Island a pier was constructed by, I understand, the Fishery Piers and Harbours Commissioners. It is a dangerous place in rough weather, and one where a considerable expenditure would have to be incurred to effect any substantial improvement.

There are a good number of fishermen at Rossadillisk, in Sillerna Electoral Division; a pier there would be a very useful work and one much required. The proposed site is rather exposed to westerly winds, so that any work undertaken there would require to be very carefully constructed.

At Leaghcarrick, east of Slackport, a harbour of refuge for boats waiting to pass Slyne Head has been suggested. The proposed place is fairly good. A breakwater about sixty yards in length is required. There are twelve feet of water on the reef of rocks on which it would be built, and a deep pool inside, where large hookers could lie in perfect safety.

(21.) Extent of salmon and freshwater fisheries. Number of men earning their livelihood therefrom.

There are two small fisheries at Ardbear and Doohulla, on which some ten men are employed in the close season at 10*s.* per week.

(22.) Banks and Loan Funds.

There is a branch of the National Bank at Clifden. There are no Loan Funds in the district.

(23.) Mineral and other resources.

A copper mine at Murvey, in the Roundstone Electoral Division, was worked for several years, but always at a loss, the ore not being sufficiently rich to pay the cost of transit to Liverpool. A marble quarry at Streamstown, two miles from Clifden, is still occasionally worked by Mr. Collins of Kilkenny, but only six men are employed.

(24.) Relative prevalence of cash or credit dealings, length of credit, interest charged, extent of barter, etc., etc.

Generally speaking most families run into debt about Christmas, and debts increase till the month of June, or later in the case of families living away from the coast; about June kelp is ready for sale, and other resources such as fish, and in Errismore early potatoes, are also available. Part of the debt due is then paid, the balance is discharged in Autumn, when cattle and sheep &c., &c. are disposed of. In bad years balances always remain due to the shop-keepers, and are carried forward into the next year's account. From 15 to 25 per cent. is charged as interest. Very little barter is carried on in the neighbourhood of Clifden, but in the remote Electoral Divisions of Sillerna and Doonloughan, and in Inishbofin and Shark Islands, it is extensively practised; eggs and fish being exchanged for tea, sugar, and tobacco. Sometimes fish also are exchanged for flour.

(25.) Estimated *cash* receipts and expenditure of a family in ordinary circumstances.

The estimated *cash* receipts and expenditure of a family of six persons in ordinary circumstances, on a holding at or under £4 valuation, are as follows:–

RECEIPTS	£	s.	d.	EXPENDITURE	£	s.	d.
Sale of 3½ tons kelp, at £4 10*s.* per ton,	15	15	0	Rent of holding,	6	0	0
" 2 pigs (profit),	4	0	0	County Cess,	0	16	0
" 3 cattle,	18	0	0	Clerical dues,	0	10	0
" 1 foal,	5	0	0	Flour at 14*s.* per cwt.,	15	12	0
" 5 sheep at 10*s.*,	2	10	0	Groceries at 4*s.* 3*d.* per week,	10	9	6
" 12 cwt. oats at 5*s.* 6*d.*,	3	6	0	Tobacco,	2	12	0
" eggs,	1	10	0	Clothes and shoes,	8	14	0
				Household goods, &c.,	2	0	0
Total,	£50	1	0	Total,	£46	13	6
Surplus,	£3	7	6				

The estimated *cash* receipts and expenditure of a family of six persons in poor circumstances, on a holding of about £2 valuation, are as follows:–

RECEIPTS	£	s.	d.	EXPENDITURE	£	s.	d.
Sale of lobsters,	8	0	0	Rent of holding,	2	0	0
" 3 tons kelp at £4 per ton,	12	0	0	County Cess,	0	5	4
" pig (profit),	2	0	0	Meal at 7*s.* per cwt.,	4	4	0
" bullock,	5	10	0	Flour at 14*s.* per cwt.,	9	16	0
" oats 6 cwt. at 5*s.* 6*d.*,	1	13	0	Groceries,	6	19	8
" eggs,	2	0	0	Tobacco,	2	12	0
" potatoes 20 cwt.,	2	0	0	Clothes and shoes,	5	10	0
				Household goods,	1	10	0
				Clerical dues,	0	6	0
Total,	£33	3	0	Total,	£33	3	0

(26.) Estimated value of home-grown food consumed, and period during which it lasts.

The estimated value of home-grown food consumed in this district is as follows:–

	£	s.	d.
About 5 tons potatoes,	10	0	0
1½ " straw,	3	0	0
1 " hay,	3	0	0
Total,	£16	0	0

(27.) Dietary of people, number of meals daily, and kinds of food throughout the year.

The people of this district take three meals daily, viz:–

Breakfast. – Tea and home-made flour bread.

Dinner. – Potatoes and fish or eggs.

Supper. – Tea and flour bread.

No matter how tea can be got it is found somewhere, and flour too. The use of Indian meal is rapidly dying out. It is everywhere admitted that the standard of living is increasing.

(28.) Clothing, whether home-made or bought, etc., etc.

See paragraph 12 of this Report.

(29.) Dwellings: kind of houses, home-life and customs, etc., etc.

The houses with walls about six feet high, and roofed with straw or rough sedge, are very small. In many there is only one apartment, but generally the buildings consist of a kitchen and one room. They have no chimney, the fire being laid on the hearth, and a hole made in the roof to allow the smoke to escape. Live stock are always kept in the kitchen during the winter months.

(30.) Character of the people for industry, etc., etc.

Whenever the people find that labour pays, they are fairly industrious and hardworking, but, on the other hand, they are easily discouraged, and have little perseverance, and magnify difficulties. Unfortunately, they have learned to look to Government for assistance in the smallest enterprise, and they never seem to think that a little energy on their part would tide them over many difficulties.

(31.) Whether any organized effort has been made to develop the resources or improve the condition of the people. If so, by what means.

I am not aware of any organized effort having been made to improve the condition of the people in this district, except an emigration scheme which was carried out by Mr. Tuke's committee in 1882 - 3 - 4, and which, I believe, was remarkably successful.

(32.) Suggestions as to any possible method for improving the condition of the people in future.

As a means by which the condition of the people could be improved, I would suggest that an attempt be made to improve the various breeds of live stock, which would confer incalculable benefit on nearly every family in the district. As regards the fishing industry, I think an effort should be made to establish at least two curing stations, one on the north and the other on the south side of Slyne Head. Aughrus Beg and Rossadillisk seem to be fairly suitable places on the northern side, while Roundstone or Bunowen, to the south of this dangerous headland, would, I think, be good centres. A curing station has already been established at Inishbofin Island.

Efforts might also be made to obtain one of the grass farms I have alluded to, so that the migration of a certain number of families from the poorest townlands might, at least, be given a fair trial.

It has also been suggested that next spring, small quantities of seed oats, barley, and rye should be supplied to occupiers of land at cost price. I think arrangements should be made to carry out this suggestion early next February.

ROBERT RUTTLEDGE-FAIR,
Inspector.

26th August, 1892.

To

The Congested Districts Board for Ireland.

CONGESTED DISTRICTS BOARD FOR IRELAND

COUNTY OF GALWAY – UNION OF CLIFDEN

REPORT OF MAJOR RUTTLEDGE-FAIR, *Inspector*

DISTRICT
OF

LETTERFRACK

STATISTICAL TABLE

ELECTORAL DIVISION.	Area in Statute Acres.	Poor Law Valuation.	Number of Ratings at and under £10 and above £4 Valuation.	Number of Ratings at and under £4 Valuation.	Population in 1891.	Number of Families in 1891.	Number of Families on Holdings exceeding £2 and under £4 Valuation.	Number of Families on Holdings at and under £2 Valuation.	Number of Families in very poor circumstances.	Number of Families which have no Cattle.
		£								
Ballynakill,	11,486	1,222	36	102	782	123	24	43	10	8
Cleggan,	4,671	748	27	153	613	116	41	21	27	18
Cushkillary,	15,079	676	15	100	465	81	26	3	7	4
Rinvyle,	13,519	1,998	147	512	2,280	401	133	72	81	15
TOTALS,	44,755	4,644	225	867	4,140	721	224	139	125	45

(1.) Whether inland or maritime.

This district is maritime. The coastline extends from Killary Bay to Cleggan Harbour, a distance of about twenty-three statute miles. More than nine-tenths of the population reside in townlands immediately adjoining the sea-coast.

(2.) Average quantity of land cultivated on holdings at and under £4 valuation, under (*a*) oats, (*b*) potatoes, (*c*) meadow, (*d*) green crops.

The returns which I have obtained show that about half an acre of oats, three roods of potatoes, and half an acre of meadow, are on an average cultivated on holdings at and under £4 valuation. Other green crops are almost nil.

(3.) Extent of mountain or moor grazing, and rights possessed by tenants, whether in common or otherwise.

In the Ballynakill Electoral Division most of the mountain grazing is in the hands of the landlords, but the people are allowed to graze their cattle and sheep on some of the townlands at fixed charges. On one property the mountains have been re-let to the tenants, *but for grazing purposes only*, and altogether distinct from the holdings on which they reside. In the Cushkillary Electoral Division the tenants as a rule have free grazing on certain portions of the adjoining mountains as a right inseparable from their holdings. The remaining mountain lands are in the landlords' hands, and are either farmed by them or let to graziers. In Cleggan Electoral Division the tenants all seem to have a good deal of rough mountain grazing which they hold in connection with their holdings, except in one townland which is all arable with no mountain attached. In the Rinvyle Electoral Division, which is owned by two landlords, Mr. Mitchell Henry and Mr. Blake, the tenants of the former have free grazing on the mountains adjacent to their holdings, but the Blake tenantry are charged at the rate of 12*s.* a year for cattle and 2*s.* for sheep for this privilege, and they have no commonage rights without payment.

(4.) & (5.) Extent and description of land, if any, which could be profitably

There are several tracts of land in this district which in my opinion are very suitable both for reclamation and the migration of families from townlands in the immediate reclaimed and added to existing adjoining holdings. Particulars as to any suitable land in district which could be obtained, and to which families could be migrated with a reasonable prospect of success.

locality which are too thickly populated to afford reasonable means of subsistence to such a large number of persons. The townland of Bunowen in Cushkillary Electoral Division, valuation £54, contains some 1,400 acres of rough grazing and bog land, which is easy to reclaim. There is only one inhabited house in this townland, while in the townland of Glassillaun, owned by the same proprietor, and only containing some 322 acres, twenty-three families reside, many of them in a state of poverty. Glassillaun is not more than two miles from Bunowen.

Again, in Ballynakill Electoral Division the trustees of the late Mr. Prior own a very extensive farm, partly arable and partly mountain, which for some time past they have, I am informed, endeavoured to sell. This farm, containing nearly 800 acres, would be very suitable for migration, as there are in the immediate vicinity several densely populated townlands, owned by Mr. Blake of Rinvyle, from which, I imagine, many families would be only too glad to migrate to Prior's farm. There are ample facilities for obtaining seaweed for manure.

There is also in Ballynakill Electoral Division a small farm called Rockfield, recently ordered to be sold by the Endowed Schools Commissioners, which would be very suitable for reclamation purposes. There is a good fall facing north and east, and drainage could be easily effected. The area of the farm is small (414 acres) as compared with either Bunowen or Prior's farm. Further, I think Rockfield will fetch a higher price as there will be more competition. The Government valuation of Rockfield is £68, and of Prior's farm £229.

(6.) Method of cultivation, manures, rotation of crops, etc., etc.

The method of cultivation is by spade labour. The land is so rocky and uneven that ploughs or harrows cannot be used. Farm-yard dung of a very poor description, and large quantities of seaweed are used as manures. "Artificials" are unknown. It is wonderful what good crops of potatoes are raised, having regard to the poverty of the soil. Oats are nearly always poor, the grain weighing very light, but the straw is valuable as fodder for cattle in winter. In this district a very considerable extent of land is meadowed far more so than in the adjoining County Mayo districts. Small plots are also sown with turnips and mangolds. This practice seems to be gradually extending. There is, however, a wide field for improvement in this respect, and I have little doubt that the value of cattle, &c., &c., would be much increased by judicious winter and spring feeding.

On the whole, the land is better cultivated in Letterfrack than in either Achill or Belmullet. This perhaps may be attributed to the training many of the peasantry received working as labourers on Mr. Mitchell Henry's large farms in the neighbourhood.

(7.) General information with regard to stock, and suggestions as to improvement of breeds – (*a*) cattle, (*b*) sheep, (*c*) horses and donkeys, (*d*) pigs, (*e*) poultry, etc., etc.

Information as to the stock of this district is as follows:–

Cattle.– These are a rough and hardy class. They are principally a cross between the ordinary country cattle and either Galloway or Polled-Angus bulls. They are of slow growth and never, under existing circumstances, really fit for sale till three or four years old, when they are eagerly sought for by Meath buyers. Some are also purchased to feed in the eastern districts of Galway. The country people complain that the "black" cattle are bad milkers. Some effort ought to be made to introduce really good bulls, and all the experienced farmers in the district are unanimous in recommending Galloways, as they say the land is too rough for Polled-Angus.

Sheep.– These are not too bad, but a distribution of black-faced rams would improve them.

Horses.– The people are well pleased that a Hackney sire was placed at Letterfrack. The stallion sent there is much admired.

Pigs.– These are small, hard, and difficult to fatten. If a few Yorkshire boars could be sold at low prices a change for the better in this respect would soon be evident.

Poultry.– There is no market for poultry, but any number of eggs can easily be sold. I would suggest that a few Andalusian cockerels be distributed.

(8.) Markets and fairs for cattle and produce of district; also statement as to where the people obtain food and other supplies, and the prevailing custom

Clifden, about fourteen miles from the centre of the district, is the market town. There, too, the principal fairs are held. There are also seven fairs held at Tully and Letterfrack, small villages in the district. Flour, meal, and groceries are obtained from the local shop-keepers with regard to the disposal of butter, eggs, and poultry; to what extent are they sold in the first instance to local shopkeepers and dealers, and, generally speaking, how old are the eggs when sold to the first buyer, and about how old when they reach their ultimate destination in Great Britain.

in these villages, and there are also a number of petty dealers scattered through the district who sell tea, sugar, and tobacco, generally bartering them for eggs. All drapery, etc., is purchased at Clifden and Letterfrack. There is very little butter sold but large numbers of eggs. The petty dealers re-sell the eggs to Westport buyers, who, in their turn, transmit them to buyers in the large English towns.

The following particulars may, perhaps, be interesting as showing the large quantity of eggs sold annually. There are over 700 families in the district. Of four families selected haphazard, the first sold in three months 380 eggs, a second in two months, 420, and a third in seven weeks 244. Prices vary from 4*s.* to 8*s.* per 120, I think 5*s.* 6*d.* may be taken as a fair average price. They are generally sold once a week, and are probably kept by the petty dealers two or three days before they are sent to Westport, and take at least four or five days more before they reach the English and Scotch towns. A few poultry are sold in the district at the following prices:– Chickens, 4*d.* to 6*d.*; ducks, 8*d.* to 10*d.*; geese, 1*s.* 4*d.* to 2*s.*, each.

(9.) Rail, steamer, sailing boat, road, postal and telegraph facilities.

The nearest railway station is Westport, thirty-four miles from Letterfrack. The construction of the Galway and Clifden Railway will improve matters a little in this respect, as when that line is opened there will be two stations, one at Clifden, eleven miles, and the other at Recess, fifteen miles, available for the Letterfrack district. A small steamer was last year run by a Westport trader to Letterfrack and Leenane, the latter a little village at the head of Killary Bay, to convey flour, meal, etc., etc. Financially the project did not succeed and it has now been abandoned. There are good roads through most of the district.

There is a telegraph office at Letterfrack, and letters are conveyed there every morning from Galway arriving at 9.30 A.M. There is a post messenger to Rinvyle, the most thickly populated portion of the district, and as the post only arrives there at 12 o'clock it is very difficult to answer letters by the return post which leaves about 1 o'clock, P.M. There is an excellent hotel at Rinvyle much frequented by tourists who suffer considerable inconvenience by this arrangement, if the post was sent on by car much additional time would be afforded, and there are many districts not half so important which enjoy that advantage.

(10.) Employment for labourers in the district, whether temporary or constant, and rate of wage.

There are about 120 men and boys afforded constant employment at wages from 5*s.* to 9*s.* per week by Mr. Mitchell Henry and other resident proprietors. In this respect, Letterfrack compares very favourably with other congested districts.

(11.) Migratory labour, average earnings per head, and where earned.

There may be said to be practically no migratory labourers in this district, but I learned that eight men left this year for Scotland.

(12.) Weaving, spinning, knitting, and sewing, whether used locally or sold, and where.

The clothing principally worn is either blue or grey frieze, which is made in the district, though some of the young men indulge in tweed suits purchased at either Clifden or Letterfrack. The fishermen wear suits made of thick white flannel, which is very durable, and well suited for rough work. It is estimated that from two to three stone of wool are required to clothe a family of six persons. There are a good many sheep in the district, and people who have not sufficient wool buy from the large graziers at prices varying from 1*s.* to 1*s.* 2*d.* per lb. To provide the required clothing, spinning and weaving is carried on to a very considerable extent. The people spin the wool in their houses; most of the older women spin well. Weaving lasts from May to about Christmas, and during that period weavers, of whom there are four in the district, can earn from 12*s.* to 16*s.* a week. There is no sale of flannel, frieze, or stockings from the district, everything made is used locally, but flannel, &c., &c., is brought from the adjoining Joyce Country district and sold at the Letterfrack and Tully fairs.

(13.) Kelp-burning, and sale of seaweed.

Over fifty families are engaged in the kelp-burning industry. In average years, about 200 tons of kelp are sold, at prices varying from £3 10*s.* to £4 10*s.* per ton. Almost all these families reside on the Blake Estate at Rinvyle, and a royalty of 25 per cent. is charged by the landlord on all kelp made on his estate. Rinvyle is a peninsula stretching far seaward, where the kelp weed, parted from its stem by stormy weather, is swept ashore by the currents which strike the headland, without entering into Killary Bay or Ballynakill, on either side.

The price of kelp is gradually recovering from the low standard to which it fell in 1879-80. Some seven years ago, £3 per ton was the highest price paid; this year I hear that £5 can be obtained for really good kelp.

(14.) Sale of turf, nature and extent of bogs.

In most townlands there is a good supply of excellent turf, sufficient to last for many years. In the townland of Dawros Beg, the bog has been all cut away, and the people have to bring turf across Ballynakill Bay in boats, a distance of some two miles. I observed in this townland that many of the tenants were cutting turf on land that had been reclaimed, and was giving good crops.

(15.) Lobster fishing, number of men and boats employed.

Thirty-two men in sixteen canoes fish for lobsters. They can earn from 12*s.* to 16*s.* per week each, from 1st May to the end of September. Lobsters are sold at Leenane to a local buyer, who sends them to Westport. The average price is 5*s.* 6*d.* per dozen.

(16.) Sea fishing. Facilities for sale of fish, and number of boats and men solely employed in fishing.

During the autumn months, a good many families fish pretty constantly when not engaged on their farms; but at other periods of the year not more than a dozen men, just sufficient to supply local demand, fish regularly. There are no facilities for the sale of any considerable quantity of fish. Very few families depend upon fishing.

(17.) Number of boats and men employed in carrying turf or seaweed or in fishing. Classification of boats.

There are twenty-six boats, all third class, and 136 curraghs engaged in fishing and carrying turf.

(18.) Fish; whether consumed at home or sold.

[See paragraph (16)].

(19.) Extent of fish-curing.

There is no fish-curing carried on in this district, except some coarse fish, which are salted for local use.

(20.) Piers and Harbours, existing and suggested, and how far those existing are adapted to wants of district.

There are three excellent harbours in the district, viz.:– Killary Bay, Salrock Harbour, and Ballynakill Bay, but lights and leading marks are sadly required to show the entrance channels, and nothing is more necessary than that they should be provided. Piers exist at Glassillaun, Tully, Derryinver, Letterfrack, and Cleggan. None of them are of much use for fishing purposes, but they are capable of improvement. The pier at Tully in its present state is almost useless. Cleggan is the landing place for Boffin Island. I think a pier should be constructed at Rinvyle if Mr. Blake gave a site and right of way. Another pier or wharf is required near Leenane, in Killary Bay, to enable goods and fish to be landed.

(21.) Extent of salmon and freshwater fisheries. Number of men earning their livelihood therefrom.

Twenty-three men are employed at salmon fishing for four months; their earnings average about 12*s.* per week during that period.

(22.) Banks and Loan Funds.

There are no Banks nor Loan Funds in this district.

(23.) Mineral and other resources.

There is a marble quarry in the Ballynakill Electoral Division, the property of Mr. F.C. Graham. I understand it was let on lease to a Belfast firm, but the difficulty of removing the marble owing to the want of a road leading to Letterfrack was so great that the lease was surrendered to the owner. During the Relief of Distress 1890-91, a road to this quarry was commenced, but was left unfinished.

(24.) Relative prevalence of cash or credit dealings, length of credit, interest charged, extent of barter, etc., etc.

Almost all flour, meal, and drapery purchased between Christmas and the following July are given on credit, and are paid for during the autumn and winter. In a bad season debts accumulate as the people are not then able to pay all their engagements, but they generally manage to pay part, and the balance is carried forward to the next account; two bad seasons in succession would be disastrous as the shop-keepers' resources are limited. Interest varies from ten to twenty per cent. for six months' credit; any per centage asked is given when balances have to be carried forward into next year's accounts. I think the rate of interest depends on the shop-keeper's knowledge of the ability of his customer to meet his engagements. Notoriously "bad pays" are always charged a higher rate of interest.

(25.) Estimated *cash* receipts and expenditure of a family in ordinary circumstances.

The estimated *cash* receipts and expenditure of a fairly well-off family consisting of six persons are as follows:–

RECEIPTS	£	s.	d.	EXPENDITURE	£	s.	d.
Sale of kelp, 3 tons at £4,	12	10	0	Rent, . .	6	0	0
„ lobsters at 12*s.* per week, .	3	8	0	County Cess, . .	0	16	0
„ three pigs, .	4	10	0	Flour, 9 bags, . .	12	12	0
„ a foal, .	5	0	0	Groceries at 4*s.* 3*d.* per week, .	10	9	6
„ two cattle at £6 each, .	12	0	0	Tobacco, . .	2	12	0
„ 8 lambs at 8*s.*, .	3	4	0	Clothing (principally home made) and shoes, . .	4	13	0
„ 4 sheep at £1, .	4	0	0	Household goods, &c., .	2	10	0
„ 8 cwt. of oats at 6*s.*, .	2	8	0	Clerical dues, . .	0	10	0
„ 1,200 eggs at 6*s.* per 120, .	3	0	0				
Total, . .	£49	10	0	Total, .	£40	2	6

The estimated *cash* receipts and expenditure of a poor family consisting of six persons are as follows:–

RECEIPTS	£	s.	d.	EXPENDITURE	£	s.	d.
Labour at 9*s.* per week,	23	8	0	Rent, . .	2	0	0
A pig, .	1	10	0	County Cess, . .	0	5	4
A bullock (one sold every two years), .	3	0	0	Meal at 7*s.* per cwt., . .	4	0	0
1,200 eggs at 6*s.* per 120, .	3	0	0	Flour, 5 bags, . .	7	0	0
Value of fish caught in autumn, (say £3), .	3	0	0	Groceries, . .	6	19	8
				Tobacco, . .	2	12	0
				Clothes and shoes . .	4	13	0
				Household goods, . .	1	10	0
				Clerical dues, . .	0	6	0
Total, . .	£33	18	0	Total, .	£29	6	0

(26.) Estimated value of home-grown food consumed, and period during which it lasts.

The estimated value of home-grown food consumed is as follows:–

	£	s.	d.
About 4 tons of potatoes,	8	0	0
1 ton of straw,	1	10	0
1 ton of hay,	2	0	0
Total,	11	10	0

(27.) Dietary of people, number of meals daily, and kinds of food throughout the year.

The people of this district take three meals daily, viz.:–

Breakfast. – Consisting of tea and baked cake made of flour, the poorer classes taking tea and potatoes.

Dinner. – Is taken about one o'clock p.m., potatoes and milk with eggs and sometimes fish is the principal food.

Supper. – Is taken at eight o'clock, tea and baked cake is generally taken; but the poorer classes cannot afford tea twice a day and use potatoes, and Indian meal stirabout and sugar, when potatoes are exhausted for this meal.

(28.) Clothing, whether home-made or bought, etc., etc.

[See paragraph (12)].

(29.) Dwellings: kind of houses, home-life and customs, etc., etc.

The houses are generally built of stone without mortar. The interior consists of one room, sometimes two rooms, and a kitchen. In the latter the cattle are kept in winter and the male members of the family sleep also. The heads of the house sleep in the room and the girls occupy the same apartment. The bedding is almost always bad, and sometimes positively filthy. In many of the houses there are no chimneys, the smoke being conveyed through a hole in the roof. The houses are seldom whitewashed, lime being scarce and expensive. The better class houses are plastered and whitewashed now and again. The people are early risers and in the remote villages of Rinvyle Electoral Division they retire to rest about 9 o'clock.

(30.) Character of the people for industry, etc., etc.

In spring and harvest the people are industrious but there is no real determination shown to overcome difficulties, work is taken up by fits and starts and after working fairly well for short periods, the people remain idle for several weeks and this for no apparent reason.

During winter and in the early spring no work is done, except to feed the cattle and bring turf and water to the houses.

(31.) Whether any organized effort has been made to develop the resources or improve the condition of the people. If so, by what means.

There has been no organized effort made to develop the resources of the people on any extensive scale. Emigration was carried out under Mr. Tuke's Committee in 1882-83-84 and a considerable number of families were assisted to emigrate. Much improvement was thus effected. During the last three years basket-making has been undertaken by Miss Sturge, an English lady. I learn that this industry is not yet self supporting; but employment has been afforded and the outlook is brighter. Miss Sturge seems to carry on her work in a thoroughly business-like manner. She does not ask for assistance from the Congested Districts Board. An iron hut containing a workshop and apartments for the teachers has been erected at considerable expense. Osiers have also been planted but it is too soon to express an opinion as to whether they can be grown successfully. At present osiers are imported and I imagine the cost of carriage and difficulties of transit, etc., add much to the working expenses. Only eight boys are employed but they get constant work and Miss Sturge tells me she finds no difficulty in disposing of the baskets and other wicker work.

(32.) Suggestions as to any possible method for improving the condition of the people in future.

The principal means of subsistence possessed by the people in this district are:–

(1.) Farming, including mountain grazing.
(2.) Employment as agricultural labourers.
(3.) Kelp making.
(4.) Sea fishing, including lobsters.

The small farms occupied by the people might easily be made to yield 50 per cent. better returns, and that with very little additional labour. For many years sub-division has been carried on to an extent which even on the West Coast is almost unprecedented, and until the townlands which are so overpopulated are thinned out, either by emigration or by migration, little can be done to help the people. I have already (paragraphs 4 and 5) pointed out places to which families might be migrated, and if the people were once scattered in this manner, with very stringent provisions against sub-division in the future, efforts might be made (*a*) to assist in fencing and drainage works; (*b*) to give instruction in an improved system of cultivation and fencing generally; (*c*) to obtain a better class of cattle and sheep.

As compared with other congested districts Letterfrack is well circumstanced for the employment of agricultural labourers, but there are two portions of the district where labour is required by the people – one at Rinvyle and the other at Baunoges.

The townlands of Ardnagreevagh and Cashleen, in the Rinvyle Electoral Division, are cut off from sea or inland communication by the want of a proper road. It is impossible to expect that persons who are unable to bring a vehicle of any kind to their dwellings can ever become really prosperous. To their villages everything has to be carried for at least one and a half miles on the people's backs. I would suggest that a road be constructed, and an outlet be thus given to the sea to enable the people to carry on fishing with better facilities than they now enjoy. The road at Baunoges to the marble quarry, commenced by the Government in 1890-91, might also be completed.

Letterfrack is so peculiarly adapted for sea fishing, owing to the safety afforded by the three natural harbours alluded to in paragraph 20, that it is difficult to realize how fishing is so little followed by the people, but on looking closely into the question it is apparent that to the want of facilities for the sale of any large quantity of fish this apathy on the part of the people must be attributed. This district will derive some benefit from the Galway and Clifden railway, but I fear the stations at Recess and Clifden will be too remote for the conveyance of fish.

If a subsidy could be given to some person in Westport who would be willing to guarantee a regular steamer service to the Killeries, Letterfrack, and Boffin, easy means of transit would be afforded. A small steamer was last year run to Letterfrack, and it was then calculated that £80 per week would pay the working expenses. This amount not being realized the steamer was taken off. During the Relief of Distress, the Government established a service for several months between Westport and Boffin and other Islands, which worked very regularly. It is of the last importance that some easy means of transit should be provided, if fishing is ever to be revived in this district.

ROBERT RUTTLEDGE-FAIR,
Inspector.

19th May, 1892.

To

The Congested Districts Board for Ireland.

Large steamers plied their trade to Leenane, at the head of Killary Bay, a natural deep-water fjord offering protection from the rough Atlantic seas.

CONGESTED DISTRICTS BOARD FOR IRELAND

COUNTY OF GALWAY – UNION OF OUGHTERARD

REPORT OF MAJOR GASKELL, *Inspector*

DISTRICT

OF

SOUTH CONNEMARA

STATISTICAL TABLE

ELECTORAL DIVISION.	Area in Statute Acres.	Poor Law Valuation.	Number of Ratings at and under £10 and above £4 Valuation.	Number of Ratings at and under £4 Valuation.	Population in 1891.	Number of Families in 1891.	Number of Families on Holdings exceeding £2 and under £4 Valuation.	Number of Families on Holdings at and under £2 Valuation.	Number of Families in very poor circumstances.	Number of Families which have no Cattle.
		£								
Lettermore,	4,037	457	30	136	1,408	239	60	150	200	From 10 to 15 per cent.
Gorumna,	7,334	897	30	372	2,506	442	130	260	400	
Crumpaun,	8,493	903	81	229	2,263	405	120	240	300	
TOTALS,	19,864	2,257	141 *	737 *	6,177	1,086 *	310	650	900 †	

* I beg to refer the Board to Appendix A. in connection with these numbers; and to the conclusion on this subject expressed in the separate paper "Average quantity of land cultivated, &c.," Appendix B.

The ratings in this district, although no doubt kept sufficiently up to date for rating purposes, give only a general indication of the distribution of the families on the holdings. Excepting three small islands, the number of families in every townland exceeds the number of ratings, the total proportion being 1,086 families to 878 ratings. The exact allocation of families to holdings is a matter requiring much time and intimate personal knowledge of the people. I have worked it out in several instances but not in all, and find that the excess of families over ratings affects chiefly the small holdings. In Appendix A. the number of families, carefully ascertained is shown for each townland.

† This number, or less in proportion to the extent of the failure of the crops, and of other sources of income, and bases of credit. The season which is bad for potatoes is bad for turf and kelp; perhaps also for fishing. Only about 10 per cent. of the population are independent of seasons. The rest are more or less in debt to landlord or shopkeeper, and their cattle unsaleable in winter.

The local shopkeeper is usually in the hands of the Galway merchant, who may at any moment, in bad times, bring pressure to bear, and close the doors of the local shops to all who cannot pay.

(1.) Whether inland or maritime.

Gorumna and Lettermore are islands in a bay off Galway Bay. Crumpaun is a narrow peninsula whose longer axis lies north and south. The southern half of each of the three Electoral Divisions may be described as maritime; the rest hybrid, between inland and maritime.

(2.) Average quantity of land cultivated on holdings at and under £4 valuation, under (*a*) oats, (*b*) potatoes, (*c*) meadow, (*d*) green crops.

I have taken all possible pains, in this District of exceedingly irregular enclosures and broken surfaces, to arrive at a correct estimate of the average quantity of land cultivated on holdings at and under £4 valuation, and I conclude that the average per family does not exceed one statute acre of potatoes and one statute acre of oats; while there is no meadowing or green crops. In a few places barley takes the place of oats. (See separate paper "Average quantity of land cultivated," Appendix B.)

(3.) Extent of mountain or moor grazing, and rights possessed by tenants, whether in common or otherwise.

As to the extent of mountain or moor grazing, and the rights possessed by tenants, I have been able in four townlands only to get the areas of the ratings from the agents of the properties, as they are not given separately in the rate books. In every townland, however, the whole of the area not included in the holdings is open to the tenants as commonage. This area varies both as to quantity and quality; the quantity being generally sufficient, if the quality were improved.

(4.) Extent and description of land, if any, which could be profitably reclaimed and added to existing adjoining holdings.

In most of the townlands of this district there is commonage land, of the same quality as that already under cultivation, which could be reclaimed with ultimate profit to the reclaimers; and which, with the consent of the landlord and of all the tenants concerned, might, before or after reclamation, be "striped" and added to the holdings. Such land, though not always adjoining existing holdings, would be within reach of them, if the necessary roads and ways of communication were made. The roadmaking, fencing, and draining could not be done by the people without substantial assistance.

Assisted Reclamation

An explanation may be looked for of the meaning which I attach to this expression.

As already stated, there is, in most of the townlands, commonage land which, with the consent of the landlord and of the tenants, might be reclaimed. The consent of the landlord would hardly be withheld, in regard to a scheme which would improve the condition of his tenants and of the land they occupy. The consent of the tenants would, I believe, be cheerfully given to a proposal to assist them in reclaiming land for themselves. My excuse for suggesting such a proposal is that reclamation on an adequate scale would be beyond their unassisted resources. They might, doubtless, borrow public money for the purpose – but that they are already heavily rented, in arrears with their rent, and subject to eviction. Nor, if their arrears were cleared, could they reclaim profitably as individuals without main drainage.

Assuming the necessary consents gained, would not the Board either

(*a*) be a "Company" within the meaning of section 31 (3) of the Land Act of 1881, and advance half the money required; receiving afterwards the other half from the Board of Works, at a rate of interest (Treasury Minute, 16th August, 1879), of 3½ per cent. for 20 years, 3¾ per cent. for 30 years, or 4 per cent. for 30 to 40 years;

Or (*b*) become the "any other security" for the tenant required by section 31 (2) of the same Act, to insure the repayment of the principal and interest within the time prescribed, of loans advanced by the Board of Works.

The work would consist in making new roads, or repairing old ones, connecting the most convenient point for landing seaweed on the shore with the land to be reclaimed; the reclamation, in fencing and draining, and probably in paring, burning, and liming the surface. It would then be possible, before final partition, to break up some of the land with a plough, which would be a novelty and an education to many of the people of this district. All work should be done, as far as possible, as piece-work, and should be paid for – partly, perhaps, in meal, on account, if absolutely required, but mainly – after measurement, and at strictly co-operative prices.

The families composing the needy population may be roughly classified as follows, in order of poverty:–

1. The mere beggars – old or crippled people, without home or means of their own – who "go about among the neighbours from place to place," universally recognised and helped.

2. Old people, who have a cabin of their own, and, perhaps, a "lockeen" of potatoes planted for them by their neighbours.

3. Widows with young children, often numerous, though the eldest may be ten.

4. Men with families, but without land.

5. Fathers of "long weak families," – the head, and, perhaps, the members of the family being sickly.

6. The same as (5), except that all are healthy.

7. Young married people, with small families.

8. Young married couples, often starting in life with little but their health and strength.

9. Families of various degrees of "strength."

It may be possible to do something for selected families from class 6; but, as a rule, classes 4, 7, 8, and 9 contain all the hopeful subjects for measures of improvement involving increased labour in cultivation.

(5.) Particulars as to any suitable land in district which could be obtained, and to which families could be migrated with a reasonable prospect of success.

Inchamakinna, – an island close to the mainland near the village of Tooreen, Carrowroe West, – 103 acres, valuation £30, present rent £75, in the occupation of one tenant, with one (herd's) house only on it, could in all probability be obtained, for migration, or reclamation in connection with the nearly adjoining villages on the mainland.

The land is accounted good; and the island is valuable on that account as well as on account of the quantity of black weed which its shores yield. It is now used for grazing purposes only. The situation must be exposed to all winds; and the 20 head of cattle which I saw coming off the island in the early spring looked weather-beaten, though healthy.

Suitable land, bog on granite, which could probably be obtained for the purpose and with the prospect stated, is Knockadav (see Sheet 52 of the Townland Survey, 6-inch scale). This Townland has at present only one house on it – that of a herd. It consists of 4,595 acres of hills and valleys, bounded on the east by the high road leading from Maam Cross to Screeb House and all traversed, north and south, by a disused bridle road (see Ordnance Map, inch scale, Sheet 947), leading from the centre of the Rosmuck promontory, on the south, to a point on the Galway–Clifden high road about 1 mile west of Maam Cross. Its western boundary may probably – if so arranged – be marked hereafter by the road, begun at its southern end last year, which is intended to lead from Inver Bridge, at the head of Kilkieran Bay – the point of junction of the Screeb–Cashel, and Screeb–Kilkieran roads – to a point not as yet determined on the Galway–Clifden road in the neighbourhood of Oorid Lough.

The whole of this Townland is let by yearly agreement, renewable in *November*, at £40 a year, to four of the Rosmuck tenants "in Co." They take in cattle to graze from this district as well as from their own. (See also separate paper on the "Cloosh Road," Appendix C.)

(6.) Method of cultivation, manures, rotation of crops, etc., etc.

Spade cultivation is the only method adopted in this district. The theory is – First year, *potatoes* manured with seaweed, the seed being set on the manure on wide ridges (lazy-beds); second year, *oats*; in the third and fourth years the tenants "rest the land." But no grass seed is sown; and the patches left to "rest" do not produce cattle food, as it is understood in agriculture. In a few places barley takes the place of oats. Rye is sown in land which "will not give oats."

(7.) General information with regard to stock, and suggestions as to improvement of breeds – (*a*) cattle, (*b*) sheep, (*c*) horses and donkeys, (*d*) pigs, (*e*) poultry, etc., etc.

The particulars with regard to the stock of this district and the suggestions as to improvement of breeds, are:–

Cattle.– The cow stock are small, light, and, at this time of year, lean and weak to an extent which must be seen in order to be realised. The improving effect of even one cross with a "Polled Angus" bull is very marked, in every particular – size, substance, and constitution; and, as I am informed, in milking properties. The one Polled bull which was owned in Crumpaun is no longer there.

Sheep.– The sheep are also very small; and it probably takes six such animals to produce a stone of wool. A breed able to exist on the poorest of "mountain" pasture, and not able to jump stone walls, would be the best breed for these tenants, if they must have sheep at all. At present much time and temper are lost, in the summer months, in keeping sheep out of the growing crops; and trespass by sheep is a fruitful source of discord.

Horses.– The horses, almost all mares, are small, active, hardy, and sure-footed.

Pigs.– There are very few pigs now. The breeding sows I have seen are of a nondescript, long nosed, lank-sided sort, which (I have authority for saying) would be best crossed by a Yorkshire boar.

Father Conway has been offered by a friend in England a boar and two sows, one of the latter in profit, from the Royal (Albert Model) Farm at Windsor. From his description, I take them to be pure "Berkshires"; but they may be of a special breed established at the Albert Model Farm by crossing the "Berkshire" with another breed.

Father Conway inquires if the Board would kindly assist him in this matter by paying the carriage of the animals from London. He would place them with one of his parishioners for the benefit of the parish.

Poultry.– The poultry are increasing in numbers; and their value as a source of income is being more recognised. A few years ago the eggs were eaten – "it was considered a shame to sell an egg." Now they are exchanged for groceries. The cockerels distributed by the Board appear to flourish. All I have seen are fine birds in good plumage and condition. They are well spoken of. In one case, the owner "had never seen such eggs as he is getting now"; in another, "the chickens appear to be getting larger."

(See separate paper on "The number of Stock," Appendix D.)

(8.) Markets and fairs for cattle and produce of district; also statement as to where the people obtain food and other supplies, and the prevailing custom with regard to the disposal of butter, eggs, and poultry; to what extent are they sold in the first instance to local shopkeepers and dealers, and, generally speaking, how old are the eggs when sold to the first buyer, and about how old when they reach their ultimate destination in Great Britain.

There is a small quarterly fair at Derrynea (near Costello Post Office) which may, some day, I hope, be *the* fair of this district. At present Spiddal, twenty miles from Carrowroe or Dangan Pass Bridge, is the place to which the cattle of these islands and Crumpaun, must be driven for sale at fairs.

The people obtain their food supplies from Galway markets, merchants, and shops. One firm of Galway merchants sells on commission through several local shops.

Butter is not sold.

The trade in eggs is considerable. (See separate paper on "Eggs," Appendix E.)

(9.) Rail, steamer, sailing boat, road, postal and telegraph facilities.

The mail car runs daily from and to Galway and Carrowroe, calling at Costello Sub Post Office. A foot messenger from Bealadangan (Dangan Bridge) Post Office meets the mail car twice daily at Costello. (This messenger, for his daily double journey of sixteen miles, six days a week, carrying mails and parcels, is paid 4*s.* 6*d.* a week). From and to Carrowroe there is a canoe post as far as Teeraneea, on the east shore of Gorumna. A Post Office in Lettermullen Island, five miles farther, is much required; and the completion of the telegraph communication round the coast, or better, across Gorumna and Lettermullen islands (fishing stations of the near future) by Kilkieran and Carna to Cashel and Recess is most earnestly to be desired.

(10.) Employment for labourers in the district, whether temporary or constant, and rate of wage.

There is no constant employment for labourers in this district except for "servant boys and girls," employed by the stronger tenants, and whose lot is indeed a hard one. There is temporary employment in seed-time for a very few; and the wages then are 1*s.* 6*d.* a day and food – tea and bread, or potatoes and eggs, for breakfast; potatoes, and either fish or eggs, for dinner. The hours of employment are 7 a.m. to 7 p.m., with one hour, 9-10 a.m., for breakfast; and one hour, 2-3 p.m., for dinner.

(11.) Migratory labour, average earnings per head, and where earned.

There is no migratory labour, except in harvest time, when spare hands go to the East Riding of Galway, and to County Clare, to dig the potatoes. The "hands" are there boarded and lodged, and receive wages of from 6*s.* to 9*s.* a week, according to the weather. All they bring home is, perhaps, a pair of boots and a new hat for each migrant.

(12.) Weaving, spinning, knitting, and sewing, whether used locally or sold, and where.

Capital sewing and knitting are done in the schools; and the women knit at home, but not for sale.

A new industry of *machine knitting* is about to be started in Carrowroe. A firm of Manchester manufacturers, introduced by the Connemara Industries Company, and who pay their workers in Manchester 10*s.* to 12*s.* a week, will supply machines and materials, and pay carriage: and they believe that girls working in their homes in Carrowroe will earn 5*s.* to 6*s.* per head per week. Father Conway, the Parish Priest, has sent off three girls to be trained in Manchester, and they, on their return, in a few weeks' time, will teach others; and so the industry will be commenced – probably in a work-room to be especially provided in connection with the building of a new National School.

P.S. – New Industry of Knitting by Hand-Machines above referred to.

This will soon be in operation. The girls sent over to Manchester for training about three weeks ago are already reported so proficient as to be earning 12*s.* a week each, equivalent to 6*s.* here when machines are supplied and carriage paid by the firm in Manchester who will take the manufactured articles. These girls are to return shortly to Carrowroe, with a female teacher specially engaged; and it is probable that a house will be required for the industry – perhaps to serve also for other industries. If Father Conway should apply for assistance to the Board, I would commend this project to their favourable consideration.

(13.) Kelp-burning, and sale of seaweed.

(See separate paper on "Kelp," Appendix F.)

The sale of "black weed" is inconsiderable. In former times it was one of the principal sources of cash income to the whole of this district, but artificial manures have come into use largely where this weed was formerly taken inland; and the demand for it at Galway was never so slack as it has been this year. Red weed is sold from Lettermullen, if not required for kelp.

(14.) Sale of turf, nature and extent of bogs.

Turf is cut for sale in five Townlands of this district. There are nine "shipping" places, at which turf is loaded into boats for Clare and the Aran Islands. Boats call wherever they can get a cargo. One boat may have many ports of call. Statistics are wanting; but the extent of the trade is limited by the power of production of the families in each of the five Townlands. (See separate paper on "Turf," Appendix G.)

(15.) Lobster fishing, number of men and boats employed.

The returns supplied to me in response to my request for the names of the owners of lobster-pots in each village are so obviously inadequate, and the oral testimony which I have taken as to the number of men who fish lobsters is so indefinite and so conflicting, that I cannot give any reliable information on the subject, but see paper "Sea-fishing," Appendix H. The industry is a considerable one, and might be extended.

(16.) Sea fishing. Facilities for sale of fish, and number of boats and men solely employed in fishing.

There is a good deal of fishing; but there are no facilities for the sale of fish. Nothing would tend so much to develop this important industry as the provision of such facilities. The coasting steamer should call *regularly* during the summer months at the mouths of the bays within certain marks. At present the population on this part of the mainland derive no advantage from the steamer. (See paper on "Sea-fishing," Appendix H.)

(17.) Number of boats and men employed in carrying turf or seaweed or in fishing. Classification of boats.

The census of boats is as follows:– Hookers, 53; sailing boats ("glothogues" and "pookhauns,"), 146 – these latter are of the same size, but differently rigged; rowing boats, 225; canoes, 181.

Hookers are chiefly employed in the turf trade, occasionally in fishing; a few belonging to shopkeepers are reserved for carrying provisions and shop goods from Galway. The "sailing boats" fetch and carry turf and weed for home use and for kelp-making, and are very useful as fishing boats, if not otherwise employed. The mode of employment depends on how the owner has been brought up. If a kelp-maker he does not fish. A hooker's complement is two men: sailing boats, when kelping or fishing, will have three men; rowing boats, three men at least; canoes, two men each, as a rule, except in the village of Trabaan, where, I am informed, the rule is three.

(18.) Fish; whether consumed at home or sold.

Gurnard, bream, cod, and ling are sold to the neighbours and in Galway; part are used, fresh and salted, at home.

(19.) Extent of fish-curing.

Fish-curing is carried on for home use chiefly, and consists of splitting the fish, and drying them on the roofs of the houses, out of the reach of cattle, pigs, and dogs. (See paper on "Sea-fishing," Appendix H.)

(20.) Piers and Harbours, existing and suggested, and how far those existing are adapted to wants of district.

There is a small pier at Costello Coast Guard Station.

There is another fishery pier at Maumeen, the home of a future fishing station, in

Greatman's Bay.

A small pier and harbour exist at Callahaigue, Carrowroe, which is very useful.

Other smaller quays exist.

(See separate paper – "Piers and Harbours," Appendix K.)

(21.) Extent of salmon and freshwater fisheries. Number of men earning their livelihood therefrom.

There is only one salmon fishery in this district – that attached to Derrynea, or Costello Lodge, at the mouth of the Cashla River, and the lakes above. In connection with this fishery, twenty-two men get £2 each per annum as keepers, and one of them, £4 extra as head-keeper. Four of them also get an occasional day in attendance on the owner of the fishery. (See Ordnance Maps, 6-inch scale, sheets 78, 79, 90, 91; inch scale, sheet 104.)

(22.) Banks and Loan Funds.

There are no Banks nor Loan Funds nearer than Galway.

(23.) Mineral and other resources.

The chief natural resources are peat, fish, and seaweed.

An extensive quartz reef, with metallic indications, is marked on the Geological Map, Sheet 104, on the Crumpaun promontory. A lead mine, near to Costello Post Office, was opened and worked (tradition says profitably for lead and silver) by the Law Life Insurance Office years ago. Metallic indications abound, according to the Geological Survey Maps.

(24.) Relative prevalence of cash or credit dealings, length of credit, interest charged, extent of barter, etc., etc.

Credit is universal, and runs on until the shopkeeper loses faith in the solvency of his creditor. This, rather than any fixed rule or calculation of the present assets of the creditor, must, I think, account for some of the amounts I have seen in books; but the rule is six months', or, at most, twelve months' credit, and the interest when charged amounts to 1*d.* in the shilling. Beyond a doubt, goods are often given, or supplied, by shopkeepers in this district to distressed neighbours, from whom there is no reasonable prospect of getting payment. On the other hand, 1*s.* a lb. on tea is a large and unreasonable profit. In some cases no interest is charged. The total indebtedness of this population to tradesmen within the district is £3,720 up to April of this year, which gives an average of £3 8*s.* 6*d.* per family.

(25.) Estimated *cash* receipts and expenditure of a family in ordinary circumstances.

(See separate paper – "Sources of possible Income, &c.," Appendix L.)

(26.) Estimated value of home-grown food consumed, and period during which it lasts.

Last year's potato crop was a particularly good one. A few families were indebted to neighbours for their Christmas dinner, but the bulk of the poorest began "buying Indian meal" in the middle of February. On the 1st of April a much larger class had consumed all their store of potatoes. On the average, the potatoes last till the 1st April.

(27.) Dietary of people, number of meals daily, and kinds of food throughout the year.

(See separate paper – "Sources of possible Income, &c.")

(28.) Clothing, whether home-made or bought, etc., etc.

The clothing is chiefly home-made, out of material manufactured at home, partly from home-grown, but more from bought, wool. Wool is bought by the people, in Galway, at about 10*d.* to 14*d.* a pound, to mix with their own. One stone of wool will make about twelve yards of flannel. (For other details, see Appendix L.)

(29.) Dwellings: kind of houses, home-life and customs, etc., etc.

The houses of the poorest class are of rubble stone work, set dry, and plastered thickly inside. The rafters are of bog-deal, sawn; and the roof covering, thatch. The floors are of mortar, which fills the inequalities of the rock surface. The simplest form of interior plan is one general living-room, with fire-place against one end wall. The next step in improvement secures one sleeping-room. I have seen a half-naked child of four to five years lying asleep before the turf fire, with his head on a rough block of wood, while the cow stood over him, as if watching and guarding the child. After dark the family and their friends sit round the fire, and the cow, heifer, calf, and pig, get as near it as they can. The poultry are also under the roof, wherever they can perch. The customs of daily life are simple and natural: and the sense and manner of the dwellers in these rude homes are such that one can never enter or quit one of them without paying a mental tribute of respect to its owner. The pig's lair in a one-roomed house is often "under the bed," especially when the pig is the mother of a litter. This I have also seen.

(30.) Character of the people for industry, etc., etc.

The people work very hard and quickly while "putting down the spring," and cutting turf. The work of carrying the turf, and of pulling sea-weed for kelp, is most laborious. I have had many proofs of the great power of intelligent work latent in the people, and which is quickly developed when an adequate motive is supplied.

(31.) Whether any organized effort has been made to develop the resources or improve the condition of the people. If so, by what means.

I believe that no organized effort has ever yet been made to develop their resources and condition, except the constant efforts of Father Conway to improve the accommodation and teaching in the schools, and the great and successful effort by which he has recently built a new and comparatively imposing chapel. The efforts of a lady representative of the Land League, who some years ago endeavoured to encourage hand-knitting in Carrowroe, led to no permanent result.

(32.) Suggestions as to any possible method for improving the condition of the people in future.

(See separate paper headed "Suggestions," Appendix M.)

W. P. GASKELL,
Inspector.

8th May, 1892.

To

The Congested Districts Board for Ireland.

Miles of drystone walls typify the Connemara landscape. Built to clear the land of rocks, they delineate the numerous small holdings of local farmers.

APPENDICES TO REPORT ON SOUTH CONNEMARA DISTRICT.

APPENDIX A.

The figures in column **P** show the number of Ratings at and under £2, *included* in the totals of the adjoining column **A**.

COUNTY – GALWAY   UNION – OUGHTERARD   ELECTORAL DIVISION – CRUMPAUN

Townland.	Area	Valuation: Total V	Valuation: Per Head	Valuation: Per Acre	Population: 1831	Population: 1891	Family Average	Ratings: £2 and under. P.	Ratings: £4 and under. A.	Ratings: £10 and under. B.	Ratings: Over £10	Total Number of Ratings	Families on the Ratings F	Averages: Column A	Averages: Column B	Averages: Valuation per family, (Columns V or F.)	Remarks.
	A. R. P.	£ s. d.	s. d.	s. d.										£ s. d.	£ s. d.	£ s. d.	
Carrowroe, North,	2,281 3 8	137 8 0	6 0	1 2	457	456	5·9	32	63	2	–	65	77	2 1 0	4 15 0	1 15 8	
* Do., South,	991 2 38	152 3 0	8 0	3 0	424	374	5·0	40	54	10	–	64	75	1 14 0	6 0 6	2 0 7	School Teacher's House (Rating, £4 5s.) included.
Do., West,	1,088 0 36	35 9 0	2 11¼	0 8	233	241	5·35	36	36	–	–	36	45	1 2 0	–	0 17 6	2 Ratings at 35s.; of the rest, 1 highest, 29s. 6d., 7 lowest, 15s. 6d.; 45 families to the 36 Ratings.
Two Islands,	12 3 35	4 0 0	–	–	–	–	12 Ratings, of which the amounts together £4, are included in the amounts of the 36, in column **A**, next above.	–	–	–	–	12(*b*)	–	–	–	–	
Rossroe Island,	57 3 30	11 15 0	8 5	4 0	34	28	7·0	3	3	1	–	4	4	2 0 0	5 15 0	2 19 0	
Muckanaghederdauhaulia,	470 1 15	38 0 0	9 0	1 7½	111	83	5·66	–	–	8	–	8	15		5 1 0	2 13 10	
One Island,	24 3 36	2 8 0	–	–	–	–	16 Ratings £40 8s., the amounts included in those of line next above.	–	–	–	–	16(*b*)	–			–	
† Barraderry,	765 0 4	121 5 0	10 4	3 2	214	235	6·7	1	3	19	–	22	35	2 8 4	6 0 0	3 9 0	The Presbytery, Rating £5 10s., included in Column A.
Δ Clynagh,	837 2 22	93 15 0	6 0	2 4½	454	336	6·0	26	40	10	–	50	56	1 6 6	4 9 0	1 15 3	Landlord's Lodge included in the Ratings, £4 10s.
Derrynea,	911 2 0	34 7 0	4 0	0 9⅔	202	174	5·44	18	21	1	2	24	32	1 6 10	4 17 0	1 11 6	The two Ratings over £10 are Costello Lodge and Fishery, £22 and £50 respectively.
§ Keeraunbeg,	708 1 5	157 7 0	9 8	4 5¼	308	325	6·0	1	7	29	–	36	66	2 13 7	4 9 0	2 7 8	
Inchamakinna Island,	108 3 21	30 0 0	1 tenant, the shopkeeper in Carraroe North.	5 7	8 herd's family	9 herd's family		–	–	–	1	1	–	–		–	1 Rating, £30. Only the tenant's herd's house on the island.
Eragh Island,	10 3 31	5 10 0		10 0	–	–	1	–	–	1	–	1	–	–	5 10 0	–	
Two Islands,	1 2 17	1 0 0		13 0	–	–	–	2	2	–	–	2	–	0 10 0	–	–	
One Island (belongs to Clynagh)	0 2 0	0 2 0	–	4 0	–	–	–	–	–	–	–	–	–	–	–	–	
	8,395 1 18	829 9 0	= 7s. 4d. per head (40s. 11½d. per family)	–	–	2,263	5.69	139	229	81 (A + B: 313+28(*b*))	3	341	405	–	–	–	
Costello Fishery, two Ratings,	180 3 23	72 0 0	–	NOTE – Deducting Costello's Fishery and £36 10s. 0d. in hands of one family (8 persons) the valuation of the E. Division is 7s. 0¼d. per head, and 39s. 11d. per family.													
	8,486 1 1	901 9 0	–	–	–	–	–	–	–	–	–	–	–	–	–	–	

* The nominal acreage of the 29 Holdings into which this townland is divided in the Estate Book, is 1,137A. 2R. 17P.: no commonage. Average per holding, 40 acres nearly. Number of Ratings, 64; of families, 73.

† Divided into 21 Holdings, averaging 21 acres each (nominal) and commonage 326 acres, according to the Estate Book.

Δ Twenty-six Holdings, together £20 (26 Ratings to 1 Valuation) and 16 Holdings averaging 9¼ acres each, nominal (23 Ratings), commonage 202 acres. One Landlord's Rating (Lodge and 2 acres) £4 13s. 0d.

§ Thirty-one Holdings, in all 523A. 0R. 16P. of which deducting 2, together 89A. 2R. 36P., there remain 29 Holdings, averaging 15 acres each, nominal, 36 Ratings, 66 families.

APPENDIX A. – *continued*

The figures in column **P** show the number of Ratings at and under £2, *included* in the totals of the adjoining column **A**.

COUNTY – GALWAY | UNION – OUGHTERARD | ELECTORAL DIVISION – LETTERMORE

Townlands	Area	Valuation			Population		Family Average	Ratings.				Total Number of Ratings	Families on the Ratings F	Averages			Remarks.
		Total V	Per Head	Per Acre	1831	1891		£2 and under. P.	£4 and under. A.	£10 and under. B.	Over £10			Column A	Column B	Valuation per family, (Columns V. or F.)	
	A. R. P.	£ s. d.	s. d.	s. d.										£ s. d.	£ s. d.	£ s. d.	
Bealadangan,	998 1 17	63 10 0	5 7	1 3¼	366	227	6·3	–	12	5	–	17	36	2 0 3	5 17 5	1 15 3	Of the 17 "Ratings," 2 are held by the landlord (together £12 17*s.*), and a third by the Dispensary Medical Officer. On the remaining 14 "Ratings," there are 36 families, the average of whose holdings is £1 5*s.* 3*d.* nearly.
Islands:																	
Annaghvaan,	311 2 31	33 10 0	5 0	2 5¾	189	153	6·65	17	18	3	–	21	23	1 2 3	6 3 4	1 13 6	
Illauneeragh,	89 2 7	15 15 0	13 9	3 6	19	23	11·5	–	–	2	–	2	2	–	7 17 6	–	
Inchaghaun,	28 1 16	9 15 0	9 3½	7 0	20	21	7·0	2	2	1	–	3	3	0 5 0	9 5 0	3 5 0	
Inishbarra,	262 1 25	59 15 0	8 0	4 7	159	152	5·4	1	12	6	–	18	28	2 11 6	4 16 2	2 2 8	
Lettermore Island:																	
Lettercallow,	1,245 1 4	108 10 0	6 0	1 9	390	361	5·55	15	32	7	–	39	65	2 3 4	5 11 5	1 13 4½	
Lettermore,	1,008 2 5	143 2 0	6 0	2 1	500	471	5·74	37	60	6	–	66	82	1 17 3	5 6 0	1 15 0	
	3,941 0 25	438 17 0 = 6*s.* 3*d.* per head (36*s.* 8½*d.* per family)	–	–	–	1,408	5·9	72	136	30	–	166	239	–	–	–	

Appendix A. – *continued*

The figures in column **P** show the number of Ratings at and under £2, *included* in the totals of the adjoining column **A**.

County – Galway   Union – Oughterard   Electoral Division – Gorumna

Townlands	Area	Valuation			Population		Family Average	Ratings.				Total Number of Ratings	Families on the Ratings	Averages			Remarks.
		Total V	Per Head	Per Acre	1831	1891		£2 and under. P.	£4 and under. A.	£10 and under. B.	Over £10		F	Column A	Column B	Valuation per family, (Columns V. or F.)	
	A. R. P.	£ s. d.	s. d.	s. d.										£ s. d.	£ s. d.	£ s. d.	
Crappagh,	117 3 28	24 0 0	15 6	4 1	39	31	7·75	–	–	–	1	1	4	–	–	–	One holding £24, in hands of the late P.L.G. for the Division.
Dinish,	95 3 3	28 10 0	7 5	3 10¼	74	50	4·55	–	12	–	–	12	11	2 7 6	–	3 6 0	
Illeuncosheen,	16 0 37	4 14 0	–	6 0	–	–	–	–	12	–	–	12	–	0 7 10	–		
Furnace,	218 3 31	49 15 0	7 7¼	4 6½	155	130	4·8	12	18	3	–	21	27	1 17 0	5 6 8	1 16 10	
Lettermullen,	787 1 30	229 11 0	8 4¼	5 10	626	549	5·49	20	64	14	–	78	100	2 9 5	5 2 2		
Golan,	34 1 1	4 10 0	–	2 8	–	–		–	6	–	–	6	–	0 15 0	–	2 7 6	
Freaghillaun More,	22 2 18	3 12 0	–	2 3	–	–	–	–	4	–	–	4	–	0 18 0	–		
Inisherk,	64 2 19	16 0 0	8 0	4 11	47	40	5 ·7	–	5	–	–	5	7	3 4 0	–	2 4 3	
Freaghillaun Beg,	26 1 9	3 0 0	–	2 4	–	–	–	–	5	–	–	5	–	0 12 0	–		
Gorumna Island																	
Creelogh,	412 3 1	21 17 0	9 6	1 0½	24	46	5·75	3	5	–	1	6	8	1 17 5	–	2 4 7½	1 holding £12 10s.
Knock,	302 2 12	27 5 0	3 7¼	1 9½	167	151	5·6	4	12	–	–	12	27	2 5 5	–	1 0 2	
Maumeen,	3,510 0 34	304 12 0	7 3¼	1 9	843	837	5 ·54	63	93	10	3	106	151	1 14 10	6 5 6	2 0 4	1 Rating £13 divided among 3 tenants; 1 £24 in hands of a non-resident; 1 of £41 18s. in hands of 1 resident tenant.
Teeranea,	1,613 1 30	165 13 0	4 11	2 0½	764	672	6·28	65	95	1	–	96	107	1 14 0	4 10 0	1 12 0	
Illaunnanownim,	24 3 14	4 18 0	–	4 0	–	–	–	–	8	–	–	8	–	0 12 3	–	–	8 Ratings, of which 1 of £2 added to the £13 rating above; the other 7, averaging 8s. 3d., to other Ratings in Maumeen.
Inishlay,	21 1 32	10 0 0	–	9 1	–	–	–	–	–	2	–	2	–	–	5 0 0	–	2 Ratings, value £10, in hands of a non-resident tenant.
One Island,	10 3 20	1 14 0	–	3 1	–	–	–	–	19	–	–	19	–	2 12 0	–	–	held by 19 of the *Maumeen* families above; total value 34s.
Two Islands,	2 0 38	0 15 0	–	7 6	–	–	–	–	14	names (difference 13)	to	1	–	0 1 0	–	–	held by 14 of the *Maumeen* families; total value, 15s.
	7,282 1 37	–	–	–	–	–	–	–	–	–	–	–	–	–	–	–	
* Two Islands (not included above).	3 2 24	0 10 0	–	–	–	–	–	–	–	–	–	–	–	–	–	–	
	7,285 3 21	900 6 0	–	–	–	2,506	5·67	167	372	30	5	394	442				
		= 7s. 2d. per head (per family 40s. 9d. nearly).†							407 (372 + 30 + 5)			13					
												407					

* Uninhabited rocks, valued for sea-weed only (belong to Crappagh).

† Note. – Or deducting £58, in hands of non-resident tenants, and of one family, resident, of 6 persons, 6s. 9d., per family 38s. 5d., per acre 2s. 5½d.

APPENDIX A. – *continued*

The figures in column **P** show the number of Ratings at and under £2, *included* in the totals of the adjoining column **A**.

SUMMARY

COUNTY – GALWAY | UNION – OUGHTERARD | ELECTORAL DIVISIONS – CRUMPAUN, LETTERMORE, GORUMNA

Electoral Divisions	Area	Valuation			Population		Family Average	Ratings.				Total Number of Ratings	Families on the Ratings F	Averages			Remarks.
		Total V	Per Head	Per Acre	1831	1891		£2 and under. P.	£4 and under. A.	£10 and under. B.	Over £10			Column A	Column B	Valuation per family, (Columns V. or F.)	
	A. R. P.	£ s. d.	s. d.	s. d.										£ s. d.	£ s. d.	£ s. d.	
Crumpaun, . . .	8,305 1 18	829 9 0	7 0¼ to 7 4	2 0	2,473	2,263	5.59	159	229	81	3	313	405	1 12 9	5 4 9	2 0 11½	Valuation reduced to 39*s.* 11*d.* per family. See "Note" at foot of Crumpaun Return.
Lettermore . . .	3,994 0 25	428 17 0	6 3	2 2½	1,643	1,408	5.9	72	136	30	–	166	239	1 19 3	5 15 0	1 16 8½	
Gorumna . . .	7,283 0 0	900 6 0	6 9 to 7 2	2 5½	2,739	2,506	5.67	167	372 One of these includes 13 names *	30	5	394	442	2 0 0	5 9 10	2 0 9	Valuation per family reduced to 38*s.* 5*d.* . See "Note" at foot of Return.
	19,582 2 3	2,168 12 0	7 0¼	2 2½	6,855	6,177	5.75	398	737	141	8	873 13*	1,086	–	–	–	
			Valuation per family, 39*s.* 11¼*d.* nearly.						886 (A, B and Over £10 bracketed)			886					

APPENDIX B.

Average Quantity of Land Cultivated on Holdings At and Under £4 Valuation.

In order to arrive at this, short of an actual survey of plots or "gardens" so irregular in shape and so broken up as to the surface by protruding rock, as to be extremely difficult to measure – I have

1. endeavoured to form an independent opinion of my own by weighing seed and measuring land; weighing seed potatoes before being cut into "sets," and afterwards measuring the land in which those "sets" or "slits" were planted; also by measuring land in which a given weight of oats was sown.
2. employed a trustworthy and careful delegate, who knows the people thoroughly, to make a field to field inspection, and to form an opinion of his own upon average plots selected by himself.

My own conclusion was that one statute acre of potatoes and one acre of oats would be a liberal but fair average to allow per family.

The delegate's returns give:–

In one village,	67½	acres	(potatoes and oats)	to 49 families.
In another,	178¼	acres	do.	to 66 do.
In a third,	158	acres	do.	to 82 do.
	403¾	acres	among	197 families

Or rather over my estimate.

Having obtained that result I inquired at the Police Barrack what their conclusion or experience in the matter is for this locality. The answer was – "*about* one statute acre of potatoes and the same of oats."

Again, the father of a "strong" family, in which there are two grown sons, "a servant boy and a servant girl" always at work, and a horse and cart when wanted, informs me that all the potatoes he could set this year are contained in about 1½ acres *Irish* – which are about 2¼ acres statute measure. But this family is of more than twice the average strength.

Lastly, I have had the cultivated patches of several small holdings, average holdings in a townland, where the weed manure has not to be carried quite the average distance, accurately measured by another delegate who thought my estimate too low. In every instance his totals are under one statute acre. The last measurement has just been brought to me:– 3 roods, 38 perches, 19 yards; an aggregate of several patches.

Subject to future correction, therefore, I have stated the "average quantity of land for farming cultivated under oats and potatoes" to be one statute acre of each. What is under potatoes this year will be sown with oats next year.

The system of cultivation is to manure for potatoes with sea weed – which must be cut from the rocks and carried to the "gardens" in baskets on the backs of women and girls. A full basket of weed weights 2 cwt. (weighed), and it takes fifty such baskets to manure a rood of ground. The work of thus "drawing the weed" is most toilsome and tedious; the amount of time occupied varying according to the distance of the "garden" from the sea. I could give further details, but have said enough, I hope, to show the importance of agricultural roads in expediting the spring work, and so enabling the people to sow a larger crop, if land and seed are available. The earlier they complete the planting of the potatoes, the more secure that crop should be from blight, and the more time will remain for other crops, which will be the sooner ripe the earlier they are sown. A strong donkey will take rather more than two woman-loads – a horse with baskets more than two donkey-loads – a cart more than two horse-loads, according to the road.

W.P. Gaskell.

19th May, 1892.

APPENDIX C.

Cloosh Road.

I fully agree with the remark of Major Peacocke that "this road, if completed, will give a much-required communication with Oughterard, more than ever useful when the Clifden Railway is built"; and I beg to commend it to the particular attention of the Board.

As shown on the accompanying map, it would almost bisect an area not far short of 150 square miles, now practically without internal roads, viz. – the area encompassed by the highroads from Oughterard to Maam Cross, from Maam Cross to Costello, from Costello to Spiddal, and from Spiddal to Oughterard; and would thus open a direct communication between the large populations bordering the coast and Lough Corrib, respectively.

From the point of view of the Board its special value would perhaps consist in the fact that it would pass through a large acreage of land, at least as suitable for reclamation as any on the granite formation; and which would be the natural outlet for the congested townlands forming the north shore of Galway Bay. The completion of the two links marked on the map as Ninna Road and Knock Road, between it and those townlands should form part of the Scheme.

The map is a tracing of the Ordnance Map, one-inch scale, with the addition of the names, area, and valuation of the reclaimable townlands on either side of the road. Of these the most important are Finnaun (7,555 acres – £35 5*s*.), Shannapheasteen (3,105 acres – £8 5*s*.), and Cloghermore (1,834 acres – £11), each of which is now let to a single tenant.

The Cloosh Road, so far as it has been made, as followed generally, and as proposed will continue to follow, an old track called "Colonel Martin's Road," laid out by him – I think, probably in 1822, which was a "famine year" – to connect the Oughterard and coast portions of the Martin property. Colonel Martin, who resided at Clareville, Oughterard, and was M.P. for Galway County from about 1820 to 1825, was the father of Mr. Thomas Barnewell Martin, the last proprietor of that name, of Ballinahinch. This track is on road material the whole way, with short exceptions; and I have authority for saying that, though it passes over hilly ground, the gradients will compare favourably with those of other roads in the county. It commands fine views from several points. The unfinished portion is about 5 statute miles long; the cost of construction would be about £400 per mile, exclusive of one bridge, marked on the map, about £150, and of a wide gullet, also marked, about £10. A bridge on the completed portion, coloured green, at the Oughterard end – marked Bealagroonan Broken Bridge – would require repair, at about £60. Total, roughly estimated – £2,250, exclusive of the repair and completion of the two "links," or feeders before mentioned.

With regard to Major Peacocke's suggestion, that each of the 4 huts built last year to accommodate labourers on the road, and described in his memorandum attached, as "of stone, 44 feet by 20 feet, with doors and windows, fitted with bunks and bedding, might make a very snug dwelling-house for a transplanted family, if sufficient land could be obtained from the landlord, around each hut." The further replies I have received are definite as regards Cloghermore townland only – (in that case *un*favourable). With regard to the other townlands I must correspond further with the Agent of the property before reporting on the possibility of obtaining land adjacent to the proposed "Cloosh Road." No. 1 hut is on the townland of Knockadoagh, on the boundary of Booroughaun, and would require land in the latter, which might perhaps be obtained. Nos. 2 and 3 huts are on the townland of Glenicmurrin, where land would not be obtained easily. No. 4 stands on Cloghermore townland, the tenant of which would probably be reasonable. Each hut would, if provided with a roof-covering more substantial than bare corrugated iron sheeting, accommodate two families for a time, there being a door at each end, and the length being divided by a central masonry partition, carried up to the roof, and containing 2 fire-places, back to back. No. 1 hut is at present 5, No. 2 about 6½, No. 3 7½, and No. 4 8½ miles from Costello Post Office (the nearest shop), and only a mile less in each case from the nearest school, marked on the map near Cashla Bridge. No. 2 hut is much coveted as a schoolhouse, for both sexes, to be used by several mountain villages, the children from which have now very long distances to go. No. 3 hut is 10 minutes' walk, and No. 4 hut 40 minutes' walk, over the bog from the nearest point of the finished road.

The actual distance saved by the Cloosh Road between Costello Post Office and Oughterard would be about 5 miles, to a population of 8,000.

W.P. GASKELL.

22nd May, 1892.

APPENDIX D.

STOCK.

I estimate the number in the district as under:

E. Division	Horses	Cattle	Sheep	Pigs	Averages per Family
Gorumna,	40	600	900	Next	H. 1 to 11 families; C.1·4; Sh. 2·0.
Lettermore,	23	400	600	to	H. 1 to 11 families; C. 1·75; Sh. 2·5.
Crumpaun,	80	850	850	none.	H. 1 to 5 families; C. 2·1; Sh. 2·1.
Totals,	143	1,850	2,350	—	Two horses to 15 families. Cattle 1·7 per family. Sheep 2·16 per family.

Probably 90 per cent. of the horses are mares. The number of cattle would be less but that fewer were sold last year than usual. Of the cattle probably about two-fifths are cows, half that number calves under 1 year, and the rest young stock between 1 and 3 years old. The prices realized for foals last winter ranged from £2 10*s*. to £3 15*s*. At the last Spiddal fair, on the 20th April, only 17 head of cattle from this district were sold. They were, I should judge, rather above than below the average in point of quality and condition; and they fetched from £3 to £3 15*s*. a head. There was no demand for sheep; and in one case a woman who offered a sheep and a lamb for 9*s*. failed to sell them.

In comparing the above figures with the Registrar General's Return it should be borne in mind that the latter are compiled before the autumn and early winter fairs, and include all ages; that foals and pigs are all sold at the end of the year, or before this time; that in ordinary years a number of cattle are sold equal probably to at least one head per family, but that last year little more than one-third of that number changed hands. Sheep are rarely sold in this district, except under pressure of process, or to procure seed, or when the price of sheep is very high. The people have them – it cannot be said that they keep them – for the sake of the little wool they yield, and which is shorn without apparent method or thought for the animal or the season. I have weighed a fleece just shorn and unwashed. It weighed 1½ lbs. The sheep was 4 years old and in fair condition. Shearing is woman's work in this district, and an intelligent woman informs me that the best fleece she ever had was 2 lbs., and that 1¼ lbs. is the rule in her experience. I have also seen one small lot of 6 in all respects useful sheep. The owner calls them Scotch, and says he has had them 4 years. They are a great contrast to the general flock. The owners of two similar lots, now on a distant pasture, inform me that they bought theirs last July in the "Joyce Country," and that they have withstood the winter well. Sheep are not taken into the houses, or fed, but are left to eke out a miserable existence among the holdings during the winter and early spring; cruelly hobbled – 3 legs being sometimes tied together – enduring starvation between the stone walls or by the roadsides; hunted by dogs, driven by children, stoned by men and women, if they "trespass" in their search for food, until the potatoes and oats are about to appear above ground. By that time some have died, and the survivors, with the new season's lambs, are sent out to the commonage for the summer. There they remain, still more or less hobbled, hunted, and herded, under conditions but little conducive to their development. Owners who can afford to do so send their sheep to larger pastures on townlands within reach, though at some distance; and there the animals fare somewhat better. After harvest all are brought back to the holdings, "to live or die through the winter." Many ewes die in the lambing season from exposure to wet and cold, in their weak state consequent upon the winter's starvation; and ill-judged shearing, early in May and at the beginning of winter, is another cause of frequent heavy losses. Quite recently a number, first stated at "about 100" but reduced on close inquiry through a trustworthy agent to 45, newly-shorn sheep perished in a single night in Gorumna. Thus the birth of lambs is said – and seeing the sheep it is easy to believe it – only to keep up, if it does so much, the general flock to its normal strength. And it would be well if the custom of attempting to keep sheep on the small holdings, and exposed wet bogs, were to die out. Then garden crops could be grown which are now out of the question, unless fenced in a manner beyond the resources of ordinary small holdings.

The cattle of the small holders are as already stated small, and at this time of the year shockingly thin and weak; but they improve rapidly on the merest suggestion of grass. Of pigs there are next to none in the district now. Here and there a breeding sow of an antiquated-looking kind; and a single litter I have seen, consisting of 5 sucklings so unequal in size that I had them weighed. The largest weighed 30 lbs., the smallest 5 lbs., and the other three 23, 18, and 15 lbs. respectively. The custom is to buy, or take, a sucking pig (bon-iv) on credit about the time the new potatoes are coming in, and to keep it till the Spiddal fair on 20th January, when it will be sold as a "slip" at from 15*s.* to 24*s.* (last January prices) according to the treatment it has received. Bought then by a tenant, perhaps a neighbour, who can afford to feed it well, it will be allowed to grow until the fair on the 20th April, when it may fetch from £2 10*s.* to £3, according to market prices, as a "pig."

I have no pathological knowledge of pigs or cattle, and only repeat common report, universally confirmed on inquiry, in stating that a frequent epidemic among pigs in this district is "cholera"; and that cattle suffer from two diseases called respectively the "pine," and the "cripple." Of the "cholera," there are two kinds; one of them rapidly fatal – death ensuing in half a day, or a day at longest, after seizure; the other marked by cramps, from which the pig may recover, but "it would be better he didn't, for he will never improve" afterwards. In the first kind the flesh of the animal attacked turns black, and cannot be used. Of "pine" and "cripple," it is said that one cures the other; the pine being peculiar to the holding, cripple to the mountain pastures. A change of air and pasture in either case, from the holdings to the "mountain" or *vice versa,* will effect a cure for a time at least. The conviction is general among the islanders that their cattle won't live the year through unless sent to the mainland pastures during part of the year. "If a calf born in the islands were to get more milk than it could drink, it would not live a year unless changed to the mainland, and the sooner the better, once it is six months old." As a rule, the island people send their store cattle out to "the mountains" in October, and bring them home in May. Many of them are then "crippled"; some so badly that they cannot stand, and must be carried in carts or boats. "I have four out on the mountains," said one of my informants in answer to my questions, "and they are bad with the cripple. But they will be able to stand about a fortnight longer, and then I must get them home the best way I can. They have lumps on their legs, but they will get better in no time when they come home. If they were laid on the ground at your feet, they would reach out their necks and eat the grass that's there (I confess I could not see it), and that will support them until they are able to get up and to walk about. Sorra bit of grass will they find on my holding yet, but they'll live there till it grows." I venture to quote these words because they were spoken honestly and illustrate fairly, in my opinion, the conditions which attach to the ownership of cattle in this district, and the lives the poor animals lead. When the market price of cattle is high, a very few owners send their "stores" to the Aran Islands for about five months from July. There they fatten, but the charge is high, 30*s.* per head of quite young stock for the season, and in the present state of the market that would not be recovered.

To unprofessional sense, it would appear that "pine" is simply starvation or consumption from actual insufficiency of food, or from weakness due to the lack of nutritive quality in the mountain grasses, and of home feeding too long deferred ("They get weaker and weaker till at last there is nothing they will eat"); and that "cripple" is rheumatism, more or less acute, due to the wetness, more perhaps than to the exposure, of the mountain lairs. It should be a very hardy breed that would thrive on such winterage, whereas most of the cattle I see are of a sort not suggestive of a robust constitution. Of the cows and young stock which are kept at home through the winter some die probably of inanition, in the beginning of spring. Within one mile of where I write, three such cases have occurred this year – in one of them a cow in-calf dying; in another, a cow a week after giving birth to a calf; in the third, a cow in-calf – a one and a half year-old heifer and a calf of a few months. Such losses, in regard to poor families, would seem irreparable, particularly at a time when Indian meal stirabout is the staple food and milk is precious. In a fourth case – which, like the three above mentioned, came to my knowledge accidentally – a family owned nine head of stock at the date of the Spiddal fair last October. They sent their best cow to the fair, but could not sell her, and brought her home. In February five head died – a three-year-old bull, three yearlings, and a calf. When I visited the holding four cows were on it and a calf born last March. The calf was lying before the fire, moribund or likely soon to be so, by the side of a crippled woman, the mother of the house. Two of the four cows were on their legs but evidently unequal to the effort of getting their own living, and I was informed that members of the family have to lift or help them up at night when they lie down in the house and try to change their position, the other two cows were able to walk.* Three of the four cows were in milk, and gave about one pint between them; which went not to the calf but to the eldest son, a man of twenty-five, who was lying sick. (The father died last January after an illness, and a grown son and daughter a year ago, so that last year's tillage was short, and the starvation of the cattle the consequence.) The only food for the calf was small potatoes, for which the ground was being searched over. My apology for inserting these details is that they appear to me to come under the head of "Particulars of Cattle," and that they are part of the life of the people.

The obvious remedy for such a state of things is sufficient holdings, and proper cultivation of them; a shed for the cattle and hand feeding. Whether comfrey should be one of the crops encouraged seems to be a disputed point, but it can hardly be good for the cattle that they should be warming their sides at a fire in a closed house at night, as I have seen them doing, and exposed to all weathers during the day.

W. P. GASKELL.

19th May, 1892.

* One of these has since died.

APPENDIX E.

EGGS.

Eggs are exchanged by the people at the shops, for groceries over the counter. Eggs are not booked, nor is money paid for them.

From the shop-keepers, in the Crumpaun Electoral Division, the eggs are collected by Galway provision dealers, who give printed receipt tickets for them, and credit the value to the accounts of the shop-keepers in their books. It may be presumed, therefore, that two profits are made on the eggs before they leave Galway. The eggs are repacked in Galway, and sent away daily by rail. One firm sends two carts, two other firms one cart each, to Crumpaun weekly; and the four carts take away between them from 15,000 to 20,000 eggs a week, during the summer.

In the islands about the same quantity of eggs are collected from the people, and sent into Galway by boat once a fortnight, by the shop-keepers.

A co-operative poultry and egg dealer is wanted.

W. P. GASKELL.

13th May, 1892.

APPENDIX F.

KELP.

Kelp is valuable, I believe, chiefly for the iodine which it contains; but also for alkaline and mineral salts, sulphate and chloride of potash, sulphate of ammonia, and common agricultural salt. I was once informed by a manufacturer that his average yield of iodine was 3 to 4 lbs. of iodine per ton of kelp; but the late Mr. Hazell, who came to Connemara fifty years ago as the agent of the Waste Lands Improvement Company, and up to the date of his death, a few weeks since, was the chief buyer of kelp from this district, assured me that an experimental ton of kelp which he had made under his own eye of pure "Ribbon-weed" (Laminaria fascia) yielded 22 lbs. of iodine. Iodine used to be worth 10*s.* per lb.; I do not know the present price. Kelp formally fetched £7 a ton. I have heard even of £11, when made of the "black weed" (Fucus vesciculosus), which grows on the rocks above low-water mark almost up to the doors of the houses; but in the last seventeen or eighteen years, and up to last year, not only has the price fallen and remained low – £3 10*s.*, £3, and less – but kelp has not been saleable at all unless made of ribbon-weed, or "red-weed" (Laminaria digitata); the former being preferred as the richer in iodine. Both these grow in deep water. The red-weed parts from its stem twice a year, in April and September, the April weed being the better both for kelp and as manure, and drifts in upon exposed shores, but not into the bays. Thus the Aran Islands, Inishbofin, &c., have a great advantage in this respect, as in others, over the inhabitants of the mainland. The ribbon-weed must be torn off the rocks, and dragged up out of from 10 to 15 feet of water with poles, about 18 feet long, having a short cross-piece fixed at one end, which when twisted takes a firm hold of the "ribbons." The kelpers, two or three men to a boat, if living where no red-weed comes ashore, sail or row out with the ebb tide five, ten, to fifteen miles, the farthest distance being off Aran Islands, to where the ribbon-weed is to be got. There they work during the last three hours of the ebb, and the first three of the flood tide, or until they have got a load. The weed is tenacious, and the work of pulling it hard; and the men sail or row home pretty thoroughly wet and tired. The rest of the family, or families, then unload the boat and spread the weed to dry. Rain will spoil it, by washing out the salts, and if rain comes on before the weed is dry, it must be gathered up and covered, to be spread again when the rain is over. Two hot summer days will dry it; and once dry it must be carefully kept so. When a sufficient quantity has been collected and dried, it is burnt or fused in long shallow kilns formed of loose stones; the result being a bluish-black cinder mass, looking like asphalte. It takes twelve boat-loads of weed to make a ton of kelp; but the kelp may pass the test if adulterated with "black weed" to the extent of about two boat-loads in twelve. Complaints of the uncertainty of the "test" are universal; and I am told that it is conducted by the buyer within closed doors, the seller not being admitted. I believe it consists simply in pouring sulphuric acid on a morsel of kelp in a glass, and judging or guessing the amount of the iodine by the colour which the acid assumes. If this is so, the eye of the expert may sometimes deceive him, or, if the kelp consist of richer and poorer weed imperfectly mixed in the burning, it is possible that the morsel selected for burning may not fairly represent the whole. However, that may be, the statement is everywhere made, with so much emphasis and circumstantial detail, that there must be something in it – that kelp rejected to-day when tendered by A will be bought to-morrow from B; or that if A takes it home, it may be accepted on another occasion either from his own, or from another boat. If this statement is founded on fact, the fact is demoralizing to the industry, and regrettable also from the manufacturer's point of view. Comparing the manufacturer's experience, which I have quoted above, with the late Mr. Hazell's experiment, I think that cases may occur of diamond cutting diamond, and that a monopolist agent buyer may take advantage of his monopoly to buy as cheaply as he can for his employers. Last year a monopoly of long standing was challenged. A second buyer entered the market; and the price touched £5, nominal standard, for a time, falling, however, to £3 when buyer No. 2 had got to the end of his tether. The effect of the competition may be estimated from the fact, that a family of ribbon-weed kelp-makers trading with buyer No. 1, received from him £4 15*s.* per ton when the competition commenced, but £3 only when it had ceased, for kelp said to have been made in precisely the same way: in spite, too, of the season's supply having amounted – as I know from inquiry at the stores last year – to little more than half the quantity on demand. Much depends upon the weather permitting the boats to work, and the weed to dry; and on the winds bringing the drift red-weed on shore. But in such a year as last year a family of three ribbon-weed kelp-makers, working even under the disadvantageous circumstances I have described, may make from £20 to £30. In Aran Islands, where weed of both kinds abounds, a similar family would make £40 or £50 much more easily; and on the mainland, wherever the supply of drift weed happens to be good, and the weather comes fine, red-weed kelp-makers can earn good wages. Last year the supply of red-weed was particularly short, until late in the summer, when the quality of drift weed is always inferior. Authentic statistics are not to be got on the spot; but adequate opportunities of observation would soon lead to a knowledge of the kelp-makers and their methods; and the ledgers of the buyers must contain a record of the results. In this district kelp is made in Lettermore, Gorumna, and Lettermullen; not much in Annaghvaan, and next to none on the mainland. Only those who are brought up to kelp-making follow it. It is a precarious industry, involving rough work and frequent disappointment during the process, and at the stores. Nevertheless, it is one which deserves the attention and countenance of the Board.

If, in conjunction with the Royal Dublin Society, or otherwise, the Board should see fit to have specimens of seaweed gathered and analyzed, and samples of kelp made under supervision, and tested by qualitative and quantitative analysis – a scientific report on the whole to follow, and a leaflet or booklet compilation from that report in English and Irish for dissemination among the people, and for use as a Reading Lesson in the local National School – I believe that great benefit, material and moral, would accrue to the kelp-makers; and that the industry would be placed altogether on a higher footing.

This year there is promise of a third buyer opening a kelp store in Carrowroe – unfortunately in connection with a shop – and that last year's prices will be at least maintained. My own impression is that kelp is worth more than is paid for it here, even at such rates.

W. P. GASKELL.

13th May, 1892.

The red-weed kelp-makers, when the supply of weed cast upon their own shore runs short, also cross to the neighbourhood of the Aran Islands, and cut the "tangle" from the bottom. For this purpose they use what they call a "crook," a long pole furnished with an iron trident, of which one prong cuts the stalk of the weed, the other two fork it up.

KELP.

P.S., 1st June. – The promise of good prices has not been fulfilled so far. There is but one buyer in the market as yet; and the price of £4 10*s.* per ton originally offered, and which, with other circumstances, stimulated production, is far from being realized.

APPENDIX G.

TURF.

Turf in the Crumpaun Electoral Division used, within living memory, to be cut close to the shore on townlands where it is now cut a mile or more inland. In one place, marked "10" on the accompanying map, it must be carried by men, women, and children, but chiefly by women and girls, the whole distance from the bog to the boat over rough ground, which it took me 28 minutes to cover, without a basket of turf on my back. In other places it is carried from the bog to the nearest road – or to a boat, if a lake or backwater be available for part of the distance, to be next loaded on donkeys or into carts. Of donkeys there are very few in Crumpaun. Carts are paid 3*s.* to 5*s.* a load, according to the distance from the boat, besides the drivers' food, and an armful of green fodder for the horse, if any is growing. Seven full "creels," or cartloads, make a boat load, of about 6 tons; a creel containing 20 average baskets. Arrived at the shipping place, the turf must be unloaded, stacked, and again loaded into the boat, when the boat is there and the state of the tide permits. A boat load thus disposed of, was worth last year 20*s.* owing to the Relief Works diminishing the supply; but the usual price is 14*s.*; and that will probably be the price this year. No new turf has yet been shipped.

It takes 14 days of the finest unbroken weather to dry turf, oftener a month. After the payment of the cart, about 8*s.* remain for the cutting and carrying of the turf, which will have occupied about 100 hours of one worker – say 1*d.* per hour. In the case of "10", the price realized at the boat is 1¼*d.* per basket, carried 1¼ mile at least; all the work of cutting and preparing the turf thrown in.

A full piled-up basket of good turf will weigh 1 cwt.; and 120 such baskets will make boat load of 7 "creels."

There are good and bad turf years, 1891 was a very good, 1890 a very bad year.

W. P. GASKELL.

13th May, 1892.

APPENDIX H.

SEA-FISHING.

Never having had an opportunity of observing a season's fishing, I can only offer the following statement as the result of a comparison of much oral testimony.

The fish caught for sale, if possible, are cod, ling, gurnard, bream, and lobsters; the first two with spillets, by those who have them; gurnard and bream with hand lines; lobsters in the usual wicker pots, and at low water of spring tides by hand. I have a list of 58 owners of spillets, throughout the 3 Electoral Divisions. The boats used are hookers, sailing boats, and canoes. The spillets all belong to canoe owners.

There is but one village in the district whose inhabitants depend chiefly on the sea for their support, viz.– *Trabaan*, on the S.E. point of Gorumna Island. It consists of 50 families, and has a fleet of canoes, of which about 30, with 3 men to each, engage in fishing. Each one of the crew has a hand line and a spillet, the latter carrying 12 score snoods and hooks on a length of 720 yards of line. The total length of the 3 spillets of a canoe is, therefore, $1^1/_4$ mile, nearly.

Another small village, *Point*, on the S.E. point of the Carrowroe promontory, has 9 canoes with 2 men each, who fish regularly. The owners of all other canoes, and of most of the sailing boats of all sizes, probably fish occasionally. Rowing boats are only used close to home for "rock fish."

A few of the old people only can mend nets; and I cannot hear of a single case in the district in which nets were used last year, or for some years previously. Yet the request for nets is in many months. In my opinion any supply of nets should be carefully regulated and limited.

Cod-fishing begins – weather permitting the canoes and boats to venture 3 or 4 miles out to sea – about the middle of December; and the fishermen endeavour to have a good supply before Christmas Eve, when the demand for "a shilling-worth" of cod-fish is general. The spillets are set overnight, and hauled in the morning. The fishing continues till February, when ling comes into season, and are fished in the same way as cod, until May. The return is about the same for both cod and ling. If a boat "gets a haul" it may mean 10 dozen fish on the combined lines; but "a haul" comes seldom, and the saying goes that "one day is as good as a month." Taking weather and other chances into consideration, I am informed that the average catch per week, by men fishing from the mainland, and inshore islands, cannot be reckoned at more than 3 dozen for each boat – or one dozen to each man. The price obtained, for a small number, may be 9*d.* to 1*s.* each. Inquiring at the Police Barrack, which is the first and one of the surest markets, I learned that the men can usually buy a "live" codfish, over 3 feet long for 9*d.* or 10*d.*, and a ling of any length for the same price. Rarely flat fish are caught on the long lines; and a shopkeeper stated to me that he recently sent to a Dublin fish salesman a turbot for which he had paid 5*s.*, besides 2*s.* for carriage, and that he only received for it 2*s.* 7*d.* It had been damaged in transit by rail.

Gurnard fishing begins about the middle to the 20th of May, and lasts till the end of June. If a canoe or boat strikes a shoal of the fish, they can be caught as fast as the lines can be let down at a depth of from 10 to 25 fathoms. Under such circumstances 6 or 7 "hundreds" of six score each, may be taken by one boat in a day, but such a "haul" comes perhaps only once in a season. The average for the season is about 3 hundreds per boat per week. The value being from 20*s.* quite at the beginning of the season, or when the supply is very short, down to 5*s.* per hundred. The gurnard are generally found some miles from the shore. They appear also to frequent Cashla Bay, but not to enter Greatman's Bay. The best chance of a haul is at spring tides.

Bream are caught from the first week in June "till the first storm of winter scatters them." They come into shallow water close to the coast, but not into Greatman's Bay; and take the bait during an hour or two at each turn of the tide; the bait being whelks, or preferably sprats caught in *home-made* bag nets. The average catch, as of gurnard, is said to be three hundred per boat per week; the average value 8*s.* to 9*s.* a hundred.

Lobster-fishing is carried on simultaneously with bream fishing – the season being the same. The Trabaan canoes use 14 "pots" each; others more, up to 20 – sailing boats, 24. The pots are examined morning and evening. A good "haul," for the coast men, would be three dozen. The average throughout the season is not more than that number per week per boat. They are sold, directly or indirectly, to a large buyer at Ballyvaughan (Mr. Scovell), who until about two years since had a lobster-pond, and two tank-hookers for collecting and cooking them. The arrangements at Ballyvaughan seem to be less complete now; but the lobsters from this district are almost all sent there. One local buyer sent there last year an average of 50 dozen per month, the catch of 22 boats – the price paid to the boats averaging 4*s.* 6*d.* per dozen during the first three months, and 8*s.* a dozen for the last three months of the season. Another buyer sent a hooker to Ballyvaughan once a fortnight, with from 20 to 30, on one occasion 35, dozen each trip, paying for them from 4*s.* to 5*s.* per dozen, and receiving a profit of 9*d.* to 1*s.* He had no means of knowing the state of the market; and his boat load would often arrive when the price was low.

My conclusion is that the coast fishing demands and deserves organization and assistance. The habits of the fish seem to be understood: but the market to be uncertain and limited. Surplus fish which can neither be used nor sold fresh are roughly salted, and taken to the shop-keepers; who keep them for sale as salt-fish, or pack them in barrels, and sell them to small dealers inland. The buyer, above referred to as sending lobsters once a fortnight to Ballyvaughan, received in all last year, including lobsters, £800 worth of fish from 113 customers, of which he sold inland 8 "thousand" (ten hundred of six score each) of salted bream – at 8*s.* to 9*s.* a "hundred" – about £34.

To judge from Trabaan, the results of sea-fishing in canoes are not satisfactory, either materially or morally. The inhabitants of this village show all the signs of great poverty, though their earnings must often be considerable. Their houses are of the worst description, and in a very exposed position. The tillage is small, and the land of the poorest. Their life entails much hardship. The improvement of their harbour is desirable, and I think practicable at small expense: the road to it should share in the improvement.

W. P. GASKELL.

24th May, 1892.

APPENDIX J.

Boats

As stated in the accompanying Report, these number 46 hookers, 164 sailing boats, 272 row-boats, and 136 canoes. A few of the hookers are owned by shop-keepers, who employ them almost exclusively in carrying goods from Galway. The rest are engaged during six months from 1st June in occasional fishing and trading with turf to the Aran Islands or County Clare. During three months of mid-winter they are of necessity idle, or nearly so; and in the three months from 1st March to 1st June do the best they can with sea-weed, and the remains of last year's turf. The profit on this turf is very small. Owing to its scarcity it is dear to buy, and from its deteriorated quality is hard to sell.

A hooker's crew consists of two men, who receive as wages "the fourth penny" each of the net profit on each trip. Half of that profit goes to the boat-owner; the other half to the crew. Thus, if the owner of the boat is one of the crew, he takes three-fourths of the profit. This rule holds good with regard to turf and "blackweed." This partition is sometimes made by giving the whole profits of the first and second of four cargoes to the owner; of the third to the captain; and of the fourth to the man before the mast. In the "red-weed" trade, the owner of the weed takes two-thirds of the price obtained, the remaining third going half to the boat-owner, and half to the crew.

The standard "load" of turf is seven creels of twenty good baskets each; of "blackweed" two rowing-boat loads of thirty-five good baskets each; of "red-weed," as much as the boat will carry, if so much can be got. The red-weed must be dried, and kept dried; and cannot be loaded in wet or showery weather. In all cases the load is put into the boat by the seller, the crew attending to the arrangement of it. Turf is put out of the boat by the crew; but the unloading of sea-weed is a first charge against the cargo. The items of that charge are, for red-weed, 2*s.* 6*d.* to three men for putting it on to the quay, and 1*s.* to two men for "trimming," catching, and heaping it up; with 6*d.* or 1*s.*, "given back" to the buyer, total 4*s.* at least. For blackweed only 2*s.* are paid for putting out and trimming, and 6*d.* to the buyer.

The price obtained for turf throughout the summer varies according to quantity and supply. I think it would be found to be on the average about twice what is paid for it. Thus, if bought for 14*s.*, it will be sold for 28*s.*, if possible, but often for less. A boatman's share of 14*s.* profit would be 3*s.* 6*d.*; and two trips a week is all a boat can make; unless in exceptionally favourable weather, which may or may not balance the delay caused by calms, and strong or contrary winds. The sails of a hooker, being made only of unbleached calico, at 6*d.* a yard, dressed with a mixture of butter and Stockholm tar, will not resist much wind pressure. Detention away from home means to a boatman the absorption of all his share of the profit of a cargo, and often more. His first act, after making a trip and discharging a cargo, will probably be to buy 6*d.* worth of bread, 6*d.* worth of tea and sugar, and 6*d.* worth of tobacco, which will not last long; this may be a charge against the cargo. In case of detention by stress of weather, if there happens to be a food cargo on board, it is a custom of the country for the boatmen to take toll from it in kind. [This custom may specially affect small consignments of seed potatoes of valuable sorts.] There may be some potatoes on board, as it seems customary in some cases for the owner to "half provision" the crew.

The following detailed statement, which I believe to be a true and correct account, of the experience of one boatman this season, will illustrate the foregoing remarks. A.B. began the spring work towards the end of March, as soon as permitted by the March winds, which were boisterous and "foul" for sailing eastward from Greatman's Bay. Turf he takes wherever he can get it best; black weed wherever he asks for it; red-weed from the Aran Islands, as it is better there than anywhere. During the four weeks from 1st April he traded black weed, carrying eight loads in all. For each of the first four the price obtained was 21*s.* 6*d.*, from which had to be deducted 10*s.* the cost of the weed, and 2*s.* 6*d.* loading and selling charges, leaving 9*s.* net profit for division. The fifth load fetched 19*s.* 6*d.*, the sixth 18*s.*, the seventh 16*s.*, and the last 10*s.* only. The last load was his own weed. He wasted two days in Galway in the hope of selling it, and was glad at last to unload it himself and to get for it, subject to the usual reductions for owner and crew, the price which he conceived he ought to have received for it at his holding without deduction, four days before. The first seven loads earned for him, therefore, 13*s.* in $3^1/_2$ weeks; and the remaining days were occupied in the venture with his own weed which he declares was at his own risk, and which if it produced for him 2*s.* 6*d.* in cash, was in other respects disappointing. On the 28th April, he took his first load of red-weed, and has carried five loads in all since in three weeks. The first two loads were sold at £3 2*s.* 6*d.* each; the third brought 56*s.*, the fourth £3, and the fifth 50*s.*, and his share of the five would be, deducting 4*s.* 6*d.* loading and selling charges for the first load, and 4*s.* for each of the others, 4*s.* 10*d.* twice, 4*s.* 4*d.*, 4*s.* 8*d.*, and 3*s.* 10*d.*; total, £1 2*s.* 6*d.* for three weeks. In the period included above, he made one short trip with a load of last year's turf, the profit on which was 5*s.* only, the usual amount, and his share 1*s.* 3*d.* Boatmen generally belong to the poorest class.

A hooker should earn for the owner, if he is himself one of the working crew, between £30 and £40 in the course of the year, against which must be set the wear and tear of sails and cordage. Cases are not wanting of boats lying idle for want of means to repair them. Some such are included in the totals given at the beginning of this memorandum.

Sailing boats, which are generally of one size, to carry three to four tons, but differently rigged, the cutter-rigged boats being called "glothogues" and the luggers "pookhauns," are, I think, the most generally useful and profitable class of boats for men who have small holdings and strong families. Such a family in one of the islands about seven years ago, were in a bad case. The sons had grown up "without ever tasting cow's milk"; the father was still able to work. A neighbour advised them to buy a boat with money borrowed from the Fishery Board. The necessary papers were obtained and filled; and the load was granted. It has been duly paid off, and the family own six head of cattle – thanks entirely to the boat; which enabled them not only to fish but to earn £20 a year at least by kelp-making. There is no denying the handiness, sea-worthiness and general usefulness of a canoe. It costs little, can be carried to and from the water at any state of the tide, is employed in all work for which other boats are used, and does it well, probably no man who has been brought up to a canoe would take to any other boat. But the labour of managing a canoe in a breeze is severe and of a fitful kind, and canoeing seems to form a habit of spasmodic effort under necessity only, followed by reaction when the absolute necessity for exertion is past. Where there is no shelter, natural or artificial, for other boats, canoes abound, and canoemen are a hardy manly class, but where shelter begins canoes gradually disappear, and the characteristics of boatmen are less marked.

W. P. GASKELL.

25th May, 1892.

APPENDIX K.

PIERS AND HARBOURS, WHETHER SUFFICIENT.

The natural harbours are Cashla Bay, Greatman's Bay, and Casheen Bay. Artificial boat harbours in Greatman's Bay are Callahaigue and Lettermore; the latter very useful, but small and incomplete; the former a benefit to the public at large, perfect as a shelter, and very commodious. In Greatman's Bay there are also fishery quays at Maumeen and Dangan Pass, which, although important works, are not now much used. A quay at Teeranea, on the other hand, which was begun in 1880, and continued by the Piers and Roads Commission of 1887, is highly appreciated and extremely useful to a large population; its prolongation a few yards to a rock which, owing to its position, is a cause of much anxiety and trouble to boats getting under weigh, is earnestly desired.

Trabaan, the large fishing village on the south-east point of Gorumna Island, has a natural harbour which is conveniently situated, and which might, I think, be much improved at a small expense by scarping a mass of rock to form a quay, and filling a hollow – perhaps also constructing a short breakwater – with the material so obtained. Material is otherwise abundant. To this harbour £45 only were allotted by the Piers and Roads Commission in 1887; and excellent work was done by the villagers with that small sum.

Lettermullen Island – which with neighbouring smaller islands, can muster forty-five sailing, and sixty-nine rowing boats – has no quay or harbour accommodation except what the rocks afford. A work much asked for is a breakwater at the head of Kiggaule Bay, to form there a harbour of refuge for hookers unable from stress of weather to pass Golam Head. The bay is very conveniently situated for such a purpose, being close to the track of vessels bound either west or east, and easy of access and egress. I have not had a chance of visiting it during a gale; and cannot give an opinion as to the shelter it would afford, or as to the possibility of entering it in rough weather; but I am assured that it is quite accessible, and that the shelter would be good and sufficient if a breakwater were built at the spot marked on the map accompanying report.

The quay at Tooreen, Carrowroe West, marked on the accompanying tracing, was completed in 1887, but shows signs of giving way in one place. The small area protected by it is too cramped for the purposes of the quay. The quay is in the form of the letter L, and the desired improvement would be effected by giving it the form of the letter I, north and south.

A quay is now much wanted at Derarta, Carrowroe North, also marked on the tracing. Since the completion of the Derarta Road by the Relief Works of last year, a great deal of turf is shipped here. On a recent occasion I was assured that seventeen hookers had loaded there the week before. The natural position is perfect, and the branch road required would be quite short. The County Surveyor has the necessary measurements.

The requirements of Derrynea Harbour have already been referred to.

Shruffane, an extremely useful quay, needs repair.

There should be a Harbour Constable, or some official, to inspect and report upon quays in each district.

W. P. GASKELL.

26th May, 1892.

APPENDI

SOURCES OF POSSIBLE INCOME AN

BUDGET FOR A FAMILY OF FIVE PERSONS:

No. of Item	SOURCES OF POSSIBLE INCOME	AMOUNT From £ s. d.	AMOUNT To £ s. d.
	The first answer I received to my first question on this head was "Well, Credit"; and credit at the local and town shop is certainly one of the means of livelihood on which the people depend. Other means are –		
1	6 hens and mate, say 12 chickens worth 5*d.* each (5*s.*); and one "hundred" (6 score) eggs from each hen in the year, at an average price (worked out) of 6*s.*:– Chickens, 5*s.*; eggs, 36*s.*; less 7 lbs. corn, at 8*d.* per stone, weekly 4*d.*, 17*s.* 4*d.* per annum, or say 16*s.*, ...	1 5 0	
2	1 pair of ducks – eggs eaten, neither set nor sold, . .	Nil.	
3	1 pair of geese – 7 goslings at 1*s.* 3*d.*; or if 3 geese, 10 goslings at 1*s.* 3*d.*, ...	0 8 9	0 12 6
4	1 "bon-iv" (sucking-pig) bought, say 1st August for 10*s.* on credit, and kept till 20th January, when it may fetch 15*s.* to 25*s.*, say 20*s.* average; less 25 weeks' keep, which has probably been potato leavings and what it could find, . . .	0 15 0	
	If kept till 20th April fair, and fed during winter and spring, it may realize £3; less cost price 10*s.*, and say 13 weeks' feeding at 1*s.* 6*d.* = £1 2*s.* 6*d.* £3, less £1 12*s.* 6*d.*; profit, . .		1 7 6
5	A brood sow. (Very few can or do keep them.) Minimum number of young (10) per annum, at maximum price of 10*s.*, .	5 0 0	
6	4 sheep (above the average number) will yield $^{1}/_{2}$ a stone of wool, worth 1*s.* per lb. at most, 7*s.*, credited on the other side of account. Sheep are rarely sold in this district, but a great number die in the lambing and shearing seasons – say 1 sold,	0 10 0	
7	1 cow = 1 calf, which may be worth at the end of the year £1, but will not be sold until 2 years old, unless under pressure, but if sold may fetch 22*s.* 6d.; less 2*s.* 6*d.* paid to the owner of the bull on the birth of the calf, ...	1 0 0	2 0 0
8	1 yearling, which may be sold at the end of the year, and bring £3 to £6 as a two-year-old, ...	4 0 0	6 0 0
9	1 mare = 1 foal, which may fetch at the end of the year £2 10*s.* to £3 15*s.*, say £3 7*s.* 6*d.* (less 7*s.*, sometimes 8*s.*) to the owner of the horse, ...	3 0 0	
	Few have carts in this district, but the owner of a cart may earn with it per annum, ...	15 0 0	20 0 0
10	Turf sold, say 6 to 10 loads at 15*s.*, less 5*s.* paid for carting, .	3 0 0	5 0 0
11	Kelp, say 3 tons at £3 10*s.* to 5 tons at £3, . . .	10 10 0	15 0 0
12	Fishing, 6 weeks' gurnard, say 3 "hundreds" a week, worth £1,	6 0 0	
	" 18 weeks' cod and ling, at 12*s.* 6*d.* per week, .	11 10 0	
	" } simultaneously { 18 weeks' bream, say 1 "hundred" per week, worth 8*s.* 6*d.*, . .	7 13 0	
	" } simultaneously { 18 weeks' lobsters, say $1^{1}/_{2}$ dozen, at 5*s.* (7*s.* 6*d.*), 18 weeks' at 7*s.* 6*d.*, . .	6 15 0	
	" 4 weeks' mackerel, say 1 "hundred" for sale, worth 8*s.*,	0 8 0	
13	Hooker, if the owner sails her, should earn for him about £33, less wear and tear, £3, ...	30 0 0	
	With regard to Items 10, 11, 12, it is obvious that a man can only do one work at a time. Kelp-making and fishing require boats. If a man, having no boat of his own, is admitted to his neighbour's to work, he shares equally with the neighbour in the produce.		
14	Boating, as boatman in a hooker, may produce £20 a year, much of which is necessarily spent away from home, .	10 0 0	
15	The out-crop, say 3 score stones of oats, sold at 8*d.* (a full price),	2 0 0	

There remains only, I believe, the items "Illicit Distillation" and "American Money". The former, if not discovered, will yield a profit of 200 per cent., on the value of the material used (£3 worth will be converted into £9 worth); the latter may be equivalent to £2 per family throughout the district, though very unequally distributed.

I heard of three men only at work on the Clifden Railway from this district. They bring home about six shillings on Saturdays.

L.

HEADS OF EXPENDITURE.

Man, Wife, and Three Children.

No. of Item	HEADS OF EXPENDITURE	AMOUNT From £ s. d.	AMOUNT To £ s. d.
	1 acre of potatoes may yield at most 640 stones, of which 100 should be kept for seed. There remain for consumption 540 stones, or 180 days' (26 weeks') supply – say from 1st August to the end of January – the family pot containing 1 stone, and being boiled thrice daily – (large pots contain 2 stones, and in large families a basket of potatoes, 6 stones, are dug and boiled daily).		
	Shop food, while the potatoes last, say 1 stone flour, 2*s.*; 6 oz. tea, 1*s.* 3*d.*; 5 lbs. sugar, 1*s.* 3*d.*; 2 oz. tobacco, 6*d.* – 26 weeks at 5*s.*,	6 10 0	
	Shop food, when the store of potatoes is exhausted – 4 stones (½ cwt.) Indian meal, at 6*s.* per cwt., 3*s.*; 1 st. flour, 2*s.*; 6 oz. tea, 1*s.* 3*d.*; 5 lbs. sugar, 1*s.* 3*d.*; 2 oz. tobacco, 6*d.*; (calico and small items will balance inaccuracies) – 26 weeks at 8*s.*, . .	10 8 0	
	Clothing – Home-grown wool ½ stone will make 6 yards of flannel. A man's jacket willl require 3½ yards, trousers 2½ yards, waistcoat 1 yard; a woman's petticoat 3½ yards, jacket 2½ yards; a child's "bawneen" (combination garment) 1 to 1½ yards, say for 3 children 5 yards. Man's suit 7 yards, woman's 6 yards, children's 5 yards; total required 18 yards. Thus 12 yards of flannel must be bought at 2*s.* 6*d.* = £1 10*s.*; to which add for weaving 6 yards (at 3½*d.*), 1*s.* 9*d.*, and for cleaning (at 1*d.*), 6*d.*, 2*s.* 3*d.*, £1 12*s.* 3*d.*; add man's hat 1*s.*, and boots 8*s.* 6*d.* to 9*s.* (8*s.* 9*d.*), 9*s.* 9*d.*, .	2 2 0	
	School pence, 2 children at 1*s.* per quarter, 1 at 1*s.* 6*d.* = 3*s.* 6*d.* per quarter, or say per annum, . . .	0 10 0	
	Church dues, 2 "stations" 1*s.* each time, 2*s.*; Christmas and Easter offerings, say 1*s.* 6*d.* each time, 3*s.*; 1 baptism, 5*s.*, . .	0 10 0	
	Rent and taxes, ...	4 0 0	
	£	24 0 0	

Notes to Table of Income.

Migratory labour is not among the sources of income in this district. Many of the young men go for three or four weeks of harvest time to other parts of the county, and to County Clare, to dig potatoes; but the wages they earn are low, and the amount brought home to the family exchequer is inappreciable. Herrings are not included among the fish caught for sale, because they have not approached this coast for two years past, and there has been no fishing for them with nets. They are due about the same time as the bream, and are of about the same value, if taken with hand lines. Mackerel come in at the same time, and are caught all through the summer by those who fish regularly in sailing boats far from the shore. The item in the Table "6 weeks at harvest time" has reference to those who fish only during a few fine autumn weeks.

Items 1 to 8 are subject to addition in proportion as the possessions of a family exceed those here assumed as a basis of calculation.

Poultry, items 1, 2, 3, is an asset capable of improvement. Peculiarities noticeable in poultry management are that the eggs of ducks are not set for hatching, and that geese often have one of their own quills thrust through the nostrils across the beak to prevent them from nesting when there are no eggs to put under them.

No. 4 often fails through "cholera." The pig does not "pay the rent," unless kept and fed till March or April which happens in a few cases only. No. 5 is rare.

No. 6 is an emergency item and a liberal estimate. The best price offered at last Spiddal fair for a "good wether" was six shillings. The mortality among ewes and newly-shorn sheep is great. Four out of seven sheep belonging to one family died in one wet stormy night this May within about twelve hours of being shorn. [These were not included in the 45 spoken of in Appendix D.]

Items 7 and 8 should be good for £5 to £6 at least to many families; subject, however, to the market, which must be strong before cattle of the description too common here are called for.

Item 9 should increase the area under tillage by about one half. If the crops grow, the family will be safe. The foal represents about £3 clear. A cart industriously employed should lift a family above want.

Item 10 depends upon the season. In finest weather turf cut on the 15th May should be ready for putting into the boats on the 1st June. This year it was cut; but it is not drying. Not only is it not drying, but it is wasting and deteriorating under the influences of alternate sunshine and rain. Rain "washes the gas out of it," according to local authority – perhaps by dissipating a volatile oil which may account for the flaming of good, as compared with the smouldering of inferior, turf. Turf-cutters can fish, if the weather permits, and if they have access to boats while the turf is drying.

No. 11 is quite as seriously affected by the weather as 10. Storms and rain interfere with the collection of the weed, in the case of those on whose shores it is not cast by the sea, and prevent the drying of it by all; thus delaying the process, as well as impairing the quality of the product. The value of the product would seem by all accounts to depend, to some extent, on the fallibility of human judgement if not on human caprice. Under fairly favourable circumstances kelp should be good for not less than £7 per man engaged.

No. 12 is perhaps the most uncertain, and dependent upon wind and weather. To realize the amounts estimated, a man must give himself up to fishing; and to make the best use of what he earns, he should be a creature different to the present fishermen of Trabaan, for instance – who, though no doubt creatures of circumstances which call for and admit of improvement, are men likely to be always poor, whatever their fishing luck may be. Ling fishing occurs during seed-time.

The estimate of expenses may be too high, but with the best will to discover where it is wrong, I cannot point to errors, nor can I alter the items without misrepresenting the facts as they appear to me now. Perhaps my failure to make the two sides of the estimated account balance is but truly suggestive of the result of the people's efforts in dealing with the reality. But against £20 to £24 a year of expenses, apart from the value of the potato crop, I cannot credit an average family with more than £10, derived from items 1, 2, 3, 4, 6, 7, 8, and 15; leaving the rest to be made up as best they can between 10, 11, 12, and 14. Items 5, 9, and 13 are exceptional; 13 depends much on 10.

I have now to state my belief that, in a "period of distress" from 60 to 70 per cent. of this population would be found "really poor"; and fit objects of any scheme of special relief.

I think I have allowed for a full yield of a statute acre of potatoes, and that any prolongation of the time, 26 weeks, during which the crop is estimated to last a family, would be due to one of two causes – either that the seed which I have supposed to be reserved would be consumed, and other bought, or that economy would be practised in filling the cooking pot. Otherwise what I venture to call the rule of the pot – its contents multiplied by the number of times it is filled daily for boiling – should determine the daily consumption as nearly as it can be calculated.

Such general distress as I contemplate would be due primarily to the failure of the crops. Risk of such failure, more or less general, there must always be with a soil so heartless, so sensitive, and so exposed to the storms and rapid changes characteristic of the climate of the West Coast, as most of this soil is. It is a quick soil which, if mixed with sand and subjected to liberal and delicate garden treatment, seems to be highly favourable to the growth of plants, especially weeds, in their early stages, but to fail them more and more as they mature, or endeavour to do so. The season which is good for potatoes is bad for oats, as last year proved. The "gardens," as the cultivated enclosures are called, following the windings of the rocky shore, and the undulations of a hilly broken surface, are small and irregular; representing, perhaps, the haphazard selection and occasional labour of the original reclaimers, and their want of time to carry farther than necessary the stones cleared off the ground. One tenant "reckoned 7½ pieces to the Irish acre, and six nice gardens, taking about 20 stones (of potato seed) each to a statute acre" – an accurate estimate, I think, of the amount of seed, if not of the average size of the "gardens." A holding is made up of many such patches, often far from each other; an arrangement which adds to the difficulties of the tenant, conduces to trespass by his own and the neighbour's sheep and cattle, and is confusing to a stranger anxious to ascertain the area under tillage.

The extension of the average area under tillage to 2 acres of potatoes and 2 acres of oats, and the improvement of the cultivation of that area, should be objects kept prominently in view: and to that end I again respectfully urge the importance of agricultural roads, assisted reclamation, and the drainage of hollows, where now drainage is impracticable without blasting, and in which the crops, late sown owing to the wetness of the ground in spring, lie often half swamped by summer rain.

The importance also of good seed, and of encouraging the use of it, is evident. The seed grown in the limestone soil of County Clare and East Galway is highly thought of in this district; and is said always to do well. This is also my own experience. The Clare men say that they could not live on the potatoes grown on this soil. One cause of the failure of the potato plants now to be noticed is said to be the *dryness* of the early spring, which caused the sea-weed to shrivel and rot, and to rot the "sets" placed on it.

In connection with the plea for roads, an instance of self-help in this direction deserves to be mentioned. Twenty years ago a man whose house is about 1,000 yards from the nearest point of the nearest road – the road leading to Dangan Pass, and along which much turf finds its way to boats – bought a cart in Galway, and brought it as near to his house as he could, building a shed for it on the roadside. This shed, having been thrice mischievously pulled down, was as often rebuilt. After eight years a relief road was made from a point near the shed to a village within a short distance of the cart-owner's house, but on the opposite side of a small bay. He then brought the cart to that village, and by degrees made an excellent road a furlong in length from his house to the shore of the bay on his side. When he requires the cart at home, it is towed, floating, behind a boat across the bay to the end of his road; but it is most used for carting turf on the Dangan Road. This man is one of the most earnest petitioners for a road through the holdings of his village.

W. P. GASKELL.

27th May, 1892.

APPENDIX M.

SUGGESTIONS.

It goes without saying that the population should be gradually thinned out, until each family has a holding sufficient for their support. It appears to me that a £4 valuation is not sufficient to secure a family against chronic distress, and that the valuation to be aimed at should be at least £5.

The improvement of agriculture by all available means; and first by the construction of agricultural roads so laid out as to facilitate and expedite the spring work of the greatest number of "gardens" within reach. Loans for carts, or the supply of carts on loan, might follow the completion of such roads, which could be made cheaply by local contracts on strictly commercial and co-operative terms as regards the workers benefited.

The recognition of the turf trade, at least for a time, as a local industry, and the organization and extension of it by the making of agricultural roads through the portions of commonage, bog most suitable for reclamation. At present the cutting of the bogs is not regulated at all, except that the people respect each others' patches. The provision of rubble quays, with top and outside courses set in cement, would be desirable in "shipping" places where none exist already, and where they would afterwards be valuable as fishery quays. Two such quays are much wanted now: one at the spot marked on the accompanying map as a "shipping" place for turf, No. "7"; the other, similarly, "10," and as having been inspected by Mr. Tuke. The former is within a short distance, measured on the 7th inst. by the County Surveyor, of a relief road completed last year; the latter touches the high road from Carrowroe to Galway.

The nursing of the fishing industry – first, by providing a regular and easily accessible market for the fish as at present caught; and then by helping, with improved apparatus if asked for, those who show themselves to be the most persevering and deserving fishermen.

Assisted reclamation of commonage land within reach of the present holdings.

The improvement of commonage pastures by drainage, and by shelter plantations, where the area is large and natural shelter deficient.

The promotion of more practical teaching of Agriculture in the National Schools, by –

(*a*) The compilation of a class book suited to local requirements, and which should at least begin by appealing in simple language to local experience, confirming what is right (if there be anything right – and I think the lazy-bed system is so), and correcting what is wrong, in local practice. Agriculture is an obligatory subject for boys from the 4th class upwards; but the teaching of Agriculture consists in reading and answering questions in a class book which will be, I hope, before the Board, called an "Introduction to Practical Farming," no doubt a most comprehensive and admirable text book; but one beyond the powers of realization of boys who have never been out of Carrowroe or Gorumna. The book is read and learnt by the 4th class as far as page 51; by the 5th class, in two stages, as far as page 122; and the whole book by the 6th class. Some of the remarks most intelligible and interesting to boys in this district are contained in pages 176 to 179, and 186 to 195; which but few of them ever see.

(*b*) The establishment in the district of a school farm where ocular demonstration may be given of the truth of what is read in the class books; and where boys may see something more than small woodcuts of ploughs and harrows, even if they cannot learn to use such implements. The information given in pages 19 and 20 of the "Introduction" might then be understood. Such a farm might include an orchard, and a vegetable and fruit garden; and the children might learn to appreciate the good things which are described in pages 52 to 63, and of which they can now learn only the names.

(*c*) The institution of small scholarships, or other means of sending a specially deserving and promising boy pupil to Glasnevin Model Agricultural School, and a girl pupil to a first-class Dairy School.

One disadvantage under which this population lies is the want of good standards and patterns, in all the details of their daily lives and observation; excepting spade work, and the building of loose stone walls. I do not doubt that, if the young are trained to better agriculture, and better models in common things, many will do credit to their training.

The promotion of the teaching of Handicrafts to boys, by assisting in the provision of workshops and the payment of teachers.

The present school programme does not contain *net-mending for boys.* As a rule, to which I have as yet discovered but one exception, the present generation here do not understand the industry (it is one of the "Home Industries" in the school programme). That exception is an intelligent man of about forty; and I submit a specimen of his work, done in my presence. It appears to be in accordance with the principles which the Rev. W. S. Green was kind enough to teach me. If no better, or more suitable, teacher be found, this man could teach net-mending to boys. One of the female teachers can *make* nets; but has yet to learn how to mend them. She could then teach the girls. Boys should be taught as well as girls in this district.

The supporting, or subsidizing, of evening classes for the teaching of Handicrafts and net-mending to boys as above; and of cooking and household work to girls. For cooking, a kitchen and apparatus would be required. A good female teacher of cooking and house work is, I believe, available for one school at least.

The extension to this district of the Example Holding System; and of other operations of the Royal Dublin Society, for the encouragement of Agriculture.

The development of the quarterly fair already held at Derrynea; and the building there of a station for a *travelling* stallion. Spiddal, the present chief fair for the district, is about seventeen and a half-miles from Carrowroe or Dangan Bridge. As the cattle of the district improve, they should be able to attract buyers to Derrynea.

The watching of the egg and kelp trades and of the other local industries – with the view not only of obtaining reliable statistics at any time, but of protecting the interests of the people; or of enabling them to protect their own interests. This end would be served by the circulation of information as to the prices of produce in which the people are interested. A notice board at each post-office, and posting thereon weekly the market reports issued by the Land Commissioners and the produce reports – as well as any information obtainable as to the value of kelp, during the kelp season – would effect this object.

The marking of rocks, to facilitate boat navigation in the bays.

The provision of seed potatoes, oats, and barley at seed-time, on commercial terms – for cash, at co-operative prices, to those who will order it beforehand, and undertake to pay for it on delivery; on special terms to a few who may be known to be unable to pay for it on delivery. If to those few the condition could be conceded of returning the seed in kind at harvest time, with or without extra measure as interest, it would be gratefully accepted, and, I feel sure, faithfully fulfilled. In their dealings with each other the people act on such a principle – for instance, the service of a bull is not paid for till the calf is dropped; and no money is taken from a neighbour for the purchase of a sucking pig ("bon-iv"). But when the "bon-iv" is sold, months afterwards, as a (more or less fat) pig, 10*s.* is paid to the first owner out of the price realized. The people will sell anything they have saleable, except the cow, for seed if they have none left when seed-time comes. In two instances a yearling calf was driven in nearly twenty miles to the last Spiddal fair to be sold for that purpose, and brought home again unsold. In many other instances men have tried to sell seaweed, in order to buy seed potatoes with the money, but tried this season in vain.

Relying upon the permission of the Chairman to "say what I think," and upon the indulgence of the Board, I submit these suggestions as a contribution only to the study of a complex question. The first governs the rest. The population must be gradually thinned out, and dispersed. Each village, and individual families, require different treatment. For some emigration is, for others migration may prove to be, the most suitable and acceptable panacea. In either case the most careful selection will be necessary. Whatever is done for the people at home, the principle should be kept in view of helping them to do better what they have been accustomed to do; and so of leading them, through their own methods, on to higher ground. In their prejudices and mutual jealousies they are strongly, perhaps perversely, conservative; but the perversity of ignorance is no new thing, and ignorance may be inferred from the school attendance records. The number of children attending school now is only about fifty per cent. of the number of school age; yet the attendance has more than doubled in the last ten years. I have not been able as yet to ascertain what the attendance was when the Commissioners of National Education established their first schools in this district about twenty years ago; but from official authority and my own observation I can state that whereas twelve years ago there were only four schools in the district, there are now twelve; greatly improved buildings, except one, as compared with the four, and supplying a higher grade of teaching. The teachers, who had then to live in local lodgings, are now comfortably "residenced." This result is largely due to the exertions of the present Parish Priest, Father Conway.

An essential preliminary, or accompanying, condition to systematic and comprehensive treatment of this district should be, I think, the establishment of a Petty Sessions Court at Bealadangan, near the Dispensary and Dangan Bridge. At present no summons can be obtained, and no case heard, nearer than Spiddal, 17½ miles from Carrowroe or Bealadangan (the Post Office at either place), and ten miles farther from Lettermullen. The population so brought within a nearer reach of the law would be 7,000 at least; and considerably more, if the Oughterard and Spiddal Petty Sessions Districts were revised.

I think I ought not to omit to mention – in case the Board should see fit to sanction work in Carrowroe or Gorumna Electoral Divisions – that under the Piers and Roads Commission in 1887 contracts were placed in the hands of Father Conway with highly satisfactory results, and that, in my opinion, all interests would be best served by requesting his co-operation in any work that may be undertaken now.

Dooleen Beaches consist of coral sand, inexhaustible in quantity by all accounts, and are within 56 perches of the end of a road which until recent years was kept in repair as a public highway. This sand would be of the highest value to the whole of this district of bog land as manure, and I beg to recommend the construction of the short piece of road required, in order to admit carts and pack horses to the Beaches. Mr. Tuke was good enough to visit the spot, and it has since been surveyed by the Galway County Surveyor, Mr. Perry. The required road is marked in *red* on the accompanying map.

Schools. – The following extracts from the "Rules and Regulations of the Commissioners of National Education" appear to apply to the circumstances of this district:–

Applicants for a School Building must be prepared to raise by local contribution, at least one-third of the whole sum, &c. (Page 2, paragraph 12).

In National Schools whose Managers desire that special provision be made for the instruction and training of externs as well as of girls who have passed through the sixth class in . . . approved branches of *industrial instruction for females* (including *net-mending* and basket-making), a salary may be awarded to a special Industrial Teacher. (Page 6, paragraph 52).

"Agriculture" (as a subject) is obligatory for boys, of fourth or higher classes . . . optional for girls. (Page 31 – note).

The Commissioners of Public Works . . . may make loans . . . for the purpose of assisting any person in the erection, enlargement, structural improvement, or purchase of a house to be used as a non-vested National School; or in the enlargement or structural improvement of any existing non-vested National School; *or in the acquisition or improvement of a farm not exceeding twenty-five acres in extent,* connected with a non-vested National School, to be used for the purpose of agricultural instruction. Such loan shall be repaid by an annual rent charge of 5 per cent. for 35 years. (Page 46).

A certificate of proficiency in Handicraft, satisfactory to the Commissioners, must be possessed by the teacher of Handicraft. (Page 57 – note).

Agriculture (4th class, boys). – To answer intelligently on the subject of crops, as treated in the "Introduction to Practical Farming." (Page 61).

Agriculture (5th class, 1st stage). – In addition to the above, to answer intelligently on cottage gardening, as treated, &c. (Page 62).

Agriculture (5th class, 2nd stage). – In addition to the foregoing, to answer intelligently on Part II. of the "Introduction," &c. (in fact, on the whole book). (Page 63).

Agricultural National Schools are schools to which farms or gardens are attached for the purpose of illustrating and introducing the most approved systems of tillage and husbandry . . . The teachers of agricultural schools must be competent to give instruction both in the theory and practice of agriculture; and must give practical instruction in agriculture to their pupils. (Page 6, paragraphs 41-48).

On or after 1st August, 1889, every *girl* who passes the 2nd stage of the 5th class shall devote the remainder of her school attendance chiefly to industrial work – including any two special industries (which may be basket-making and *net-mending*). (Pages 64-65).

The following extra branches can be taught *to girls only*:–

Practical Cookery. Management of poultry. Dairying. (Page 70, last 2 lines).

In any National School *to which a dairy is attached* having at command a sufficient supply of milk and proper appliances, dairying may be recognized as an extra branch (page 73). The Teacher must hold a certificate of dairying competency.

Domestic Economy and Hygiene (but *not domestic work*) can be taught in the schools to "females." (Pages 73 and 74).

[Practical Cookery may be taught by any ordinary literary teacher – no special certificate being given to Teachers for this branch, but a proper kitchen and utensils must be provided by the management. The National Board will contribute to the building, but not to the fittings.*]

Management of poultry will not be paid for as an extra subject where there is not a poultry yard attached to the school; available for, and made use of in, the practical instruction of the pupils. (Page 69).

Evening Schools.

Teachers are paid partly by salary, partly by results fees . . . The salary is £1 per month for each teacher (under certain conditions). A school will not be examined for results fees unless it has been in actual operation as a National School for at least six continuous months. (Page 36).

Under no circumstances should a day school pupil be presented for examination in an evening school . . .

In an evening school *not more than two* extra branches can be taught. (Page 68).

The Commissioners admit into the Albert Model Agricultural National School, at Glasnevin, a limited number of free, and also of paying, resident pupils.

W. P. GASKELL.

11th May, 1892.

* I have this from the local Inspector of Schools, but as yet cannot quote the page of the "Rules" &c., on which it appears. The word "Cookery" is not in its place in the index, nor do I find "Apparatus."

CONGESTED DISTRICTS BOARD FOR IRELAND

COUNTY OF KERRY – UNION OF CAHERSIVEEN

REPORT OF MR. BUTLER, *Inspector*

DISTRICT

OF

CAHERSIVEEN

STATISTICAL TABLE

ELECTORAL DIVISION.	Area in Statute Acres.	Poor Law Valuation.	Number of Ratings at and under £10 and above £4 Valuation.	Number of Ratings at and under £4 Valuation.	Population in 1891.	Number of Families in 1891.	Number of Families on Holdings exceeding £2 and under £4 Valuation.	Number of Families on Holdings at and under £2 Valuation.	Number of Families in very poor circumstances.	Number of Families which have no Cattle.
		£								
Caher,	10,899	3,181	245	451	3,388	595	138	313	76	61*
Canuig,	8,156	580	68	44	693	111	24	20	17	10
Ballinskelligs,	7,500	1,209	103	169	1,688	316	65	104	46	29†
Emlagh,	8,799	1,680	101	115	1,621	270	55	60	38	26
St. Finan's,	3,579	622	43	20	515	81	3	17	10	6
Teeranearagh,	6,508	849	61	63	848	148	23	40	12	13
Bahaghs,	9,660	817	50	38	745	106	12	26	9	3
Castlequin,	13,450	1,909	129	163	1,417	251	42	121	18	14
Derriana,	23,077	909	76	37	784	119	10	27	15	13
Killinane,	12,732	971	86	171	1,041	187	40	131	20	6
TOTALS,	104,357	£12,727	962	1,271	12,740	2,184	412	859	261	181

* Principally in town of Cahersiveen. † Mostly in village of Dungeagan.

(1.) Whether inland or maritime.

All these Electoral Divisions are partly inland and partly maritime, with the exception of Canuig, Bahaghs, Derriana, and Teeranearagh.

(2.) Average quantity of land cultivated on holdings at and under £4 valuation, under (*a*) oats, (*b*) potatoes, (*c*) meadow, (*d*) green crops.

There are about 3 acres on an average cultivated on holdings at and under £4 valuation in the following way:–

Oats,	1 acre
Potatoes,	1½ acres
Green Crops,	½ acre

(3.) Extent of mountain or moor grazing, and rights possessed by tenants, whether in common or otherwise.

The extent of mountain or moor grazing in the several Electoral Divisions comprising the district is as follows:–

Electoral Division	Extent	How held
	Acres.	
Caher,	1,602	In common
Canuig,	2,468	” and 200 acres held by two or more
Ballinskelligs,	942	”
Emlagh,	746	”
St. Finan’s,	508	”
Teeranearagh,	997	”
Bahaghs,	2,453	” and 310 acres held by two or more
Castlequin,	4,967	” and 309 acres in landlords’ hands
Derriana,	13,064	” and 1,200 acres held jointly by two or more and 200 acres in landlords’ hands
Killinane,	4,104	” and 1,024 acres held by two or more

(4.) Extent and description of land, if any, which could be profitably reclaimed and added to existing adjoining holdings.

There is a large extent of slob-land lying between the Electoral Divisions of Caher and Castlequin, extending from Caher racecourse to the mouth of the Festa river, which might be reclaimed by embanking; it is covered over at high tide by four to seven feet of water; the soil consists of mud and sand.

The value of this land when reclaimed would, however, not be sufficient to warrant the necessary outlay.

(5.) Particulars as to any suitable land in district which could be obtained, and to which families could be migrated with a reasonable prospect of success.

There is no suitable land in this district which could be obtained to which families could be migrated with any reasonable prospect of success.

(6.) Method of cultivation, manures, rotation of crops, etc., etc.

Cultivation is carried on in this district altogether with the spade and shovel: a large quantity of sea-weed, and sometimes sea-sand, with a little farmyard manure is used, which might be increased both in quantity and quality with much benefit to crops and land.

The usual course of rotation is as follows: potatoes for two and often three years, then oats, with sometimes a little green crops, turnips, cabbages, &c.; growing more of these would much improve the small farmer and his stock. After the oats is cut (the docks and other weeds as a rule are left standing), the land is left to nature to grow weeds with a little of the coarser natural grasses.

The method of cultivation is as follows:–

First year, the land being in grass. In February and March the land is prepared for potato sowing by stripping furrows 18 inches wide and 1½ or 2 inches thick, leaving beds between, 4 feet wide: sea-sand is then sprinkled over, and seaweed laid over the grass part of the beds, and on the seaweed a little farm-yard manure is thrown. On the manure the potato sets are spread, some 9 inches apart, during the month of February, and then all is covered with soil from the furrows. After May 1st the potatoes are earthed up with soil from the furrows; this, in wet land, acts as temporary drainage, and often saves a crop from rotting. The potatoes are dug and stored in pits during October, leaving sufficient of the smaller potatoes in the ground for seed the following year.

Second year: In February seaweed or dung is laid on the beds, and the beds deeply dug, fixing the seed left in the ground from last year with the manure in each cut as the digger goes along, then earthed up and dug clean out, and stored the same as in the first year.

Third year: The potato land is dug out level about April; oats is then sown and covered with the bush harrow; after cutting oats in the following August, the land is left to struggle back to even an inferior pasture to what it was before being broken up, as an abundant supply of weeds have as a rule grown along with the potatoes, the seeds of which remain in the ground and choke and smother the few natural grasses struggling for an existence.

Another rotation sometimes followed is:– (First year) Oats or sometimes green crops are sown in beds 4 feet wide. After the oats are cut, and during the winter seaweed is laid on the beds. In March the beds are trimmed up and potatoes are planted often for two years. Then oats are sown again, and the land left idle afterwards. This rotation is more common than it used to be.

(7.) General information with regard to stock, and suggestions as to improvement of breeds – (*a*) cattle, (*b*) sheep, (*c*) horses and donkeys, (*d*) pigs, (*e*) poultry, etc., etc.

Cattle.– The classes of cattle seen in this district are Kerries and cross-breeds. The Kerry has much improved of late years, but might be further improved by the introduction of good Kerry Bulls. The district is not suitable for larger cattle.

Sheep.– The breed of sheep is poor and small. Rams of better breeds than those in the district – for instance, well bred Shropshire rams would do best.

Horses.– These are small, badly bred, and much deteriorated. The introduction of a few good hackney and farm sires would be advantageous.

Donkeys.– These are fairly good, and very numerous. A few Spanish donkeys might be introduced with advantage.

Pigs.– The breed of pigs is fairly good.

Poultry.— These are small and of a poor breed, and are mostly kept for the sake of their eggs.

Poultry might be greatly improved by introducing a larger and better laying breed, such as Plymouth Rocks, Wyandottes, &c.

(8.) Markets and fairs for cattle and produce of district; also statement as to where the people obtain food and other supplies, and the prevailing custom with regard to the disposal of butter, eggs, and poultry; to what extent are they sold in the first instance to local shopkeepers and dealers, and, generally speaking, how old are the eggs when sold to the first buyer, and about how old when they reach their ultimate destination in Great Britain.

Monthly fairs and weekly markets are held at Cahersiveen, where the people of the district chiefly get their food supplies. Butter and eggs are sold to local dealers and shop-keepers. The eggs are sold weekly by the producers on market days, the average age being four days. Dealers often keep them three or four weeks, the average time being twenty-three days; in transit to consumer another three days must be added, so that the average age of the eggs when they reach the consumer would be about twenty-eight to thirty days.

(9.) Rail, steamer, sailing boat, road, postal and telegraph facilities.

There is a railway in course of construction between Killorglin and Valencia, which will be completed about August, 1893. The Clyde Shipping Company's steamer sails weekly between Cork and Cahersiveen, and Messrs. Russell & Co.'s steamer weekly between Limerick and Cahersiveen. The roads throughout the district are good. There are post and telegraph offices at Cahersiveen, Waterville, and Valencia (Knightstown), and post offices at Ballinskelligs, Kells, Mastergeehy, and Portmagee.

(10.) Employment for labourers in the district, whether temporary or constant, and rate of wage.

There is temporary employment in this district for farm labourers at 2*s.* per day, but higher wages are paid during spring and harvest work.

(11.) Migratory labour, average earnings per head, and where earned.

There are no migratory labourers in this district.

(12.) Weaving, spinning, knitting, and sewing, whether used locally or sold, and where.

There is no weaving, spinning, knitting or sewing carried on in this district, except for home use; coarse flannel and tweeds, also some stockings are made.

(13.) Kelp-burning, and sale of seaweed.

There is no kelp-burning carried on in this district; there is no sale of seaweed, except in Castlequin Electoral Division, where a little is sold to inland farmers for manure.

(14.) Sale of turf, nature and extent of bogs.

The bogs in this district are extensive, and good everywhere. A little turf is sold in Cahersiveen, for consumption in the town.

(15.) Lobster fishing, number of men and boats employed.

In Castlequin Electoral Division there are eight men and two boats engaged in lobster fishing; in Killinane two men and one boat, and in Ballinskelligs and St. Finan's thirty men and five boats. Mackerel, herrings and lobsters are chiefly sold in the English markets. A little coarse fish is caught, but nearly altogether for home consumption.

(16.) Sea fishing. Facilities for sale of fish, and number of boats and men solely employed in fishing.

In Castlequin Electoral Division there are 176 men and forty-four boats engaged in fishing; in Killinane forty-four men and eleven boats; and in Ballinskelligs and St. Finan's 133 men and twenty-seven boats. Of the above, sixty-eight men and eight boats fish salmon during the season (June and July), and forty men and eight boats fish lobsters part of the season, as mentioned in the foregoing paragraph.

(17.) Number of boats and men employed in carrying turf or seaweed or in fishing. Classification of boats.

There are in this district 330 men and seventy-eight boats employed in fishing and carrying turf and seaweed; the boats are all open row-boats, from twenty to thirty feet long. There are no canoes in this district. Of the above, twenty-one men and seven boats carry sand and seaweed alone, chiefly for manure.

(18.) Fish; whether consumed at home or sold.

Mackerel, herrings, lobsters and salmon caught off this district are generally sold; other fish are mostly consumed at home.

(19.) Extent of fish-curing.

In Castlequin Electoral Division 198 barrels of mackerel were cured and sent to American markets in 1891. There is no fish-curing carried on in any other parts of the district.

(20.) Piers and Harbours, existing and suggested, and how far those existing are adapted to wants of district.

At Caher there are good piers, and at Ballinskelligs there is a pier little used. There is a half-tide pier at Emlagh, built by Trinity College, for landing sand and seaweed chiefly. There is a boat-slip at Reenard Point, in Caher Electoral Division. Boat-slips on small piers are very badly wanted at Coonnana or Coomscroum, in Castlequin Electoral Division; at Kells, in Killinane Electoral Division, and at St. Finan's Bay, in St. Finan's Electoral Division.

(21.) Extent of salmon and freshwater fisheries. Number of men earning their livelihood therefrom.

There are no salmon nor freshwater fisheries in this district.

(22.) Banks and Loan Funds.

There are branches of the National and Munster and Leinster Banks at Cahersiveen. There are no Loan Funds in the district.

(23.) Mineral and other resources.

There are indications of good slate in Caher Electoral Division, but it is not worked. There is building stone everywhere, but no limestone.

(24.) Relative prevalence of cash or credit dealings, length of credit, interest charged, extent of barter, etc., etc.

Credit dealings are almost universal in this district, except at fairs and markets, when cattle and butter are paid for in cash. The length of credit varies from six to eighteen months; no actual interest is charged, but all credit prices are higher than cash. Banks advance money on bills at about 7 per cent. There is no barter carried on in the district.

(25.) Estimated *cash* receipts and expenditure of a family in ordinary circumstances.

The estimated *Cash* receipts and expenditure of a family of eight persons, possessing six cows, on a holding of say £7 10*s*. valuation, are as follows:–

Receipts	£	*s.*	*d.*	Expenditure	£	*s.*	*d.*
Sale of butter,	18	0	0	Rent of holding,	9	0	0
" young stock,	12	10	0	Poor Rate,	0	11	0
" pigs,	12	0	0	County Cess,	1	17	6
" sheep and lambs,	5	0	0	Young pigs bought,	4	0	0
" eggs, wool, etc.,	3	0	0	Food, breadstuffs, etc.,	22	0	0
				Groceries,	5	0	0
				Clothes, tobacco, etc.,	8	0	0
Total,	£50	10	0	Total,	£50	8	6

This estimate does not include fish, which varies according to season and locality.

(26.) Estimated value of home-grown food consumed, and period during which it lasts.

The estimated value of home-grown food consumed is about £15, as follows:– 1½ acres of potatoes, yielding four tons to the acre, at 2*s.* 6*d.* per cwt.; total, £15. Eggs and milk are also consumed. In a very good year potatoes last for twelve months; in an inferior season seven to nine months. There is no home-grown grain used for food.

(27.) Dietary of people, number of meals daily, and kinds of food throughout the year.

The dietary of the people of this district consists of potatoes, bread, flour, Indian meal, tea, fish, eggs and milk. Three meals are taken daily. *Breakfast* – Bread and tea. *Dinner* – Potatoes and milk, with eggs, fish, or meat sometimes. *Supper* – Potatoes and milk, or tea and bread.

(28.) Clothing, whether home-made or bought, etc., etc.

A good deal of coarse flannel is made at home, and used for underclothing; also some coarse tweed. A great deal of the clothing is bought, either ready-made or otherwise. A large trade is done in the town of Cahersiveen on fair and market days, by hawkers selling second (or more often third) hand ready-made clothes to the country people. It is an amusing sight watching a country man trying on and bargaining for a coat, &c.; he will often try on a dozen before he is pleased, and eventually he will buy a coat for perhaps three shillings; this class of garment gives no wear.

(29.) Dwellings: kind of houses, home-life and customs, etc., etc.

In Caher Electoral Division about one-fifth of the houses are slated, elsewhere about one-eighth; all the rest are thatched. They consist generally of two or three rooms and a loft; they are tolerably clean and comfortable, but without any sanitary arrangements whatever. In the poorer class of houses the horse and cow generally occupy a corner of the kitchen, not to mention cocks and hens, a few calves and always a dog or two.

(30.) Character of the people for industry, etc., etc.

The people of this district are neither industrious nor thrifty as a rule; they are generally sober, except on market days, fair days or holidays, when they visit the villages and invariably come home the worse for drink. They are by nature indolent, and have no care for to-morrow, time being a matter of no consequence, and never doing to-day what can possibly be put off till to-morrow.

(31.) Whether any organized effort has been made to develop the resources or improve the condition of the people. If so, by what means.

No organised effort has been made to develop the resources or improve the condition of the people of this district, except that in Caher and Castlequin Electoral Divisions the landlords – Lord Lansdowne and Trinity College have, from time to time, laid out considerable sums in providing better dwellings, drainage and other works for their tenants.

(32.) Suggestions as to any possible method for improving the condition of the people in future.

This district and other districts, will be much improved and opened up when the Killorglin and Valencia Railway is completed. The agriculture of this district might be much improved in the following ways:– Induce the farmer not to overstock his land; the common practice being to keep three half-starved cows on the grass of two, and to rear three wretched stunted calves, instead of one or two good ones; there is always (even in the worst times) a demand for a good beast; a stunted and half-starved beast is becoming more unsaleable every day. I would recommend the use of better seeds, better cultivation, more reclamation, the making and collecting of more farm-yard manure, and above all things the keeping of the land free from weeds, etc.; all these are much neglected. It is no uncommon thing to see a miserably poor crop of potatoes struggling to grow through a most luxuriant crop of weeds; in fact I have often seen a man mowing the weeds off the beds, so as to be able to dig his potatoes. I would say that at present at least one-fourth of this district is growing weeds instead of grass, &c. The leaving in the ground of the immature and often unripe small potatoes for seed the following year is a practice much to be condemned, being a certain means of insuring an inferior crop and one subject to disease. The getting in of both the hay and corn harvest in time, is much neglected, the meadows being grazed too late in spring and often not cut till October. The use of a better class of sires and doing away with the bad ones is most desirable. In my opinion no stallion ought to be allowed to serve in any district without a government certificate, backed by a local veterinary certificate, saying that the horse is a fit and proper one to serve in the district and free from hereditary unsoundness. I would carry out the same plan with bulls if possible.

A few well-bred Shropshire rams scattered through the district would be of much service, as the breed of sheep have greatly deteriorated, owing to careless and too close breeding.

The fisheries might be developed as suggested in my special reports on certain piers, landing places, &c.

Much planting might be done with benefit were it possible to get up the land from the occupiers.

The tourist traffic between Cahersiveen and Kenmare, where the scenery all along is unrivalled, the hotel accommodation good, sporting, both fishing and shooting, excellent and much sought after, might be much encouraged by making a new line of road (and building a bridge across the river Eeny), about three miles in length, in Emlagh Electoral Division, which would avoid a bad and dangerous hill, shorten the distance from Cahersiveen to Waterville and a very large area beyond, and be an immense benefit to the entire district.

The excessive poor rates in some of the poorer Electoral Divisions in Cahersiveen Union are almost swamping the poorer rate-payers. A list of the rates struck November 23rd, 1892, accompanies this report: for instance, in Loughcurrane Electoral Division the Poor Rate is 5*s.* in the £, and the County Cess as much more. In Ballinskelligs Electoral Division the Poor Rate is 4*s.* in the £, and in the other Electoral Divisions from 1*s.* 6*d.* to 3*s.* in the £. I would suggest that a small annual grant be made to relieve these over-rated Electoral Divisions.

The general condition of the people might be improved by doing away with about half the public-houses in the town of Cahersiveen, and preventing the sale of whiskey in the same shops with meal, flour, and other goods; the public-houses now number over sixty. I would prevent a concoction of vitriol, &c., being sold as whiskey, which maddens the drinkers and helps to fill Killarney asylum with lunatics, now numbering over 400. I would suggest the establishment of a coffee-room in the town of Cahersiveen to be opened on fair and market days; also the introduction of the teaching of cooking and more plain needle work into the National Schools. An effort should be made to induce the people to be more cleanly and thrifty, and to keep their houses and yards cleaner and in better repair, to be more liberal-minded, and more anxious to improve both their own condition and that of their neighbours.

J. E. BUTLER,
Inspector.

21st December, 1892.

To

The Congested Districts Board for Ireland.

CONGESTED DISTRICTS BOARD FOR IRELAND

COUNTY OF KERRY – UNIONS OF KENMARE AND KILLARNEY

REPORT OF MR. BUTLER, *Inspector*

DISTRICT

OF

KENMARE

STATISTICAL TABLE

ELECTORAL DIVISION.	Area in Statute Acres.	Poor Law Valuation.	Number of Ratings at and under £10 and above £4 Valuation.	Number of Ratings at and under £4 Valuation.	Population in 1891.	Number of Families in 1891.	Number of Families on Holdings exceeding £2 and under £4 Valuation.	Number of Families on Holdings at and under £2 Valuation.	Number of Families in very poor circumstances.	Number of Families which have no Cattle.
		£								
Ardea,	8,422	1,045	67	61	916	140	37	6	2	about 190‡ (Ardea to Kilgarvan)
Banawn,	16,387	986	68	32	790	120	13	2	0	
Dawros,	12,806	1,102	76	45	792	141	22	2	3	
Glanlee,	15,265	653	31	13	509	80	6	4	8	
Glanlough,	10,390	784	40	8	602	82	3	1	8	
Glanmore,	18,113	916	69	*87	995	142	25	11	5	
Kenmare,	13,452	3,412	170	†278	2,661	420	65	68	20	
Kilgarvan,	16,735	1,889	67	†91	1,563	230	21	27	18	
Coolies,	7,171	878	25	60	610	92	18	38	13	10
TOTALS,	118,741	£8,665	613	675	9,438	1,447	210	159	77	110

* There are 17 ratings at 6*s*., and one at 8*s*. in Glanmore in the townland of Knockowen, which is uninhabited and used as a mountain grazing by tenants of an adjoining townland.

† Many of the small ratings in Kenmare and Kilgarvan are for townparks, held by inhabitants of the town and village.

‡ Including families living in Kenmare town, and the villages of Kilgarvan and Cross Roads.

(1.) Whether inland or maritime.

Ardea, Dawros, Glanmore, and Kenmare are partly maritime, the remaining Electoral Divisions are inland.

(2.) Average quantity of land cultivated on holdings at and under £4 valuation, under (*a*) oats, (*b*) potatoes, (*c*) meadow, (*d*) green crops.

In the Electoral Divisions of Kenmare Union there are about 3¼ acres on an average cultivated on holdings at and under £4 valuation in the following way:–

Oats,	½ acre.
Potatoes,	1 "
Meadow,	1½ acres.
Green crops,	¼ acre.
Total,	3¼ acres.

In Coolies Electoral Division (Killarney Union) there are about 5½ acres on an average cultivated on holdings at and under £4 valuation in the following way:–

Oats,	1	acre.
Potatoes,	1¼	acres.
Meadow,	3	„
Green crops (cabbage only),	¼	acre.
Total,	5½	acres.

(3.) Extent of mountain or moor grazing, and rights possessed by tenants, whether in common or otherwise.

There are in this district about 90,000 acres of mountain or moor-grazing, chiefly held in common by tenants of townlands.

(4.) Extent and description of land, if any, which could be profitably reclaimed and added to existing adjoining holdings.

In Kenmare Union there are about 5,000 acres of bog which could be reclaimed, but there would be great difficulty in dealing with the tenants who have grazing rights, usually in common, over it.

In Coolies Electoral Division (Killarney Union) there are about 40 acres of moorland in Gortdromakiery, and 20 acres in Faghcullia which could be reclaimed.

(5.) Particulars as to any suitable land in district which could be obtained, and to which families could be migrated with a reasonable prospect of success.

There is no suitable land in the district which could be obtained, and to which families could be migrated with a reasonable prospect of success.

(6.) Method of cultivation, manures, rotation of crops, etc., etc.

As a rule, in this district the cultivation is of a most primitive description, and in most parts spade husbandry only. For manures, on the coast seaweed and seasand are used; elsewhere farm-yard manure of a poor kind, chiefly composed of furze and heather, with small quantities of lime and artificial manures. On the coast potatoes are grown in bog year after year; elsewhere the rotation is oats, potatoes for two or three years, oats, and then leave to nature to produce grass; the first crop of oats is often omitted. On good land and large holdings the rotation is potatoes, turnips, oats, and hay seeds.

(7.) General information with regard to stock, and suggestions as to improvement of breeds – (*a*) cattle, (*b*) sheep, (*c*) horses and donkeys, (*d*) pigs, (*e*) poultry, etc., etc.

Cattle and Sheep.– These are, as a rule, very poor and degenerated: the first step towards improvement would be to get rid of the wretched bulls which wander over the mountains and replace them by Kerries, and to introduce well-bred Shropshire rams.

The cattle in Ardea, Dawros, and Glanmore are particularly bad. Lord Lansdowne has endeavored to improve them, but his efforts failed, as all efforts must, until, as above suggested, the present bulls are got rid of.

Horses.– Good Hackney stallions are required.

Donkeys.– In places where these are used a larger breed of Jacks is required.

Pigs.– These are fairly good.

Poultry.– The poultry are small, but they are good layers and suited to the country; they might be improved by crossing with black Spanish fowl.

(8.) Markets and fairs for cattle and produce of district; also statement as to where the people obtain food and other supplies, and the prevailing custom with regard to the disposal of butter, eggs, and poultry; to what extent are they sold in the first instance to local shopkeepers and dealers, and, generally speaking, how old are the eggs when sold to the first buyer, and about how old when they reach their ultimate destination in Great Britain.

For Kenmare Union there are twelve fairs annually in Kenmare, and six at Cross Roads. There are markets weekly at Kenmare and Kilgarvan for butter. Provisions, &c., are bought at Kenmare, and to a small extent at Kilgarvan. There are two or three local provision dealers in Tuosist parish. There is a creamery at Kenmare, which so far has proved successful.

In Killarney Union, Coolies Electoral Division, there are thirteen fairs in the year at Killarney; food &c., is procured there.

Butter in both Unions is now generally sold locally and fresh; some, however, is sent in firkins to Cork.

Eggs are sold to local dealers when about one week old, and reach their ultimate destination in another week, or when a fortnight old.

(9.) Rail, steamer, sailing boat, road, postal and telegraph facilities.

In Kenmare Union there is a weekly steamer service from Cork to Kenmare; coal, &c., are also sent there by steamers and sailing vessels from England, Cork, and Limerick. Occasionally cargoes of timber arrive there from America – St. John, N.B.

There is a railway in course of construction, which will be open for traffic early in 1893.

There are Post Offices at Kenmare, Banawn, Ardea, and Lauragh, and a Telegraph Office at Kenmare.

In Killarney Union, Coolies Electoral Division, there is railway connection at Killarney, also a Post Office and Telegraph Station. There is a Post Office at Muckross.

Roads throughout the district are good and plentiful.

(10.) Employment for labourers in the district, whether temporary or constant, and rate of wage.

Twenty or thirty labourers are employed constantly at Kenmare, at farm-work and discharging vessels, at 12*s.* per week. There are no other labourers employed in Kenmare Union, except in Spring and harvest time, at 2*s.* 6*d.* per day. Large farmers employ servant-men at about £5 and diet for spring quarter.

Labourers in Coolies Electoral Division get constant employment from gentry and farmers, at about 9*s.* a week without diet.

(11.) Migratory labour, average earnings per head, and where earned.

There are no migratory labourers in this district.

(12.) Weaving, spinning, knitting, and sewing, whether used locally or sold, and where.

Except round Kenmare there is no weaving, spinning, knitting or sewing carried on except for home use. In Kenmare some flannel and tweed is sold, There is a woollen mill near Kenmare, but it is not worked to any extent. If it could be taken up and worked a trade would probably be established, and a market created for local grown wool.

Some lace-making and needlework is carried on at Kenmare Convent.

(13.) Kelp-burning, and sale of seaweed.

There is no kelp-burning or sale of seaweed carried on in the district.

(14.) Sale of turf, nature and extent of bogs.

There is no turf sold in the district, except a little at Kenmare. The bogs in Kenmare Union are very extensive, and all tenants have free turbary.

In Coolies Electoral Division there is hardly any turbary, the bogs having been cut away, except about 120 acres, most of which is too wet for turbary. The people buy turf on adjoining lands not scheduled as congested.

(15.) Lobster fishing, number of men and boats employed.

There is no lobster fishing carried on in this district.

(16.) Sea fishing. Facilities for sale of fish, and number of boats and men solely employed in fishing.

There is one trawler of about 12 tons at Kenmare. There are no other boats solely employed in fishing. The fish caught are chiefly sent to hotels in Killarney, some is sold in Kenmare and the rest used at home.

(17.) Number of boats and men employed in carrying turf or seaweed or in fishing. Classification of boats.

Besides the trawler mentioned in the last paragraph there are two second-class and six third-class boats, with forty-three men, registered in the district; they, however, only fish occasionally for bream, &c. There are no boats used for carrying turf or seaweed.

(18.) Fish; whether consumed at home or sold.

Some of the fish caught off the district is sold at Kenmare and Killarney, but most of it is used at home.

(19.) Extent of fish-curing.

There is no fish curing carried on except for home use, in the district.

(20.) Piers and Harbours, existing and suggested, and how far those existing are adapted to wants of district.

There are piers at Kenmare and Bunaw (Killmakillogue Harbour.) New piers for boats are required at Ormond Harbour, Dawros, Reencaragh (in Feorus West Townland), and Lehid.

Kenmare pier now dries at low water; if lengthened thirty feet there would be five feet of water at the end at low-water springs, and at an hour's flood fishing vessels, or small carrier steamers, could reach it and land fish for dispatch by rail when the railway is opened. Mackerel in Spring are now landed at Garinish and Cuolagh Bay; they are carted to Castletown Bear, sent by steamer to Bantry, forwarded by rail thence to Cork, carted across the city, and sent to Dublin by rail. By improving Kenmare pier fish could be landed there, carted one mile to the railway, and sent direct to Dublin – one transhipment instead of three.

(21.) Extent of salmon and freshwater fisheries. Number of men earning their livelihood therefrom.

There are four salmon fisheries, all close to Kenmare, at the Sound, Sneem, Gortalinny, and Roughty, employing about fifteen men for three months.

Two men in Coolies are employed in a salmon fishery at Muckross.

(22.) Banks and Loan Funds.

There are branches of the National Bank and Munster and Leinster Bank at Killarney, and a branch of the latter Bank at Kenmare. With the exception of the Sea and Coast Fisheries Fund, there are no Loan Funds in the district.

(23.) Mineral and other resources.

There is limestone in the neighbourhood of Kenmare, but, with this exception, there are no mineral nor other resources in the district.

There were copper mines worked near Kilgarvan, but they have long been disused, as at the present price of copper they could not be made to pay.

(24.) Relative prevalence of cash or credit dealings, length of credit, interest charged, extent of barter, etc., etc.

Credit dealings are almost universal, save at fairs and markets. The length of credit varies from six months to two years; no interest is charged, but credit prices are higher than cash.

In dealing with local shop-keepers there is usually a pass-book and running accounts, never cleared except in an unusually good year. Banks, of course, advance money on bills at about 7½ per cent. There is no barter carried on.

(25.) Estimated *cash* receipts and expenditure of a family in ordinary circumstances.

It is impossible to form a positive estimate as to the *cash* receipts and expenditure of a family in ordinary circumstances. As nearly as I can tell for a family of six persons having four cows, £30 to £35 would be the receipts and expenditure in an ordinary year, viz.:–

Receipts	£	*s.*	*d.*	Expenditure	£	*s.*	*d.*
Sale of butter, . .	12	0	0	Rent, . .	6	0	0
” 2 calves (2 years' old), .	8	0	0	Roor Rate (tenant's proportion)	0	7	0
” 2 pigs, .	7	10	0	County Cess, . .	1	0	0
” sheep and lambs, .	3	0	0	Bon-ivs (or young pigs) .	2	0	0
” eggs, wool, fowl, &c., .	2	0	0	Food – bread stuffs, . .	15	0	0
				Groceries, . .	3	0	0
				Clothes, tobacco, &c., .	5	0	0
Total,	£32	10	0	Total,	£32	7	0

In a bad year the receipts would be less and the expenditure more, in a good year the reverse. In the majority of cases the expenditure is very much regulated by the receipts and the amount of credit obtainable.

(26.) Estimated value of home-grown food consumed, and period during which it lasts.

Potatoes and milk are the only home-grown foods. In a good year potatoes will last nine or ten months, in a bad year half that time. The value of home-grown food consumed, of course, varies with the year; the average is about £10 to £16.

(27.) Dietary of people, number of meals daily, and kinds of food throughout the year.

The dietary of the people of this district consists of potatoes and milk while they last. At other times bread made half of flour and half of Indian meal is eaten. Tea is much used of late, and in Coolies the poorer classes take coffee.

In Kenmare Union salt-fish is much used with potatoes, but not with bread. Three meals a day – breakfast, dinner, and supper – are the rule.

(28.) Clothing, whether home-made or bought, etc., etc.

The clothing of the people of this district is mostly bought, except inner clothing, for which home-made flannel is often used. In Kenmare Union some home-made frieze or flannel is used.

In Coolies the people sell their wool and buy clothing.

(29.) Dwellings: kind of houses, home-life and customs, etc., etc.

In Kenmare Union about half the houses are slated, the rest thatched; the latter usually consist of a kitchen and lofted sleeping room.

In Coolies there are about a dozen slated houses, the rest are thatched.

There is nothing peculiar in the customs or home-life of the people of this district; as a rule, they are quiet and orderly, but are much given to wasting time at fairs, markets, wakes, funerals, &c.

(30.) Character of the people for industry, etc., etc.

The people of this district work very hard in Spring and harvest, but at other periods are rather indolent, and very thriftless. They have very little idea of order or neatness, though in this respect the National Schools are producing some improvement.

(31.) Whether any organized effort has been made to develop the resources or improve the condition of the people. If so, by what means.

Some of the landlords in this district have expended money in making roads, building houses, &c., under the Board of Works, and Lord Lansdowne started a local cattle-show at Kenmare, but it was a failure. No other attempt has been made to improve the condition of the people, or develop the resources of the country, except by the construction of the railway to Kenmare by the late Government.

(32.) Suggestions as to any possible method for improving the condition of the people in future.

It is very hard to see how the condition of the people of this district can be improved while they are so entirely dependent on the land, and have such small farms. Improved dairies and getting rid of the dung-heaps and cess-pools, which are up to their doors, would of course improve the quality of their butter. The sanitary officers at present, unless there is an outbreak of illness, do not take any trouble in this matter. I think the Constabulary might be made useful in enforcing greater cleanliness. Instruction in dairying and in agriculture generally would be useful, but I fear it would take many years before any improvement could be effected, as the people cling most tenaciously to their old habits.

If manufactories of any kind could be introduced they would, of course, be the best. As a beginning, I would suggest that the Kenmare woollen mills should be taken in hands; with a practical, energetic manager who would try to push a trade, I believe it could be made to pay, and besides giving employment, it would create a market for local wool.

Of course the improvement of stock, &c., as suggested in paragraph (7) of this report, is one of the first matters to be attended to if the condition of the people is to be improved.

If the railway was opened to Kenmare, and a small steamer put on the river as a "carrier," I think the fisheries might be made a source of great wealth.

The smaller tenants whose valuation does not amount to £7, and who cannot therefore claim loans from the Board of Works for improving their farms, are often the most industrious, and, as far as they have means, the most improving. It would be a great matter if loans could be made to them on their getting securities in the same way, as fishery loans are now made from the Sea and Coast Fisheries Fund.

Planting for shelter would be of use in some localities.

J. E. BUTLER,
Inspector.

6th October, 1892.

To

The Congested Districts Board for Ireland.

Tunnels through the Kerry mountains on the Glengarriff Road, near Kenmare.

CONGESTED DISTRICTS BOARD FOR IRELAND

COUNTY OF KERRY – UNION OF CAHERSIVEEN

REPORT OF MR. BUTLER, *Inspector*

DISTRICT

OF

VALENCIA

STATISTICAL TABLE

ELECTORAL DIVISION.	Area in Statute Acres.	Poor Law Valuation.	Number of Ratings at and under £10 and above £4 Valuation.	Number of Ratings at and under £4 Valuation.	Population in 1891.	Number of Families in 1891.	Number of Families on Holdings exceeding £2 and under £4 Valuation.	Number of Families on Holdings at and under £2 Valuation.	Number of Families in very poor circumstances.	Number of Families which have no Cattle.
		£								
Portmagee,	4,080	750	36	154	908	180	33	121	25	*20
Valencia,	6,371	2,053	80	221	2,050	336	59	162	50	40
TOTALS,	10,451	2,803	116	375	2,958	516	92	283	75	†60

* Not including residents in Portmagee Village and (Chapeltown) Valencia.
† Most of these are cabin holders with little or no land. No family having the grass to keep a cow is without one.

(1.) Whether inland or maritime.

Maritime.

(2.) Average quantity of land cultivated on holdings at and under £4 valuation, under (*a*) oats, (*b*) potatoes, (*c*) meadow, (*d*) green crops.

There are about two and a quarter acres on an average cultivated on holdings at and under £4 valuation, in the following way:–

Oats,	1	acre.
Potatoes,	3/4	"
Meadow,	1/4	"
Green Crops,	1/4	"
Total,	2 1/4	acres.

(3.) Extent of mountain or moor grazing, and rights possessed by tenants, whether in common or otherwise.

In Portmagee Electoral Division there are 200 acres of grazing held in common between two tenants, and 1,360 acres held in common by forty-nine tenants holding farms adjacent to mountain.

In Valencia Electoral Division there are 1,010 acres in landlords' hands, the grazing of which is let yearly.

Grazing rights on mountains, possessed by tenants of lowland holdings, are almost altogether in common – in proportion to the valuation of their farms. Poor Rates and County Cess are paid for such grazing rights in a similar proportion.

(4.) Extent and description of land, if any, which could be profitably reclaimed and added to existing adjoining holdings.

There may be said to be practically no land in this district which could be profitably reclaimed and added to existing adjoining holdings.

(5.) Particulars as to any suitable land in district which could be obtained, and to which families could be migrated with a reasonable prospect of success.

There is no suitable land in this district to which families could be migrated with any prospect of success.

(6.) Method of cultivation, manures, rotation of crops, etc., etc.

The method of cultivation is this district is almost altogether by the spade and shovel. The manures used are a large amount of seaweed and sea-sand, with a certain amount of farm-yard manure.

The usual rotation of crops is potatoes, two and often three years, oats and sometimes green crops, and then grass, or rather weeds, as neither before nor after cutting the oats is grass seed sown. Weeds of all sorts are prevalent. I shall refer more fully to this subject in my report on Cahersiveen District.

(7.) General information with regard to stock, and suggestions as to improvement of breeds – (*a*) cattle, (*b*) sheep, (*c*) horses and donkeys, (*d*) pigs, (*e*) poultry, etc., etc.

Information with regard to the stock of this district is as follows:–

Cattle.– These are mostly Kerry and cross-breeds.

Sheep.– These are of the small, mountain breeds.

Horses and Donkeys.– The breed of the former is very poor; of the latter fairly good.

Pigs.– These are of good quality, of the White (Yorkshire) breed.

Poultry.– The poultry are good in Valencia Electoral Division, but small and poor in Portmagee Electoral Division, and are kept, in the latter division, solely for the sake of their eggs.

It is suggested that in Portmagee Electoral Division much might be done by introducing a few good Kerry bulls and some better class rams, and also a larger and better breed of laying poultry.

In Valencia Electoral Division much was done by the late Knight of Kerry to improve the Kerry cattle, sheep, and poultry. The latter are of better quality than usual in this part of the county Kerry.

(8.) Markets and fairs for cattle and produce of district; also statement as to where the people obtain food and other supplies, and the prevailing custom with regard to the disposal of butter, eggs, and poultry; to what extent are they sold in the first instance to local shopkeepers and dealers, and, generally speaking, how old are the eggs when sold to the first buyer, and about how old when they reach their ultimate destination in Great Britain.

There are fairs monthly at Cahersiveen, and markets weekly at that town for butter, eggs, &c. Food is obtained either in Cahersiveen or from local shop-keepers in Valencia or in Portmagee village. Butter and eggs are sold chiefly to local dealers in Cahersiveen; there is no sale of poultry.

Eggs are sold weekly by the producers, the average age then being	3 days
Dealers often hold them for three or four weeks for a market – average time,	20 „
Average time in transit to consumers,	3 „
Average age when the eggs reach the consumer,	26 days

(9.) Rail, steamer, sailing boat, road, postal and telegraph facilities.

There is a railway (Branch of the Great Southern and Western Railway) in course of construction between Killorglin and Valencia. There is a weekly steamer service between Cahersiveen and Cork and Limerick. The roads in the district are good.

A postal and telegraph office is at Knightstown (Valencia) and there are post offices at Valencia (Chapeltown) and at Portmagee.

(10.) Employment for labourers in the district, whether temporary or constant, and rate of wage.

The labourers in this district are temporarily employed, at about 2*s.* per day, in spring and harvest. The few employed constantly get 10*s.* a week.

Girls employed by farmers at dairy work, &c., get from £6 to £8 a year, living with the family.

(11.) Migratory labour, average earnings per head, and where earned.

There are no migratory labourers in this district.

(12.) Weaving, spinning, knitting, and sewing, whether used locally or sold, and where.

There is some coarse flannel woven for home use, and knitting of stockings, jerseys, &c., is carried on at Valencia. See paragraph (31.) of this report.

(13.) Kelp-burning, and sale of seaweed.

There is no kelp-burning nor sale of seaweed carried on in the district.

(14.) Sale of turf, nature and extent of bogs.

There is very little turf sold, but Portmagee possesses about 1,000 acres of good bog, and Valencia about 100 acres of fair bog.

(15.) Lobster fishing, number of men and boats employed.

There is no lobster fishing carried on at Valencia, but Portmagee employs twenty-seven men and nine boats. These men and boats fish for mackerel, &c., part of the season, and are included in the number of men and boats employed in fishing, mentioned in paragraph (17.) of this report.

(16.) Sea fishing. Facilities for sale of fish, and number of boats and men solely employed in fishing.

Nearly all the mackerel (fresh), herring, and lobster caught in this district are sent to English markets. Most of the other fish (trawl and line) taken is consumed in the country; some, however, is sent to the English markets.

The following table gives statistics of the amount of fish taken in 1891:–

—	Mackerel	Herrings	Lobsters	Cod, Ling, and Hake	Other Fish
			Dozens	tns. cwt. qrs.	tns. cwt. qrs.
Portmagee, ...	239,000	627,600	192	44 11 0	6 10 0
Valencia, ...	375,590	198,000	–	3 10 1	2 2 0
Total, .	614,590	825,600	192	48 1 1	8 12 0

In 1890 nearly double the above number of mackerel were taken, but only about one-fourth as many herrings.

(17.) Number of boats and men employed in carrying turf or seaweed or in fishing. Classification of boats.

Portmagee employs 64 boats and 268 men, and Valencia 45 boats and 158 men; total, 109 boats and 426 men. In Portmagee both wooden four and six-oared open boats and canvas canoes are used, fishermen, as a rule, prefer the canoes as being handier and lighter. This is the most southerly point in Ireland where canoes are used.

The fishermen here are very averse to using the larger and better kind of boats. Two fine boats, fully equipped with nets, &c., were sent to Portmagee a few years ago, but the men would nor fish or learn how to work them. Consequently the boats were taken elsewhere, and the nets were neglected and went to the bad.

(18.) Fish; whether consumed at home or sold.

Nearly all the mackerel, herrings, and lobsters are sold; the cod, ling, hake, and scad are partly consumed at home and partly sold.

The mackerel caught in July and August are mostly consumed at home, being small and considered of inferior quality.

(19.) Extent of fish-curing.

The extent of fish-curing in 1891 was:–

Portmagee,	201 barrels of mackerel.
Valencia,	118 " "
Total,	319 " "

These barrels were of about 200 lbs. net weight each, and contained about 240 mackerel each. They were sent mostly to American markets, where they fetched from £3 to £4 per barrel.

(20.) Piers and Harbours, existing and suggested, and how far those existing are adapted to wants of district.

There are deep-water piers and boat-slips at Knightstown (Valencia), and at Portmagee, and a landing-slip at Tennies (Valencia), built by Trinity College, Dublin. There is also good anchorage in three to ten fathoms in Valencia Harbour. This harbour might be greatly improved by clearing the north entrance. A boat-slip is badly wanted at Portmagee ferry (Valencia side).

Portmagee pier might be rendered much more serviceable by being extended a little on the north side, so as to cover a reef of rocks which hinders vessels of six feet draught from lying alongside.

A boat-slip is much wanted at Dohilla, Valencia. (See special Report.)

(21.) Extent of salmon and freshwater fisheries. Number of men earning their livelihood therefrom.

There are no salmon or freshwater fisheries in this district.

(22.) Banks and Loan Funds.

There are branches of the National Bank and of the Munster and Leinster Bank in Cahersiveen.

There are no Loan Funds in the district.

(23.) Mineral and other resources.

There are extensive slate quarries in Valencia, worked for many years, but closed since 1884. They produced very high class slabs, largely used for water tanks, billiard tables, and such like purposes; also good and durable roofing slate, but heavier and coarser than the Welsh slate. It is doubtful whether the thin and brittle Welsh slate will stand this climate; it has only been recently introduced. There is no doubt that the *native* slate makes a much more durable roof. There is *no* limestone in the district.

(24.) Relative prevalence of cash or credit dealings, length of credit, interest charged, extent of barter, etc., etc.

Credit dealings for food, clothing, &c., are almost universal, but butter and cattle are always sold for cash.

The length of credit is from nine to eighteen months, interest is added, and an increased price charged, as a rule, in the first instance. There is no barter carried on in the district.

(25.) Estimated *cash* receipts and expenditure of a family in ordinary circumstances.

The estimated *cash* receipts and expenditure of a family of eight persons, having four cows and occupying about thirty acres of land, and mountain grazing in proportion, are as follows:–

Receipts	£	s.	d.	Expenditure	£	s.	d.
Sale of butter, 90 lbs. per cow				Rent, . .	6	0	0
at 8*d.* per lb., .	12	0	0	Half poor rates and County Cess,	1	8	0
„ young stock, . .	7	0	0	Food – meal, flour, etc., .	12	0	0
„ sheep, . .	2	0	0	Groceries, . .	3	0	0
„ eggs, wool, etc., . .	3	0	0	Clothes and incidentals, .	8	0	0
„ pigs, . .	7	10	0				
Total, . .	*£31	10	0	Total, . .	£30	8	0

* This does not include fish sold, which would vary from £5 to £40 according to the season.

(26.) Estimated value of home-grown food consumed, and period during which it lasts.

The estimated value of home-grown food consumed would be about £12 to £14, and would last in a good year from ten to twelve months, and in a bad one from seven to nine months.

(27.) Dietary of people, number of meals daily, and kinds of food throughout the year.

The dietary of the people of this district consists of potatoes, bread, fish, Indian meal, milk, eggs, and occasionally meat. The people take three meals daily, viz.:–

Breakfast.– Tea or milk and bread.

Dinner.– Potatoes, milk, eggs or fish, and very occasionally meat.

Supper.– Tea and bread, or potatoes and milk.

Note – Meat cannot be looked upon as part of their weekly diet.

(28.) Clothing, whether home-made or bought, etc., etc.

Inside clothing is mostly home-spun and home-made, but of recent years most of the outside clothing is bought in shops ready made.

(29.) Dwellings: kind of houses, home-life and customs, etc., etc.

In Portmagee about one-eighth of the houses are slated. The rest are thatched, but comfortable and of fair size; they consist of two, sometimes three rooms, with a loft.

In Valencia nearly one-half of the houses are slated, and of a superior class, but kept in very bad repair.

The people of this district are not by any means as industrious, either as farmers or fishermen, as they might be.

Home life is primitive, and the customs casual – the cow, pig, horse, and poultry often sharing the living-room with the family.

(30.) Character of the people for industry, etc., etc.

The people of Valencia are fairly industrious and hardworking by fits and starts.

When fishing is successful a considerable portion of their earnings goes in drink, which often prevents their availing themselves of the most favourable circumstances for continuing the fishing. Many of them seem quite unable to resist the temptation when they have money in their pockets.

In Portmagee most of the snooding for the long-lines is spun by the fishermen, and is considered superior to any that can be bought.

(31.) Whether any organized effort has been made to develop the resources or improve the condition of the people. If so, by what means.

In the Electoral Division of Valencia Miss FitzGerald, of Glanleam, commenced in 1881 teaching the women and girls of the neighbourhood to knit stockings, socks, jerseys, &c., and a considerable industry has since sprung up under the management of the Misses FitzGerald, and women and girls to the number of sixty to eighty annually were taught high class knitting – Miss FitzGerald supplying materials, paying for the work done at fixed rates, and finding a market for the manufactured articles. These knitters for several years supplied jerseys on contract to the White Star Line of steamers.

A village hospital has been built, at a cost of £450, and is maintained by private subscriptions, proving most useful to the islanders.

In the Electoral Division of Portmagee attempts have been made from time to time to help the fishermen by grants of boats, and nets and gear, but without much apparent result.

The landlords of these Electoral Divisions (the Board of Trinity College, Dublin, and the late Knight of Kerry) have from time to time spent large sums of money in making roads, drains, and fences, and building houses.

(32.) Suggestions as to any possible method for improving the condition of the people in future.

The Electoral Divisions of Portmagee and Valencia being almost entirely maritime, and the inhabitants therefore mostly depending on fishing for their living, any efforts to improve their condition must be made in that direction.

The improvement of the pier at Portmagee and the construction of a boat-slip on the Valencia side of Portmagee ferry would be useful works; also the construction of a landing place at Dohilla, Valencia Island. See special reports.

The fishermen of this district are very slow to take advantage of opportunities of improving their class of boats, &c.

The reopening of the slate quarries in Valencia Island would give a considerable amount of employment, and ought if properly worked to pay.

The teaching of the boys and girls at the National Schools to make and repair nets and other fishing gear would be a step in the right direction.

The knitting industry in Valencia has done much good, and ought to be encouraged and extended. (See previous paragraph.)

The railway from Killorglin to Valencia will very much improve and open up this district.

J. E. BUTLER,
Inspector.

31st August, 1892.

To

The Congested Districts Board for Ireland.

CONGESTED DISTRICTS BOARD FOR IRELAND

COUNTY OF CORK – UNION OF SKIBBEREEN

REPORT OF MR. ROCHE, *Inspector*

DISTRICT

OF

BALTIMORE

STATISTICAL TABLE

ELECTORAL DIVISION.	Area in Statute Acres.	Poor Law Valuation.	Number of Ratings at and under £10 and above £4 Valuation.	Number of Ratings at and under £4 Valuation.	Population in 1891.	Number of Families in 1891.	Number of Families on Holdings exceeding £2 and under £4 Valuation.	Number of Families on Holdings at and under £2 Valuation.	Number of Families in very poor circumstances.	Number of Families which have no Cattle.
		£								
Cape Clear,	3,916	1,314	105	95	1,216	213	17	32	20	80 (Cape Clear and Tullagh)
Tullagh,	4,262	1,686	93	119	2,101*	235	47	28	20	
Aghadown, Sth.,	5,090	2,691	95	84	1,605	260	21	19	40	80 (Aghadown, Sth. and Castlehaven, South)
Castlehaven, South,	4,600	1,857	107	48	1,208	212	20	25	60	
TOTALS,	17,868	£7,548	400	346	6,130	930	105	104	140	160

* The population of Tullagh Electoral Division includes that of the town of Baltimore, 1,032 – of whom 566 were person on board shipping.

(1.) Whether inland or maritime.

The district is maritime.

(2.) Average quantity of land cultivated on holdings at and under £4 valuation, under (*a*) oats, (*b*) potatoes, (*c*) meadow, (*d*) green crops.

There are about $3\frac{1}{4}$ acres cultivated on an average on holdings at and under £4 valuation in the following way:–

Oats,	1 acre.
Potatoes,	1 ,,
Meadow,	1 ,,
Green crops,	$\frac{1}{4}$,,
Total,	$3\frac{1}{4}$ acres.

(3.) Extent of mountain or moor grazing, and rights possessed by tenants, whether in common or otherwise.

There are in this district about 1,700 acres of rough grazing held almost entirely in severalty.

(4.) Extent and description of land, if any, which could be profitably reclaimed and added to existing adjoining holdings.

There is very little land in this district which could be profitably reclaimed and added to existing adjoining holdings.

(5.) Particulars as to any suitable land in district which could be obtained, and to which families could be migrated with a reasonable prospect of success.

There is no suitable land in this district to which families could be migrated with a reasonable prospect of success.

(6.) Method of cultivation, manures, rotation of crops, etc., etc.

Cultivation is carried on in this district mostly by the spade; on the larger holdings, ploughs are used. The manures used are farm-yard, seaweed, shells, and sand. Potatoes, oats, and meadow form the usual rotation.

(7.) General information with regard to stock, and suggestions as to improvement of breeds – (*a*) cattle, (*b*) sheep, (*c*) horses and donkeys, (*d*) pigs, (*e*) poultry, etc., etc.

Cattle.– The breed is very inferior, and their improvement, by the introduction of good bulls, would be beneficial. Half-bred Shorthorns are, in my opinion, suitable.

Horses.– These are very inferior; an improvement by the introduction of Hackney stallions would also be beneficial, one of the latter stationed at Skibbereen would serve for this district.

Pigs.– These, too, need improvement. Large white Yorkshire boars, I consider best for the purpose.

Poultry.– The hens are of a very inferior class, and are not kept to as great an extent as they ought to be.

(8.) Markets and fairs for cattle and produce of district; also statement as to where the people obtain food and other supplies, and the prevailing custom with regard to the disposal of butter, eggs, and poultry; to what extent are they sold in the first instance to local shopkeepers and dealers, and, generally speaking, how old are the eggs when sold to the first buyer, and about how old when they reach their ultimate destination in Great Britain.

Cattle, sheep, pigs, butter, and eggs are mostly sold at Skibbereen and Ballydehob fairs and markets. Food and clothing are bought there, and at Baltimore and Castletownsend. Butter is sold fresh at the weekly markets to local dealers, and the representatives of Cork merchants. Eggs are sold weekly, and are, on an average, four days old when first sold, and fourteen days old when they reach the consumer.

(9.) Rail, steamer, sailing boat, road, postal and telegraph facilities.

The railway is being continued from Skibbereen to Baltimore, and will be completed before the end of the year. Road accommodation is fair. Sufficient facilities exist for coasting steamers and sailing boats. There are Post Offices at Aghadown, Castletownsend, Baltimore, and Sherkin Island, but there is no post to Cape Clear, where 584 persons reside; there is a telegraph station at Baltimore.

(10.) Employment for labourers in the district, whether temporary or constant, and rate of wage.

The adult male inhabitants of this district are mostly small farmers and fishermen; there are few labourers in the ordinary sense.

(11.) Migratory labour, average earnings per head, and where earned.

There is no migratory labour in this district.

(12.) Weaving, spinning, knitting, and sewing, whether used locally or sold, and where.

Weaving, spinning, knitting, and sewing is carried on only to a very small extent, and that only for home use.

(13.) Kelp-burning, and sale of seaweed.

There is no kelp-burning or sale of seaweed carried on in this district.

(14.) Sale of turf, nature and extent of bogs.

There is no sale of turf in this district, and not much extent of bogs.

(15.) Lobster fishing, number of men and boats employed.

There are forty lobster boats employing 120 men in the Electoral Division of Aghadown, South, engaged in summer at lobster fishing.

(16.) Sea fishing. Facilities for sale of fish, and number of boats and men solely employed in fishing.

It is almost needless to say that this district is one of the most important fishing centres in Ireland. Two hundred and seventy boats visited it this year, including 86 Manx, 28 English and Scotch, 7 French, and 149 Irish. Two hundred and eleven boats are registered with the Coastguards as owned in the district, viz.:– 56 first class boats, and 155 second and third class boats: they give employment to about 1,000 men.

Facilities for the sale of fish are good, and the extension of railway communication to Baltimore will further increase them. Buyers attend from England and Scotland, and there are several local dealers.

(17.) Number of boats and men employed in carrying turf or seaweed or in fishing. Classification of boats.

See previous paragraph.

There are no boats employed in carrying turf, and few in carrying seaweed, except for their owners' use. When the fishing season is over, a large number of the second and third class boats are used occasionally to collect seaweed, and carry turf from the mainland to the islands.

(18.) Fish; whether consumed at home or sold.

Some of the fish caught in the district is consumed at home, but most of the fish is sold.

(19.) Extent of fish-curing.

1,112 barrels of mackerel were cured in this district in 1891, of which 410 were cured at the Baltimore Fishery Industrial School.

(20.) Piers and Harbours, existing and suggested, and how far those existing are adapted to wants of district.

There are piers in this district at Baltimore, Cape Clear, and Sherkin Island. If funds were available, a larger pier is required at Baltimore, on to which the railway would run, and at which fish could be landed, and moved direct into the railway trucks.

A boat-slip was built on Hare Island, and one repaired on the mainland, both in Aghadown South Electoral Division, as relief works in 1891. The latter work was not quite finished. Both are useful works. There is no slip or pier in Castlehaven South Electoral Division; and consequently there is but little fishing. A slip is much needed there. Tralegan strand is said to be the most convenient and suitable place for it.

Complaint has been made that the break-water at Cape Clear is so placed that the harbour does not afford sufficient shelter to 17 large fishing boats worth perhaps £8,000, which are owned there, and which have consequently to lie at Baltimore, nine miles away from their owners, and nine miles further from the fishing grounds. I was informed that Mr. Manning, late engineer to the Board of Works, had visited this place, and made plans to remedy this defect.

(21.) Extent of salmon and freshwater fisheries. Number of men earning their livelihood therefrom.

There is a salmon fishery in this district in the river Ilen, between Baltimore and Skibbereen. Twelve boats and 48 men are employed in it from June 1st to October 1st.

(22.) Banks and Loan Funds.

The branches of the Provincial and Munster and Leinster Banks in Skibbereen afford banking accommodation to the district.

There are no Loan Funds.

(23.) Mineral and other resources.

There are no mineral or other resources in the district. Copper mines were formerly worked in Aghadown South Electoral Division; they have been disused for years.

(24.) Relative prevalence of cash or credit dealings, length of credit, interest charged, extent of barter, etc., etc.

The produce of the district – cattle, sheep, pigs, eggs, and fish – are usually sold for cash, and to a large extent the supplies of food and clothing required are bought for cash also. There is no barter.

(25.) Estimated *cash* receipts and expenditure of a family in ordinary circumstances.

The *cash* receipts and expenditure of a family in ordinary circumstances depends altogether on the fishing, and it is very difficult to make a reliable estimate – in an average year probably £50.

(26.) Estimated value of home-grown food consumed, and period during which it lasts.

The estimated value of home-grown food consumed is as follows:–

	£	*s.*	*d.*
Potatoes,	10	0	0
Fish,	5	0	0
Milk,	5	0	0
Total,	20	0	0

If the potato crop is good it lasts throughout the year; in a bad season it is used in three months.

(27.) Dietary of people, number of meals daily, and kinds of food throughout the year.

The people of this district take three meals daily. Bread and tea or milk for breakfast; potatoes, fish and milk for dinner; bread and tea or milk for supper. When potatoes are very abundant they may be used for a second meal.

(28.) Clothing, whether home-made or bought, etc., etc.

The clothing worn by the people is almost all bought.

(29.) Dwellings: kind of houses, home-life and customs, etc., etc.

Three-fourths of the dwellings are slated, and contain two or more rooms. One-fourth are thatched, and some of these contain but one room.

(30.) Character of the people for industry, etc., etc.

The people of this district are reputed for industry, and bear a high character as intrepid and skilful fishermen.

(31.) Whether any organized effort has been made to develop the resources or improve the condition of the people. If so, by what means.

A remarkable and conspicuously successful effort has been make by the Rev. C. Davis, P.P., to develop the fishing industry, and his exertions have been largely aided by the generosity of Lady Burdett-Coutts. Where, a few years ago, as I was informed, only a very poor hamlet existed, there is now a thriving and well-built town, and the place has been made one of the chief fishing centres in the south.

It is the rendezvous annually of a large fishing fleet. A Fishery Industrial School has been established, which is licensed for 150 boys, and is always full, and in connection with which there has already been started the business of fish-curing, and the trade of net-making. If resources were available other cognate trades and industries might probably be added.

(32.) Suggestions as to any possible method for improving the condition of the people in future.

Though in this district farming may be regarded as subsidiary to fishing, yet the prosperity of the former may be very much promoted by improving the breeds of cattle, sheep, and pigs, by the introduction of better bulls, rams, and boars; fowls, too, might be kept in larger numbers, and with more profit, if some attention were paid to breeding kinds, suitable for table use and equally good egg layers.

There seems to be a desire to adopt the new method of butter making, and a butter factory is about to be opened at Skibbereen, but it will only serve for a radius of three to four miles around. Parts of the district would be suitable for the growth of early potatoes and other vegetables. The soil is good, the localities are well-sheltered, and sea manure is convenient, but to develop any attempt in this direction, instruction and a ready market are essential. A market would be found among the crews of the fishing fleet that visit Baltimore annually, even if no other were available.

The operations of the Fishery School might be extended to the manufacture of fish boxes and barrels, the manufacture of sails, and even to boat building, but for one serious obstacle. At present the boys can only be legally committed to the school until they are sixteen years old. They have, consequently, to be discharged at an age when they cannot have acquired any trade sufficiently, and it would be of great advantage to them, if they could be then apprenticed to some trade taught in the school for which they had an aptitude for three, four, or five years, some public official or body being constituted guardian to arrange the term of apprenticeship. If some arrangement of this kind could be made, the operations of the school might be widely extended and its utility increased.

I have already referred to complaints as to the north harbour at Cape Clear which is worthy of attention. Application has been made for the erection of a boat-slip at Toe Head in the Electoral Division of Castlehaven South, the work seems to be a useful one for the locality.

In the Electoral Division of Aghadown South, my attention was called to a small pier in Roaring Water Bay, which was repaired and raised as a relief work in 1891, but was not quite finished. So much having been done, the little that remains to complete it might be accomplished.

As regards the people living near the coast and in the Islands, who are all fishermen, it is stated that more accommodation in the way of slips and shelters is needed in various places. It is also said that many of them have not means to procure boats and gear instead of those which have now become unserviceable from age, and that assistance to do so would be welcomed.

A very interesting effort is being made by the Mercy Nuns in Skibbereen, to establish a flax-spinning and weaving industry. Though the raw material has to be imported or procured from the North of Ireland, the attempt has so far been successful, and goods of a very superior quality are produced. The idea is to train up young girls to the work, which they might afterwards carry on in their own homes, and if it succeed, it would be a great benefit to the locality by supplying employment to the adult female population at home. I wish to bring this work under the notice of the Board, as I consider the project worthy of attention and assistance.

An application has been made to the Board for assistance to erect a permanent lighthouse at the entrance to Castlehaven in substitution for a temporary light which has been kept up there for some years past. The light would stand at Reen Point in the Electoral Division of Myross, and would mainly benefit the town of Castletownsend, which is in the Electoral Division of Castlehaven North. Neither of these Electoral Divisions is scheduled, and the figures or circumstances do not present a case for adding them to the list of congested districts. The valuation per head of population in Myross is £1 15*s*., and in only four townlands out of twenty-two is it under 30*s*. In Castlehaven North the valuation is £1 13*s*. 9*d*. per head, and if the fishing population (not permanent residents) who are included in the Census were excluded, it would give £2 7*s*. per head. Castlehaven, however, is an important fishing station; 259 fishing boats called there in 1891. Four first class and twenty-nine second and third class boats are registered as owned locally, and 1,300 barrels of mackerel were cured there last year. That the residents who are interested are satisfied a leading light to the harbour is necessary is proved by the fact that they have maintained for some years past at their own expense a temporary light. The actual cost of the erection of the lighthouse and light-keeper's residence is estimated at £300, and its maintenance at £60 a year, and it is an important consideration whether the dues that may be authorized would provide sufficient funds to meet the annual expenditure.

REDMOND ROCHE,
Inspector.

7th January, 1893.

To

The Congested Districts Board for Ireland.

The old and the new (left) – with funding assistance from the Congested Districts Board, many families were able to build new houses and live in relative comfort.

CONGESTED DISTRICTS BOARD FOR IRELAND

COUNTY OF CORK – UNIONS OF CASTLETOWN AND BANTRY

REPORT OF MR. ROCHE, *Inspector*

DISTRICT

OF

CASTLETOWN BEARHAVEN

STATISTICAL TABLE

ELECTORAL DIVISION.	Area in Statute Acres.	Poor Law Valuation.	Number of Ratings at and under £10 and above £4 Valuation.	Number of Ratings at and under £4 Valuation.	Population in 1891.	Number of Families in 1891.	Number of Families on Holdings exceeding £2 and under £4 Valuation.	Number of Families on Holdings at and under £2 Valuation.	Number of Families in very poor circumstances.	Number of Families which have no Cattle.
		£								
Adrigole,	15,385	1,199	98	189	1,540	264	86	44	30	
Bear,	4,381	1,090	83	72	967	162	30	8	10	
Coulagh,	10,097	1,992	125	270	1,763	301	74	60	50	
Curryglass,	9,159	1,169	91	240	1,075	174	41	34	20	300
Killaconenagh,	10,698	2,968	172	250	3,142*	344	54	72	40	
Kilcatherine,	14,951	2,068	160	325	2,579	431	89	85	40	
Kilnamanagh,	8,774	1,567	107	64	1,323	202	16	14	10	
Kilcaskan,	16,541	1,254	57	142	1,572	264	76	49	30	
Glengarriff,	11,098	1,783	68	104	1,175	204	25	47	50	40
TOTALS,	101,084	£15,090	961	1,656	15,136	2,346	491	413	280	340

* The population of Killaconenagh Electoral Division includes 2,076 in the town of Castletown, of whom about 900 were on board shipping and not permanent inhabitants.

(1.) Whether inland or maritime.

The district is maritime.

(2.) Average quantity of land cultivated on holdings at and under £4 valuation, under (*a*) oats, (*b*) potatoes, (*c*) meadow, (*d*) green crops.

There are about 4¾ acres on an average cultivated on holdings at and under £4 valuation in the following way:–

Oats,	1½	acres.
Potatoes,	1½	”
Meadow,	1½	”
Green crops,	¼	”
Total,	4¾	”

(3.) Extent of mountain or moor grazing, and rights possessed by tenants, whether in common or otherwise.

There are about 61,000 acres of mountain or moor grazing land in this district, of which 36,000 acres are used in common, and 25,000 acres held in severalty.

(4.) Extent and description of land, if any, which could be profitably reclaimed and added to existing adjoining holdings.

As to the extent of land which could be profitably reclaimed it would be difficult to make a reliable estimate. The great bulk of the area is rough mountain, in which there are at intervals patches of reclaimable land, but what the extent of these bits is in the aggregate, I can form no opinion.

(5.) Particulars as to any suitable land in district which could be obtained, and to which families could be migrated with a reasonable prospect of success.

There is no suitable land in this district to which families could be migrated with a reasonable prospect of success.

(6.) Method of cultivation, manures, rotation of crops, etc., etc.

Spade cultivation prevails generally. Two crops of potatoes, followed by one of oats and one of grass is the usual rotation. Seaweed, sand, and dung are the manures employed.

(7.) General information with regard to stock, and suggestions as to improvement of breeds – (*a*) cattle, (*b*) sheep, (*c*) horses and donkeys, (*d*) pigs, (*e*) poultry, etc., etc.

The live stock of the district generally are of an inferior description.

Cattle.– These are a mixture of various breeds, and have lost any distinctive character. An improvement is urgently needed. The district has the same physical characteristics as the adjoining portions of county Kerry, and I am of opinion the Kerry breed of cattle would be suitable. In the better parts Red-polled Norfolk or half-bred Shorthorns would suit. Some of the farmers I met have a liking for Ayrshire, of which there is a strong strain in Bantry and Macroom Unions.

Sheep.– These are numerous, and of a very inferior class. The male lambs are allowed to run uncut on the mountains, and breed promiscuously with their kindred, leading to the degeneracy of the breed and the sterility of the ewes. The mountains are dry, but elevated and exposed. I think good-sized Scotch Highland sheep would suit best, but Mr. Somers Payne, agent of the estate of the late Lord Bantry, which comprises a large part of the district, informed me he tried the use of Shrop rams with the mountain ewes successfully. Highly priced and finely-bred sheep are not adapted to the district.

Horses.– These are of a very poor class.

Poultry.– There is room for great extension in the number and improvement in the description of poultry. At present there are fewer kept in proportion to the population than in any of the adjoining districts.

(8.) Markets and fairs for cattle and produce of district; also statement as to where the people obtain food and other supplies, and the prevailing custom with regard to the disposal of butter, eggs, and poultry; to what extent are they sold in the first instance to local shopkeepers and dealers, and, generally speaking, how old are the eggs when sold to the first buyer, and about how old when they reach their ultimate destination in Great Britain.

Cattle, sheep, and pigs are mostly sold at fairs held in:– Castletown, 15 in the year; Bantry, 13 in the year; Allihies, 6 in the year; Ardgroom, 7 in the year; and Eyeries, 8 in the year. The two first named are well attended.

Food and other supplies are bought for the most part in Bantry and Castletown, and to some extent in the country villages. Butter is almost all sold fresh in lumps at weekly markets, held in several towns and villages through the district, which are attended by buyers from Cork and Bantry who export it to England and Scotland. Eggs are sold weekly at those markets also to small dealers who re-sell to shippers in Bantry and Cork. They average four days old when first sold, and fourteen days old when they reach the consumer.

(9.) Rail, steamer, sailing boat, road, postal and telegraph facilities.

There is no railway in the district, the nearest station is Bantry, ten miles from the nearest and forty from the remotest part of the district. There is a steamer between Bantry and Castletown. In the summer it plies once each way daily, in winter on alternate days each way. Roads are wanted in many parts of the district and some in existence are not kept in repair. There are Post Offices in Castletown, Bear Island, Adrigole, Allihies, Eyeries, Glengarriff, and Lehanmore, and Telegraph Stations at Allihies, Castletown, Glengarriff, and Lehanmore.

(10.) Employment for labourers in the district, whether temporary or constant, and rate of wage.

There are but few labourers in the district in the ordinary sense, nearly all the agricultural population being small farmers; the wages for them are about 1*s.* a day and diet. Some of the younger members of the families who do not own boats are employed at the fishing by other boat owners, the employment is precarious and the earnings depends on the take of fish. A number of persons in Adrigole and Kilcaskan raise and sell sea-sand to inland farmers. The price is 8*s.* to 12*s.* per boat-load of four to six tons.

(11.) Migratory labour, average earnings per head, and where earned.

About fifty persons from Adrigole and Kilcaskan Electoral Divisions go to Wales annually to work in the iron works. They remain usually from April to December, and bring home on an average £15 each.

(12.) Weaving, spinning, knitting, and sewing, whether used locally or sold, and where.

There is very little weaving, spinning, knitting, and sewing carried on in this district, and such is only for home use.

(13.) Kelp-burning, and sale of seaweed.

There is no kelp-burning in this district, and seaweed is not sold to any great extent.

(14.) Sale of turf, nature and extent of bogs.

There is no sale of turf except to a small extent near the town of Castletown, in Bantry, and at the hotels at Glengarriff. There is no large tract of bog, but there are a number of detached plots in the valleys and recesses of the mountains, the area of which I am unable to estimate.

(15.) Lobster fishing, number of men and boats employed.

There are twenty boats and about eighty men occasionally employed in the lobster fishing, but it does not seem to be pursued in a regular manner.

(16.) Sea fishing. Facilities for sale of fish, and number of boats and men solely employed in fishing.

The sea, west of this district, is one of the principal mackerel fishing grounds of the coast. The boats engaged in it mostly shelter in Bearhaven, and dispose of the fish there. In the season buyers attend from various parts of England and Scotland, who ship direct to the nearest port to their respective markets in steamers specially chartered for the purpose. When the quantity taken is not so large as to attract buyers from a distance the fish is bought by local buyers, who sometimes forward it by steamer to Bantry, thence by rail, or, in the autumn season, cure it. During my visit 174 boats were assembled at Castletown; 69 French, 18 Manx, and 87 Irish, of which latter 75 were from Arklow. There are 194 boats registered as owned in the district, of which seven are first class deep sea boats, 32 second class yawls, and 165 third class. Some of the second class boats fish seines, but most of the second and third class with lines only. There are 1,024 men employed to man the local boats, but a large number of the inhabitants besides are employed on the strange boats which frequently come short-handed.

(17.) Number of boats and men employed in carrying turf or seaweed or in fishing. Classification of boats.

See previous paragraph.

There are but few boats employed carrying turf and seaweed, except occasionally for the owners.

(18.) Fish; whether consumed at home or sold.

Mackerel in the spring and early summer is sold fresh. In the autumn it is cured, part is sold and part kept for home consumption. Hake, whiting, and flat fish are sold fresh also. Three hundred pounds worth of winkles were sold from November 1891, to April 1892, in Castletown alone, and I was informed much more might be made of this industry, at which children and women are only employed, if carried on more perseveringly.

(19.) Extent of fish-curing.

Garinish is the principal curing station. During the past three years £6,000 worth of mackerel were cured there. It is greatly to be regretted that the curing of herrings is not carried on more systematically.

(20.) Piers and Harbours, existing and suggested, and how far those existing are adapted to wants of district.

There is a pier at Castletown which it is said is not large enough for the trade of the place and requires extension. There is a pier also at the east end of Bear Island (Lawrence's Cove), which is said to be built in the wrong place and of little use; a pier at Ballycrovane Coastguard station which is rendered almost useless by the fact that the road to it is nearly impassable; and one recently built on Dursey Island which is very useful. A pier is asked for at Garinish; a boat-slip is required at Bear Island, in a central position opposite Castletown; a slip built as a relief work at Aghabeg wants to be completed; a slip is wanted at Ballydonegan near the Coastguard station; and a slip is also said to be required between Adrigole and Glengarriff to accommodate the sand traffic. There is a boat-slip at Glengarriff.

(21.) Extent of salmon and freshwater fisheries. Number of men earning their livelihood therefrom.

There are no salmon nor freshwater fisheries in this district.

(22.) Banks and Loan Funds.

The Munster and Leinster Bank has a branch at Castletown Bear, and the Munster and Leinster, and Provincial have branches at Bantry. There are no Loan Funds in the district.

(23.) Mineral and other resources.

There were very extensive copper mines worked formerly in this district, first by Mr. Puxley, a private owner, and after by the Bearhaven Mining Company, which bought them from him. They have been idle for several years, and the buildings have gone to ruin. An asbestos mine is said to exist at Black Ball Head, six miles from Castletown Bear.

(24.) Relative prevalence of cash or credit dealings, length of credit, interest charged, extent of barter, etc., etc.

Cattle, sheep, pigs, butter, eggs, and fish are sold for cash. Food and clothing are bought largely on credit, which would probably average twelve months. Interest is not charged, but somewhat higher prices are paid than if bought for cash. There is no barter carried on in the district.

(25.) Estimated *cash* receipts and expenditure of a family in ordinary circumstances.

The *cash* receipts of a family in ordinary cirumstances depend, to a very great extent, on the success of the fishing which fluctuates widely from year to year. In an average year the receipts would be about £50. The expenditure varies according to the receipts.

(26.) Estimated value of home-grown food consumed, and period during which it lasts.

Potatoes, milk, and fish are the only foods consumed which are not bought. The value would probably be – potatoes, £18 (if a good crop), milk, £5, fish, £5, total £28. If there is an abundant potato crop it lasts throughout the year; a bad crop may be consumed by Christmas.

(27.) Dietary of people, number of meals daily, and kinds of food throughout the year.

The people of this district take three meals daily, viz.:– bread, and milk or tea for breakfast, potatoes, fish, and milk for dinner, bread or potatoes, and milk for supper.

(28.) Clothing, whether home-made or bought, etc., etc.

The clothing worn by the people of this district is almost all bought. Some home-made frieze, and flannel are worn.

(29.) Dwellings: kind of houses, home-life and customs, etc., etc.

The dwellings, as a rule, and especially in Adrigole, Coulagh, and Kilcaskan, are very inferior, and badly kept. There are 2,142 inhabited houses in the district. Of those not more that a fourth are slated, and contain two or more rooms, the remaining three-fourths are thatched, and half of these contain only one room.

(30.) Character of the people for industry, etc., etc.

The people have the reputation of being industrious, but there is too much drinking, especially among the fishermen.

(31.) Whether any organized effort has been made to develop the resources or improve the condition of the people. If so, by what means.

There has been no organized effort made to develop the resources or improve the condition of the people of this district except in connection with the fishing industry, and more has been done in that by strangers than by the natives. The failure of the Bearhaven Mines had a disastrous effect on the western side of the district, these attracted a large population who have remained on in the place trying to make a livelihood by other means. Taking it altogether, it is the poorest district I have seen in the South.

(32.) Suggestions as to any possible method for improving the condition of the people in future.

The people of this district live by farming and fishing. They have adjacent to their shore a splendid fishing ground, but of 174 boats employed in deep sea fishing this year only seven belong to this district. The great majority of people fish in 1st and 2nd class boats, and mostly with lines. They are skilful fishermen, and would probably participate more largely in the deep sea fishing, if they could procure suitable boats and gear on easy terms as to the repayment of the cost. It is said that in many ways the deep sea fishing may be assisted. At present it is dependent for a market on the attendance of buyers from England and Scotland. If fish is not caught in sufficient quantity to make it worth those buyers' while to stay and keep steamers chartered at great expense they go away, and the fishermen have no market. The great difficulty in the way of creating a local trade in fresh fish, is that the buyers who may engage in it have no stores of ice or means of procuring it when required. Herrings frequent the coast in enormous numbers, and it is strange that a cured herring industry has not been established.

Persons who have local knowledge say that attempts have been made which have proved failures, and they attribute this to the fact that Irish cured herrings will not bring the price in foreign or even home markets, which branded Scotch herrings will. It is alleged that the inspection and branding of herrings here as in Scotland would greatly help to create an industry. Much more might be done in the curing of autumn mackerel, but facilities are required for producing salt and barrels in sufficient quantities and storing them, as well as a repetition of instruction in curing and packing. Greater facilities for transit are urgently needed also.

A boat on alternate days at certain seasons between Castletown and Bantry is not sufficient for fish traffic, and the only alternative is conveyance by road on carts a distance of forty to fifty miles. Complaints too are made that the high railway freight rates from Bantry to English towns sometimes absorb the entire price obtained for the fish. Pilchard curing is another industry which might be pursued here. The fish, other than mackerel and herrings, are mostly caught by the smaller boats and are sold fresh. Many of these boats are too small, and I have been told their owners are anxious to replace them by a better class of boats and gear if enabled to do so by loans on easy terms of repayment.

Representations are made that boat slips are much needed at Ardgroom, at Ballydonegan (where an old rotten wooden jetty erected for the use of the mines when working, is still used at great risk), at Bear Island and at Coolieragh or thereabouts. It was also stated that a ferry boat, sufficiently capacious to convey horses and cattle between Bear Island and the mainland, is greatly required. At present these animals, when being conveyed to or from a fair, have to be either fettered, thrown down and lifted into a small boat, or to swim across. It seems to me a ferry boat would be very useful to the islanders. The proposed pier at Garinish would be a costly work. It seems from the correspondence to have had the approval of the Fishery Inspectors. Upon the questions whether its advantages would be commensurate with its cost, or whether it would afford sufficient shelter to any considerable number of large boats I am unable to give an opinion; I was told that the boat which up to a short time ago tended the lighthouse on the Bull rock always lay there with safety when not on service. As an alternative to the erection of a pier it was suggested that a timber jetty, erected at a moderate cost, might be put up, which would last for many years, and afford a test whether any such trade can be developed there as would justify the larger expenditure on a pier. It is stated that if landing stages where erected at Adrigole and on Bear Island, the steamer plying between Castletown and Bantry would call at those places, which would be a great advantage.

The entire of the district is very mountainous. The mountain pastures, which are very rocky, cover three-fifths of the area. On the lowlands dairy cattle are kept, on the hills a large number of sheep. The breeds of both are of the worst description, and nothing would be more beneficial to them than the introduction of suitable bulls and rams. As regards the rams it should as far as possible be insisted on that those now in use should be sold or castrated.

A Hackney stallion stationed in Castletown would be a great benefit, and so too would some large white Yorkshire boars. There are not as many fowl kept as there ought to be, and no pains are taken as to their breeding, as they are kept for the sake of the eggs only. It would be a great service if better breeds were introduced, and the people learned the gain that might be derived by producing fowl for table use. Notwithstanding the proximity to the sea, trees seem to do well in the few places where they are planted. Shelter is very necessary, and I was informed there are many who would plant trees on their holdings if they were taught how, and got the trees.

Several parts of the district possess many advantages for the growth of early potatoes and other vegetables, mild climate, a good aspect, light friable soil, and abundant sea manure amongst others.

In the creation of such an industry there are two great obstacles: (1) the ignorance of the people and the difficulty of getting them out of the old grooves; (2) the want of a market at their doors. If the newly-formed Garden Produce Company in Cork succeed in overcoming those difficulites they deserve every assistance and encouragement.

REDMOND ROCHE,
Inspector.

20th December, 1892.

To

The Congested Districts Board for Ireland.

CONGESTED DISTRICTS BOARD FOR IRELAND

COUNTY OF CORK – UNION OF BANTRY

REPORT OF MR. ROCHE, *Inspector*

DISTRICT

OF

SHEEPSHEAD

STATISTICAL TABLE

ELECTORAL DIVISION.	Area in Statute Acres.	Poor Law Valuation.	Number of Ratings at and under £10 and above £4 Valuation.	Number of Ratings at and under £4 Valuation.	Population in 1891.	Number of Families in 1891.	Number of Families on Holdings exceeding £2 and under £4 Valuation.	Number of Families on Holdings at and under £2 Valuation.	Number of Families in very poor circumstances.	Number of Families which have no Cattle.
		£								
Glanlough,	3,770	614	41	92	678	102	33	17	10	
Seefin,	5,001	835	49	76	762	115	19	20	15	50 (Glanlough, Seefin, Sheepshead)
Sheepshead,	6,009	888	50	123	863	129	24	36	25	
Durrus East,	4,156	997	32	30	535	92	7	16	20	40* (Durrus East, Durrus West)
Durrus West,	5,202	1,420	56	78	919	159	26	38	40	
TOTALS,	24,138	4,754	228	399	3,757	597	109	127	110	90

* Mostly residents in Durrus village.

(1.) Whether inland or maritime.

The district is maritime.

(2.) Average quantity of land cultivated on holdings at and under £4 valuation, under (*a*) oats, (*b*) potatoes, (*c*) meadow, (*d*) green crops.

There are about 3¼ acres on an average cultivated on holdings at and under £4 valuation in the following way:–

Oats,	1 acre.
Potatoes,	1 "
Meadow,	1 "
Green crops,	¼ "
Total,	3¼ acres.

(3.) Extent of mountain or moor grazing, and rights possessed by tenants, whether in common or otherwise.

There are about 13,000 acres of mountain or moor grazing in this district, of which 3,000 are used in common, the remainder in severalty.

(4.) Extent and description of land, if any, which could be profitably reclaimed and added to existing adjoining holdings.

There are only small portions of land in this district which could be profitably reclaimed and added to adjoining holdings. These lands lie at the base and in the recesses of the range of mountains which runs through the centre of the peninsula from north-east to south-west. It is impossible to form a reliable estimate of the area.

(5.) Particulars as to any suitable land in district which could be obtained, and to which families could be migrated with a reasonable prospect of success.

There is no suitable land in this district to which families could be migrated with a reasonable prospect of success.

(6.) Method of cultivation, manures, rotation of crops, etc., etc.

Cultivation is carried on in this district, on the larger holdings by the plough, and on the smaller by the spade. The manures used are farm-yard, sand, and seaweed. The usual rotation is two crops of potatoes followed by oats and grass.

(7.) General information with regard to stock, and suggestions as to improvement of breeds – (*a*) cattle, (*b*) sheep, (*c*) horses and donkeys, (*d*) pigs, (*e*) poultry, etc., etc.

The cattle in the district are of a mixed breed, and an inferior class. An improvement is much needed.

A gentleman of great experience and knowledge of the district, Mr. J.E. Barrett, J.P., considers half-bred Shorthorns the best kind of bull to improve the breed; the district is too bleak and cold for pure-bred cattle. A large number of sheep are kept on the mountains; they are very small and inferior, and better rams are required. Leicesters are recommended, but they should not be too finely bred or brought from rich pastures. Horses, pigs, and poultry also require improvement. Hackney stallions and large white Yorkshire boars are, in my opinion, most suitable. Poultry are not kept to as large an extent as they ought to be. Plymouth Rocks, or any other breed of fowl that would increase the size without impairing the laying powers, would suit.

(8.) Markets and fairs for cattle and produce of district; also statement as to where the people obtain food and other supplies, and the prevailing custom with regard to the disposal of butter, eggs, and poultry; to what extent are they sold in the first instance to local shopkeepers and dealers, and, generally speaking, how old are the eggs when sold to the first buyer, and about how old when they reach their ultimate destination in Great Britain·

The cattle, sheep, and pigs of this district are mostly sold at Bantry. Eggs, and fresh butter in lumps, are sometimes sold at weekly markets in the villages of Kilcrohane and Durrus, which buyers from Cork and Bantry attend, but chiefly at Bantry. Food and clothing are bought for the most part in Bantry. Eggs are, on an average, four days old when first sold, and a fortnight old when they reach the consumer.

(9.) Rail, steamer, sailing boat, road, postal and telegraph facilities.

The nearest railway station for this district is Durrus Road, which is three miles from the nearest, and twenty miles from the most remote part of the district. There is no communication by steamer or sailing boat. The road accommodation has been extended and improved by some relief works in 1891, but is still deficient. There is a Post Office at Kilcrohane, and a Postal and Telegraph Office at Durrus.

(10.) Employment for labourers in the district, whether temporary or constant, and rate of wage.

As the inhabitants of this district are nearly all small farmers whose families supply the necessary labour, there may be said to be few labourers in the ordinary sense.

(11.) Migratory labour, average earnings per head, and where earned.

There is no migratory labour in this district.

(12.) Weaving, spinning, knitting, and sewing, whether used locally or sold, and where.

Weaving, spinning, knitting, and sewing is carried on only to a small extent, and this only for home use.

(13.) Kelp-burning, and sale of seaweed.

There is no kelp-burning or sale of seaweed carried on in this district.

(14.) Sale of turf, nature and extent of bogs.

There is no sale of turf in the district: there is one large bog and some scattered plots, the area of which it is difficult to estimate.

(15.) Lobster fishing, number of men and boats employed.

There is no lobster fishing carried on in the district.

(16.) Sea fishing. Facilities for sale of fish, and number of boats and men solely employed in fishing.

There are fifty-five second and third class boats engaged in fishing, employing 220 men. There is no sale of fish within the district as buyers do not attend: it is sold chiefly in Bantry.

(17.) Number of boats and men employed in carrying turf or seaweed or in fishing. Classification of boats.

For the number of men and boats employed in fishing, see previous paragraph: the fishing-boats are occasionally used for collecting seaweed for the use of their owners.

(18.) Fish; whether consumed at home or sold.

The fish caught in the district are partly sold and partly consumed at home.

(19.) Extent of fish-curing.

I have been informed that 900,000 herrings were cured at Gerahies alone and sold in Bantry at about 8*s.* per 1,000.

(20.) Piers and Harbours, existing and suggested, and how far those existing are adapted to wants of district.

There is a pier in Durrus West in bad repair. Small piers or boat-slips would be useful at Kilcrohane in Sheepshead Electoral Division, and at Ahakista in Glanlough Electoral Division.

There are several natural coves round the coast, but on the whole it is very exposed and comparatively shelterless. The cove at Gerahies was much improved by clearing boulders, building a sea wall, and making an approach, in 1891, as "Relief Works."

(21.) Extent of salmon and freshwater fisheries. Number of men earning their livelihood therefrom.

There are no salmon or fresh-water fisheries.

(22.) Banks and Loan Funds.

There are no Banks or Loan Funds in the district. The branches of the Provincial and Munster and Leinster Banks in Bantry supply whatever Banking accommodation is required.

(23.) Mineral and other resources.

There are no mining operations carried on at present in the district. There seems to be a good deal of slate through the district, but it has not been systematically worked.

(24.) Relative prevalence of cash or credit dealings, length of credit, interest charged, extent of barter, etc., etc.

The produce of the district – cattle, sheep, pigs, butter, eggs, and fish – are sold for cash. Food and clothing are, to a large extent, bought on credit; about twelve months' credit is usual. A moderate addition to price is charged in lieu of interest. There is no barter carried on.

(25.) Estimated *cash* receipts and expenditure of a family in ordinary circumstances.

The estimated *cash* receipts and expenditure of a family in ordinary circumstances, and in an average year, would be about £40, but it depends largely on the fishing.

(26.) Estimated value of home-grown food consumed, and period during which it lasts.

The estimated value of home-grown food consumed is as follows:–

	£	*s.*	*d.*
Potatoes,	12	0	0
Milk,	5	0	0
Fish,	5	0	0
Total,	22	0	0

A good potato crop lasts through the year; a bad crop, like that of 1890, is consumed in three months.

(27.) Dietary of people, number of meals daily, and kinds of food throughout the year.

The people of this district take three meals daily. Bread, potatoes, fish, milk, and tea are the staple articles of food.

(28.) Clothing, whether home-made or bought, etc., etc.

The clothing worn by the people is all bought. Some home-made frieze and flannel are used.

(29.) Dwellings: kind of houses, home-life and customs, etc., etc.

The houses in this district are rather inferior. About half are slated, and contain two or more rooms; the other half are thatched, and many contain only one apartment.

(30.) Character of the people for industry, etc., etc.

The character of the people of this district for industry is good.

(31.) Whether any organized effort has been made to develop the resources or improve the condition of the people. If so, by what means.

No organized effort has been made to develop the resources or improve the condition of the people of this district.

(32.) Suggestions as to any possible method for improving the condition of the people in future.

The most necessary and beneficial thing that can be done is to improve the breeds of cattle, sheep, pigs, horses, and poultry.

The district has a seaboard of 36 miles; the coast is rock-bound, and, owing to the want of shelter, large boats cannot be kept. There are 55 second and third class boats, and the number could be largely increased if the fishing industry were better worked. Remoteness, and want of facilities of communication, tend to prevent a large trade in fresh fish, but curing might be much more extensively practised. Curing sheds, salt depots, and instruction in fish-curing are the great needs. Here, as at Castletown, the necessity for inspecting and branding the herrings is urged. It is alleged the value of the fish would be considerably enhanced thereby. A better organization for the disposal of cured fish, too, is needed.

The fishermen require better boats and gear, and are desirous to obtain loans for the purpose. The district in many places is very suitable for the growth of early potatoes and other vegetables.

Some gentlemen interested in the Electoral Divisions of Durrus East and Durrus West are anxious that an attempt should be made to get up a woollen manufacturing industry in the village of Durrus, which they believe would be successful, and would give considerable employment. There is a small mill there, worked by water power, which, it is said, could be purchased or rented on moderate terms. It is at present used to grind corn for hire for the farmers, and to card wool. If the Board desires to make further inquiry as to the project, the Rev. Micheal Kearney, P.P., Durrus, or Mr. James Gilhooly, M.P., Bantry, would afford information.

REDMOND ROCHE,
Inspector.

20th December, 1892.

To

The Congested Districts Board for Ireland.

Report upon Emigration to Canada, by the Hon. Horace Plunkett

To the Members of the Congested Districts Board

Gentlemen, – At the informal meeting of the Congested Districts Board held at the Irish Office, London, on the 30th July last, it was agreed that the time which was to elapse before the Board held its first formal meeting should be utilized by individual members for investigations into the various conditions with which we should have to deal, and into the feasibility of the alternative remedies indicated in the 39th Section of the Land Purchase Act of 1891. The study of Irish emigration, which would naturally fall to the lot of Mr. J. H. Tuke, the highest authority on the subject, but which seemed to require an extended tour in the United States and Canada, was entrusted to myself, as being available for the journey, and so, as soon as I could make the necessary arrangements, I sailed for Canada, and landed at Montreal on the 7th of September. Lord Fingall accompanied me throughout and rendered valuable assistance to me in my inquiries.

As I was obliged, from the necessity of the case, to act without definite instructions, it is well that I should state briefly the nature and scope of the inquiry which I had undertaken. The Board, I was aware, might or might not at some future time see fit to assist emigration. Other remedies so far as practicable would be preferred. At the same time in some districts the chief remedy would be "amalgamation of holdings," and this would involve migration or emigration. Some families would surely choose the latter alternative, and it would in those cases be the duty of the Board at least to furnish them with such information as would lead to their going to places where their condition would be improved. Quite apart, too, from any influence which the Board may exert, it is not to be expected that the human stream from Ireland to America will altogether cease to flow, and much good might be done by discouraging promiscuous uninformed emigration, such as has hitherto prevailed. I set myself, therefore, in the light of recent immigration and the laws relating thereto, to consider what opportunities the New World offered to the West of Ireland immigrant, whether as a field for labour or settlement on the land. The necessary visits to public men prompted the ubiquitous interviewer to magnify a tour of investigation into the elaboration of schemes which would materially affect the distribution of people on the surface of the globe. I need hardly say that I confined myself to ascertaining facts to lay before the Board.

I will only add, by way of introduction, that the field of inquiry was so enormous that it could not be covered in the time at my command. We had only six weeks and two days ashore. One week was lost through sickness. My inquiries in Canada were fairly satisfactory to me. But I had intended to take four more weeks in the States, when I heard that the Board was to meet on October the 29th, and had to hasten my return. I, therefore, hold over my report as to the United States for the present, hoping that I may get further information when my own business takes me to America in the autumn of 1892. It should be borne in mind that any information obtained or suggestions offered with regard to emigration, apply solely to such emigrants as would start from the Congested Districts of Ireland or of Scotland.

Canada.

The Census of the present year shows an abnormally small increase in the population of Canada, especially in rural districts. This is a matter of bitter disappointment to the Canadians, but it has brought immigration into high favour.* It is true that the Government had been in recent years forced by pressure from the Labour organizations to abandon the payment of steamship fares. But the opposition to this policy related only to skilled labour, of which the supply is quite equal to the demand. Hence, the Government has been able to substitute for assisted passages cash payments to actual settlers on the free grants of Manitoba and the North-West Territories.†

It was soon evident that such opportunities as might be found for successful immigration must almost exclusively exist to the west of Winnipeg. In Quebec, Montreal, Ottawa, and Toronto we made inquiries into the possibility of settling poor families on farms in the old settled districts of Upper and Lower Canada, and as to the demand for unskilled labour in the towns.

* Mr. J. G. Colmer, C.M.G., Secretary to the High Commissioner for Canada in London, has pointed out, in an article in the *Fortnightly Review*, October, 1891, that, in the recent Canadian Census, changes in the method of enumeration were adopted which accounted to some extent for the disappointing results.

† The scale of these bonuses is as follows:–

"To settlers from the United Kingdom taking up such land within six months of their arrival in the country:– Fifteen dollars (£3 1*s.* 8*d.*) to the head of a family, seven dollars fifty cents. (£1 10*s.* 10*d.*) for the wife and each adult member of the family over twelve years of age, and a further sum of seven dollars fifty cents. (£1 10*s.* 10*d.*) to any adult member of the family over eighteen years taking up land."

Many instances were laid before us of farms being offered for sale by growing families needing more room and moving west. But in no case could we learn, as had been suggested, that the circumstances under which these farms had been abandoned indicated their availability for colonization in small holdings. Where clearing of the forest was required, land was cheap enough, but the backwoods offered no such inducements as the western prairies. Where the land was cleared the price was prohibitive, and the capital required for working it for the Eastern market comparatively high.

In the province of Ontario, and some parts of Quebec, there seemed to be a definite though limited demand for farm labour, and unquestionably a certain number of fairly "strong" families could be provided for.

In the ports of Quebec, Montreal, and in the large inland towns there are "Dominion Government Agents," who constitute the staff of what is practically an immigration bureau, charged with the duty of giving information to newcomers as to the demand for labour, rate of wages, cost of transportation, board and lodging, &c. From these agents, who all seemed to be men of large experience, we gathered that we could count on their organization, which is especially efficient by virtue of the co-operation existing between them, to assist in looking after any immigrants on landing. With a month's notice they all felt confident that a limited number of families could be provided with employment if they came out in the early spring. In Toronto, the Dominion agent, Mr. J. A. Donaldson, who has some fifty years' experience, said, "I can place any number of 'strong' families in Ontario. A good workman, with a grown son, could be placed with any amount of family, and a good workman, with a wife, could be placed with a young family, the latter not to exceed four or five children." He thought the want of labour was being severely felt by the Ontario farmers, and that many of the large ones could be induced to build houses to shelter labourers and their families. The other Dominion agents we saw spoke in the same sense and left no doubt on our minds that, through this agency, selected families preferring farm labour to the responsibilities of colonization on farm lands, could be provided for. If fifty families were to offer themselves as an experimental consignment, they would be given a fair chance of improving their condition, and might open the way for many followers.

Wages for farm hands would probably be £2 15*s.* to £3 10*s.* per month, with board. It would greatly improve the condition of the labouring emigrant if he could be taught to milk before he left home, and if he could also handle a plough he would qualify as a skilled hand. These accomplishments ought to form a part of our scheme of technical education in the Congested Districts.

We could hear of no large works, such as the construction of the Rideau Canal or the Canadian Pacific Railway, which formerly provided employment for, and gave a start to, many Irishmen in past years, though it was suggested to us that the enlargement of existing canals and the dock works at Sault St. Marie would require a large amount of labour for some time to come.

We only found one other employment outlet worth mentioning, and that applies to nearly the whole of the North American Continent, namely, domestic service for women. For this there is an almost unlimited demand. Wages for absolutely untrained girls would be in Canada from 20*s.* to 30*s.* a month in the Eastern provinces, and double these figures in the West. Washing would add 3*s.* to 5*s.* a month to their earnings, and plain cooking would command from £3 to £4 a month in the East, £5 to £6 in the West. In the United States (except, perhaps, some of the Southern States) the scale would maintain a higher average. It has always been a puzzle why the Irish emigrant in America is so little tempted by the high wages and comparatively enviable position attaching to domestic service. It may be largely explained by want of tact on the part of mistresses unaccustomed to the employment of domestic servants. Some knowledge of their business on the part of the latter would enormously reduce this friction and popularise a splendid opening for poor Irish girls.

I venture here to suggest that the Congested Districts Board would do well to encourage and assist any conventual or other institution which undertook to instruct young women and female children in common housework, laundry work, and cooking. Such an education would brighten their prospects, whether they sought employment in Ireland or elsewhere, and if they never sought employment at all, would exercise a most civilising influence on the lives of the poor at home. The profitable tourist traffic in the Congested Districts is restricted more by the difficulty of finding local help for the house-maiding in first-class hotels than for any other reason.

It is now time to consider that part of the Dominion which lies west of Winnipeg as a field for emigration, namely – Manitoba, the North-West Territories, and British Columbia.

The last-named we did not visit, because it would have taken more time than we had at our disposal. There is undoubtedly much to be said for the climate of British Columbia, which resembles, but is in many ways an improvement on that of our own Atlantic coast. An agent from the Government of that Province is known to have entered into negotiations with Her Majesty's Treasury for a loan towards a scheme for the transference of from 1,000 to 1,250 Crofter fishermen's families from the Western Islands and Highlands of Scotland to British Columbia.*

* Since the above was written the whole of the United Kingdom has been included in the scheme, which has been sanctioned by the Imperial Parliament.

The emigrants were to be established on grants of free land on the coast and islands of British Columbia, and to be provided with dwellings and means of livelihood.

Thus settled, it was expected that they would develop both the fishing and agricultural resources of the country. Nothing, so far as I am aware, has come of the negotiations, and I believe that members of Parliament and others interested in the scheme have, after a local investigation, expressed a doubt as to its probable success. In any case, before anything is done in the matter, the Treasury will be in possession of the fullest information. The opportunity may be worth watching in view of the exceptional conditions of climate and proposed pursuits. In the meantime, the growth and progress of British Columbia, which is, generally speaking, too remote for direct emigration, has an indirect relation thereto by virtue of the market which it is creating for the live stock and agricultural products of certain districts in Alberta, which will be referred to hereafter.

The suitability of Manitoba and the North-West Territories for immigration from Irish and Scotch Congested Districts has been very warmly debated. In further examination of this question, it was quite unnecessary for us to make any lengthened inquiry into the agricultural resources of the country. The widely-published report of "The Visit of the Tenant Farmer Delegates to Canada in 1890" has been accepted as the best authority on this point. The terms upon which the land can be acquired, the cost of transportation to the lands, the capital required to support a family in the various districts, and other similar details can be found in the Canadian Government's publications and Parliamentary reports. The most useful inquiry that we could make seemed to be such local investigations as would illustrate in the light of past settlements the conditions of successful immigration. As we were only concerned with the class of immigrant that would have, in some form or other, to be assisted, and as a deportation of families to such a country, without further provision for their welfare, is out of the question, the feasibility of colonization was our chief head of inquiry.

This naturally led us to an examination of the Crofter settlements, upon which we determined to form an independent opinion. Until the contrary has been proved by experiment, it may be assumed that the population of the West Coast of Ireland being of the same race, and living in similar climate and under similar circumstances, has much the same physical and moral characteristics as these Crofter immigrants, though, perhaps, the latter have a little the advantage of the former in the point of education. It is true that the Western Irish would be almost entirely Roman Catholic, but from all that we learnt the Catholic Crofter families had shown at least as much ability to cope with the difficulties of their new environments as those of any other denomination.

It is not necessary to give any detailed report of our visit to the Crofter colonies of Killarney in Southern Manitoba and Saltcoats in Assiniboia. The fullest detail as to their foundation and subsequent progress can be found in the Crofter Colonization Report of 1890 and 1891 (Blue Books C. 6067 and C. 6287). Our notes refer to a period twelve months later, and we may say generally that in both the colonies the progress reported in the Government Returns above mentioned has been fully maintained.†

In Killarney, the older settlement of the two, consisting of thirty-three families which emigrated in 1885, the prosperity of the emigrants was most satisfactory. Many of them were crying out for more land, which the growing willingness to exchange labour between neighbours has fitted them to manage. The story they told us was briefly as follows: They expected before the end of the year to have commenced their repayments under the Scheme. Nothing would induce them to go back to their old houses unless they were well educated in school and were in the best of health. They were rich enough to live without labour. Their children's work was continuous but not hard. At first they had to rely upon outside work, but now their farms took all the labour they could devote to them. The women had at first been oppressed by a sense of loneliness, but now were reconciled to the life as they knew it was best for their husbands and children. A man who knew them well told us that the only reason he had to fear for the future of these people was their willingness to incur debt. They were regular attendants and liberal buyers at "credit sales." It must be admitted that the selection of the land for the location of the Killarney crofters was exceptionally favourable, and it is doubtful whether such good land could now be obtained.

The Saltcoats Settlement, consisting originally of forty-nine families, of which eighteen left the colony the first year, was located on the Manitoba and North-West Railway in 1889. The district was newer and the soil apparently not quite so good as at Killarney. In this colony we especially sought out the known malcontents with the object of getting to understand the personal difficulty of colonizing this class of immigrant. I will quote from notes taken during an interview with the most hopeless case that we came across – a man whose face indicated a discontented ne'er-do-weal.

> "I was sent out with four young children and given two dry cows, pork and flour unfit for human food. It made my daughter sick. Whatever hardships a man has to suffer elsewhere, he will suffer worse here. My oats is done – can't get it cut. My wheat is no use. I owe 100 dollars, besides what I owe to the Government. I won't be able to pay anything back to them. I paid taxes all my life to the Government, and they must pay my passage back."

† Since above was written the 1891-92 report of the Colonization Board has been published, showing further progress in detail. See Blue Book C. 6693. (1892.)

The others we saw were fairly prosperous and likely to succeed. Their wives were pleased with the prospect, and those children who were old enough to form any judgment on the matter especially delighted in the change. The whole colony had suffered from the frost (frozen wheat), and all the more intelligent seemed to see their salvation in mixed farming. They had heard dreadful accounts of the climate, but they said it was not too bad, and that they and their families were generally in the best of health.

On the whole the Saltcoats experiment bids fair to show a high percentage of success with those families which gave the colony a fair trial. The country was evidently better adapted to mixed farming than to dependence on wheat, and what is true of the country in this respect is equally true of the Crofters and West-coast Irish.

There is another Crofter Colony on the Line of the Canadian Pacific Railway, near the eastern boundary of Assiniboia, at Moosomin, which was established in 1883 and 1884. I have not with me a record of the exact number of families in this colony. They appear to have been sent out by private enterprise, and so far as we could see were doing very well. There has been a great deal of trouble in getting them to meet their obligations. In the years of their settlement almost everything that was supplied to them cost nearly double the present prices, and consequently their outfits had been so curtailed that their progress had been very much delayed. But the best opinion seemed to be that they would ultimately discharge their liabilities and become prosperous owners of their farms.

In our travels we did not confine our attention to the Crofters, who are still too few to illustrate the capabilities of the country, but learned all we could about bodies of immigrants who were prospering in their new homes. We found almost every European nationality represented, and doing very well. Two instances we thought especially instructive. Some 1,100 families of Mennonites from Southern Russia settled in 1884 and 1885 on the Red River. They had on an average under £15 in cash per family when they began to farm. The Dominion Government set apart a tract of country for their use, and advanced to them about £17 to carry them over. Although in their first year they were visited by a plague of grasshoppers, they are now almost out of debt – mostly owning their farms, and own a large quantity of stock besides. They are looked upon as model settlers, and the following extract from a letter which I have received from an informant who knows them well, gives an insight into the cause of their prosperity:–

> "They had a system of living in villages when they first arrived, but this is gradually breaking up, and they are working out on their farms. This system, while perhaps objectionable in some ways, in leaving so much of the country unoccupied by buildings, and giving it an unsettled look, was, perhaps, for them the best thing they could have done, and was a great saving. For instance, one well would serve the village at the beginning, while the cattle for the whole village would be herded by one herd boy, and no fences were required. The land for cultivation was allotted in proportion to the quantity of good land fit for cropping on each one's particular homestead. Their buildings have been very much improved, and most of them are very comfortable log buildings and log stables with thatched roofs. Some of them have got frame buildings. They have a large amount of stock, and it has been remarked that their horses are always in splendid condition, and of a very good class."

The persecution which this strange sect suffered equally at the hands of Protestants and Catholics in the Reformation times seems to have bred in them the same attributes of success which the Jews display when seeking a refuge from oppression in a new country.

A far more instructive instance is that of 113 Icelandic families which settled, in the years 1881 to 1890, in Argyle County, Southern Manitoba, as the circumstances of the immigrants are strangely analogous to those of people in the poor districts of Ireland and Scotland. The population of Iceland was, when these people first came in 1881, in the truest sense "congested," and as we heard the country described by one of the emigrants, it reminded us strangely of the worst districts we had visited in the West of Ireland. We were told of a country with hardly any agriculture, except a little spade cultivation, and which therefore has to import all its bread stuffs; with no subsidiary industries except fishing and the feather trade; whose commerce is conducted almost entirely by barter; a country without wheeled vehicles; a population with an abnormal proportion of paupers, but displaying dangerous liberality in providing demoralising relief: a people quickwitted, of high moral character, but living in a climate that precludes continuous labour – all these conditions make it particularly interesting for us to watch their progress when they are forced by circumstances to seek a new country where continuous exertion is absolutely essential to success.

I have been fortunate enough to obtain in the utmost detail, which I have condensed below, a correct statement both of the material condition on arrival and in 1891 of these 113 Icelandic families.

Date of Settlement.	Number of Families.	Number in Families.	Acres Broken.	Acres under Cereals.	Roots, &c.	Neat Cattle.	Horses.	Sheep.	Swine.	Poultry.	Value of Land and Buildings.	Value of Implements.	Starting Capital.	Present Debts.	Total Resources.	Present Nett Worth.
1881	7	46	745	496	4	240	25	77	15	282	$28,920	3,480	1,185	5,050	39,063	34,013
1882	17	72	1,832	1,378	8	508	63	65	27	620	$53,700	7,914	2,935	17,455	78,287	60,832
1883	14	67	967	710	6½	440	37	140	18	525	$32,700	4,770	1,990	12,385	50,172	37,787
1884	18	95	1,152	858	9	588	41	103	41	557	$36,200	7,573	1,305	14,460	57,357	42,897
1885	10	41	500	426	5	260	18	81	16	325	$15,300	3,519	1,136	8,150	25,259	17,109
1886	10	53	493	393	5	288	19	86	15	218	$13,600	3,079	940	5,725	23,144	17,419
1887	11	49	418	275	5½	254	14	24	11	240	$18,300	2,119	1,730	3,660	25,472	21,812
1888	9	36	352	237	5½	144	2	11	13	146	$11,800	927	1,188	3,705	14,187	10,482
1889	15	57	504	340	7½	160	15	3	4	170	$17,550	2,577	2,040	7,310	25,017	17,677
1890	2	10	23	14	1	14	–	–	1	10	$1,100	–	100	–	1,265	1,265
–	113	526	6,986	5,127	57	2,896	234	590	161	3,093	$229,170	35,958	14,549	72,930	339,223	261,293

The figures speak not only for the material resources of the country, but also for its effect upon the people who settle in it. It is noticeable that while in the earlier years the emigrants were mostly men of enterprise, in later years they were in many cases "assisted" by the community on which they had been a burden. They were now all independent. They at first tried to subsist on a small green crop and a few sheep and ponies, as a means of making a livelihood. But they had now adopted the wheat-growing of the country. Their children are bilingual, and go to the English schools. In the rising generation all clannishness bids fair to disappear. The only advantage they have over Scottish and Irish emigrants is the greater ease with which they endure the cold.

In all the districts in this country which we had hitherto seen the farmers mainly depended on wheat for their profit. This crop grown upon the virgin soil and in favourable seasons pays well enough; but unhappily in these latitudes its repeated partial destruction by frost shows it to be a very speculative one. Early sowing and the introduction of a new variety of wheat has greatly lessened the risk. Nevertheless, the tendency of the country is towards mixed farming, and, as above suggested, the class of immigrants in whom we were interested would be far better adapted to the care of stock than to cultivation which has to be conducted, in order to be profitable, in a rough and ready but very expeditious manner.

We therefore determined to look over a district much farther west, with which I happened to have been acquainted as manager of a ranching company a few years ago, namely the portion of the Alberta Territory lying along the "foot-hills" of the Rocky Mountains between Calgary and Edmonton. The locality to which we went was about sixty miles north of Calgary, and is known as the Red Deer Country, being situated on the river of that name. It was a fair sample of a considerable area open for settlement. We found an excellent soil for cultivation, and many conditions which would be of the utmost advantage to poor settlers. There was an ample supply of running water, and well-water could be obtained at a moderate depth. The country was well wooded, and the pasturage was far finer than anything we had seen in the districts further east. Timber was much more plentiful for both building purposes and fuel. The climate, although quite as severe in its extremes and less suitable for growing wheat, was far better adapted for handling stock, because a greater rain and snow-fall produced luxuriant pasturage, which gave both better and more abundant hay for use in the winter time.

At the same time the snow did not lie as long in the winter owing to the well-known "Chinook" wind which periodically crosses the mountains from the Pacific Coast, sometimes sweeping away six to ten inches of snow in a single night. Cattle here would do without hay for ten months in the year, whereas in Manitoba they would probably have to be fed for six months.

The chief disadvantage would be the extra cost of some provisions, and a considerably higher freight on agricultural machinery, implements, &c., from, and all products to, the eastern markets. But a market is likely to develop in British Columbia, where the area of agricultural land is disproportionately small in comparison with the mining, fishing, timber, and other industries. Calgary, many people think, will develop into a large city. Its market already absorbs, at good prices, the products of the surrounding country. While we were there two companies were establishing extensive cold storage plants for beef, mutton, and pork. It would also cost more to get the emigrants to this country, the railway journey being from 300 to 500 miles further than to the districts already colonized. But the cost of maintenance would be greatly reduced where cows could be cheaply kept. I might add that the early settlers, at any rate, would be able to avail themselves of such an abundance of game (prairie chicken, willow grouse, ducks, geese, &c.) as we had never before witnessed. I must not go into further detail; but I may say that we thought this country more suitable for emigration purposes than any of those already mentioned.

From Alberta we hurried back to Winnipeg, having made arrangements before leaving Canada for the United States to confer with the representative men of the Provincial and Dominion Governments, and with prominent officials of the Railways, the Hudson Bay Company, and the various Land and Financial Agencies. Among the many who showed us the utmost courtesy, and gave us the most valuable information, I may mention Mr. H.H. Smith, the Dominion Land Commissioner, Mr. A.F. Eden, Land Commissioner of the Manitoba and North Western Railway Company, and W.B. Scarth, of the Canada North-West Land Company.

What has been said above tends to show that the free lands of Manitoba and the North-West Territories can be successfully availed of for the purposes of colonization. When the emigrants are industrious they can undoubtedly repay borrowed capital, and quickly secure independence. I have not gone into the resources which the country affords for assisted emigration without subsequent provision for the emigrant, as no action in this direction could be undertaken by the Congested Districts Board. But it is worth while to note that the country absorbs all its immigrants, and even those who leave these settlements to seek their fortunes independently manage to subsist without being supported by the community. Probably the most unsuitable emigrants ever sent out to Canada were a certain twenty families who were sent from the East-end of London in 1884, to farm lands in Assiniboia. They were utterly unacquainted with country life and to-day only five of them remain upon their farms. Eight have settled in the little town of Moossomin, in a quarter nicknamed Whitechapel, and are profitably following various trades. The seven others are scattered about in various parts of the West of Canada, and are believed to be doing well.

The difficulties of the climate are, I believe, greatly exaggerated. Looked at only from a thermometric point of view, it is unquestionably severe. But all classes of immigrants seem to become quickly acclimatised, and we could hear of no cases in which any considerable number of people, not previously affected by disease, had suffered in health from the change. It must, however, be admitted that the newness of all conditions, the bleak inhospitable prairie, the absolute necessity for energetic and continuous effort, and the many necessary hardships incidental to the settler's life, to say nothing of grievances fostered by visitors who had politically disapproved of the scheme, exercise a most discouraging effect upon emigrants from poverty-stricken districts, and render it extremely difficult to conduct them through the early period of dependence and indebtedness to a state of independence and ownership. This can only be accomplished through the elaboration of a financial and administrative plan based on a thorough knowledge of the personal characteristics of the emigrant, and of the various conditions of the localities selected.

It should always be borne in mind that there are others interested in the success of the emigrants than the Government of the country assisting them to emigrate. A scheme of colonization should rely upon the co-operation of all parties benefited, as far as possible in proportion to the amount of the benefit. The Dominion Government could hardly be expected to go beyond their grant of 160 acres of free land and their bonus to settlers. The land available for settlement being quarters of alternate sections (square miles), the owners of the other sections have a direct interest in seeing the Government lands occupied, as it increases the value of their own lands.*

In many districts the Hudson Bay Company are largely interested in this way. The Railway Companies are also interested in the settlement of the lands along their lines, and I have no doubt that they could be induced to carry immigrants and their goods at a rate which would cover the actual cost of transportation. Generally also the Railway Companies are owners of enormous tracts of land and are therefore interested in a double capacity.

By the co-operation of these Companies can the problem of colonization best be solved. This has been recognised by the Colonization Board who have had charge of the Killarney and Saltcoats Settlements, for they have appointed an advisory Board in Winnipeg which includes representatives of the Agencies above mentioned. The difficulties with which they have had to contend are enormous, and the ability with which they have been surmounted is beyond praise, especially when it is considered that the services of these gentlemen have been gratuitous. I am quite convinced that, by using the experience which they have gained in past experiments, they will be able to devise a scheme under which the same class of emigrants with which they have hitherto dealt could become independent and repay the cost of the outlay on their removal and settlement.

I shall, I presume, be expected to suggest in what way the Congested Districts Board, if forced to apply the emigration remedy, could do so in Canada. Single labouring families could be dealt with as suggested at the beginning of this Report. For any large scheme of colonization I should strongly urge the Board to confine itself to the reception of applications for families desiring to emigrate, to starting arrangements, and to a limited financial responsibility. The further administration of the scheme could not possibly be in better hands than those of the Colonization Board. This Board had recently been reorganized for the purpose of including in its operations the Congested Districts of Ireland, and of utilising therefore a certain fund alloted for emigration purposes under the Land Law (Ireland) Act, 1881, sec. 32. It seems to have been overlooked that clause 4, sec. 35, of the Purchase of Land (Ireland) Act, 1891, Part II., repeals the above section, and there are, therefore, no funds available, but it would be within the power of the Congested Districts Board to obtain funds for the purpose on the security of its income.

It is essential that the emigrants should understand that they do not deal directly with the Government at home, or with any body whom they looked upon as equivalent to the Government, and that they will be made to meet their obligations. It would be well if one of the agencies I have mentioned, or a joint agency, including representatives from them, could be induced to undertake the work. A loan to such a body, at a low rate of interest, and with easy terms of repayment, with possibly a small capital rebate, provided the colonization were carried out on some such lines as those laid down by the Colonization Board, and under their control, would, probably, be the most feasible plan for starting a new colony.

With regard to the financial risk the matter stands thus:– The settlement of the *right kind of settler* and of his family, without capital of his own, is a sound investment for parties interested in the settlement of the land advancing the money. If, on the other hand, as might be the case with settlers from the Congested Districts of Ireland, the material were not quite suitable for the experiment, some risk would be incurred, and it is the amount of this risk that the Congested Districts Board would have, in some way or other, to bear. For example, the Manitoba and North-Western Railway, who assisted the Saltcoats Colony, is now itself advancing large sums to settlers who have been forced to leave their farms in Dakota, United States, and are coming, in large numbers, into Manitoba and Assiniboia. The Railway Company does not expect to lose any money, but to reap considerable profit by its advances, but it is not willing to take the same risk with settlers of the Crofter type. No doubt a sum could be named that would compensate it for limitation in the selection of the settlers, but such a sum would have to be provided by the Congested Districts Board in the case of Irish immigrants, if the Colonization Board, acting for the Congested Districts Board, were to make terms with the Manitoba and North-Western Railway, which, chiefly through Mr. Eden's exertions, have the best scheme of colonization I have seen.

To sum up the foregoing, a limited emigration to the older settled parts of Canada might be assisted, if encouraged by the Dominion Government. In Manitoba and the North-West Territories a position may be earned by the West of Ireland emigrant far beyond the possibilities of life at home, but this can only be obtained by an elaborate system of colonization which I believe the Colonization Board could render successful.

* Ordinary settlers are in many ways a great acquisition to a new district. All classes of commodities cheapen as the population increases. In thinly inhabited districts, it is extremely hard to start and maintain schools. Neighbours are essential, not only for the sake of company, but also on account of the necessity for the exchange of labour, implements, &c.

It is only right to mention that the many Ministers and Government Officials whom we met, and the officers of the Canadian Pacific Railway and Hudson's Bay Company, did all in their power to assist us to obtain information. Their courtesy and hospitality were unremitting.

HORACE PLUNKETT.

May 15, 1892.

Since the above was written, Mr. Davitt has published an article in the *Nineteenth Century* of April, 1892, which appears to substantiate the facts, and to differ little from the conclusions of this report.

One of the original members appointed in 1891, Horace Plunkett remained on the Congested Districts Board until 1918. He was the founder of the Irish Agricultural Organisation Society (1894) and a leading figure in the co-operative movement in Ireland. He was knighted in 1903.

THE "CONGESTED DISTRICTS" AND THE WORK OF THE CONGESTED DISTRICTS BOARD

BY

FRANCIS S. SHERIDAN, *Barrister-at-Law,*
Chief Clerk to the Congested Districts Board.

[FEBRUARY 1915]

EDITOR'S NOTE: The following is the final part of Sheridan's Report, with a concluding summary of the Board's operations. ***The beginning of the report may be found on pages 1-4 of this book.***

§ 3. LAND PURCHASE AND RESALE BY THE CONGESTED DISTRICTS BOARD.

In treating of the *land itself* as distinguished from the use that can be made of it, it should be mentioned that although the general powers given by the Act of 1891 to the Board at its inception were wide, and although the Act indicates the enlargement of holdings on the estates of private owners as one of the objects of its attention, the *purchase* of estates was not expressly authorised, and the Board could hold land only in the name of the Land Commission. The provisions of the Act of 1891 for amalgamation of small holdings on *private estates* was found to be inoperative, so in 1893 an Act was passed giving the Board power to acquire land for enlargement of holdings and to hold it by means of trustees.

In 1894, another Act was passed to enable the Board when selling an estate to give a guarantee to the Land Commission for the regular payment of instalments by the purchasing tenants. Thus no guarantee deposit would be retained by the Land Commission out of the purchase money. The Act also incorporated with the Congested Districts Board Acts the provisions of the Land Clauses Acts so far as they relate to the taking of land by agreement.

In 1896 the Land Law Act gave power to the Land Commission to make advances to enable the Board to buy estates. The advances were to be made in Guaranteed Land Stock, subject to an annuity of 4 per cent. (consisting of $2\frac{3}{4}$ per cent. interest and $1\frac{1}{4}$ per cent. sinking fund). This Act put a difficult restriction on the Board as regards re-sale of their lands, for it provided that the Land Commission should not make an advance to a tenant to buy a holding unless the ratable valuation was over £10. Most of the holdings in the congested districts were "small holdings" (i.e., under £10 valuation) and the Board could not then obtain sufficient untenanted land to bring all their tenants' holdings up to £10 valuation, owing, among other things, to the operation of Section 40, which gave temporary tenants a priority in buying their holdings in the Land Judge's Court, thus preventing such lands from coming into the possession of the Board who would have used them for the enlargement of small holdings. The Board could not, therefore, expect to be in a position to re-sell much land through the Land Commission and of course the disqualified tenants had not cash to buy direct from the Board. The disability was removed by the Act of 1899 which suspended the operation of Section 40 on the Board making an offer to purchase an estate in the Land Judge's Court, thus preventing a "Court tenant" purchasing grass lands until the Board's offer for purchase of the estate had been considered. The Act also enabled the Land Commission to make advances for redemption of the head rents affecting estates purchased by the Board. This had formerly to be done by cash out of the Board's slender income. The Act also removed the barrier as to sale of "small holdings," and increased the Board's income by about £15,000.

The next Act passed for the Board was the Act of 1901 which gave them power to deal with a tenant who obstructed the re-arrangement of holdings on estates purchased. The Act further empowered the Board to enter on non-judicial holdings to make arrangements at to turbary, etc., – a fruitful source of trouble in the West of Ireland. The Purchase of Land Act (No. 2) of 1901 deals with the annuity payable on a holding to which lands had been added – treating as *one* holding the old portion and the enlargement.

The most important of the Land Purchase Acts so far was that of 1903 which reverted to cash advances instead of land stock, gave vendors a *bonus* of 12 per cent. on the purchase-money of estates sold, to facilitate negotiations for sale of *estates,* as distinguished from *holdings* (the system heretofore in operation) and enabled a vendor when selling his estate to obtain an advance to repurchase his demesne as if he were a tenant. The Act further placed a limit on advances for purchase of Court lettings in the Land Judge's Court, increased the maximum limit for county advances, reduced the annuity payable by tenant purchasers to 3¼ per cent. (interest as before at 2¾ per cent., but sinking fund at ½ per cent.) for 68½ years at a uniform rate instead of 4 per cent. as formerly with decadal reductions, enabled the Board to settle accounts with the Land Commission after sale of each estate instead of by county groups as formerly, facilitated re-sales to tenants, and added £20,000 to the Board's income. This Act was most successful in causing numerous landlords to agree to enter into negotiations for the sale of their estates, but unfortunately it did not sufficiently secure priority of attention to the claims of the congested districts. The new annuity of 3¼ per cent. had some years before in the case of Clare Island been devised by the Board, who saw the advantage of reducing the sinking fund rate to ½ per cent. and enabled sales to be arranged at a 3¼ per cent. annuity that could not have been brought about on the old 4 per cent. basis.

The Land Act of 1904 sanctioned the payment of the bonus to landlords who were tenants-for-life for their own use and benefit, freed from any trust or other claim. This had the effect of stimulating sales of estates which had been retarded by tenants-for-life.

Owing to the success of the 1903 Act outside the congested districts delay occurred in paying landlords their purchase-money and the Treasury could not continue to make prompt cash advances for financing sales as fast as they were arranged.

The Act of 1909 accordingly re-introduced payments in Land Stock at 3½ per cent. (interest 3 per cent. and sinking fund ½ per cent.). It re-constituted and increased both the powers and income of the Board as a result of the Inquiry held from 1906 to 1908 by the Dudley Royal Commission on Congestion. The Board's income was raised to £250,000 a year, of which £19,000 is paid to the Department of Agriculture and Technical Instruction for Ireland to meet expenditure in connection with the powers and duties transferred to the Department from the Board under Section 47 – viz.:

(*a*) the provision of seed potatoes and seed oats;
(*b*) agricultural instruction or practical husbandry; and
(*c*) aiding and developing of forestry, or the breeding of live-stock or poultry.

The 1909 Act created a scheme for advances for purchase either in land stock, or cash, or partly in each, the intention being to settle priority and facilitate the completion of sales where cash to pay off the vendors would not be provided by the Treasury for several years to come, under the terms of the Act 1903. The fixed 12 per cent. bonus was altered to one on a sliding scale varying up to 18 per cent. and details were revised as to limits for advances, as to turbary, etc.

It will convey some idea of the magnitude of the Board's operations in connection with the purchase, re-arrangement and re-sale of lands to give the following summaries up to the 31st. March, 1914:

TABLE II. – *Estates purchased or offered for sale between 1891 and 31st March, 1914.*

Period	No. of Tenants	Area	Estimated Purchase-price
		acres	£.
(a) Purchased under Acts prior to 1909	15,727	497,484	2,260,551
(b) Purchased under Act of 1909	29,737	1,178,698	3,983,329
(c) Offered for sale since 1909 but not yet purchased	22,800	904,975	3,820,325
Totals	68,264	2,581,157	10,064,205

TABLE III. – *Estates re-sold by the Board up to 31st March, 1914.*

Period	No. of Tenants	Area	Estimated Purchase-price
		acres	£.
Prior to Act of 1909	9,371	246,394	1,167,846
Since Act of 1909	3,497	93,758	571,301
Totals	12,868	340,152	1,739,147

Since the Act of 1909 the greater number of the Board's Estates Staff have been engaged upon operations and arrangements in connection with *purchase* of Estates which were offered for sale and for which it was considered desirable to settle terms of purchase without delay. As the negotiations for purchase are now drawing to a close in the majority of cases of estates offered, it is being arranged that more rapid progress shall be made henceforth in carrying out improvements and re-distributing lands for *re-sale* to tenant purchasers.

§ 4. Redistribution of holdings.

So much for the Board's operations in the handling of land itself and aiding in the transfer from the dual to the single ownership in a way which will, as far as it is possible, allow the new peasant–proprietors to make a living out of their land. But the Board are fully aware that many of the purchasers cannot live on the produce of the land alone, because there is not enough land in Connacht for enlarging holdings so as to give every tenant-purchaser a holding out of which alone he can support his family. The improvement of house accommodation and the provision of out-houses for live-stock by means of a scheme of free grants and loans to tenants will be some of the most important results of the Board's work.

Therefore the Board have to exercise a discretion in the allotment of land – a task that is made easier by a prohibition in the Act of 1909 against giving land to *landless men*, the only classes to which the Board can give holdings being tenants, tenant-purchasers, and herdsmen.

Before referring to the Board's efforts to develop husbandry and the conditions of life *on* the land, it may be pointed out that in the West the people have for generations in several hundreds of cases been unable to live on the patches of poor land they held – rarely in one compact lot, but divided and sub-divided among families from time to time at rents varying from a few shillings to a few pounds. With these holdings there are usually rights to cut turf for fuel and sometimes for sale, while on the sea-board there are rights to cut sea-weed for manure as well as to burn for kelp manufacture, and there is also frequently some grazing or commonage appurtenant. On the sea-board, too, the resources are augmented by fishing and by the cheap carriage of foodstuffs, etc., while there and elsewhere there are weaving, knitting, lace-making, and such home industries to help the family in making a living. Other subsidiary sources of income, varying according to localities, are the English and Scotch harvesting operations and gifts from relatives abroad. A substantial addition to the comfort of the "congests" for the past few years is the Old Age Pensions, of which the West gets a large proportion owing to the poverty and longevity of the people. Referring to the British harvesting and other work the receipts may average about £10 per man profit at the end of the season.

To return to the Land Purchase procedure, the several Acts enable the Board by advances for the Land Commission to buy out the landlords, and the Board then devote a part of their income to various improvements on the estates, the work being done under the supervision of Inspectors by the tenants and their families. When the estates are ready for sale they are sold to the tenants at prices which recoup the Board for about half of the money spent on improvements. It is estimated that the irrecoverable expenditure in estate improvements will amount to about £100,000 per annum. Sales to tenants are made through the Land Commission and the Board's advances for purchase are cancelled by the advances (loans) made to tenant-purchasers. Thus the Board are intermediaries or agents in bringing about the purchase, improvement, and transfer of estates from landlords to small tenant-purchasers, the land and the social and economic condition of the people being improved while the estates are in the Board's hands. Of course the Board have to buy relatively good estates in certain localities in order to have untenanted lands to enlarge small holdings in the neighbouring district; but when holdings are comparatively well-circumstanced there is no need for the Board to intervene and the owners may, and in some cases do, sell *direct* to the tenants through the Estate Commissioners without reference to the Board.

The fact of holdings being small in size is not the only drawback in settlement, for sometimes holdings by the repeated splitting up among families become under the "rundale system" exceedingly complicated and involved. A patch of a few acres in area might be made up in some cases of as many as 30 to 40 detached plots without any sufficient boundaries, being only marked by stones or a strip of grass – some plots being as far away as 3 miles from the tenant's house. It is obvious that any attempt at a proper system of agriculture is exceedingly difficult, if not impossible under such circumstances. In dealing with these cases the Board has to value all interests and re-divide the entire estate into new compact holdings as far as practicable. It may be remarked that under the Land Purchase Acts while lands are subject to the control of the Land Commission sub-division is illegal.

A matter of prime importance in the redistribution of land among small landholders unaccustomed to manage good farms is that if, after purchasing, they were left to work out their own economic salvation on enlarged holdings without any guiding influence or advice as to the management of their farms under their new circumstances, the increase of land merely would only half-equip the new tenant-purchasers. But the Board make loans to tenant-purchasers for purchase of live-stock, for improvements in dwellings, etc. (loans to over £10,000 for house improvements have been made); and by arrangements between the Board and the Department of Agriculture and Technical Instruction, the Department is arranging to supply agricultural instruction for the owners of the new holdings. This co-ordination of the two Departments appears to be well calculated to make the most of the operations of the Land Purchase Acts, and to render the practice of agriculture in the congested districts as skilful and profitable as it is practicable to make it.

§ 5. Improvement of housing.

The housing conditions of the people have always received special consideration owing to the importance of the subject in the work of re-generation.

Until the inhabitants of the Western Districts are provided with clean and healthy homes, with proper out-offices for the live-stock, instead of their present insanitary dwellings, no substantial improvement could be expected in the general tone of life.

The following figures will show the work done by the Board and their tenants and the amount of money spent on housing:

Table IV – *Money spent on housing improvement.*

Number of new houses erected by the Board on their estates	1,956
Number of new houses erected by Board's Tenants with assistance from the Board	1,523
Number of houses improved by tenants with aid from the Board	2,880
Total amount spent by the Board in grants and advances to tenants for new houses or improvements in existing ones on Board's Estates	£427,112

Nor are the Board's efforts to improve housing conditions in the congested districts confined to the estates which pass through their hands. They have devised a plan for "helping the people to help themselves" under what is known as the *Parish Committee Scheme.* In this the Board set apart out of their income a lump sum and apportion it for the benefit of the parishes in their area, the annual expenditure on the scheme at present being £20,000. A local Committee, comprising clergy, doctors, rural district councillors and six elected persons, is formed to administer the grant given to the parish under regulations prepared by the Board. This Committee selects from among the applicants for aid a number of the poorest landholders below £7 ratable valuation and votes grants for approved works – usually the building of new or improvement of old dwellings, the addition of a room to a house, the building of out-offices, etc.

In making selection of recipients for grants, the Parish Committee are instructed to adopt the cases where the people are most in need of aid and make the best offers by their own work to carry out improvements – the more the tenant binds himself to do the better chance he has of obtaining a grant. Under the rules no one can get assistance who does not offer to turn out a job worth in capital value at least 3 or 4 times the amount of the grant, and the competition for grants may bring out work worth from 5 to 10 times the value of the sum voted. Thus the spirit of self-help is fostered and the best efforts of the people drawn out to improve their housing.

Roughly the advances made are intended to barely cover the out-of–pocket expenses for purchase of materials or wages of skilled labour (masons and carpenters, etc.), all the rest of the work being done by the family of the grantee. Many a poor landholder would in days gone by with or without the aid of a mason or carpenter be anxious to put up an out-house if he could purchase the timber or roofing materials, but the work remained undone and he continued in miserable surroundings for want of the ready cash to start the work and owing to a fear that he would be charged more rent on account of the improvement of his holding. For it must be remembered that the custom in Ireland (differing from the English system) is for the landlord to merely let the soil and the tenant has to do everything in fitting up buildings, fences, etc. The Board's Parish Committee in this way supplies the necessary motive power to stimulate improvements in social and material well-being.

The following is a summary of the work of the Parish Committees. It should be noted that these grants are made apart from the Board's estate-improvement schemes.

TABLE V. – *Grants under the Parish Committee Scheme for Housing Improvement.*

	Number	Amount of Grants paid to Recipients £	Estimated value of the work done for the sum paid as in previous column £
New dwellings erected	1,116	5,590	40,996
Improvements to existing houses	27,151 *	36,585	152,101
Total	28,267	42,175	193,097

(*) Under the scheme several grants may be made from year to year towards gradual improvements to the same house or out-offices.

The Board have also a scheme for granting loans to *tenant-purchasers* of holdings not exceeding £7 ratable valuation who desire to undertake the erection or improvement of houses after they have purchased their holdings, either through the Estates Commissioners or through the Board. It was found that in many cases tenants who were not properly housed at the time they bought their holdings were afterwards anxious to come into line with their neighbours who had improved their dwellings under one or other of the Board's schemes, thus showing the stimulating effect of seeing the houses around them improved. The Board, therefore, in order to meet the desire of these people decided to lend them money on solvent security. The scheme has only been in operation a short time, but so far the following cases have been dealt with:

Table VI – *Loans to Tenant-Purchasers for Housing Improvement.*

	No. of Loans	Amount lent
New Dwellings erected	245	£7,852
Improvement to existing dwelling	156	£3,133
Totals	401	£10,985

It is thus seen how the effect of a healthy rivalry creates or increases a desire of the people to improve their dwellings and surroundings. People who remember the condition of the houses and farms of the West about 20 years ago and compare it with that of to-day testify to the wonderful improvement they see in the appearance of the whole face of the country. As proving the extent to which the general impression of the observer is borne out by a house-to-house survey, attention is drawn to the Returns of the Census Commissioners regarding Housing for 1891 and 1911 which when compared show that in the rural districts of the Counties Donegal and Kerry, and of Connacht there is an *increase* of 21.5 per cent. in the number of first class houses while there is a *decrease* of over 5 per cent. in the 2nd. and 3rd. class, and a *decrease* of 78.4 per cent. in the number of fourth (or worst) class of houses! This last figure is very remarkable and points to a marvellous improvement in the home surroundings of the congested districts which cannot fail to have an up-lifting effect on the habits as well as physical condition and social well-being of the people. It shows what can be, and has been, done by the Board, local bodies, and the people working together to improve housing accommodation; and when people are decently housed improvements in other respects inevitably follow.

§ 6. IMPROVEMENTS IN AGRICULTURE, LIVE-STOCK, ETC.

Apart from the Board's dealings in *the land itself* in the earlier years of their work, they gave (having regard to their small income) earnest attention to the advantages accruing from improvement in the breeding of horses, donkeys, cattle, sheep, pigs, and poultry, in bee-keeping, and also in giving practical instruction with the object of improving the methods of cultivation in the congested districts. Itinerant instructors were appointed, example plots were cultivated, and example holdings fully worked, all operations being clearly explained for the information of the neighbouring farmers. When the Local Government Act was passed in 1898 and the Department of Agriculture and Technical Instruction established in 1899, it was found that there would be over-lapping if the Board and the Department were to continue working in the same localities. The Board could not legally operate *outside* the congested districts, the

Department could not legally expend their funds *inside* the congested districts, and the new County Councils could not levy rates for County Agricultural Committees to spend on agricultural schemes except over entire county areas comprising both congested and non-congested areas. Accordingly a working arrangement was made by which the entire work of agricultural development in the congested districts was taken over in 1904 by the Department of Agriculture, the Board paying a fixed sum to defray the cost of the work undertaken in the congested districts. This subsidy was reconsidered when the congested districts were enlarged in 1909, and it was fixed for a term of years at £19,000 per annum under the Land Act of 1909, when the work was by Section 47 formally transferred to the Department, as already explained.

The Board's efforts for agricultural improvement were necessarily small as compared with the systematic and comprehensive schemes instituted by the Department with their larger funds and their staff of highly trained agriculturists. Every year benefits are being conferred upon farmers, among which may be specially mentioned the provision of veterinary surgeons and the establishment of veterinary dispensaries in parts of the country where such advantages had not existed.

In a short paper like this the details cannot be stated of all the Board's live-stock schemes, one of the most interesting phases of their work. Besides, the transfer of these duties to the Department of Agriculture would more properly place a record of the results obtained within the scope of a report on the Department's activities. The Board took steps to improve the breed of live-stock by importing hardy strains, and improved poultry, both for table and laying, by crossing the home-breeds and exchanging eggs, to avoid the evils of in-breeding. Bee-keeping was given special attention owing to its peculiar suitability as a cottage industry, and the capital required is so very little while a very high percentage of profit is obtainable. It has been estimated that one hive may in a good year produce as much profit as a pig.

§ 7. The fishing and allied industries.

In order to be in a position to decide upon plans for improving the condition of the residents of the congested districts littoral, the Board first examined the condition of affairs along the whole western sea-board from Donegal to Cork, and they found that while in the counties south of the Shannon the fisheries were in a fair state of development, so far as markets and transit facilities were concerned, allowing for the difficulties in landing fish, in Connacht and Donegal the transit and market arrangements were defective, as well as the landing accommodation. Along the whole coast there was a dearth of capital to provide boats and gear to properly work the fisheries, and except in a few places there were no fleets of decked fishing boats such as were worked regularly in Irish waters by French, Dutch, Manx, and British fishermen. This survey enabled the Board to deal with local suggestions and applications for aid of various kinds.

As regards suitability for the Coasts where there are no natural harbours capable of accommodating large boats, it may be mentioned that open boats that can be hauled up on a beach are more suitable for the local fishermen (who are usually also small farmers) than either yawls or large boats requiring shelter, because the crews can carry the light boats to safety, whereas heavy boats would have to take their chance lying at anchor. In stormy weather – and the West Coast is open to all the force of the Atlantic gales – the anchored boats are sometimes driven ashore and smashed while open boats and the "curraghs" (or small canvas-covered canoes) are deposited high and dry. Hence these canoes, though they may look primitive, are found to better suit the requirements of the fishermen–farmers than large boats. These men have little capital and do not fish all the year round. It would not pay them to invest capital in large boats, even if they had it, for unless fishermen who go in for such boats continue at it all the year round, and make it their sole occupation, they cannot make fishing pay a proper dividend on their outlay. The canoes cost very little, and therefore suit the class of men who use them when fishing seasons and weather warrant. But they often pay in results as high remuneration for work done as if the men were engaged during the same time as "hands" on board a big fishing boat. They will for this reason continue to be used, even though there has been a revolution of late years in the working of large boats.

With the object of encouraging fishing, the Board in many instances met local demands by erecting piers, slips, and quays to provide means of landing fish and giving boats reasonable safety.

In considering the fishing industry, a broad line is drawn between "freshing," or the marketing of fresh fish, and the curing or preservation of fish for export as well as home trade. "Freshing" can only be carried on where there are regular and quick means of transit, chiefly to the English markets, the principal sources of consumption. This trade involves much preparation – fish boxes, ice, ice-hulk, etc. – and in their operations the Board provided all necessary plant and started fresh-fish centres, notably for spring-mackerel fishing at Aran Islands (Galway Bay), and some mainland centres in Galway and Mayo, the fish being despatched over the Midland Great Western Railway system to Dublin and thence to England. The Board's object was not to become fish merchants themselves but to afford an object-lesson in starting the industry, to demonstrate that it could be made to pay. Having done this, the Board retired, and now there are fish-merchants carrying on the trade on commercial lines. To aid the industry, the Board subsidised a few steamer services from outlying places to the railway.

In the cured-fish trade on the other hand much capital has to be sunk in providing the necessary curing-sheds, stores, salt, barrels, hiring of coopers and curers, etc. Having done this at several centres where curing was previously unknown or forgotten, the Board leased or sold their stations and left the development of the industry to the enterprise of commercial fish-curers. The result has been most encouraging, particularly in County Donegal where the headquarters of the Board's herring-trade is located. At Downings Bay in a few years they converted a poor locality where a cured fish trade was unknown into one of the busiest of herring-centres, and fleets of over 200 Scotch and Irish boats have made the place a hive of industry, giving employment to great numbers of men and women. And considerable employment is also given in carting the fish. The herrings taken off the Donegal coast and cured at Downings at first won the highest place in the world's markets and were specially sought for at the leading foreign centres of consumption but as the steam-drifters came to the coast in recent years and intercepted the shoals out at sea, the quality of the herrings has sunk nearer to the average, as the Downings herrings in earlier years did not acquire their peculiar quality until they had arrived close to the shore.

Various kinds of fish-curing are carried on in the Board's stations according to the class of fish found in the locality (cod, ling, etc.), but the herring and mackerel from the industrial point of view are those out of which the biggest earnings are made by fishermen and fish-merchants.

In these ventures of pioneer fishing and curing, the Board had to risk loss, and some big reverses have been sustained here and there by the loss of boats that could not be insured, but the Board consider it part of their duty as pioneers to test the different fishing centres in the congested districts and thus encourage the people to embark on new grounds when it has been proved that they are safe, or at least hold out reasonable prospect of success.

One of the important functions of the Board is to make loans to fishermen to enable them to procure suitable boats and gear with which to pursue their calling. In no case do the Board advance cash to a borrower. They either purchase what is required and hand it over to the fisherman on receiving proper security for repayment of the loan, or arrange to allow him to purchase where he wishes and then pay the account direct on proof of delivery, usually in the presence of the local representatives of the Board. Loans are also made in special cases to assist in fish-curing operations, and the Board occasionally import cargoes of barrel-making materials, selling them on credit along the coast to curers on a quick-repayment system. By these means the Board are slowly working small but enterprising merchants into a position of being capitalists capable of largely extending their trade.

Another and more complicated system of aiding fishermen to become owners of large boats is to enter into an arrangement known as the "share-system." Under this procedure the Board supplies the boat and gear to a selected crew who undertake by an agreement to work the boat; and the proceeds of the earnings are divided into shares, the agreement running until the Board's share of proceeds repays the purchase outlay, when the boat and gear become the property of the crew. The Board retain plenary powers of dealing with the crew while the agreement is in force, in order to ensure proper discipline and control of the boat and its operations. An instructor is placed in charge who acts as "skipper" of the boat as well as teacher of the crew. This system was first tried in Donegal and was found very successful in the case of decked sailing boats until the advent of *power* fishing boats, since when the crews of sailing boats have not been so successful.

In developing the fishing industry, the Board have had to make arrangements for training men as fishermen, and in the case of large boats intended to proceed to deep-sea fishing grounds, they had to train them to be sailors as well as fishermen. Many of the men had never seen a compass until taught its use on the Board's boats, but they soon became proficient in their new sphere of activity. In the early years of the Board's work they engaged experienced Scotch fishermen to teach the local crews, and the instructor was make the skipper of the boats (whether loan or share-boats). Now many Irish fishermen are fit to act as instructors for young crews. In addition to instruction in fishing and fish-curing, the Board have classes for instruction in net-mending, and mounting of nets, but this subject is now included in the routine of fishing and all crews have to prepare and care for their own nets.

During the past quarter of a century the fishing industry has kept pace with the progress in ship-building generally. The introduction of steam-trawling was followed by the building of steam-drifters and motor-boats and the time is fast approaching when the old-time sailing craft will be "crowded out" of competition at large fishing centres by the various forms of modern power-boats. Even sailing craft are being fitted with steam capstans for hauling nets and gear. To keep up to date with the times, the Board have procured for experimental purposes, and as instruction-boats for the training of crews, various kinds of steam-drifters and motor-boats and in the light of their experience (which they place at the disposal of local fishermen) they make loans to enable enterprising fishermen to fit out motor-boats of a suitable design.

To meet the demands of the increasing fishing industry, the Board opened some boat-building yards under skilled instructors and designers, and also sent instructors to work in private yards to aid local builders in designing and building fishing boats, the idea of the Board being to give instruction rather than to make money in boat-building. Another form of the Board's activities in assisting mackerel and herring-curing was to open barrel-making workshops under skilled coopers who took in local hands as apprentices to be trained. In the course of years there have been numerous men trained who are now working as coopers and curers, and the barrels made in the Board's workshops are sold to local fish curers when their own stock of barrels runs short.

For assisting the Board to carry on satisfactorily their various fishery operations, and for providing a ready way to inspect the coast work of the staff, it was considered desirable to build a special steamer suitable for cargo-work and at the same time possessing sufficient accommodation for those employed in inspection duty. She also does some police duty in preventing illegal trawling in prohibited areas, the responsibility of this public service being under the Department of Agriculture.

One of the side-issues of fishery development is the necessity of looking after the social well-being of the men, and coffee stalls were opened at some places where fishermen could be supplied with tea, coffee, etc., and have accommodation for letter-writing and social intercourse. These stalls are much appreciated by the men, especially those away from home.

The results of the Board's operations in developing the fishing and allied industries have been far-reaching, for not merely is work found for the men, but also for their wives and daughters who obtain employment on shore at cleaning, salting, packing of herrings and mackerel. Indirectly all the local people benefit by the circulation of money, and the general standard of comfort is raised. There is an increased demand for food-stuffs and thus even the farmers and shopkeepers in the neighbourhood benefit from the development of a fishing centre in their districts.

§ 8. Cottage-industries and other industrial development.

In this branch of their administration, the Board decided to devote their energies to fostering and initiating home and cottage industries and domestic training. Weaving, spinning, knitting, embroidery, and the making of various descriptions of lace and crochet work thus came in for attention. In County Donegal where the home-spun woollens had obtained some celebrity, the Board encouraged the industry by giving premiums for high-class work, and the weavers competed keenly for the "stamp" of the Board, which was affixed to an approved web after a careful examination and measurement of the whole piece by the Board's Inspector of Home-spuns.

In County Mayo the Board assisted a newly established woollen factory at Foxford nearly 20 years ago by making a loan to develop the factory. The result was most gratifying, for the repayment instalments were made regularly for several years, and the balance outstanding was paid up some years ago. The factory is now a commercial success and is giving a large amount of local employment were none existed before.

In County Donegal facilities were given for the erection of buildings to enable a Scotch firm (Messrs. Morton, of Darvel, Ayr) to start a branch of their hand-tufted carpet factory. This venture has also been most successful, the Irish "hands" being found most capable, intelligent, and satisfactory in every way. New branches have been formed in the county by the firm, who are pleased with their experiences of the Donegal peasantry. A lace curtain factory was subsequently started by the same firm in Connemara, and it was aided by the Board paying the salaries of some Swiss instructors brought over to train the local workers.

In lace making, embroidery, fine-knitting, and kindred industries the Board establish "classes" under salaried teachers to instruct the girls of the locality who attend. The teachers market the output with the assistance, when desired, of the Board's Inspector of Industries, who keeps up his knowledge of markets and of the changes of fashion, the workers being thus in touch with the latest designs on the Continent and in America, so that the up-to-date demand may be kept supplied. Of late one district has taken up the knitting of soft woollen golf-coats, which happen now to be fashionable, and they find a ready sale at good prices. In most districts the girls are, as fashions change, able to adapt themselves to new work. There are over 100 lace, crochet, embroidery and similar classes working with a turnover of about £30,000 per annum.

It is only in the poorest parts where farm work is not extensive or pressing, or where other more profitable sources of earning do not exist, that the girls can spare the time, or poverty supplies the incentive, to take up lace-making and other needle-work and make it remunerative. The earnings of the girls vary of course according to ability and the time spent at the work. The greatest drawback to such industrial earnings is that they are very frequently used to enable girls to emigrate to the United States of America.

Another form of class instruction is that for domestic training, at which, however, no earnings are made. The Board have a staff of nine itinerant instructors who are sent to centres to give a four-months' course to the local girls. The classes are then moved on to the next selected centre. These classes are very successful, for they bring home to girls in backward places an education that would otherwise be beyond their reach. The girls appreciate these classes so much that they often walk some miles a day to attend. As the cottages in which the girls live give them no opportunity of learning the requirements of domestic service in ordinary or large houses, these girls when employed were heretofore only fit at first for the roughest household or farm work at low wages. Now after a course of instruction they can, at a better rate of wages, take on a higher grade of work requiring a knowledge of cookery, laundry, and general housewifery.

The primary object of the course is to improve the homes by training the girls in habits of neatness and order as well as in the acquisition of useful information, thus raising the standard of ideas as to comfort and health. With technical knowledge, girls are enabled to earn better wages as servants if they leave home, or to use the knowledge in their own homes if they remain. Even if the girls emigrate they are able to obtain situations at higher wages than if they went into service as "green hands." They have then more money available to send home to the old people and in this way the relatives at home indirectly benefit from the domestic training as well as the emigrants.

The Board have helped some other industries such as basket-making, home carpentry, etc., and they pay the fees of pupils in technical schools to learn such crafts as are likely to aid them in becoming wage-earners and useful citizens. Under the head of "Technical Instruction" the Board include the salaries of Fishery Instructors and the various classes of teachers engaged in imparting knowledge to enable pupils to start in industries which would be closed to them without such technical skill. There are at present two itinerant carpentry instructors and during winter when work is slack in the country the Board employ four other instructors to teach boys home and farm carpentry so that they may be able to do work at farm buildings, construct rough carts, and make home furniture suitable to their wants and surroundings.

The question has been seriously considered by the Board and discussed with the Department of Agriculture and Technical Instruction whether the Board ought to continue to provide instruction in domestic economy and in carpentry. Both the Board and the Department agree that such educational work falls within the province of the Department, but so far arrangements have not been made for handing it over to the Department, as each body finds a difficulty in agreeing to the financial settlement proposed by the other on a transfer of the work.

§ 9. Engineering works.

On completion of their first survey of the congested districts, an outstanding need was apparent for the erection of piers, breakwaters, boatslips, and beacons or lights, to develop fisheries and afford transit facilities; for the making of roads to open up communication between the outside world and backward parts of the scheduled area, the erection of bridges over rivers which formerly had to be forded, the carrying out of main drainage operations to reclaim lands and the cleaning of river and old drains to save districts from perennial flooding. These operations involved the appointment by the Board of an engineering staff who, having executed the most urgent works the Board had in mind, were in course of time transferred to the Department of Agriculture, which had some time previously been established and required such a staff to carry on work outside the congested districts.

Of late years the Board have a working arrangement with the Department by which the services of the staff are lent to the Board at fixed rates to carry out any small works which have been decided upon by the Board. In the early years the Board themselves undertook the *entire* cost of the most urgent work, carrying them out either departmentally or through a contractor, but of late years they are slow to undertake engineering works unless the localities concerned are willing to contribute towards the cost and thus prove the necessity for the work. Usually such works are now undertaken by the county authorities, the Board granting a proportion of the cost – say one-half or one-third, according to circumstances – the remainder being raised by local taxation. Since the establishment of the Board they have spent £99,596 on marine works, and £76,994 on inland works of various kinds, making a total sum of £176,590.

Owing to financial and legal difficulties the Board have not been able to carry out arterial drainage outside their own estates to the extent they would wish, for no work would be more reproductive or add more to the agricultural value of the land. The Board, however, did carry out a few extensive schemes on their estates in the County Mayo while re-arranging and preparing them for re-sale to the tenants. Over £20,000 was spent in this way reclaiming and improving lands, and it is estimated that the money spent on the works will earn a "dividend" for the localities of over ten per cent. per annum in increased value to agriculture. A Vice-regal Commission in recent years reported on the subject of Drainage in Ireland and the Board await legislation to enable them to start operations in this fruitful field for improvement of the soil, subject to funds being available. Meantime the Board and the Development Commissioners have formulated a scheme to cost about £15,000 in County Sligo, the Commissioners lending £12,000 repayable in 20 years without interest, the Board to carry out the scheme as contractors to a Drainage Board to be created by the Board of Works and bear all cost over the amount of the loan, the work to be done as usual in such cases under the Drainage Acts through the Board of Public Works.

The Development Commissioners are further co-operating with the Board by voting liberal grants to enable large engineering works to be carried out at selected centres, and a loan to the Board is also being made by the Commissioners for the building and equipment of power fishing boats.

§ 10. Miscellaneous schemes.

Apart from the various schemes under the several heads mentioned, the Board carry out certain financial arrangements to aid generally in their procedure. For instance under the Workmen's Compensation Acts they underwrite their own risks since they have developed large undertakings involving the employment of large numbers of workmen, instead of insuring through an Insurance Company as they did formerly when the number of men employed was small. On similar lines, the Board carry on a live-stock insurance under which owners of stock who place animals on the Board's lands for grazing can be protected by payment of a small premium from what would probably be a crushing loss in the event of death of animals.

The Board make grants to the Post Office on foot of guarantees to enable the Department to open telegraph offices, money order offices, and post offices in backward places with a view to bringing the inhabitants into touch with modern commercial connections, thus facilitating the development of business. This is particularly the case in the fishing centres where telegraphic information as to the prices of the day in the leading markets is of prime importance, and sales can be arranged by telegraph.

Another item of the Board's miscellaneous work is the building of a few nurses' residences in out-of-way places to bring the people within the benefits of the Lady Dudley Nursing Fund. It is difficult to estimate the advantages of this scheme to the poor who are far distant from regular medical assistance, and the nurses are greatly appreciated by the dispensary doctors and the people in the districts where they are employed.

***

The foregoing is a summary (though not an exhaustive one) of the leading features of the Board's various activities in improving the condition of the people of the congested districts. The writer desires it to be understood that his views are personal regarding transactions in which he has always taken the deepest interest, and that the article is not written as representing with any authority the ideas of the Board.

EPILOGUE

Editor's Note: *The following is an extract from the concluding chapter of* **History of The Congested Districts Board (1925)** *by W. L. Micks, first Secretary and later Member of the Congested Districts Board of Ireland. Micks here gives a personal assessment of the benefits of the workings of the Board.*

The amount of money deposited in local Post Office Savings Banks is an indication of the improved financial position of the population living in congested districts. The House of Commons Return (No. 272 of 1913), from which the figures in the following table are taken, does not state the amount deposited in 1891, the date when the Board started, but on the other hand 1912 is the last year given, and it is probable that the amount of deposits increased greatly in subsequent years. It is therefore probable that the ratio between 1881 and 1912 might not differ substantially from the ratio between 1891 and (say) 1918.

Deposits in Post Office Savings Banks

Counties	**Amount of Deposits on 31st December, 1881**			**Amount of Deposits on 31st December, 1912**		
Counties	**£**	*s.*	*d.*	**£**	*s.*	*d.*
Donegal	44,403	7	10	409,151	9	11
Galway	59,589	3	1	388,643	18	9
Kerry	24,981	14	6	381,331	15	3
Leitrim	13,432	12	4	147,051	16	9
Mayo	48,875	7	0	518,695	2	9
Roscommon	20,538	15	1	198,495	4	2
Sligo	31,318	19	11	221,706	19	1
Totals	**243,139**	**19**	**9**	**2,265,076**	**6**	**8**

Notes: Figures are not given for the Counties Clare and Cork, as only part of these Counties was congested. The amount deposited in 1912 is $9\frac{1}{3}$ times as much as what was deposited in 1881. The amount of local deposits in Joint Stock Banks cannot be ascertained.

To one who, like myself, was familiar with the general conditions in the West of Ireland before 1891 – in my own case as far back as 1860, as I spent some years of my boyhood in the County Mayo – the change is simply marvellous. Unhealthy hovels, then broadcast in the districts, have in most cases been obliterated or turned into cattle sheds. Compact holdings of increased acreage have taken the place of small holdings in numerous scattered plots, some of the plots no more than an unfenced single ridge in a small field. The first steps (no more is claimed here) have been successfully taken by making new holdings and by improving the mode of agriculture and the breeds of live stock and poultry. The farmers, as they now may be called, in East Connacht and similar areas are in a position much more favourable for taking advantage of such future, and far too long deferred, agriculture developments as made Denmark prosperous in a very few years.

I lay stress on the independence of the Board, as its work is a most interesting and valuable illustration of what Irishmen, possessing full powers, though with relatively small funds, were able to do for the improvement of the poorest and most backward districts of their country within the very short space of thirty-two years in the lifetime of a nation. The Board insisted upon its freedom of action, except for a few years. If such insistence had not been persevered in, or if the projects of the Board had been subject to the criticism of Dublin Castle and British Treasury officials personally unacquainted with local conditions, the result undoubtedly would have been that nothing, or next to nothing, would have been effected.

I venture to say that the moral to be derived from a consideration of the Board's work is that in the future, as in the past, bodies charged with the development of the resources of the country should be given, within the limits of funds placed at their disposal by the Oireachtas, a wide and unfettered discretion, free from the objections or modifications of clever administrative or financial officials, but who are without the special knowledge that ought to be possessed by those to whom functions for development are entrusted.

I attribute such success as the Board has achieved to its complete independence and to its power to take prompt and immediate action for carrying out its plans, subject to keeping expenditure within its yearly income, and subject to the obligation to satisfy the Auditor-General that the expenditure was within its powers, and that all payments were duly and strictly vouched. Such was the procedure in the case of the Congested Districts Board, and I believe that only under such a system can successful development be carried out.

Every man, or body of men, must fail in some instances, but surely a few failures with freedom of action are preferable to cramped, curtailed or spoiled efforts by a spanceled body. The Board did not always succeed at first, but their initial experiments did not involve much financial loss. It is so with any successful business firm or company, and opportunities would pass away if every idea or project had to run the gauntlet of outside officials without the special knowledge requisite for developing the resources of the country.

It had been the intention of the Government of Saorstát Eireann to transfer the industrial functions of the Board to the Ministry of Industry and Commerce, but it was decided upon reconsideration to transfer these functions to what is now the Department of Fisheries and Rural Industries. Personally I was glad of this change, as Mr. L.C. Moriarty, the Secretary to that Department, had been at the head of the Board's staff in the Dublin office dealing with rural industries and previously with fisheries. He had also acted as an inspector in both branches, and had acquired a good knowledge of circumstances and individuals in the country. He has a natural aptitude for the work, with a greater number of years' experience, so I felt that the Minister of Fisheries under whom he serves would have an ideal official in advisory and executive functions.

The end of the Board was obviously at hand as soon as the Parliament at Westminster and Oireachtas at Dublin confirmed the Treaty that had been made between representatives of Great Britian and of Ireland. The Board in 1891 had been made independent of the Government of the day, including the Treasury and Dublin Castle, because there was not confidence in Ireland as regards the inclination, knowledge and ability of the British Government in England and Ireland to remedy the deplorable condition of the inhabitants of the congested districts. As soon as an independent Irish Government was established the reason for the continuance of the Board ceased to exist, and its operations came temporarily under the supervision and control of the Ministry for Agriculture in Saorstát Eireann. Mr. Patrick Hogan, the Minister for Agriculture, requested the Board to carry on its work as before, pending legislation for the distribution of its functions and funds among appropriate Ministries. During this transition period the work of the Board went on as before, except that any matter of unusual interest or importance was referred to Mr. Hogan, with a statement as to the views of the Board, for his decision. In fact the Board worked as a department of Saorstát Eireann, and its operation went on with as much smoothness as before owing to the interest and sympathy that Mr. Hogan felt for the work of the Board.

At its meeting on the 8th of May 1923, a letter was received by the Board from Mr. Hogan stating that:–

> "On the 31st March last, as a result of the Transfer of Functions Order the office of the Commissioner of the Irish Land Commission ceased to exist and the Government are now under the necessity of constituting a Land Commission. It has been decided that the new body shall administer all services in connection with Land Purchase, that is to say, that it shall include the Land Purchase function of the former Land Commission and of the Congested Districts Board.
>
> "It is proposed to give effect to this decision in a Land Purchase Bill and a Ministries Bill, both of which will be introduced in the Dáil within this month. The passing of these Bills will not in any way prejudice the positions of the existing staffs or of officials who have been superannuated.
>
> "In coming to this decision the Government had in mind not only the necessity for economy but also the fact that the Ministries of Industry and Commerce and of Fisheries have been constituted and that, in the normal course, the functions of the Congested Districts Board in regard to industries and fisheries would be transferred to these Ministries.
>
> "The Government fully realise that in the absence of an Irish Parliament it was of the utmost importance that the administration of land purchase, and particularly its most urgent aspect the relief of congestion, should be in the control of a representative Irish Board and *they feel that they are speaking for the whole country in offering to the members of the Congested Districts Board the nation's thanks for their unselfish services and for the efficient and lasting work which they have accomplished.*"

INDEX

Due to the standard format of the Congested Districts Board's Reports, the same subjects are covered in each report in relation to a district and will therefore not be covered in this index *unless there is a specific and/or exceptional reference to a subject.* These standard subjects include, in their order of reference in the Reports: cultivation of land, crops grown, grazing, reclamation of land, migration schemes, cultivation methods, manures, crop rotation, livestock, breeds, markets and fairs, railways, steamers, sailing boats, post and telegraph offices, labourers in district and migratory, wages earned, weaving, spinning, knitting and sewing, kelp-burning, seaweed, turf and bogs, lobster fishing, sea fishing, boats, fish and fish-curing, piers and harbours, salmon and freshwater fisheries, banks, loan funds, minerals, cash or credit dealings, barter, expenditure of families, home-grown food value, dietary, clothing, dwellings, home life and customs, character of the people, and improvements suggested.

NOTE: The abbreviation *ff* (for folios) after a page number indicates further mentions on following pages of that individual Report.

– L –

– M –

– T –

– U –

– V –

– W –

– Y –

– Z –

PICTURE CREDITS

Photographs reproduced with the kind permission of:

The Trustees of the National Museums and Galleries of Northern Ireland (Ulster Museum)
pages 28 (Robert Welch), 64, 82, 85 (Robert Welch), 108, 115 (Robert Welch), 171 and 211

The National Library of Ireland
38, 50, 54, 142, 149,
front cover and back cover

The Royal Irish Academy
pages 17 (Robert Welch), 35 (Robert Welch), 62, 94, 96, 139 (Robert Welch), 163 (Robert Welch) and 201

Irish Co-operative Organisation Society
page 228